FACING THE CAMBODIAN PAST

SELECTED ESSAYS 1971–1994

DAVID CHANDLER

Silkworm Books

ISBN 978-974-7100-64-8

First published in 1996 by
Silkworm Books
6 Sukkasem Road, T. Suthep, Chiang Mai 50200, Thailand.
E-mail: info@silkwormbooks.com
www.silkwormbooks.com

Set in HPJansonText 11 pt. by Silk Type.

ACKNOWLEDGMENTS

The essays in this book approach the Cambodian past from several angles, reflecting changes in my interests and my thinking as well as developments in Cambodian historiography.

I've arranged the essays into five parts. The first of these deals with Angkor and pre-colonial Cambodian culture. It is followed by one that treats several aspects of nineteenth century Cambodia. Essays in the third part cover the colonial period (1863–1954) while those in the fourth deal with the Khmer Rouge era (1975–1979) and its aftermath. The final section contains two essays, written fifteen years apart, about what I have called the tragedy of Cambodian history.

I've introduced each part with some remarks that place the essays in context.

In preparing the collection I haven't adjusted my findings, second-guessed my opinions or brought the bibliographical references up to date. I've tinkered with the style of several essays, however, and I couldn't resist adding some new information to the essay "Royally Sponsored Human Sacrifices in Nineteenth Century Cambodia."

In my notes to the essays, I've acknowledged the help I received from friends and colleagues while the papers were being prepared. I owe a special debt to Dr Tej Bunnag, who as editor of the *Journal of the Siam Society* in the 1970s offered a home and helpful comments for several early essays. Papers prepared in connection with conferences sponsored by the Social Science Research Council (SSRC) in 1978 and 1981 owe a good deal to the remarks of other participants and to the editorial comments of Dr David Szanton, who convened the meetings

For the remaining essays, I'm grateful to the conveners and editors concerned for their helpful suggestions and advice.

A list of all the people who have inspired and helped me with my writing over the years would read like a "Who's Who" of Southeast Asian studies, but I'm happy to record the special and numerous debts I owe to May Ebihara, Kate Frieson, Steve Heder, Charles F. Keyes, Ben Kiernan, Judy Ledgerwood, Ian Mabbett, Jacques Nepote, the late Eveline Poree-Maspero, Craig Reynolds, Serge Thion, Michael Vickery and Hiram W. Woodward, Jr. Finally, I'm grateful to my publisher at Silkworm Books, Trasvin Jittidejarak, who suggested that I assemble the collection and has shepherded it into print.

David Chandler

Bellagio, Italy
March 1996

CONTENTS

Part I   Angkor and Memories of Angkor 1
Folk Memories of the Decline of Angkor in Nineteenth
    Century Cambodia (1978) 3
An Eighteenth Century Inscription from
    Angkor Wat (1970) 15
Maps for the Ancestors (1975) 25

Part II   Cambodia before the French 43
Normative Poems (*Chbap*) and
    Pre-colonial Cambodian Society (1982) 45
An Anti-Vietnamese Rebellion in Early Nineteenth
    Century Cambodia (1973) 61
Songs at the Edge of the Forest (1978) 76
Going through the Motions (1979) 100
Royally Sponsored Human Sacrifices in Nineteenth
    Century Cambodia (1973) 119

Part III   The Colonial Era 137
The Assassination of Résident Bardez (1981) 139
The Duties of the Corps of Royal Scribes (1975) 159
The Kingdom of Kampuchea,
    March–October 1945 (1985) 165
Cambodian Royal Chronicles (*Rajabangsavatar*) (1976) 189

Part IV   Cambodia since 1975 205
Transformation in Cambodia (1976) 207
Revising the Past in Democratic Kampuchea (1982) 215

Seeing Red (1982) 233
A Revolution in Full Spate (1982) 255
Cambodia in 1984 (1984) 276

Part V   Tragedy and History 295
The Tragedy of Cambodian History (1979) 297
The Tragedy of Cambodian History Revisited (1994) 310

Index 327

For Susan

PART I

ANGKOR AND MEMORIES OF ANGKOR

The essays in this section were published in the *Journal of the Siam Society*. "An Eighteenth Century Inscription from Angkor Wat" was drafted in 1969 at the University of Michigan where I was studying under Professor David Wyatt. I wrote "Maps for the Ancestors" in 1974, using documents I had copied in the Institut Bouddhique in Phnom Penh in 1970 and 1971. In that essay I dealt with overlapping notions of truth, memory and history, using two nineteenth century royal documents that simultaneously remembered and forgot the reign of Yasovarman I almost a thousand years before.

The themes of memory and forgetting recur in the essay on the "leper king" at Angkor, written in 1978.

FOLK MEMORIES OF THE DECLINE OF ANGKOR IN NINETEENTH CENTURY CAMBODIA: THE LEGEND OF THE LEPER KING

One of the intriguing features of the European 'discovery' of Angkor in the mid-nineteenth century A.D. was that the supposedly forgotten ruins and much of the statuary came equipped with Cambodian names. Recent research has shown that in some cases these names were historically accurate while others, in somewhat garbled form, are folk memories of the kings and divinities associated with a particular site.[1]

This paper argues that the association of a statue and three toponyms with the phrase *sdach komlong* ("leper king") in nineteenth-century Cambodia constitutes a folk memory of this kind, quite possibly of an otherwise all but forgotten king, Indravarman II (reigned c. 1220–1243?) who left no inscriptions of his own.

Evidence to support this argument comes from an examination of the statue and the toponyms, from a study of myths about a leper king from Cambodia and Thailand, from the research

In preparing this paper, I profited from discussion and correspondence with L.F. Brakel, M.C. Subhadradis Diskul, Ian Mabbett, the late Eveline Porée-Maspéro, Saveros Pou, Craig Reynolds, Khin Sok, Michael Vickery and O.W. Wolters. This paper was first published in *Journal of the Siam Society*, Vol. 67, Part 1, January 1979, reprinted with permission.
[1] See Saveros Lewitz, "La toponymie khmere", *Bulletin de l'Ecole Française d'Extrême Orient (BEFEO)*, LIII (1966–1967), pp. 375–451, for a detailed discussion of toponyms. For the persistence of some Angkorian ones, see David Chandler, "Maps for the Ancestors", below p. 25.

of the late Victor Goloubew (who came to the conclusion that Indravarman II's predecessor, Jayavarman VII, was a leper), from the only inscription that mentions Indravarman, and from the testimony of Chou Ta-Kuan, the Chinese envoy who visited Angkor in A.D. 1296. Chou, in discussing illness at Angkor, mentions that lepers could be seen "from time to time" ("*de distance à distance*") along the roads nearby, and adds:

there was a sovereign who contracted this disease; for this reason, people do not speak of it contemptuously (*avec mépris*).[2]

The story of a leper king at Angkor, then, dates from at least the thirteenth century A.D., and no earlier references are known. By the mid-nineteenth century the story had become embedded in Thai and Cambodian chronicles as well as in popular folklore.[3] Some people even believed that a leper king had built Angkor.[4] In the Cambodian chronicle (which, incidentally, makes no mention of the heyday of Angkor), the leper king is placed in the tenth

---

[2] Paul Pelliot, *Oeuvres posthumes*, vol. III, *Memoires sur les coûtumes du Cambodge de Tcheou Ta Kouan* (Paris, 1952), pp. 23–24.

[3] Versions of the myth can be found in Dr. Angier, "Le lèpre au Cambodge", *Annales de l'hygiène et medicine coloniale 6* (19d3), pp. 176–180; Etienne Aymonier, *Le Cambodge*, vol. III (Paris, 1904), 488; A. Benazet, "De quelques pratiques de la medicine chez les cambodgiens", *L'Ethnographie*, 1932, pp. 29–44; James Campbell, "Notes on the antiquities . . . of Cambodia", *Journal of the Royal Geographical Society*, 1860, 182–199; Adhemard Leclère, *Cambodge: contes et légendes* (Paris, 1899), pp. 112–143; Claude Notton, *Légends d'Angkor et chronique du Bouddha de cristal* (Limoges, 1960), 22–25; C. Notton, *Légendes sur le Siam er Le Cambodge* (Bangkok, 1939), 48–52 and 97–104; Eveline Porée-Maspéro, *Etudes sur les rites agraires des Cambodgiens*, 3 vols. (Paris and The Hague, 1962–1969), pp. 258, 669, 678, 704, 745 and 847.

[4] See Campbell, op. cit., p. 194, where Rama IV reports the rumor, and C. Naudin, "Receuil des documents pour servir à l'Histoire des temples du groupe d'Angkor", *Bulletin de la Societé des Etudes Indochinoises (BSEI)*, III–IV (1928), pp. 5–134 at 32.

Rama IV's fascination with Cambodian history and with Angkor in particular would reward detailed research. A good place to start would be the royally sponsored attempt, in 1859–1860, to dismantle two small towers of the twelfth-century A.D. The passage that refers to his contracting leprosy reads as follows.

One day the king summoned all of his ministers to a meeting. When he had done so, he noticed that one of the ministers, named Neak (i.e. "naga", or dragon), refused to prostrate himself. Filled with anger, the king took his sacred sword and smote the minister. When he did so, venomous spittle fell on him, and he became a leper. People called him the leper king [*sdach komlong*] and he was no longer recognizable as a king. He died at the age of sixty-nine, having reigned for fifty-nine years.[5]

Other versions of the myth say that the king contracted leprosy by cheating a Hindu magician or by being kissed by a leprous woman.[6] Mme. Porée-Maspéro has shown that the myth penetrated deeply into Cambodian folk-lore; Stieng and Cham versions, moreover, have been reported. [7]

Against this impressive body of myth is Chou's matter-of-fact statement which suggests that his interlocutors were referring

century temple of Ta Prohm and transport them to Bangkok. The temple was in Thai territory at the time but the attempt failed when Thai foremen attempting to dismantle the temple were murdered by local people. See Christopher Pym (ed.), *Henri Mouhot's Diary* (Kuala Lumpur, 1966), p. 109 and Aymonier, op. cit., III, pp. 32–33, as well as C. Flood (trans.), *The Dynastic Chronicles; Bangkok Era, the Fourth Reign* (Tokyo, 1967), I, 222–223 and 226–227 and *chotmai het ratchakan thi 4* ("Collected Documents from the Fourth Reign"), cs 1221/70 and cs 1222/80, in the National Library in Bangkok-a reference kindly supplied by Chalong Soontravanich.

[5] *Brah raja bangsavatar mahaksat khmaer* ("The Royal Chronicle of Cambodia"), manuscript from the Buddhist Institute in Phnom Penh, photographed by the Institute of Far Eastern Studies in Tokyo (available on microfilm), p. 43. See also Jean Moura, *Le royaume du Cambodge* (Paris, 1883), II, p. 15, which paraphrases an earlier recension of the chronicie.

[6] Cf. John Audric, *Angkor and the Khmer Empire* (London, 1972), 151–152 and Charles Danguy, *De la ville des hommes à la cité des dieux* (Paris-Saigon, 1940), pp. 221–224.

[7] Porée-Maspéro, op. cit., 514 and Paul Mus, "Deux légendes chames", *BEFEO*, XXXI (1931), p. 97.

to an historical personage, perhaps within the living memory of some. It is not impossible, of course, for a myth to have its basis in fact; many twentieth-century Cambodian myths can be traced to real events.[8] However, if the story of a leper king at Angkor had no basis in 1296, what follows is pure speculation.

Because of its unusual appearance, the statue known as the *sdach komlong*, located in the *tilean sdach komlong* ("terrace of the leper king"), is difficult to date.[9] Most experts, however, date it, cautiously, to a period slightly later than the statuary of the nearby Royal Terrace – i.e. to the early years of the thirteenth century A.D.[10] A short inscription on the base of the statue, dated by Cœdès on linguistic grounds to the fourteenth or fifteenth century, identifies the statue not as a king but as *Dharmajara*, or Yama, the divine assessor of virtues and defects.[11] Its placement in what is believed to have been the royal cremation ground suggests that it occupies its original position.[12]

By the mid-nineteenth century the statue was revered as a representation of the leper king, and was associated by some

[8] See, for example, Buddhist Institute (comp.), *Brajum rioeṅ preṅ* ("Collected Folk Stories"), VIII (Phnom Penh, 1972), pp. 125–129 and 185–190, where cults involving ancestor spirits (*nak tā*) are traced to twentieth-century events.

[9] See N. Filoz, *Cambodge et le Siam* (Paris, 1889), pp. 75 and 81; Henri Mouhot, *Voyage dans les royaumes de Siam . . .* (Paris, 1863), pp. 201–202 and Pierre Benoit, *Le roi lepreux* (Paris, 1927), pp. 117–118 (a fictional account). For a description of the statue (a seated, nude, male figure without sexual organs and with disorderly hair, fangs and rudimentary modelling of the torso), see Jean Boisselier, *La statuaire khmère er son évolution* (Paris, 1955), I, p. 191.

[10] On dating, see Boisselier, loc. cit. (by inference); M.C. Subhadradis Diskul (personal communication). H.W. Woodward, however, perceives no fool-proof date (personal communication).

[11] G. Cœdès, "Le date du Bayon", *BEFEO*, XXVIII (1928), pp. 81–112 at 84. This dating has been confirmed by Saveros Pou (personal communication). In 1940, Cœdès apparently leaned toward the fifteenth century: Cœdès, "La destination funeraire des grands monuments cambodgiens", *BEFEO*, XL (1940), pp. 315–343 at 338.

[12] Cœdès, "La destination . . . ", pp. 338–339.

with Yasovarman I, the founder of the city of Angkor.[13] Visitors to Angkor throughout the nineteenth century saw the statue sheltered in a small hut, in the manner of a Cambodian ancestor spirit, or *nak tā*[14] Perhaps its 'leprosy' was connected with lichenous growths that flourished on it. On the other hand, it is possible that the phrase *tilean sdach komlong* means "the terrace of the king who was a leper" rather than "the terrace where a statue, now called the leper king, has been found." The suggestion that the place has named the statue, rather than the reverse, is strengthened somewhat by the existence of a near-replica of the statue found at *Wat* Khnat which was not reportedly known as a *sdach komlong.*[15]

In addition to the terrace, only two toponyms in nineteenth-century Cambodia contained the phrase. Both are in the Angkor region. One is on Phnom Kulen – a small brick building, five metres by ten, opening to the east, roofless, known as the *prasat dot sdach komlong* or "temple of the leper king's cremation."[16] In the 1870s it sheltered a stone lingam. According to Aymonier, local traditions held that the leper king had been cremated on the roof of the building; according to Moura (who did not visit the site) a statue similar to the leper king mentioned above was found nearby.[17]

Near the site of the temple, a large slab of sandstone in a streambed has been carved with innumerable small lingams. Local people told Aymonier that the leper king had bathed in

[13] Aymonier, op. cit., III, p. 487. Notton supports his identification of the statue and the real leper king with Indravarman III (r. 1296–1308) by the dubious contention that representations of this king are "well known" at Angkor. Notton, *Légendes de Siam . . .*, p. 50n.

[14] E. Lunet de Lajonquière, *Inventaire descriptif des monuments du Cambodge*, III (Paris, 1911), pp. 56–57.

[15] Lunet de Lajonquière, op. cit., III, 281–282. Cœdès, "La destination . . .", 339n. remarks that the *Wat* Khnat statue lacks the fangs (*crocs*) of the one found at Angkor Thom. The *Wat* Khnat statue, incidentally, turned up between the visits of Aymonier, who fails to mention it, and Lunet de Lajonquière.

[16] Aymonier, op. cit., III, 416, and Lunet de Lajonquière, op. cit., III, pp. 236–237.

[17] Moura, loc. cit.

this portion of the river, a belief shared by their counterparts almost a century later. Inscriptions found at the site in the 1960s, however, date these carvings to the ninth and tenth centuries A.D.[18]

Aymonier, incidentally, who is cautious when confronted by many Cambodian historical myths, believed that the leper king was an historical person.[19]

The second toponym is in Chikreng district, to the east of Angkor, and refers to a temple visited by Aymonier known as the kampheng *sdach komlong*, or "leper king's fortress"; the name dropped out of use toward the end of the nineteenth century.[20]

Aymonier found two inscriptions at the site, on stones reused in the construction of the temple.[21] A third inscription, published by Cœdès in 1953, is dated on calligraphic grounds to the thirteenth century, and, although fragmentary, is of markedly Sivaite character.[22] In 1940 Cœdès had suggested that the temple had been built during the reign of Jayavarman VII, attached to one of the hospitals constructed by that monarch throughout the kingdom.[23]

Both sites, then, are of markedly Sivaite character, while the terrace of the leper king is not. The Chikreng temple, like the terrace, probably dates from the end of the twelfth or early

---

[18] Jean Boulbet, "Kbal Spean: The stream of a thousand lingas", *Nokor Khmer*, No. 2 (January-March 1970), pp. 2–17. The mountain is dotted with monuments and statuary from all periods of Angkorian history. See Philippe Stern, "Travaux executés à Phnom Kulen", *BEFEO*, XXXVIII (1938), pp. 152–175. Danguy, loc. cit., and Notton, *Légendes d'Angkor*, p. 25, connect the leper king with this site. Notton's text (dating in its Thai version from 1932) reads: "[the king] being leprous, did not recover. He went with his cortège of concubines to cure himself on the eight-peaked mountain of Koulen. Getting no better, he died of old age. His body and those of his concubines turned into stones, which can be seen today."

[19] Aymonier, op. cit., II, p. 417. Contrast this with his criticism of the mythologizing impulse in nineteenth-century Cambodia at III, p. 326.

[20] Aymonier, op. cit., II, pp. 448–450; Lunet de Lajonquière, op. cit., I, p. 373.

[21] These are catalogued by Cœdès as K. 170 and K.171.

[22] K.764. See G. Cœdès, *Les Inscriptions du Cambodge*, IV (Paris, 1953), p. 318.

[23] G. Cœdès, "Les hôpitaux de Jayavarman VII", *BEFEO*, XL (1940), pp. 344–347 at 346.

thirteenth century while the Phnom Kulen site, impossible to date, is associated by local people with a leper king whom Aymonier believed to have been a real man. The myth of the leper king fascinated Victor Goloubew of the Ecole Française d'Extrême Orient (1876–1945). In a series of intense, informal studies begun in 1922 and extending into the 1930s, Goloubew became convinced that the leper king was a real person and came to associate him with Jayavarman VII.[24] This association is attractive for several reasons, and fits some of the evidence nicely. In the late 1930s it was accepted, tentatively, by Cœdès;[25] more recently, and with less caution, it has been advanced by B.P. Groslier.[26]

The evidence for Goloubew's claim included a lintel to a hospital temple, depicting Lokeśvara and a leper; bas-reliefs from the inner courtyard of the Bayon, showing a man being treated for the disease; and tantalizing evidence from southern India and Ceylon which indicated that at an unspecified date a Cambodian king, afflicted with leprosy, had visited both places and been miraculously cured. Another piece of evidence, which Goloubew did not use, is the association between a *sdach komlong* and a hospital-temple of Jayavarman VII, discussed above. A smaller bit, drawn from Chou Ta Kuan's account, is the phrase translated

[24] See Louis Malleret, "La vingtième anniversaire de la mort de Victor Goloubew", *BEFEO*, LIII (1966–1967), pp. 331–373, especially pp. 345, 352–353. Goloubew never published all the results of his research; nor did his fellow-Indianist, Silvain Levi, who shared his fascination with the leper king: see V. Goloubew, "Silvain Levi et Indochine", *BEFEO*, XXXV (1935), pp. 351–367. Portions of it, however, appeared in V. Goloubew, "Un idole khmer de Lokesvara au Musée de Colombo", *BEFEO*, XXIV (1924), pp. 510– 512 and V. Goloubew (with Louis Finot), "Rapport sur un mission archéologique à Ceylan", *BEFEO*, XXX (1930), pp. 627–643. See also V. Goloubew, "Sur quelques images khmères de Vajradhara", *Journal of the Indian Society of Oriental Art*, June-December 1937, pp. 97–104. G. Cœdès, "Le mystère du Bayon", *Cahiers de l'EFEO*, X (1937), pp. 25–30 summarizes Goloubew's research and tentatively accepts his conclusions. See also G. Muraz, "Les scènes medicales et domestiques dans les bas-reliefs des temples d'Angkor", *La Géographie*, LXIV (1935), pp. 103–120, especially fig. 14.
[25] G. Coedes, *Angkor* (Hong Kong, 1963), pp. 93–94.
[26] B.P. Groslier, "Les inscriptions du Bayon", in J. Dumarçay and B.P. Groslier, *Le Bayon*, (Paris, 1973), p. 255.

by Pelliot as "*de distance à distance*". While the phrase can as easily mean "from time to time" it is just possible that it is a veiled reference to Jayavarman's hospitals, still being used as leprosaria nearly one century after his death.[27]

Goloubew's hypothesis is useful in explaining some of the idiosyncratic features of Jayavarman VII's reign, such as the hospital-building program and what looks like an effort to finish his building program before what may have been a predictable death from the disease.[28] Perhaps, as Cœdès suggests, the king sought to obtain merit in this way, or better, to counter the demerit implied by his affliction.[29]

Goloubew seems on less firm ground, however, when he suggests that the Bayon bas-reliefs represent Jayavarman VII. Several authorities date these bas-reliefs well after Jayavarman's death, and perhaps to the period of Hindu-inspired iconoclasm at Angkor.[30] Goloubew's evidence from Ceylon and southern India is likewise hard to use, although it strengthens his contention (and mine) that the leper king was a real person. The Khmer statuette of Lokeśvara found in Ceylon is difficult to date, although it may be from the Bayon period; we do know that one

[27] I am grateful to Professor O.W. Wolters who checked the original Chinese for reducing my enthusiasm for this interpretation (personal communication).

[28] In the last years of his reign, Jayavarman VII sponsored no inscriptions, nor do other inscriptions mention his activities. This suggests retirement, consonant with leprosy, perhaps, but just as easily with Jayavarman's advanced age.

[29] Cœdès, *Angkor*, loc. cit., Angier, op. cit., mentions that Cambodians in the early twentieth century thought that leprosy was hereditary.

[30] These bas-reliefs have been dated well after Jayavarman VII. See Philippe Stern, *Les monuments khmers du style du Bayon et Jayavarman VII* (Paris, 1965), p. 164 and G. de Coral Remusat, *L'art khmer : les grandes étapes de son évolution* (Paris, 1951), 85–86. B. Dagens, "Etude sur l'iconographie du Bayon", *Arts Asiatiques*, XVI (1969), pp. 123–167, argues that the death of Indravarman II, perhaps in A.D. 1243 (see below) ushered in a new style at the Bayon; however, too little is known about the tastes and policies of this monarch to be sure. If the bas-reliefs represent Jayarvaman (merely) as a leper, one must assume a deeper change in attitudes toward kingship than Chou Ta-kuan's account half a century later implies. If, however, the reliefs were carved after the death by leprosy of a more insignificant (or unmeritorious) king, perhaps the aura of *lèse majesté* would be less.

of Jayavarman VII's sons went to Ceylon to study Buddhism.[31] However, if the royal visitor was Jayavarman VII, and especially if he was as myths suggest miraculously cured it is surprising that no inscriptions in Cambodia record this event. A visit by a less pretentious monarch seems more likely; and if this monarch is to fall in the memory-span of people alive in A.D. 1296, it would have to be Indravarman II.

The closing years of Jayavarman VII's reign are shrouded in mystery. So is the reign of Indravarman II.[32] This period, moreover, is crucial to understanding the shifts and changes that added up to the decline of Angkor as a major power. The period was marked by declining Cambodian influence abroad,[33] by Hindu iconoclasm at Angkor (hitherto unknown),[34] by the rise of Theravada Buddhism at the expense of Jayavarman's Mahayana beliefs, and by a steep decline quantitatively and qualitatively in temple construction, stone-carving and inscriptions.[35]

The argument that Jayavarman's successor was a leper must be a tentative one. All we know about Indravarman II is that he was dead in A.D. 1243.[36] He may have been Jayavarman's son, but this is by no means certain.[37] He is mentioned in only one inscription, K.488, composed at the end of the thirteenth century, which

[31] G. Cœdès, *Les états hindouisés d'Indochine et d'Indonésie* (Paris, 1964), p. 323.

[32] See G. Cœdès, "Inscriptions de Prasat Chrung", *Inscriptions du Cambodge*, IV (Paris, 1953), p. 230ff. In his discussion of these inscriptions, found at the four corners of Jayavarman's capital city, Cœdès points out the decline in the skill of the versification from the beginning of the reign to the end, and adds that, perhaps at Jayavarman's death, the inscriptions on certain steles were left unfinished. See also G. Cœdès, "L'année du lièvre AD 1219", in *India Antiqua* (Mélanges Vogel), (Leiden, 1947), pp. 83–88.

[33] This decline is summarized in Cœdès, *Les états*, 328–330. See also L.P. Briggs, *The Ancient Khmer Empire* (Philadelphia, 1951), pp. 238–239.

[34] Cœdès, "Le mystère du Bayon", 30 and Cœdès, "Le date du Bayon", 97.

[35] Cœdès, "Inscriptions de Prasat Chrung", *passim*. See also Briggs, op. cit., pp. 243–244.

[36] See below, notes 38 and 39. Scholars have perhaps been hasty in accepting this year as the one in which Indravarman II actually died.

[37] For a discussion of four of Jayavarman VII's sons, see Cœdès, *Les états . . .*, 328. They would seem to have been born too early to have reigned in 1243.

describes the life of a Brahmin, Çri Jaya Mahapranjana who served Jayavarman VII as well as Indravarman's two successors.[38] The stanza which mentions Indravarman reads as follows;

> In the year 1165 (*saka*; AD 1243) [he went] to offer homage to Śiva in Bhimapura (P'imai) for the peace of Indravarman, who was gone.[39]

Several things about the stanza are enigmatic. One is that Indravarman's posthumous name – if he had one – is not mentioned, although this is not crucial, since the posthumous names of other dead kings mentioned in the inscription are not included either. Another point is that the Brahmin seems to be careful to demonstrate his awareness of the continuity of Cambodian kingship from Jayavarman VII to Indravarman III (r. 1295–1308) in whose reign the inscription was presumably incised. But he is just as careful, it seems, not to praise Indravarman, or to mention his services to him. The voyage to P'imai, moreover, may not have been merely to pray for Indravarman (an odd reason for such a long trip, in any case); the inscription mentions that the Brahmin met and married a young woman there who later gave birth to his six children. That the Brahmin prayed to Siva may indicate that Indravarman II was a Sivaite but not necessarily, for the Brahmin had served Jayavarman VII, a Buddhist, while still a Hindu himself. The brevity of the mention, finally, suggests that in some unspecified way Indravarman II failed to live up to the kings who came before and after him. Would this merely indicate pique on the Brahmin's part? Perhaps, but if so we might expect at least one other mention of the king in the corpus of Cambodian inscriptions.

---

[38] Louis Finot, "Le temple de Mangalartha à Angkor Thom", *BEFEO*, XXV (1925), pp. 393–406.

[39] Ibid., p. 398 (Sanskrit text). I.W. Mabbett has translated this for me, pointing out that the phrase translated as "is gone" is a reconstruction by Finot; the initial character (*ga* of *gatasyn*) is effaced.

None of these remarks, of course, proves that Indravarman was a leper and it would certainly be anomolous, to say the least, if a leprous prince were allowed or encouraged to accede to power. It is fair to assume that if Indravarman was a leper, he contracted the disease as a reigning monarch – a suggestion echoed by the myths.

Aside from this inscription, what can we infer about his reign? For one thing, Jayavarman's successor must have been responsible for carrying on his building program, especially at the Bayon and the royal terraces. Perhaps work on the hospitals continued in Indravarman's reign as well, for only 32 temples that can be linked to Jayavarman's hospitals, out of the originally planned 102, have come to light.[40] Without venturing into psychohistory we can assume, by the absence of inscriptions, that if Indravarman was a Buddhist, his religion was less public and far less verbalized than Jayavarman's had been. It is possible that he was Hindu, or that he changed religions at some point in his life, as Jayavarman himself may also have done.

Perhaps he did so when he contracted leprosy. In this regard, Chou Ta Kuan's statement that the king's disease had been greeted with magnaminity among the people does not, I think, ring true. It is more likely that the knowledge that a reigning king was afflicted with this disease (and thus, in the words of the chronicle, "unrecognizable as king") would have called into question the legitimacy of Cambodian kingship, especially of the grandiose, individualistic variety celebrated by Jayavarman VII. Of course, this crisis of confidence would perhaps have been even greater had Jayavarman himself been a leper; but again had this been common knowledge, it seems unlikely that the inscription which barely mentions Indravarman would have been so fulsome about Jayavarman VII. Instead, I suspect that a king's leprosy would be interpreted, throughout the society, as a judgment and a

[40] Cœdès, "Les hôpitaux", *passim.*

13

curse. In 1860, judging his own reign to have been unmeritorious, the Cambodian king, Duang, stipulated that his body be exposed for birds of prey.[41] Perhaps Indravarman, afflicted with leprosy, made a similar assessment of his reign, and retired with his retinue to Phnom Kulen.

But this is speculation. What we know for certain is that Cambodians from the thirteenth century onward believed that Angkor had once been ruled by a leper king.

Like the toponyms associated with Yasovarman I, discussed in another paper,[42] the myth of the leper king suggests that folk memories of Angkor were more persistent and more accurate than many nineteenth and twentieth century French savants were willing to grant. The uses to which Angkor was put by Cambodians, right up to its 'discovery' by the French, would also repay detailed study. Why was Angkor Wat, rather that the Bayon, a Buddhist pilgrimage site? Might the abandonment of the Bayon, and the rest of Jayavarman's city, reflect an assessment of the obscure period in Cambodian history associated in the popular mind with the catastrophe of a leper king? Until a better explanation comes to light for the rapid decline after about A.D. 1200 in construction at Angkor and for the silence that surrounds early thirteenth-century kingship there, it is worth suggesting that the story of a leper king, so often denigrated as myth, not only held its own in popular thinking, but represented the memory of an historical event.

---

[41] Eng Soth, *Akkasar mahaboros khmaer* ("Documents about Cambodian Heroes"), (Phnom Penh, 1969), pp. 1096–1097. See also Manuscript P-31 (fonds EFEO, Phnom Penh) in the Ecole Française d'Extrême Orient, Paris. and pp... below.

[42] Chandler, "Maps for the Ancestors", *passim*. Another folk memory of Angkor, perhaps specifically of Jayavarman VII, is reported by Albrecht, "Reconnaissance de l'anciennes chaussées . . .", *BSEI*, 1904, pp. 1–17 at 7: "in former times, the old people say, on the great road which leads to Angkor, each stage of the journey was marked by a monument". See G. Cœdès, "Les gîtes d'étape à la fin du XII siècle", *BEFEO*, XL (1940), pp. 347–349.

AN EIGHTEENTH CENTURY INSCRIPTION FROM ANGKOR WAT

Between 1541 and 1747 AD some thirty Khmer inscriptions, numbered collectively by Professor Coedès as K. 301,[1] were incised onto pillars in the galleries (Brāh Bān) connecting the second and third enclosures of Angkor *wat*.[2] Generally, these inscriptions commemorate Buddhist ceremonies performed in the galleries at the behest of secular worthies and contain valuable information about religious practices and monastic structure. Others also give dates when monarchs or high officials visited the temple. The 1747 inscription is interesting for these reasons and because some forty of its seventy-six lines are given over to the partial biography of an important Cambodian official.

This paper was first published in *Journal of the Siam Society*, July 1971, Vol. 59 Part 2, reprinted with permission.

[1] George Cœdès (ed.), *Inscriptions du Cambodge*, Vol. 8 (Paris, 1966), 129. The inscriptions in question are printed in *Silajarik Nokor Vatt* (Inscriptions of Angkor Wat, Phnom Penh, 1958); for the 1747 inscription, see pp. 111–117. See also Etienne Aymonier, "Les inscriptions de Preah Pean (Angkor Wat)", *Journal Asiatique (JA)* 19 (1899), pp. 493–529. Throughout this essay, except in the case of topynyms, I have generally followed the transcription system proposed in Saveros Lewitz, "Note sur la translittération du Cambodgien", *Bulletin de'l Ecole Francaise d' Extrême Orient (BEFEO)* 55 (1969), pp. 163–170.

[2] The popular name Brāh Bān ("sacred images") refers to the Buddha-images collected there. See Au Chhieng, "Ban et rnnoc, deux thèmes de réflexion méthodologique pour l'étude de vieux khmer" in *Mélanges d'Indianisme à la mémoire de Louis Renou* (Publications de l'Institut de Civilisation Indienne, Vol. 28), pp. 44–51. The name dates at least from the seventeenth century: see *Silajarik*, 32 (inscription of 1629 AD).

The years covered by this part of the inscription (1737–1747) coincide roughly with those generally given for the third and last reign of the Cambodian monarch Thammrājā IV.[3] Little is known about his personality, beyond the fact that he spent the thirty years between his second and third reigns in semi-retirement in Siam. During this period, Cambodia was governed alternately by two kings, each of whom reigned twice. The first, Ang Im (reigned 1710–1722 and 1729–1730) was related to Thammrājā IV by marriage.[4] He abdicated twice to his son, Sāttā (reigned 1722–1729 and 1730–1737), but seems to have maintained considerable power, for a struggle to overthrow Sāttā ensued immediately after his father's death in 1736. The chronicles relate that Sāttā's wife, Sijhātā, and her relations plotted against Sāttā. After losing battles to them the king fled into those parts of the Mekong delta which were under Vietnamese control.[5] At this point, the biographical portion of the 1747 inscription begins.

[3] Western-language sources for this period of Cambodian history are Jean Moura, *Le royaume du Cambodge* (2 vols, Paris 1884); Etienne Aymonier, *Le Cambodge* (3 vols., Paris, 1900–1904) and Ahémard Leclère, *Histoire du Cambodge* (Paris, 1914). In Khmer, the only detailed source is Eng Sut (ed.) *Akasār mahāboros khmaer.* (Documents about Cambodian heroes, Phnom Penh, 1969) which draws heavily on manuscript sources. Two Thai translations of Cambodian chronicles (not yet printed in Khmer) are also useful: *Ratchaphongsawadan krung kamphucha* (Royal chronicle of the kingdom of Cambodia, Bangkok, 1917, reprinted 1970) and *Phongsawadan Khamen* (Khmer chronicle), which appears as part of the first volume of the series *Prachum phongsawadan* (Collected chronicles, Bangkok, National Library edition, 1963). A copy of the Cambodian manuscript which the *Ratchaphongsawadan* purports to translate, the so-called Nupparot chronicle of 1878, is in the National Library in Bangkok. Although the *Ratchaphongsawadan* often constitutes more of a treatment than a translation, the portions of the Nupparot chronicle covering the years 1737–1747 (pp. 94–97) are accurately translated in the *Ratchaphongsawadan*. For a discussion of these sources, see George Cœdès, "Essai du classification des documents historiques cambodgiens. . . ." *BEFEO* 18. 9 (1918), pp. 15–28.

[4] Ang Im's wife was the daughter of Thammrājā IV's father, King Jai Jesthā, who reigned four times in Cambodia and died there in 1729. Ang Im's wife's half sister, Sijhata, married Ang Im's son, Sāttā.

[5] Eng Sut, pp. 861–862, says that Sāttā personally sought help from the Vietnamese monarch, who refused it.

The inscription itself concerns three major characters: the narrator, an unnamed Cambodian offcial bearing three successive titles; his patron, Thammrājā IV, both before and after he came to power, and the narrator's wife, who accompanied him to Angkor *wat*. These persons appear in the inscription under the titles they bore at the moments of history being discussed—in other words, with several different names.

In December, 1747,[6] the inscription begins, a Cambodian official entitled *okñā voṅsā aggrāj*, accompanied by his wife, convened monks at Brāh Bān to recite prayers associated with memorial services for the dead.[7] The inscription then doubles back to trace part of the narrator's career, beginning at an unspecified date (earlier than January, 1738) when he was in Siam with Thammrājā IV and bore a title which translates roughly as minister of war.[8] The "ruling monarch" of Cambodia, the inscription tells us, had recently left Ayudhya and had reached the district of Chantabori on the coast.[9] Here he ordered the narrator to go to the town of Lovek to meet "the lesser prince", entitled *brāh kaev fā*. We know from the chronicles that Thammrājā IV travelled from Ayudhya to Chantabori in 1737, and it seems likely that the "lesser prince" was his nephew Cān, a cousin of Sāttā's

---

[6] The date appears in the inscription as Thursday, thirteenth waxing day of the month *magsir*, 1669 *saka*, year of the hare. Most of the other dates in the inscription are in the form of animal years.

[7] This prayer is given in the inscription as *baṅsukul annicā*. I am grateful to mahā Prahsan Bunprahkong of the Department of Fine Arts for identifying it. See also Evéline Porée-Maspéro, *Cérémonies Privées des Cambodgiens* (Phnom Penh, 1958), p. 76.

[8] This title, *copañā montri sanggrām*, still existed in the 1790s, but apparently went out of use at some point in the nineteenth century. See Prince Damrong Ratchanuphap (ed.) *Tamtra tamniap bandasak krung kamphucha* (Guide to the rankings of the royal household of Cambodia, Bangkok, 1922), p. 5, and *Phongsawadan Khamen*, 237. This officer was responsible for the flintlock weapons of the *upayoraj*, the prince who has abdicated. It was probably given the narrator by Thammrājā IV when he abdicated leadership of the Cambodian court at Ayudhya to his son, an event which Leclère (p. 377) places in 1732, and Eng Sut (pp. 857–858) five years later.

[9] Before leaving Ayudhya, Thammrājā IV probably obtained permission to do so from the Siamese king, Baromokot, who also provided him with troops. See Eng Sut, p. 864, and *Phongsawadan Khamen*, p. 198.

rebellious wife.[10] The chronicles place Cān at about this time in Lovek, north of the traditional Cambodian capital at Udong, gathering troops to overthrow King Sāttā.[11]

We do not know if the narrator's mission was a success, but the inscription says that by January, 1738, he was already "sad, poor, without riches or possessions". At this point an aunt visited him in Lovek, accompanied by an unmarried female cousin named Sor.[12] These women gave him clothes and he "hurried after" them to Samrong Sen, a swampy region north of Lovek, near the mouth of the Tonle Sap.[13] Here he encountered a "young queen, princes, princesses, royal nephews and royal nieces; he also saw his own aunt, and his relations to seven degrees of kinship".[14] The "young queen" was probably Sāttā's rebellious wife, Sijhātā, who was in Samrong Sen at about this time.[15] During the narrator's stay there (and perhaps this is why he had gone) he courted and married a young woman, Pau, who had "large quantities of goods and slaves". When the couple returned to the "fortified city" (presumably Lovek)[16] they received titles from the "great prince", Thammrājā IV's eldest son. This prince, who bore his father's name and was to succeed him to the throne in 1748,

---

[10] *Ratchaphongsawadan*, 114, and Eng Sut, 861. Although Ang lm had been known by this title (bestowed on him in 1699 by his father-in-law, King Jai Jestha) for most of his life, he had assumed the title of *upayoraj* when he abdicated for the last time in 1730.

[11] Lovek, the capital of Cambodia throughout most of the sixteenth century, had been reoccupied in 1732, and made the capital again, by King Sāttā. Sāttā abandoned Lovek following his father's death in 1736. See *Ratchaphongsawadan*, p. 115; *Phongsawadan Khamen*, 195, and Eng Sut, p. 855.

[12] Aymonier, *Le Cambodge*, Vol. 3, p. 31, suggests that the narrator was in prison, but the form his rescue took makes this unlikely.

[13] The region has been famous since the 1870s for the neolithic artifacts discovered there. For its strategic importance, see Aymonier, *Le Cambodge*, Vol. 1, p. 354.

[14] For the concept of seven degrees, see Solange Thierry, "Contribution à une étude de la societé cambodgienne", *L'Ethnographie* 58–9 (1964–1965), pp. 63–70.

[15] *Ratchaphongsawadan*, 115; *Phongsawadan Khamen*, 198; Eng Sut, p. 866.

[16] See Saveros Lewitz, "Quelques cas complexes de dérivation en cambodgien", *Journal of the Royal Asiatic Society* 1969, Part 1, p. 43.

had preceded his father into Cambodia, travelling to the capital *via* Angkor *wat*.[17] The narrator's new title, *okña surinthrāthibbāti*, carried with it, in the nineteenth century at least, revenues from the district of Roleia Pear, south of the Tonle Sap.[18] More interestingly, his wife's new title, *comtav sri ratna kesrā*, combined those of his aunt (*ratna kañña*) and his deceased mother (*kaññā kesrā*). This fact reveals the narrator's deep sense of obligation to these two women and suggests that his wife may even have been his aunt's daughter, if not the girl Sor mentioned earlier in the inscription.[19] No date is given for these events, which probably occurred in 1739 or 1740.

In 1741–1742, the inscription goes on, a royal personage referred to as the "revered father"—probably Thammrājā IV— gave the narrator the title he still bore in 1747—*okñā voñsā aggrāj*. In the eighteenth century, this official shared responsibility with the minister of justice (the *yommrāj*) for the supression of disorders.[20] In the nineteeth century, with similar duties, the office was part of the parallel administrative structure alloted to the second princely house, that of the *obbayorāj*, or prince who has abdicated.[21] This connection, and the absence of the phrase "ruling monarch" from the titles attached to the "revered father", suggests that in 1741–1742 Thammrājā IV was not fully in control of the kingdom. By 1744–1745, however, this situation appears to have changed, for the inscription tells us that a ruling monarch with some of the same titles as the "revered father" ordered the narrator to subdue bandits operating in five districts a!ong the southern shore of the Tonle Sap. The narrator may still have had

---

[17] This prince expected to be crowned himself, according to Leclère (p. 377).

[18] A. Fourès, "Royaume du Cambodge. Organisation politique", *Excursions & Reconnaissances* 13 (1882), pp. 169–211. In the 1790s, the title was associated with the ministry of justice: see Prince Damrong, p. 11.

[19] For the mother's title, see *Silajarik*, p. 117. The Khmer word *pan*, although frequent as a proper name, also means merely "younger".

[20] Ahémard Leclère, *Les Codes cambodgiens* (2 vols., Paris, 1898), Vol. 2, 32, mentions this officer in connection with a law promulgated by King Sāttā in 1723. See also Leclère, *Histoire*, 408, and Aymonier, *Le Cambodge*, Vol. 1, p. 236.

[21] Etienne Aymonier, *Le Géographie du Cambodge* (Paris, 1876), p. 42.

duties connected with one of these districts, Roleia Pear, and his expedition was apparently a success.[22]

In the summer of 1747, the narrator was ordered to raise troops to fight a "princess who was the daughter of the prince *brāh kaev fā*". No other source mentions her or this rebellion. However, we know from the chronicles that the *brāh kaev fā* originally named by Thammarājā IV, prince Cān, had died in 1743. His widow, whom he had married when Thammrājā IV assumed the throne, soon married one of the king's own sons. Another son was then appointed *brāh kaev fā*.[23] This sequence of events may have insulted Cān's relations, who had been helpful in returning Thammrājā IV to power. A daughter from Cān's earlier marriage, owing nothing to the monarch, might thus have been able to rally troops whose loyalty was primarily to Cān. In any case, the rebellion apparently failed. For his generalship the narrator was offered the position of *okña tejō*, with which to administer the important territorial division of Kompong Svay, north of the Tonle Sap.[24] This part of the inscription is obscure, but the narrator apparently refused the promotion, perhaps temporarily, choosing instead to travel to Angkor *wat*.[25] His wife, his aunt, and several female relations went with him.

Here the biography stops, and the last lines of the inscription describe the ceremonies at Brāh Bān in which the family took part. A curious feature of these ceremonies was the temporary entrance into religious life of several women, including the narrator's wife and aunt, but not the narrator himself. For

---

[22] The inscription says that after the bandits were surpressed "commerce flourished, and goods went in and out", suggesting that the bandits had disrupted internal commerce at a time when Cambodia's access to the sea was blocked by the prcsence of a group of Sino-Vietnamese who administered the ports on the gulf. See Emile Gasparadone, "Un chinois des mers du sud", *JA* 240 (1952), pp. 363–386.

[23] Eng Sut, 872; *Phongsawadan Khamen*, p. 201

[24] For a discussion of this post, see Jean Imbert, *Histoire des institutions khmères* (Phnom Penh, 1961), p. 67.

[25] Despite his refusal, the monarch appears to have given him the regalia of office.

their services in reciting prayers and the great Jataka, monks at the temple were offered silver, cloth and other objects. The inscription closes by recalling the narrator's mother and father, in whose honor an inscription had been incised onto a neighboring pillar in 1703.[26]

The 1747 inscription is the last extensive one at Angkor *Wat* and reveals the importance of the temple in Cambodian religious life barely a century before it was "discovered" by the French. The inscription itself is helpful for the political and social information it conveys. For example, the importance of women in the narrator's career, in the religious ceremonies at Brāh Bān, and in the two dynastic revolts mentioned in the inscription throws an interesting side-light onto the question of the dynamics of power in Cambodia at this time. The inscription also reveals a continuity of patronage and functions within a single bureaucratic career. Finally, the inscription provides valuable support for the chronicles and offers some claritications in matters of dating. The length of time between Sāttā's departure and Thammrājā IV's assumption of power, the inscription suggests, lasted at least from 1737 to 1741–1742, and perhaps longer. The chronicles obliquely confirm this delay without stressing dates by spelling out the extensive set of patronage and marriage arrangements which Thammrājā IV made among his potential supporters before resuming the throne.[27] These arrangements seem to have disintegrated when Thammrājā IV died, in 1747–1748, and the dynastic turmoil which followed lasted for over thirty years.

---

[26] This earlier inscription dates from Thammrājā IV's first reign.
[27] Eng Sut, pp. 873–877.

TRANSLATION

[To those who read what follows] greetings, good health, prosperity, victory.

In the year 1669 *saka*, year of the hare, month *magsir*, thirteenth waxing day, a Thursday, at an auspicious moment all the ranking members of the sacred order assembled, the lords of the ever prosperous community superiors, teachers, elders and novices in the right proportions, as requested by *okñā voṅsa aggrāj* and the lady *sri ratna kesrā* who had gone up [the steps] to [perform a ceremony with which to] earn merit, and had invited the monks to recite *baṅsukula aunicā* at Brāh Bān.

When *okñā voṅsa aggrāj* was still [entitled] *copoña montri sanggrām*, the ruling monarch [of Cambodia] bid farewell and left Krung Thep, the great city (Ayudhya) and came to the region of Chantabori, where he ordered *copoña montri sanggrām* to come first to the fortified city of Lovek and meet the lesser prince, whose title was *brāh kaev fā*.

In the year of the dragon, month *magh* [the narrator] was in difficulty, sad, poor, without riches or possessions. Then the lady *ratna kañna*, the younger sister of one of his parents, and an unmarried girl named Sor, a cousin, sent a silk skirt and a jacket to *copoña* in Lovek. He hurried after his relations to the region of Samrong Sen, where he met a young queen, princes, princesses, royal nephews and royal nieces; he also saw his own aunt and his relations to seven degrees of kinship. He courted and took in marriage a young woman Pau who had large quantities of goods and slaves.

[Having returned to] the fortified city, the great prince, whose title was *sri thammrājā*, bestowed the title of *okña surinthrathibbāti*, and on the woman Pau that of *sri ratna kesrā*. Later the revered father, *baromnit brāh bāt baromobupit*, bestowed the title of *okñā voṅsa aggrāj*, in the year of the cock. In the year of the rat, the ruling monarch, *brāh bāt baromnit brāh bāt baromobupit* ordered *okñā voṅsa aggrāj* to assemble soldiers, slaves, dependants and relations to go out and subdue bandits in the districts of Roleia

Pear, Borbaur Klong, and Krakor. [The narrator] defeated the bandits, and made them resume their fealty to the ruling monarch. Then there was plenitude and abundance in the country; and the people were happy and at ease. Commerce . . . flourished* and goods went in and out.

On Friday, the 3rd waning day, month *asadh*, year of the hare, *jai jesthā thirāj rama thibbāthi baromanadh brāh bāt barombupit*, the ruling monarch, commissioned *oknā voṅsā* agg . . . to be a general. He accepted the royal command . . .* bowed, bid farewell, and went out to gather soldiers, conscripts, dependants and relations to confront and wage war against a princess who was the daughter of the *brāh kaev fā*. He fought the princess and defeated her, driving out, dispersing, seeking out and disintegrating [the enemy forces] so that they became aware of the ruling monarch's power. [Indeed, the victory was due to] the strategy, intelligence and tactics of *okñā voṅsa aggrāj*, who planned and carried out attacks throughout the countryside, cutting across every road and path, until the forces, slaves and goods of the princess were led in [to the capital] and offered up [to the king].

Then *brāh bāt baromnit brāh bāt baromobupit*, the ruling monarch, prepared an edict, benevolently bestowing upon *okñā voṅsa aggrāj* the title of *okñā tejō*, to consume (administer) the province of Kompong Svay. [The narrator] implored the king, and did not accept the reward; (but ?) the king honored him with a gold plate and a four-tiered umbrella. [The narrator] bowed low and bid farewell to *brāh bāt baromnit brāh bāt baromobupit*. He went away and came to earn merit at Brāh Bān.

[There he] entered into religious life the lady ratna kanna, his aunt; his wife, the lady *sri ratna kesrā*; a young woman Kim, who was a relative by marriage; and two nieces. These entered as nuns to earn merit on a single day. For his aunt, the following monks were invited to recite *baṅsukul annicā*: two superiors, five abbots, and eleven teaching monks. To recite on behalf of *okñā voṅsa*

---

* *Lacuna* in original.

aggrāj were one superior, one abbot, and two teaching monks. For the lady *ratna kesrā* there were one superior, two abbots, and six teaching monks. The following contributions were made: for each superior, an ounce of silver; for teaching monks, eight strings of coins per monk. [When the monks had] finished reciting, the two superiors and the three abbots were each offered an ounce of silver, and teaching monks were offered two *baht*. The two novices who had recited prayers were offered one *baht*, and the seventy novices who had [joined in chanting] *baṅsukul annicā* each received a string of coins.

Then the congregation was asked to recite the great Jataka, once, and Kuṅ, an eight-year-old boy, was offered to the Law, along with three *baht*, and was repurchased for seven ounces of silver. The congregation was asked to record these actions, and to record the honor [which fell to those who] entered religious life. Other offerings [to the monks] included a carved box, a shoulder-bag, a length of white cloth, and a silk scarf for betel. The cost of musicians was seven *baht*. All the offerings totalled three *jing* of silver.

Those who made the offerings were *okñā voṅsa aggrāj*, the son of *okñā krālāhom* senabortes and of lady *kañña kesra*: the lady ratnā kesrā; and Hiṅ, Prom, and Kuṅ. All of these people were eager to gain merit, and made these offerings to their parents and ancestors, to seven degrees of kinship.

They ask further to be granted great age, reaching five thousand rainy seasons, as well as wisdom and riches resembling those of (a mythical merchant named) Jotikasetti. Finally, they beg to be granted health and happiness until the time that they enter Nirvana.

MAPS FOR THE ANCESTORS:
SACRALIZED TOPOGRAPHY AND ECHOES OF ANGKOR IN TWO CAMBODIAN TEXTS

This paper will be concerned with invocations to local spirits, known generically as *me sa*, which are found in two Cambodian texts: one dating from 1859[1] and the other, printed in 1946, dating at least from the 1880s.[2]

The first text tells us that halfway through the month of *srap* (July-August) 1859, the Cambodian king Duang (r. 1848–1860) sponsored a ceremony at his capital, Udong, to cleanse his kingdom of demerit by offering gifts to its guardian deities and spirits, summoned by name in prayers recited by his

In writing this paper, I benefited from correspondence and discussions with R.I. Heinze, Charles F. Keyes, Ian Mabbett, the late Eveline Porée-Maspéro, Saveros Pou, Thong Thel, Craig Reynolds, Michael Vickery and Hiram W. Woodward, Jr. This paper was first published in *Journal of the Siam Society*, July 1976, Vol. 64, Part 2, reprinted with permission.

[1] *Bakya prakasa devata knung Brah rajabidhi parunasastra* (Text of a decree to the spirits in a royal ceremony connected with Varuna) in Buddhist Institute (comp.) *Brah rajabidhi dvad samasa* (Royal Festivals of the Twelve-Months' cycle), Phnom Penh, 1951, 172–179, translated (with several omissions) as Adhémard Leclère, "Les fêtes locales au Cambodge. Un *pithi plieng* (rain-summoning ceremony)", *Revue Indochinoise* (*RI*) 1906, pp. 90–99. A text with the same title in Leclère, *Cambodge, Fêtes civiles*, Paris, 1916, does not include the full list of toponyms.

[2] Kingdom of Cambodia, *Saccā pranidhān samrap broe nau sālā jumnum knung kambujā* (Oath to be used in the courts of Cambodia), Phnom Penh, 1946 (Text MCC 56.036 in the archives of the Buddhist Institute). I am grateful to Pech Thinh for providing a typescript of this text. The first lines of the invocation are identical to those in the oath cited in part by Leclère, *Fêtes civiles*, pp. 634ff., (collected in Kampot in the 1880s).

court brahmans, or *baku*. Another purpose of the ceremony, normally conducted somewhat earlier in the year, was to ask these guardians for rain.[3] The invocation runs to some eighty lines of print. About half of these are addressed to recognizable Indian gods. The last thirty five lines, however, invoke roughly a hundred local spirits identified with toponyms and topographical features throughout Cambodia. About two-thirds of these can easily be identified.

The second text to be examined is a civil oath (Saccā Praṇidhan) the first two-thirds of which is taken up by a similar list of *me sa*, running to over two hundred names which, as Mme. Porée Maspéro has written, pose "arduous problems of identification".[4] Five of the names in this list (two of which also appear in the 1859 text) are associated with archaeological sites from the reign of Yasovarman I (r. 889–c. 910), the founder of Angkor. These names are clustered together in such a way as to suggest "memories" of Angkor that are absent from other Cambodian sources including post-Angkorean inscriptions, folk tales and the chronicles or *bangsavatar*.

The lists themselves are interesting for several reasons. In the first place, similar toponymical invocations have been recorded in Laos[5] and among Indo-Chinese tribal peoples,[6] but they do not

---

[3] Rainmaking ceremonies were normally celebrated in April and May, according to *Brah rajabidhi*, II, pp. 170–171; see also Evéline Porée-Maspéro, *Etude sur les rites agraires des cambodgiens* (*Etude*), 3 vols., Paris, 1961–1969, I, 237. The festival was delayed in 1859 because of Duang's temporary absence in Kampot.

[4] Porée-Maspéro, *Etude*, 12, n.1. In identifying toponyms in the text, I have relied on G. Cœdès, "Index alphabetique pour *Le Cambodge* de M. Aymonier", Bulletin de la Commission archaeologique de l'Indochine, vol. 1(1911) pp. 85–169, and United States Army Topographic Command, Geographic Names Division, Cambodia, Washington, 1971.

[5] See Anonymous, "Prestation du petit serment à l'occasion du nouvel an laotien" *Bulletin de l'Ecole Française d'Extrême Orient* (*BEFEO*) XXIX (1929) pp. 530–532; P. Nginn, "Invocation aux devata dans le cérémonie du serment" *France-Asie* (*FA*) VIII (1951) pp. 573–576, and Thao Viboun, "Le Basi", *La Revue Française* No. 34 (Jan. 1952) pp. 91–93. See also Charles Archaimbault, "La fête du T'at a Sieng khwang (Laos)" *Artibus Asiae* (*AA*) XXIV, 3–4 (1961) pp. 191–2, n.16, and Archaimbault, "Les cérémonies en l'honneur des *phi f'a* (phi célestes) à Basak (Sud Laos)" *Asie du Sud-Est el Monde Insulinde* (*ASEMI*) VI/I (1975) pp. 85–114.

[6] For examples, see J. Boulbet, "Börde au rendez-vous des genies" *Bulletin de*

seem to have been a feature of Thai ceremonies, either at court or in the countryside, in spite of the extensive exchange of cultural baggage among the Thai, Lao and Khmer in the centuries that followed the abandonment of Angkor.[7] Another interesting feature of the lists is that they are the only written maps, on a national scale, that have come down to us from pre-colonial Cambodia. The absence of pictorial maps (which survive from nineteenth century Thailand and Vietnam)[8] is less important when approaching the Angkorean echoes, for example, than the presence of these recited ones which are suggestive of Cambodian notions, probably extending back at least to Angkor, of sacred space, ethnicity and jurisdiction.[9] The lists, like those found in the inscriptions at the ground level of the Bayon, a Buddhist temple built at Angkor at the end of the twelfth century, are in some senses an inventory of the kingdom, a map of and for the

la societé des études indochinoises (*BSEI*) XXX (1960) p. 640; Bernard Jouin, *La mort et la tombe*, Paris, 1949, p. 227, and Albert Maurice, "Trois fêtes agraires rhade" *BEFEO* XLV (1951–1952) p. 191.

[7] I am grateful to Ruth Inge Heinze, Charles F. Keyes, Craig Reynolds, and Hiram W. Woodward, Jr. for their (fruitless) efforts to unearth Thai toponymical litanies. One possible exception is the short list of ancestor spirits, some associated with places, in the fourteenth century Thai oath translated in A.B. Griswold and Prasert na Nagara, "The Pact Between Sukhodaya and Nan. Epigraphical and Historical Studies No. 3", *JSS*, 57/1 (January 1969) 57–109 at pp. 80–82.

[8] For Thai examples see Victor Kennedy, "An Indigenous Early 19th Century Map of Central-Northeastern Thailand" in Tej Bunnag and Michael Smithies (eds). *In Memoriam Phya Anuman Rajadon*, Bangkok, 1970, 315–348 and Klaus Wenk, "Zu einer "Laadkarte" Sued und Ostasiens" in Siam Society, *Felicitation Volume of Southeast Asian Studies presented to H. H. Prince Dhaninivat*, Bangkok, 1965 (2 vols) I, pp. 119–122. See also the "map" of Burma and Siam described in F.A. Neale, *Narrative of a Residence at the Capital of the Kingdom of Siam*, London, 1852, 55, where Siam and Burma are depicted as two people, with Siam the larger. For reference to Vietnamese maps, see A.B. Woodside, *Vietnam and the Chinese Model*, Cambridge, Mass. 1971, p. 257; P. Huard and M. Durand (comps.), *Connaissance du Vietnam*, Hanoi 1954, p. 4, and Nguyen van Huyen, "A propos d'une carte de repartition des génies tutelaires dans le province de Bac-Ninh" *Institut Indochinois pour l'étude de l'homme* III (1940) pp. 137–155.

[9] For a stimulating discussion of ethnicity, see Robert A. Levine and Donald Campbell, *Ethnocentrism: Theories of Conflict, Ethnic Attitudes and Group Behaviour*, New York, 1972, especially pp. 82–110. See also June Helm (ed.) *Essays in the Problem of Tribe*, Seattle 1968.

use of the ancestral spirits, or *nak tā*, being summoned from their normal dwelling places to be revered.[10] It is interesting to see how the toponyms are arranged. In both texts, they seem to proceed in a clockwise spiral, beginning to the east of Udong and gradually enclosing it within a *mandala*, or circle, keeping it to the right in a process known as *pradakṣinā*.[11] The act of recital, it would seem, and the shape formed by names recited in a given order perhaps as an aid to memorization were at least as important to the celebrants because, in a sense, the recital "built" the kingdom as much as the accuracy of the names themselves.

Since only twenty-two toponyms are common to both lists, it is unlikely that they spring from a common source or were compiled with reference to each other. In very general terms, the 1859 text appears to stress toponyms in the vicinity of Udong at the expense of those elsewhere. The oath has a greater number of toponyms associated with archaeological sites.[12] But so many toponyms in both lists cannot be identified that it is impossible to contrast the lists usefully in terms of the way the names they contain are distributed over the landscape.

Aside from Vietnam, which benefited from China's rich cartographic tradition,[13] scientific mapmaking was slow to develop

[10] See J. Dumarçay and B.P. Groslier, *Le Bayon*, Paris, 1973, pp. 113–134. The most succinct analysis of the cult of *nak tā* is Porée Maspéro, *Etude*, I, pp. 3–16. For various legends about them, see Buddhist Institute (comp.) *Brajum rioeñ preñ* (*BRP*) (Collected Old Stories) VIII, Phnom Penh, 1971. There is an exasperated "definition" of the phrase in Jean Moura, *Le royaume du Cambodge*, Paris, 1883, I, p. 172 :"Sortes de divinité locales, des génies tutelaires, d'anges gardiens d'une territoire, d'une forêt, d'une montagne, d'une île, d'une rivière, d'un arbre, d'un village, des bêtes féroces d'une contrée." On *me sa*, see below, p. 184.

[11] Evéline Porée-Maspéro, personal communication. On the process in general, see J. Przyluski, "*Pradaksina* . . . en Indochine" *Festschrift für M. Winternitz*, Leipzig, 1933, pp. 326–332, F.D.K. Bosch, "La procession du feu sacré" *UEFEO*, XXXII (1932) 7–21, and Groslier, *Bayon*, p. 194. There is an interesting set of Biblical parallels in E. Nourry, "Le tour de la ville et la chute de Jerico", Ch. 4 of his *Essais du folklore biblique*, Paris 1922.

[12] The oath also has more references than the 1859 text to mountains (23 to 7, with 2 overlaps), islands (15 to 3) and forests (14 to 2), but many of these are unidentifiable. It is not surprising that more than half of the identifiable toponyms in both texts represent sites within reach of Udong.

[13] See Joseph Needham and Wang Ling, *Science and Civilisation in China*,

on the mainland of Southeast Asia, and only one indigenous map of Cambodia-of dubious authorship-drawn earlier than the colonial era has survived.[14]

The absence of cartographic tradition in Cambodia can be traced to the isolation of villages from each other, the sedentary quality of Cambodian life and the absence of systematic cadastral records transmitted from one generation or regime to the next. In their everyday lives, Cambodians had little use for national or even supra-village maps, although there is abundant evidence that smaller scale ones existed.[15]

The absence of national maps, however, should not be taken to mean that Cambodians lacked notions of national space or internal divisions, especially as these were rendered sacred by local, royal and Buddhist ceremonies.[16] For ceremonial reasons at least Cambodia was divided for most of the nineteenth century into five *di* or "earths"[17]: Tboung Khmum to the east of Udong, Ba Phnom to the southeast, Trang to the southwest, Pursat to the

Vol. 3, Cambridge 1959, pp. 491–590.

[14] Anonymous, "Notes to accompany a map of Cambodia", *Journal of the Indian Archipelago*, 1851, pp. 306–311; the map was "compiled for the purpose of registering some items of geographical information" brought to Singapore by a Cambodian trade delegation. The reference to a "Cambodian geographical work" in Charles Gutzlaff, *Three Voyages along the Coast of China*, London 1833, p. 43, is probably spurious. In 1867, the Cambodian king presented the Societé Géographique with a map of Cambodia that had been prepared by the French; see H. Cordier, *Bibliteca Indosinica*, Paris, 1912 col. 2661.

[15] See inscription K. 466, for example, dated 1006 A.D., which includes a small map. The spacing of rest-houses along Cambodian roads in the twelfth century, and the distribution of Yasovarman's digraphic inscriptions also suggests fairly sophisticated notions of space. See G. Cœdès, "Les gîtes d'étape à la fin du XII siècle", *BEFEO*, XL (1940) pp. 347–49, and G. Cœdès, "A la récherche du Yasodharasrama", *BEFEO*, XXXII (1932) pp. 84–112. See also G. Cœdès, *Inscriptions du Cambodge* (IC) I. 193 (K806) and III, p. 19 (IC. 207).

[16] On Buddhist rituals, see M. Giteau, *Le bornage rituel des temples bouddhiques au Cambodge*, Paris 1969, and Luc Mogenet, "Notes sur la conception de l'éspace a Louang Phrabang", *Bulletin des Amis du Royaume Lao*, Nos. 7–8 (1972) pp. 166–96. On Vietnamese cults, see L. Cadière, "Sur quelques faits religieux ou magiques observés pendant une epidémie de cholera en Annam", *RI*, 1912, p. 116, and Cadière, "Le culte des bornes" *BEFEO*, XIX (1919) pp. 40–47.

[17] E. Aymonier, *Géographie du Cambodge*, Paris 1876, p. 29.

west, and Kompong Svay (known today as Kompong Thom, and before about 1700 as Santhuk) to the north.[18] These fell under the jurisdiction of five high-ranking officials, referred to in some sources as *sdach trān* or "regional kings".[19] Purely administrative districts, known as *sruk*, were governed by officials of lower rank.[20]

The origins of the *di* and *sdach trān* are obscure, although the motif of five sites, four grouped at cardinal points around a centre, is deeply rooted in Indian cosmology and frequently evident at Angkor.[21] The divisions as they stand are certainly post-Angkorean, however, if only because no *di* is centered at Angkor.[22]

[18] Adhémard Leclère, *Codes cambodgiens* Paris 1900, p. 119n.

[19] References to stac trān, as such, are rare in Cambodian texts, which usually refer to these officials by their administrative titles. For French references, see Leclère, *Codes cambodgiens*, p. 114ff., A. Leclère, *"Le sdach meakh"*, *Revue Indochinoise*, XI, 1905, pp. 1378–1384, and E. Aymonier, *Le Cambodge* (3 vols.) Paris 1900–1914, I, p. 280. A quartering of the kingdom was in effect under Jayavarman VII, according to Groslier, *Le Bayon*, 131, and Ceylonese governors in classical times were referred to as "the quarters" (Hocart, "The Four Quarters", *Ceylon Journal of Science* (1926) pp. 105–111 at 108). See E. Porée Maspéro, *Etude*, p. 384, for a Khmer legend about *stac trān* collected in southern Vietnam. The institution may well have been post-Angkorean (Michael Vickery, personal communication).

[20] Groslier, *Bayon*, 131, argues that the kingdom was divided into twenty four districts under Jayavarman VII. A century later, a Chinese visitor said there were "more than ninety" districts (P. Pelliot, *Memoires sur les coûtumes du Cambodge de Tchou Ta-kuan*, Paris 1951, p. 32). In the nineteenth century, the number fluctuated from around thirty to around fifty. Interestingly, only two-thirds of the districts in effect at any point in the nineteenth century appear in the oath, and less than a third appear in the 1859 text-an indication that the *baku* did not choose to proceed in compiling the "maps" from an administrative vantage-point.

[21] An excellent description of this pervasive notion is Paul Mus, "Barabadur, Les origines du stupa . . ." *BEFEO*, XXXII (1932) pp. 398–411, *passim*. See also A.M. Hocart, "The Four Quarters", and William H. Alkire, "Concepts of Order in Southeast Asia and Micronesia", *Comparative Studies in Society and History*, XIV/4 (1971) pp. 484–493, and H.W. Shorto's influential article, "The 32 myos in the medieval Mon kingdom" *Bulletin of the School of Oriental and African Studies (BSOAS)* 26 (1963), pp. 571–591. On directional symbolism, see B.L. Gordon, "Sacred Directions, Orientation, and the Top of the Map", *History of Religions (HR)* 10 (February 1970), pp. 211–227.

[22] Originally, the central *dī* may have been Ba Phnom. See David Chandler,

Aside from this "quartering" of the kingdom, what was important about the *sdach trān* was their ceremonial role, and their relationship to the king. French sources assert that they shared with the king the power to impose death sentences;[23] another role they played, according to Leclère, was to preside on the king's behalf at new years' ceremonies in the *di*, including those known as *loeñ nak tā* or "raising the ancestors", at which litanies of guardian spirits (and oaths of loyalty) were probably recited, and at which human and buffalo sacrifices occasionally took place.[24] At Udong, one manuscript suggests, the *sdach trān* represented the *di* at royal ceremonies, and came under the supervision of the *baku*.[25] Incidentally, all five of the *di* are mentioned in the oath, but only two (Pursat and Tboung Khmum) appear in Duang's text.

Before examining the lists in general terms, a particular group of toponyms-numbering perhaps fifteen (some may have been intended as combinations, and others are unidentified) in the oath deserves detailed attention. Seven of them are easily identifiable. They are all from Siem Reap, in the vicinity of Angkor; six of them are archaeological sites. Of these, five contain temples (and in two cases inscriptions) from the reign of Yasovarman I. The sixth site, Bakong, is a temple built in 881 A.D. by Yasovarman's father, Indravarman I (r. 869–889). Two of the six – Phnom Krom and Phnom Bakheng – also appear in the 1859 text, as does an unidentifiable one (Phnom Prah). The cluster of toponyms in the oath, which falls roughly half-way through the first one hundred names, is as follows:

"Royally Sponsored Human Sacrifices in Nineteenth Century Cambodia: the Cult of *nak tā* Uma Mahisāsuramardini at Ba Phom" below p. 118.

[23] E. Aymonier, *Cours de Cambodgien*, Saigon 1876, 125 and A. Leclère, *Réchêrches sur le droit publique des cambodgiens*, Paris 1894, pp. 188–9.

[24] Porée Maspéro, *Elude*, 246, p. 248.

[25] France, Bibliothèque Nationale, Fonds Indochinois 387, (Collection Adhémard Leclère)-an undated Cambodian manuscript that contains (p. 37) a diagram of temporary buildings put up by the *stac trān* at the capital. See Leclère, *Cambodge, Fêtes civiles*, 610, for the assertion that *stac trān* took orders from the *baku*, and also Leclère, "Bandenh trah reachea", *Revue Indochinoise*, XI, 1906, pp. 581–86.

1. *Phnom di* ("mountain of earth")

There are four sites of this name in present-day Cambodia,[26] Two are in Siem Reap, and one of these is a small hill, 272 metres above sea-level, north west of the Angkorean complex, where a temple dedicated to Harihara, and an inscription dated 893 A.D., was discovered by the French in 1914.[27] Cœdès and B.P. Groslier have argued that the hill is one of four temple sites grouped roughly at the cardinal points around Yasovarman's "central mountain" of Phnom Bakheng (number 15, below).[28] Another site of this name, west of Siem Reap, was visited by Aymonier in the 1870s, and is associated nowadays with a powerful *nak tā*.[29]

2. *promnat rusrei* (untranslatable)

Not identifiable as a toponym.

3. *brah indrachar* ("lord Indra the teacher")

Possibly an oblique reference to Indravarman I, or to one of his temples at Hariharalaya, but not identifiable with a particular site.

4. *jung khnes* ("point of a scraper")

Nowadays and presumably in the nineteenth century a floating village at the mouth of the Siem Reap river, near the base of Phnom Krom (below), with which it may be meant to elide in the text.

5. *phnom krom* ("lower mountain")

A small hill, 140 metres above sea level, "below", (i.e. south of) the Angkor complex.[30] The site is also mentioned in the 1859 text.

---

[26] U.S. Army Topographic Command, Cambodia, 194.

[27] G. Cœdès, "L'inscription du Phnom Dei", *BEFEO*, XVIII/9 (September 1918), pp. 13–14.

[28] See IC, IV, p. 98, n.2, and Groslier, *Bayon*, p. 156, These scholars agree that four of the five mountains are Bakheng, Phnom Krom, Phnom Dei, and Phnom Bok. The fifth, to the north, is the Phimeanakas, according to Groslier. For a discussion of the alignment of temples at Angkor, see P. Paris, "L'importance rituelle du nord-est et ses applications en Indochine", *BEFEO*, XLI (1941), pp. 301–333, with maps. Cœdès suggests that the fifth site should be to the west of Bakheng, but no elevated site associated with Yasovarman has been located in that direction.

[29] Aymonier, *Le Cambodge*, II, p. 369. See also Buddhist Institute, *BRP*, VIII, pp. 57–61.

[30] On Cambodian directions, see S. Lewitz, "Récherches sur la vocabulaire cambodgien, VI. Les noms des points cardinaux" *Journal Asiatique* (*JA*) (1970).

On its summit is a temple attributed by scholars to the reign of Yasovarman I.[31]

6.   *prek banteai dom* ("stream of the lofty fortress [es]"?)

Not identifiable; perhaps an oblique reference to the Siem Reap River, which flows through the Angkor complex.

7.   *prek banteai tvea* ("stream of the fortress [es] at/of the gate")

Not identifiable, unless as a reference to the Siem Reap river. There is a twelfth century temple, Athvea, between Phnom Krom and Siem Reap.[32]

8.   *phnom prah* ("mountain of the sacred"?]

This toponym also occurs in the 1859 text, where Leclère identifies it as a village near Udong "whose *nak tā* is very powerful".[33] There is a small hill called Prah Phnom ("sacred mountain") in western Siem Reap, with three inscriptions indicating devotions at the site to Siva.[34] The toponym is perhaps intended to merge with (9) below.

9.   *our chay* ("beautiful stream"?)

Unidentifiable, even if read with (8) above.

10.   *baray tuk thla* ("dam of clear water")

Unidentifiable, but perhaps a reference to the catchment area built at Angkor by Yasovarman, the Yasodharatataka, known today as the Baray, where four inscriptions of Yasovarman have been found.[35]

---

[31] M. Glaize, "Le dégagement du Phnom Krom", *BEFEO*, XL (1940) pp. 371–81.

[32] Aymonier, *Le Cambodge*, II, 400 ff. See also G. Cœdès, "La grotte de Bon Prah Thvea", *BEFEO*, XI (1911) 398–400, which describes a site on Phnom Kulen dedicated to Siva.

[33] Leclère, "Fêtes locales", p. 98, note 23.

[34] See G. Cœdès, *Incriptions du Cambodge*, III, p. 121.

[35] G. Cœdès, "A la récherche du Yaçodharaçrama" discusses inscriptions K. 279–282, as well as Yasovarman's digraphic inscriptions (note 50, below). The Yasodharatataka is mentioned in thirty-two inscriptions, including the digraphic ones.

11. *mahasiek rithi* (siek is not translatable; maha . . . rithi means "great power")
Unidentifiable: possibly intended as attributes of an unidentified person or deity.

12. *lolei* (not translatable; perhaps a garble for Hariharalaya)
An archaeological site near the village of Roluos in Siem Reap, located near temples built by Indravarman I at his capital of Hariharalaya. The site is marked by a four-towered brick temple erected (or completed) by Yasovarman I in honour of his ancestors in 893 A.D. The temple contains several of his inscriptions : one (K. 323) from 889 A.D. and the others (K. 324–338) from 893 A.D.[36]

13. *bak dong* ("broken dong tree")
Although there is a village of this name in Kompong Thom, the phrase probably refers to the temple-mountain of Bakong, erected by Indravarman I at Hariharalaya in 881 A.D.[37]

14. *phnom bok* ("hump-back mountain")
A small hill, 212 metres above sea-level, about 10 kilometres northeast of Angkor Thom, crowned with a temple attributed to Yasovarman I. Statues of Brahma, Siva and Visnu have been found there; the presence of these three resembles an arrangement noted by Maurice Glaize at Phnom Krom, and he suggests that the two temples were built at the same time, in alignment with Phnom Bakheng (number 15 below).[38]

15. *bakheng* ("ancestor kheng" or "mighty ancestor")
A small hill, about 100 metres above sea-level, located inside the archaeological complex of Angkor Thom, and covered with an elaborate pyramid, dedicated to Siva, which contains seven

[36] M. Glaize, *Les monuments du groupe d'Ankgor*. (Paris 1963) pp. 259–261. G. Cœdès, "La date du Bayon", *BEFEO*, XXVIII (1928), p. 91 suggests that the temple was originally intended to include six towers, and that work was suspended after Yasovarman moved his capital to Angkor. The inscriptions from Lolei are K. 323–338 and 947.

[37] Glaize, *Les monuments*, 250–254. Fourteen inscriptions have been found at this site : K. 304–308, 825–826, 829, 870, 882, 894–895 and 915.

[38] M. Glaize. "Phnom Bok. Dégagement", *BEFEO*, XXXIX (1939), pp. 340–341. See also Jean Boisselier, *Le Cambodge*, Paris 1966, 290. Like its "sister" temple at Phnom Krom, the site has no inscriptions.

inscriptions from the seventh to the fifteenth centuries A.D.[39] In 1932, V. Goloubew identified it as the "central mountain" (*phnom kandtal*) associated, in the eleventh century inscription of Sdok Kak Thom, with Yasovarman's devotion to the cult of the *devaraja*.[40] The site is also mentioned in the 1859 text.

The toponyms discussed above clearly represent less than fifteen real places, but the occurrence of five sites associated with Yasovarman is extraordinary not only in a text which is not otherwise systematic, but also because verbal "memories" of this kind are difficult to find elsewhere in Cambodian literature.[41] Two questions immediately arise: Why these sites, and not others? and why Yasovarman, and not another king?

Neither text mentions any of the monuments erected by Cambodia's greatest builder-king, Jayavarman VII (r. 1178–c. 1219), unless the reference to Angkor Thom in Duang's invocation

[39] Jean Filliozat, "Le symbolisme du montagne de Phnom Bakheng", *BEFEO*, XLIX (1953) p. 527ff. None of the inscriptions is from Yasovarman's reign.

[40] V. Goloubew, "Le Phnom Bakheng et la ville de Yasovarman", *BEFEO*, XXXIII (1933) 319–44, and Goloubew, "Nouvelles récherches autour de Phnom Bakheng", *BEFEO*, XXXIV (1934) pp. 576–600. For the eleventh century reference, see G. Cœdès and P. Dupont, "Les stèles de Sdok Kak Thom, Phnom Sandak at Prah Vihar" BBFEO, XLIII (1943–1945) pp. 156–154 at 113.

[41] The question of "memories" of Angkor would repay detailed research. The so-called "modern" inscriptions of Angkor *Wat* date from the sixteenth century to 1747 A.D. (S. Lewitz, "Les inscriptions modernes d'Angkor Wat", *JA*, 1972, 107–129) but ten identifiably nineteenth century inscriptions (IC, VIII, 10) are all from southern Cambodia. A poem entitled "The poem of Angkor Wat" was written in 1620 (S. Pou, "Note sur la date du *Poème d'Angar Vat*", *JA*, (1975) 1 19–124) and attributed the temple to a celestial architect, a theme echoed in the modern Khmer folk-tale, "Prasad Angkor" *BRP*, V, 1–2 5, trans. by P. Fabricius in *Nokor Khmer*, 2, (January-March 1970) pp. 47–61. Although the word Yasodharapura, Yasovarman's name for the city he founded, remained part of Cambodian royal titles until at least 1602 (N. Péri, "Essai sur les relations du Japon et de l'Indochine au XVI et XVII siècles", *BEFEO*, XXIII (1923), p. 129, Yasovarman's role in the construction of Angkor and his connection with the temples mentioned in the oath, were not clarified until the colonial era, by French scholars. On "post-Angkorean" Angkor, see B.P. Groslier, *Angkor et Le Cambodge au XVI siècle*, Paris, 1958, esp. pp. 90–139. In Khmer folk-beliefs their loss of the skills evident at Angkor is traced to the Thai theft, following the capture of Lovek in 1595, of Cambodian sacred texts (*kbuon*) concealed inside a sacred ox (*brah ko*) – Thong Thel, personal communication. See also E. Porée-Maspéro, *Etude*, 111.

refers to Jayavarman's capital, and neither text mentions Angkor Wat, even though this was familiar to eighteenth and nineteenth century Cambodians as a pilgrimage site.[42] Indeed, with a few exceptions, the identifiable toponyms in both documents reflect post-Angkorean conditions. Only one toponym in the 1859 text (Nakorn Ratchasima, in northeastern Thailand), and two in the oath (Basak in southern Laos, and Medaeng in southern Vietnam) can be located beyond the frontiers of eighteenth century Cambodia; these two, however, are probably references to sacred hills.[43]

Another anomaly about the fifteen sites is that they appear under their present-day names rather than their Sanskritized, Angkorean ones. There is no mention of Yasovarman's capital city, Yasodharapura, for example, or of its predecessors, unless Lolei is a reference to Hariharalaya. There is no way of telling, of course, when these popular names caught hold and whether, for example, the "ancestor" in the phrase *ba kheng* is Yasovarman himself, Siva, the name of the hill as Yasovarman found it, or, in different ways, all three of these.[44] With only two texts to refer to, it is also impossible to determine when, if, or why names were taken off or added to the lists, and thus, by implication, which

---

[42] Set David Chandler, "An Eighteenth Century Inscription from Angkor Wat", above pp. 3–24.

[43] Interestingly, neither list includes toponyms connected with Cambodian settlements in southern Vietnam, as listed in L. Malleret, "Anciens toponymes du delta du Mekong", *L'archeologie du Delta du Mekong*, 4 vols., Paris 1959–1963, IV, pp. 192–197. on Khmer settlement patterns, see B.P. Groslier, "Pour une géographie historique du Cambodge", Les cahiers d'outre-mer, 104 (October-December 1973) pp. 337–379. On Me Deng, see Paul Wheatley, "The Mount of the Immortals: a Note on Tamil Cultural Influence in Fifth Century Indochina", *Oriens Extremus* 21/1 (June 1974) 97–109. On Bassac, Ma Tuan Lin (tr. Marquis d'Hervey de St. Denis) *Ethnographie des peuples étrangers à la Chine*, Geneva 1876, 483 (the reference is to the mountain in c. 600 A.D.); Groslier, "Pour une géographie" 347 says that *Wat* Ph'u was a Khmer pilgrimage site in Angkorean times.

[44] See S. Lewitz, "Récherches sur la vocabulaire cambodgien. VIII, Bakong", *JA* (1970) pp. 147–149. Bakheng is mentioned as a Buddhist shrine in an unpublished post-Angkorean inscription, K. 1006, from Phnom Kulen, dating from the fifteenth or sixteenth century: Michael Vickery, personal communication.

regions and which ancestral spirits rose or diminished in power between Yasovarman's reign (or earlier) and the time when the texts assumed their present form.

The answer to some of the anomalies, I believe, lies in what we know, from inscriptions about Yasovarman's reign, which was marked by self-consciously proclaimed continuities with Cambodia's pre-Angkorean past, by bold architectural innovations, religious tolerance (or eclecticism) and centralized control, or at least suzerainty, extending throughout and well beyond the areas of present-day Cambodia.

On his mother's side, Yasovarman traced his ancestry to the ruling families of Vyadharapura, Sambhupura, and Anindita-pura – regional power centres associated with the kingdoms known to the Chinese as "Funan" and "Chenla".[45] On his father's side, he was a great-nephew of the first Angkorean king, Jayavarman II, under whose auspices the cult of the *devaraja* was allegedly introduced in 802 A.D.[46]

Architecturally, Yasovarman was the first Cambodian king to build extensively in stone rather than in brick and he seems to have had a personal preference for building monuments on the top of natural hills. Here, too, perhaps, he was self-

---

[45] See Claude Jacques, "*Etude*s d'epigraphie cambodgienne. VII. Sur l'emplacement du royaume d'Aninditapura", *BEFEO*, LIX (1972) pp. 193–205 and O.W. Wolters, "Jayavarman's Military Power: the Territorial Foundation of the Angkor Empire", *Journal of the Royal Asiatic Society (JRAS)* 1973, pp. 21–30.

[46] Four studies of *devaraja* are G. Cœdès, "Le veritable fondateur du culte de la royauté divine au Cambodge" in H.B. Sarkar (ed.) *R.C. Majumdar Felicitaiion Volume*, Calcutta, 1970, pp. 56–62; H. Kulke, "Der *devaraja* Kult", Saeculum, XXV/1 (1974) 24–55; I. W. Mabbett, "Devaraja", *Journal of Southeast Asian History (JSEAS)* X/2 (1969) pp. 204–209 and H. Mestier Du Bourg, "A propos du culte de dieu roi (*devaraja*) au Cambodge". *Cahiers d'Histoire mondiale*, 11 (1908–1969) pp. 499–516. See also K. Bhattacharya, "Hari Kambujendra", *Artibus Asiae* 27 (1964) pp. 72–76 and Jean Filliozat, "New Researches on the Relations between India and Cambodia", *Indica*, III (1966) pp. 95–106. Cœdès' synthesis in "Le veritable fondateur", p. 57, is impossible to improve:

"Les enterprises d'unification et d'hegemonie telle que celle de Jayavarman II s'accompagnaient regulièrement de l'etablissement sur une montagne naturelle ou artificielle du culte d'une divinité étroitement associé à la personne royale, transcendant les cultes locaux, symbolisant l'unité du royaume, et doublant sur le plan réligieux une action politique."

consciously identifying himself with his forebears, the "kings of the mountain"; Goloubew has speculated that Yasovarman saw Phnom Bakheng as the successor to earlier sacred hills (also honouring Siva) at Ba Phnom and at *Wat* Ph'u (Lingaparvata) in southern Laos.[47] Stylistically, too, the art of Yasovarman's reign marked a recognizable development from the past, and the beginnings of the so-called "Angkorean" style.[48]

The king's religious eclecticism has been discussed by Cœdès and L.P. Briggs,[49] but his primary devotion was to Siva, the deity mentioned most frequently in Yasovarman's so-called "digraphic" inscriptions, and the one to whom Bakheng was dedicated. The digraphic inscriptions – fourteen in all, with identical texts, except for one variable line, have been found throughout Cambodia, as well as at locations in southern Laos and eastern Thailand.[50]

In this context, we can speculate that the survival of five toponyms associated with Yasovarman, rather than with another king, arose in part from the fact that he founded Yasodharapura not only as the site of a personal shrine but as a national capital with the centre of the nation at Phnom Bakheng and digraphic inscriptions (as well as temples carefully placed at four cardinal points around the capital) indicating the extent of the new king's jurisdiction. Yasovarman was a map-maker himself, and it is likely

---

[47] Goloubew, "Phnom Bakheng . . ." p. 344. In the 1870s, Ganesa, the offspring of Siva and Kali, was thought to be the guardian of Phnom Bakheng; see J. Moura, "De Phnom Penh à Pursat en compagnie du roi du Cambodge", *Revue d'Extreme Orient*, I (1882), p. 100.

[48] Boisselier, *Le Cambodge*, 246 refers to several stylistic innovations whereby Yasovarman sought to "place Angkorean power on a new footing".

[49] Cœdès, "A la récherche" 106, L.P. Briggs, *The Ancient Khmer Empire*, Philadelphia, 1951, p. 112, and K. Bhattacharya, *Les religions brahmaniques dans l'ancien Cambodge*, Paris 1961, pp. 29–30.

[50] See Cœdès, IC, VIII, 17: inscription K. 323 at Lolei says that Yasovarman "made, at all the cardinal points, a hundred asrami". Aymonier, *Le Cambodge*, II, pp. 482–483 suggests, in view of their stylistic uniformity, that they were carved by a single artist. See Briggs, *The Ancient Khmer Empire*, p. 103, map 9, which shows that while the inscriptions are fairly evenly distributed to the east, southeast, south, centre and north (the two inscriptions from Laos, not shown on the map) nothing appears to the southwest, a "dead zone" for temples, as Groslier has suggested (*Le Bayon*, p. 125).

that toponymical litanies of a national sort were introduced, made popular or refined during his reign.[51] Yasovarman's ordering of toponyms in and around Yasodharapura – and thus to an extent his animation of the landscape – is what survives from his reign in these toponymical texts. Another reason for the survival of the names may be that the king's devotion to Siva found echoes at other levels of Cambodian life (such as village ceremonies of "raising the ancestors", for example) which Jayavarman VII's esoteric and grandiose Buddhism did not.[52] Finally, there is the fact that the successors of Yasovarman's court brahmins, who presided over such non-Buddhist rites as rainmaking ceremonies and oaths of loyalty in the nineteenth century, also retained custody of the lists.

Another interesting feature of the lists is the phrase *me sa*, written *me sar* in the 1859 text. Some thirty toponyms in Duang's invocation and eleven in the oath are preceded by these words. In some cases, *me sa* apparently should be read as a plural; in others, it is connected with only one toponym. The phrase is used inconsistently in the two texts attached to archaeological sites, administrative divisions, and oddities of the landscape.[53]

---

[51] See Inscription K. 286 (IC, I-V, p. 58) for a description of Yasovarman's frontiers. The fact that an eleventh century oath of office, with the two hundred-odd officials associated with specific *sruk*, is incised at the Phimeanakas, a temple with connections with Yasovarman (see above, note 28) may also indicate such a "memory". The ceremony may have included some ritualistic blood-letting; see note 52 below. See IC, III, pp. 207–216.

[52] See P.C. Bagchi, "On some Tantrik Texts Studied in Ancient Cambodia", *Indian Historical Quarterly*, 5 (1929) pp. 754–769. One of the texts, mentioned in connection with the *devaraja* cult by the Sdok Kak Thom inscription, the Ciraccheda ("Beheading") may also have been recited at the expiatory ceremony conducted prior to his coronation by Jayavarman II in the vicinity of Ba Phnom, recorded in inscription K956, (IC, VII, 128–129). See Claude Jacques, "La carrière de Jayavarman II", *BEFEO* XLIX (1972) pp. 105–120.

[53] Thus, in the oath, the first *me sa* is associated with Ba Phnom (a site not mentioned in Duang's text); others in the oath are archaeological sites (e.g. Santhuk, Basak) or not identifiable (e.g. Prek Aeng, Sbat Sbay). The *me sa* in 1859 text are more widely distributed, and include Angkor Thom (the popular name for the Angkor complex), Pursat, and Bakheng, as well as several sites near Udong.

Its meaning of "guardian spirit" is fairly clear, but the link between this guardian spirit and toponyms is not. In an earlier paper, I accepted Mme. Porée Maspéro's suggestion that the phrase be taken as a slurred contraction of the name Uma Mahisāsuramardini – Siva's consort killing a demon buffalo.[54] The suggestion is tempting, as a statue of the divinity was worshipped as *me sa* at Ba Phnom as recently as 1944. But there seems to be no correlation in the lists between places where statues of the goddess have been found (or a cult in her honor mentioned in an inscription) and the inclusion of the phrase. Although *me sa* at one time may have meant "guardian spirit of the kingdom, of the sort worshipped at Ba Phnom" this meaning seems to have faded by the nineteenth century, when the word may have retained echoes of this connection and one with the word *mahisa* alone, Khmer, *via* Sanskrit, for "buffalo".[55]

Why should toponyms be associated with buffaloes, or with a goddess in the act of beheading one? Here the evidence is clearer, for there are amply documented connections between buffalo-sacrifices and village religion throughout much of Southeast Asia and especially in Laos, Cambodia and among hill tribes[56] and it is possible that the cult of the *devaraja* took hold in Cambodia (and in Java) when it did because it was based on centuries of local sacrifices to naga spirits, *nak tā*, *me sa*, and Indian gods like Siva and Uma.

The toponyms therefore – or at least some of them – may well represent places where sacrifices took place annually or at one time: this is not to suggest, however, that the names on the lists are confined to such places, or that sacrifices were identical from

[54] Porée-Maspéro, *Etude*, 9.

[55] For an investigation of connections between the Sanskrit word for "buffalo" and the Javanese word for "tomb", see L. Damais, "Etudes Javanaises. I. Les tombes musulmanes datées de Tralaya", *BEFEO*, XLVIII (1956–1957) pp. 357–359, n.2. No such connection is possible in Khmer, according to Saveros Pou (personal communication), but this does not rule cut links between the phrase *me sa* and the word, *mahisa.*; L.F. Brakel (personal Communication).

[56] See Chandler, "Royally Sponsored Human Sacrifices", notes 36–38.

place to place or era to era. Many of the places, clearly, were the sites of some odd event of the sort that has produced devotions in recent times to particular *nak tā*.[57] There is no evidence to suggest that the lists are limited to the *nak tā* most honoured in Cambodia at a given time. In some cases, such as the sites associated with Yasovarman, what it was that had rendered the sites powerful in the tenth century-among the common people, who used popular names for the sites-had been forgotten, in a sense, by the nineteenth.

And yet something had been "remembered": the toponyms related to Yasovarman are grouped together in the oath, and the most important of them, Bakheng, appears in both texts. One reason for this survival – perhaps more inclusive than others – may be Yasovarman's well-documented devotion to Siva. As Paul Mus and others have shown, the worship of this god was widespread in Southeast Asia, and linked in many places to tombs, the propitiation of ancestors, the use of stone, the fertility of the soil and the sacralization of places.[58] One aspect of Yasovarman's devotion, the cult of the *devaraja*, may have involved ritual beheadings, and the link between this kind of sacrifice and the installation (or celebration) of authority was echoed annually in the Cambodian *sruk*, after having been repeated – although this is uncertain-at the four corners, or quarters, of the kingdom. These rituals subdued the landscape by summoning the *nak tā* to renew their contracts with the world of the living – a process

---

[57] *BRP*, VIII, especially pp. 175–195. For Indonesian parallels, see J. Knebel, "Legenden over de plaatsen. . ." *Tijdschrift Bataviaasch Genootschap* 48 (1906) 527–565, 50 (1908) 388–406 and 51 (1909) 377–430. See also C. Stevan Harrell, "When a Ghost Becomes a God" in Arthur P. Wolf (ed.) *Religion and Ritual in Chinese Society*, Stanford 1974, pp. 195–206.

[58] See Paul Mus, "Cultes indiens et indigènes au Champa", *BEFEO*, XXXIII (1933) pp. 367–410 and Paul Mus, "La tombe vivante, équisse d'une série ethnographique naturelle", *La Terre et la Vie*, VII (1937) pp. 117–127. The transmissions and reshaping of beliefs, as discussed by Mus, are refined in the last chapter of S.J. Tambiah, *Buddhism and Spirit Cults in Northeast Thailand* (Cambridge 1970) pp. 367–378, which attacks the problem of "levels". See also Filliozat, "Recent Researches", p. 104, for the strong but unverifiable statement, "In Cambodia there were no sacred places when the Saiva religion came".

with parallels to rituals in classical China. At each level they also announced a celebrant's territorial jurisdiction and only the king (or, technically, his *baku*) had access to, or power over, the lists of "national" *me sa*.[59] The names they recited and the order they took summoned and synthesized the kingdom, seen as an amalgamation of ancestors, place-names, and features of a landscape. In some cases – but not these texts – the definition was stretched to include "Lao" spirits, perhaps because they too responded to buffalo sacrifices, whereas Thai and Vietnamese counterparts did not;[60] but "Cambodia" in general was the sum of places, arranged in *mandala* form, where *nak tā* were honored and sacrifices took place. This notion endured from Yasovarman's reign through the collapse of Angkor and Cambodia's "dark ages" at least until 1969, when officials of Lon Nol's government met to swear loyalty to him and to Prince Sihanouk by summoning spirits to come and witness their oath.[61]

[59] This monopoly may explain why the litanies do not appear in French descriptions of the annual oath-taking ceremony; cf, Jean Moura, *Le royaume du Cambodge* (2 vols.) Paris 1883, I, 251, and R. Mennetrier, "Les fêtes du Tanh Tok à Phom Penh", *RI*, 1912, pp. 334–345.

[60] For a bas-relief at Angkor depicting buffalo sacrifice, see Henri Dufour and Charles Carpeaux, *Le Bayon d'Angkor Thom: Bas Reliefs* 2 vols., Paris, 1910–1914, plate 9, reference supplied by Hiram W. Woodward. The rarity of buffalo-sacrifices in Thailand – and the rarity of statues of Uma Mahisāsuramardini (frequent in Cambodia and on Java) – poses interesting historical problems, probably connected with the ways and times it was "Indianized". For an instance of ethnic Lao in Thailand sacrificing buffaloes, see Mary Cort, *Siam or the Heart of Further India*, New York, 1886, pp. 362–363–a reference pointed out to me by R.I. Heinze. For an example of a Cambodian *nak tā* speaking "Lao", see *BRP*, VIII, p. 121.

[61] *Realités cambodgiennes*, 22 August 1969. See *Kambuja*, 22 October 1943 for a discussion of the links between toponyms, local deities, and the administration at Angkor after Yasovarman's reign, see Groslier, *Bayon*, pp. 113ff., 264–66, and G. Cœdès, "Les expressions *vrah kamraten an et kamraten jagat* en vieux-khmer", *The Adyar Library Bulletin* XXV, 1961, pp. 447–460.

PART II

CAMBODIA BEFORE THE FRENCH

My doctoral dissertation dealt with the political history of Cambodia between 1794 and 1848. It was based to a large extent on the chronicle histories of Thailand, Vietnam and Cambodia, but also used some archival materials available in Cambodia, Thailand and France. All but one of the essays that follow, in a sense, are "spin-offs" from my doctoral research.

The paper on *chbap* was prepared for a panel at the Association for Asian Studies (AAS) annual meeting in San Francisco in 1983. Like "Songs at the Edge of the Forest", the essay uses literature to gain access to the thought world of the Khmer and thereby to heighten our understanding of Cambodia's past. Without the invaluable edition of the *chbap* prepared by Saveros Pou, referred to in the notes, the essay would have been impossible to write.

"A Holy Man's Rebellion" was written in 1974 and draws on some of the materials I consulted in writing my dissertation.

Millenarian rebellions like the one described were frequent in pre-colonial Southeast Asia and essays about them were *à la mode* in the scholarship of the 1960s and 1970s, when many writers were looking for precursors and forerunners to anti-colonial movements and revolutionary wars. When the essay was being written, Cambodia was mired in its fourth year of civil conflict.

"Songs at the Edge of the Forest" was prepared for a conference sponsored by the Social Science Research Council (SSRC) in Ithaca NY in August 1978, shortly before the demise of the Pol Pot regime. The essay draws on two Cambodian folk tales that I had translated in 1976 and also uses a nineteenth century verse chronicle that I had consulted in my earlier research. "Songs" is my favorite of all my papers. I feel that it manages to convey some of the poignancy and richness of the sources on which it is based.

"Going through the Motions" was written for an SSRC conference that convened in Santa Cruz California in November 1978. Like "Maps for the Ancestors" in Part 1, it attempts to link royally sponsored rituals with the way that nineteenth century Cambodians conceived of national history and presented it in their chronicles.

NORMATIVE POEMS (*CHBAP*) AND PRE-COLONIALCAMBODIAN SOCIETY

Order is always a burden to the individual. Disorder makes him wish for the police or death. Such are the two extreme conditions in which human nature is not at ease. The individual's wish is for a perfectly enjoyable era, in which he is completely free, yet completely cared for. He finds it toward the beginning of the end of a social system.

—Paul Valéry, "*Persian Letters*"[1]

Using the *chbap* to analyze pre-colonial Cambodian society is difficult because these gnomic, normative poems are only incidentally concerned with the ways in which that society was put together.[2] Moreover, it is·hard to determine how firmly

This paper was first published in the *Journal of Southeast Asian Studies*, Vol. XV, No. 2, September 1984, reprinted with permission. In revising this paper, I benefitted greatly from the comments I received from the late Lucien Hanks and May Ebihara.

[1] Paul Valéry, "Persian Letters" in *History and Politics* (London: Pantheon, 1963), pp. 215–26; quotation at p. 219.

[2] The Cambodian texts of the poems discussed in this paper, as well as transliterations and French translations, will be found in successive volumes of the *Bulletin de l'École Française d'Extrême Orient* (*BEFEO*) beginning in 1975, edited by Philip N. Jenner and Saveros Pou under the running title, "Les *cpap* ou 'codes de conduite' khmers", as follows: "*Cpap* Kerti Kal" (hereafter C-1). *BEFEO*, LXII (1975), pp. 369–94; "*Cpap* prus" (hereafter C-2), *BEFEO*, LXIII (1976): 313–50; "*Cpap* kun cau" (hereafter C-3), *BEFEO*, LXIV (1977), pp. 167–215; "*Cpap* Rajaneti" (hereafter C-4), *BEFEO*, LXV (1978), pp. 361–402;

they are anchored in the times when they were written: how useful is a seventeenth century *chbap* in helping us to understand eighteenth-century society? Another problem with using them is that they often provide an idealized picture, suggesting norms of behavior rather than describing or analyzing the ways in which people behave. Because of this, the poems belong to more than one century at a time. Finally, like anything written down in a largely illiterate society, the *chbap* encapsulate and pass on the ideology of a minority élite. It can be argued that this ideology in pre-colonial Cambodia at least was rarely at odds with the ideology of the rural, illiterate poor; but this may be a circular argument, brought on by the widespread popularity of the *chbap* themselves, imposed by the élite over several centuries.

Before turning to the poems, these questions can be dealt with briefly. First, no other pre-colonial texts are *more* useful for reaching an understanding of Cambodian society. This is because the *chbap*, unlike chronicles or inscriptions, are concerned with the activity of the entire society, and not merely the ceremonial behavior of the élite. They are also useful because for the pre-colonial period Cambodian historical documents are of little use in writing Cambodian history. They are frequently inaccurate, seldom detailed and contain wide chronological gaps.[3]

It can also be argued that Cambodian institutions changed very slowly between the seventeenth century and the nineteenth. Nineteenth-century Cambodians, listening to the recitation of a seventeenth-century *chbap*, would have had little trouble recognizing the social arrangements depicted in the text.

"*Cpap* Kram" (hereafter C-5), *BEFEO*, LXVI (1979), pp. 129–60; "*Cpap* Trineti" (hereafter C-6), *BEFEO*, LXX (1981), pp. 135–93. For an overview of the genre, see S. Pou, "La littérature didactique khmere: les *cpap*", *Journal Asiatique*, CCLXIX (1981), pp. 453–66.

[3] For a discussion of these issues, see Michael Vickery, "The Composition and Transmission of the Ayudhya and Cambodian Chronicles", in Perceptions of the Past in Southeast Asia, ed. Anthony Reid and David Marr (Singapore: Heinemann, 1979), pp. 130–54.

Similarly the idealization of society in the *chbap*, which frees the poems from the particularities of the times when they were composed gives us an indigenous standard against which to measure several centuries of pre-colonial history. This is what the *chbap* themselves were intended to do, recited over the years by worthy men. Moreover, while it is difficult to say at what point they reflect a particular century's concerns, they always reflect *Cambodian* ones, for, as Saveros Pou has argued,[4] the genre itself does not appear to be borrowed from somewhere else. Finally, the question of whether texts of this kind are effusions of the élite is connected with the choices we make to build our models of society and periods of history. If these can be constructed most helpfully in the Cambodian case in terms of conflict between social groups, the *chbap*, which emphasize the propriety of hierarchies, rote-learning, and tradition, will obstruct our understanding. If, on the other hand, the hierarchical arrangement of Cambodian society in pre-colonial times was agreed upon by nearly all participants (most of the time), and if, therefore, there is not much of a gap between the ideology of the texts and the *praxis* of pre-colonial society, we can use the *chbap* as windows opening onto an otherwise obscure period of history.

The alternative, given the nature of the sources that have come down to us, is to walk away from Cambodia's past, and to relegate Cambodians to the outer darkness of people "without history" – which, of course, has never been the case.[5]

The Cambodian word for "society" (*sangkum*) does not appear to have entered the spoken language before the 1930s. The same is true of a great many social and political terms which we and

---

[4] Pou, "La littérature didactique", pp. 459.

[5] For a discussion of this problem, see Guy Lardreau, "L'*Histoire* comme nuit de Walpurgis". *Cahiers de l'Herne: Henry Corbin* (Paris: Herne, 1981), pp. 110–21. Lardreau contends (p. 120. n. 11) that "people without history" are those who "ignore the *historian*" (his emphasis); as a result, "the forms, and images under which [they] subsume themselves are not deployed in the format: the history of the time".

Cambodians nowadays take for granted. On the other hand, precolonial Khmer is rich in words and phrases that denote relative status (within a family, for example) and the maintenance of social relationships that keep hierarchies in place is one of the concerns of the *chbap*. They legitimize the "lop-sided friendships" implicit in the educational process, for example; recited *de haut en bas*, the poems were to be accepted as the work of teachers (*kru*), trained and aged specifically to compose and recite poems of this kind. Naturally, the *chbap* often praise the wisdom of teachers, and several of them suggest that a particular author – blending, as his name is mentioned, with the *kru* reciting a particular poem – was very old and for that reason deserving of respect. The age of the text, the age of the poet, and the age of the teacher blend into one another; and what comes out of the past, *via* the old, has an intrinsic value. As one poet expresses it,

I have composed this text using the *brahma* meter
In the same way as my father used it
When he was busy with my education.[6]

While honoring the past, each poet and each teacher expects to be honored in due time by his pupils and descendants – *in exactly the same way*. Repetitions are proof that one's lineage has endured, along with appropriate behavior. The two are linked. Having a lineage sets "good people" (*nak chea*; the phrase in nineteenth century Khmer also meant "free people")[7] apart from those beyond the reach of the *chbap*, such as fools, animals, and hereditary slaves (*nak ngea*, or "task people"). A severe insult in this era was to accuse another of not knowing his or her

---

[6] C-2, p. 343. Citations throughout the notes are to the French translations although my English versions have been checked against the Khmer.

[7] On *nak chea*, or "healthy people", see C. Janneau, "*Le Cambodge* d'autrefois", *Revue Indochinoise* (1914), pp. 617–30. Janneau's study first appeared in Saigon in 1870; it is a penetrating study of Cambodian society on the brink of colonial transformation. See also Pou and Jenner's comment on the term at C-1, p. 382, n. 7. There are some interesting parallels between the notion of *nak chea* and the Burmese concept of *athi*, discussed in Michael Aung-Thwin. "Athi, Kyun-

grandparents' names. Such ignorance was "wild" (*prei*), beyond the reach of reason. There seems to have been an ingrained set of contrasts in much pre-colonial Cambodian thinking between what is tame, repeated, sociable and humane and what is wild, ad hoc, singular and bestial. The *chbap* are on the civilized side of the balance and were seen by Cambodians as playing an important part in the civilizing process.[8] They are efficacious, and so the ways they are presented, as well as their poetic form, are as important as their content; the combination made them recognizable as *chbap*; and so when new *chbap* were composed, in the nineteenth and twentieth centuries, they followed traditional models, like reproduced antiques.

The forms of social behavior encouraged by the poems appear at first merely to echo and legitimize the pre-colonial *status quo*, almost as if power and merit were to be thought of as conterminous.[9] The audiences, after all, were always less educated than the poet, and we might expect them to be "mystified" by the supposedly élite values foisted on them from "above". In fact, the poets do not seem to have seen society in terms of power or status so much as in terms of the difference between human, meritorious behavior on the one hand – i.e., civilization as it was understood – and wild, unacceptable behavior on the other. If princes were thought of as meritorious, the poor were not by definition animals, or in some sense "worse" as human beings.

The poems examine a selection of social relationships, and the contrasts they set up between haves and have-nots, well-born

thaw. hpaya khun: Varieties of Commendation and Dependence in Pre-Colonial Burma", in *Slavery, Bondage and Dependence in Southeast Asia*. ed. Anthony Reid (St. Lucia: University of Queensland Press, 1983), pp. 64–90. especially at p. 67.

[8] For a discussion of this idea in a Cambodian context, see David Chandler "Songs at the Edge of the Forest: Perceptions of Order in Three Cambodian Texts", below p. 76. See also C-1, p. 384. n. 8.

[9] The best discussion of this issue is Lucien Hanks, "Merit and Power in the Thai Social Order", *American Anthropologist*, LXIV, No. 6 (December, 1962), pp. 1247–61.

people and hereditary slaves, patrons and clients, teachers and pupils, and so on are themselves ways of examining wholeness and complementarity, rather than friction between opposing segments of society:

> The kite flies because of the wind.
> An official reaches the heights because
> his men support him.[10]

In another *chbap*, a king's subjects

> Can be compared to fish
> And his officials to water;
> When the water becomes too hot
> The people feel themselves in danger
> Because they lack support.[11]

There is no way of water and fish going separate ways; only the relationship between the two can alter. When the water becomes "hot", therefore,

> Officials, civil and military,
> Are comparable to tigers
> Or spotted snakes.
> Whenever the people come to them
> Seeking assistance
> They change immediately into demons
> Without compassion.[12]

Here is a case where some officials behave as if they were impervious to *chbap*, while ordinary people, respectfully seeking assistance, are acting meritoriously, i.e., just as they ought to act. As so often in the Cambodian version of the *Ramayana*,

---

[10] C-4, p. 387.
[11] C-6, p. 169.
[12] Ibid.

the *Reamker*, such people have more merit (*bon*) than tyrannical princes.[13] This notion is never pushed very far, however, and the ideal remains Prince Rama, rather than any of his helpers.

Discovering one's place in society and acting in accordance with it is one of the messages of the *chbap*. Failing to do so leads to conflict:

> Stupid people hate instructed ones,
> Poor people, deprived of knowledge,
> Hate those who have acquired fortunes;
> Wives in their jealousy
> Detest the favorite female slave . . .[14]

One virtue imparted by the poems is sociability, which implies the acceptance of one's status and obligations, as well as those of other people, cementing connections "upwards" and "downwards" in the family, the village, the capital, and the state. The act of listening to the poems as a group, of course, enhanced "horizontal" ties as well.[15] What is to be feared is loneliness, without the security implied by these relations:

> True solitude is being an orphan, lonely, desolate;
> It is possessing learning, but not teaching others,
> It is not having children to love you.[16]

The second line is peculiarly strong in Khmer, for the words translated as "learning" and "teaching" are closely related (*robien* = "something learned"; *brien* = "teach"; cf. *rien* = "learn").[17]

---

[13] See S. Pou, tr. *Ramakerti* (Paris: EFEO, 1977). and also S. Pou, Lan Sunnary and Kuoch Haksrea, "Inventaires des oeuvres sur le Ramayana khmer", *Seksa Khmer* 3–4 (December, 1981), pp. 111–26.

[14] C-4, p. 386.

[15] See Amin Sweeny, *Authors and Audiences in Traditional Malay Literature* (Berkeley: University of California Press, 1980) for an interesting discussion of this concept.

[16] C-6, p. 18.

[17] See Philip N. Jenner and Saveros Pou, "A Lexicon of Khmer Morphology", *Mon-Khmer Studies* M-X (1981), pp. 265–66.

Three forms of solitude then, are when one lacks parents, students, and children. Another is to be without a teacher:

> To "know" by oneself
> Is like being lost in the middle of a forest,
> Or like a blind man
> Left to himself, who sets out on his way
> With no one to take his hand
> And when he looks for the path
> He never finds it
> But wanders into the forest instead
> Because he has learned things by himself
> With no one to take his hand.[18]

Living in such a world meant that everyone needed people to guide them and people to guide; they needed to honor ancestors so as to be honored by descendants. It meant being a link in a chain. Being "free" (*srei*) in such a society meant not being formally enslaved, rather than being "independent" in a twentieth-century sense, which was thought to be the same as being lost, or blind.

In their discussions of poems, Jenner and Pou point out the distinction that they make between rules of social behavior (*chbap*) and laws of the universe (*dharma*),[19] although the poems occasionally infer that intimations of *dharma* can arise from intense concentration on the meanings of *chbap*. On these occasions, the texts become mantras, with a liberating function:

> Whoever has the chance to listen
> Whoever has the chance to hear
> Whoever has the chance to meditate

---

[18] C-5, p. 154.
[19] C-2, p. 343, n.3; C-3, p. 203, n. l; C-6, p. 174, n. 4 and p. 179, n. l.

On the essence of this *dharma*,
Which is a code of conduct (*chbap*)
Will have gained the power
Of achieving *nirvana*.[20]

The *chbap* often make the point that benefits which can be summarized as "peace of mind" accrue to those who understand the poems. Similarly, they suggest that disaster will strike a society whose leaders ignore the poems and mislead the people. They do not propose any sanctions or constraints on those in power, however, or suggest places of refuge for anyone else. They merely assume that awareness of the *dharma*, stimulated in part by internalizing the messages of the *chbap*, can lead to personal salvation. Collective awareness, however, is not discussed.

Like most literature anywhere before the nineteenth century, the *chbap* take it for granted that well-born people have greater access to virtue than others, and by being *well placed* are therefore "born to rule". However, the poems do not suggest that Cambodian society actually worked according to this pattern for *dharma* manifested itself in part, by chance and so

The intelligent man can be beaten by an imposter,
The faithful servant can be beaten by a favorite,
The meritorious man can be beaten by someone luckier,
The student of the law by someone with an easy manner.[21]

In another stanza, we learn that

The good man can become evil,
The modest man can become prosperous,
A man of noble lineage can become confused
With ordinary people.[22]

[20] C-4, p. 397.
[21] C-4, p. 389.
[22] Ibid.

How are such mutations to be predicted, or warded off? Perhaps primarily by accepting them when they occur, and by adjusting one's priorities:

The *dharma* is the way
Which protects and defends all beings,
And assures them of success.
It is better to lose a fortune
Than to die; but it is better to die
Than to lose the essence of the law.[23]

The "success" offered by the *dharma*, therefore, has nothing to do with politics, manipulation or money. The virtues of the poems are those that accrue to educated men who are trained to step away from the turmoil of competition. This indifference to the world, however, should not be confused with torpor. The poets repeatedly urge their listeners to be alert:

When you hear someone speaking "good words"
You must inform yourself
About his lineage and his ancestors,
Whether good or bad so as to figure out
Whether the speaker is really "high" or "low".[24]

Similarly, much of the advice given by the poems is very specific, relating, for example, to sensible agricultural practices and household management. The virtues emphasized are always those of balance and proportion . If a tree has too many fruits, for example:

The leaves will suffer.
Too many fish trouble the water;
Too many goods are difficult to keep;

[23] C-4, p. 392.
[24] C-4, p. 390.

Too few of them will make you worry. . .
Learn and reflect on everything.
Whatever you say, be faithful to the truth.[25]

What use are these poems in helping us to understand pre-colonial Cambodian history? The emphasis they place on the teacher-pupil relationship, when considered alongside the profusion of *chbap* manuscripts that survived into the colonial era and beyond it, suggests that they present a continuous and popular attitude toward education which blended the past, the *kru*, his audience and ideas about the *dharma*. The generally quietist message which the poems transmit, in turn, along with the hope they extend for individual salvation reflect the appeals of Theravada Buddhism to post-Angkorean, village-oriented Cambodians.

We have no way of knowing if the *chbap* circulated freely in the élite-oriented state centered on Angkor for no popular literature that can be dated to the Angkorean era has survived. It seems unlikely, however, that villagers at Angkor had access to teachings of this kind before they adopted Theravada Buddhism in the thirteenth century; the *chbap* dealing with kingly virtues are also suffused with Buddhist thinking, and do not portray a powerful, urbanized state.

The endurance of the *chbap* throughout post-Angkorean times suggests also that they were helpful to a majority of people in this period – or at least to those receiving a rudimentary education. Had this not been the case, the genre would have disappeared, or diminished in importance, just as the kings at Angkor and their temples did. Instead, the *chbap* became the principal textbooks of pre-colonial Cambodia. Their popularity and longevity reflect the backward-looking orientation of literate Cambodian society; for generations of Cambodians, the *chbap* delivered a distillation of village-centered common sense. Of course, since printing only came to

---

[25] C-1, p. 386. For an example of agricultural advice, see C-2, pp. 335–36.

Cambodia at the end of the nineteenth century, *chbap* texts were accessible in written form only to monks or to the relatively well-to-do.[26]

The poems were experienced in oral form, as part of ceremonial, controlled occasions. which may have increased the distance between the literate poet and his illiterate audience, as well as the sacred qualities of what was said, although we cannot be sure, if the evidence of *wayang* is any guide, that the majority of listeners *heard* the entire poem so much as they *attended* its recitation.[27]

The received wisdom of the poems however, is not what guided Cambodians in the acquisition of wealth or in the exercise of power. Instead, it tends to be what they called on to confront, evade, or better the harsh conditions of everyday life. Much of this harshness, of course, came from inequalities in the distribution of power, labor, and rewards, but the *chbap* do not resort to such analyses, which are seen (if they are perceived at all) as *out of place*. Instead, they make family life the focus of morality. They also suggest that it is prudent to obey masters outside the family. Honoring one's betters, looking fondly at the past, and praising the acuity of old people were ways of insuring that rice-growing villages and the families inside them survived in peace, unharmed by suzerains, ancestors, or by those enjoying day-to-day control.

Pre-colonial Cambodian society was disorganized, brutal and unjust, but the people who wrote, recited and overheard *chbap* had no alternative arrangements to suggest. None of them had

[26] It would be rewarding to study pre-colonial Cambodia and its literature in terms of Cambodia being a partially literate society in which recited, overheard and memorized *chbap* played a far greater role than the perusal of written texts. The problem is addressed in a stimulating way by Rhys Isaac, *The Transformation of Virginia*, 1740–1790 (Chapel Hill, N.C., 1982), pp. 121–31. For a generalized discussion see Jack Goody. ed., *Literacy in Traditional Societies* (Cambridge University Press, 1968), especially pp. 27–38 and 85–131.

[27] See Barbara Hatley, *Ketoprak Theatre and the Wayang Tradition* (Clayton, Australia: Monash University Centre of Southeast Asian Studies, Working Paper No. 19, 1980), and also Amin Sweeney, *Authors and Audiences, passim*.

ever seen a truly different society at work. The texts available to the poets (in Pali, Khmer, and Thai) had no improvements to propose; the poets and the people who listened to them shared the view of pre-colonial Cambodian officials, the colonial regime, and Cambodian governments since World War II that social groupings which transcended particular occasions and lacked the sponsorship of the government or the *sangha* were probably subversive of the social order. Although rebellious figures, bandits, and men claiming supernatural powers (*nak mean bon*) attracted followers and caused disruption throughout these years, the *chbap* say nothing about them or the messages of liberating hope they occasionally spread. In the view of the *chbap*, the best way of lessening political injustice was to put one's mind on something else. To reverse Mao Zedong's famous adage, politics was not allowed to take command.

Although the poems are benign they are not particularly optimistic. Preferable eras are in the past; former societies are better than those in which we live.[28]

It is possible to examine the poems in terms of Cambodia's history from 1700 to 1848, a period which marked the low tide of Cambodia's political power and when the poems proliferated at least in manuscript form.

At that time, Cambodia came under pressure from new dynasties in Vietnam and Siam while its own central authorities seem to have lost their grip on provincial administration. The reasons for the breakdown in Cambodia's institutions in the eighteenth century have not been examined in detail. The Tayson rebellion in Vietnam and dynastic turmoil in Siam following the Burmese sacking of Ayudhya in 1767 were undoubtedly important causes, and had effects on Cambodian institutions. In trying

---

[28] Buddhist time-reckoning is numbered forward from the death of Gautama Buddha (in 543 B.C.) until the year 5000. when the world is to come to an end. This concept echoes Indian ones, whereby we are inhabiting the last of several eras. It seems likely in fact that time-reckoning seen in terms of *decline*, rather than in terms of cycles, repetition, or forward movement, is more widespread than we might suppose. See Paul Veyne, *Les grecs ont-ils crus a leurs mythes?* (Paris: Seuil, 1983), 146, n. 40.

to work out the *mentalité* of this period, we are hampered by a scarcity of sources, and by the reluctance of those we have to take a "national" point of view. It does seem clear that during the period of Vietnamese hegemony (roughly 1810–45) the influence of the monarchy on the countryside almost disappeared. Until the brief rekindling of Cambodian institutions under King Duang (reigned 1848–60), Cambodia's élite survived with little royal inspiration.[29] This meant, among other things, that the idea of *satria* officials, so deeply rooted in Javanese political thinking even in periods of decline, was largely absent from the *chbap*, although it crops up in popular novels. Class differences had become too blurred to inspire anyone, or to be maintained, and in the words of one *chbap*,

> This is how power diminishes.
> One hears the sound of gongs
> But not the sound of the royal drum;
> There is a ruler but no queen,
> There is a royal city, but no fortification.[30]

In the late 1840s when thousands of Cambodians emerged from hiding they were able to rebuild a Theravada kingdom because of traditions kept alive for them by their monks, their teachers and the *chbap*. These traditions were also rooted in the villages that gradually came back to life, where boys studied in *wats* before rejoining their parents in the fields and later becoming parents themselves and where everyone, in theory, was exposed to recitations of *chbap*.

Knowing how to behave in a family, a *wat*, a village and a market were essential to the peaceable enactment of Cambodian life. The monarchy and the *Reamker* were not essential in the same way. However, the organization of Cambodian society with officials and the reigning monarch at the "top" only made sense

---

[29] For a general discussion of this era, see David Chandler, *A History* of Cambodia (Boulder, Colorado: Westview Press, 1992), pp. 99–136.

[30] C-6, pp. 175–76.

if the villagers were located near the "bottom". It was important for some people to believe that they were "higher" than others; but those "beneath" them were probably less conscientious in their own pursuit of an appropriate position. Besides, in the jumble of the nineteenth century, much of the "top" had been destroyed and, by being inefficacious, probably had been called into question as well.

The poems form an accompaniment, then, to the eclipse of the Cambodian state in the early nineteenth century, and also to its tentative rebirth. Poems about behavior with politics left out, the *chbap* contributed to the apparent inertia and repetitiveness of Cambodian life in later eras. The attitudes which the poems foster and reflect may explain in part why the French often spoke of Cambodians as "asleep", and why governments and demagogues since independence were unable to draw people away from their families to pursue supposedly higher frames of reference. The world picture transmitted by the *chbap* is one where deference and fatalism take up more space than rebelliousness or hope. The same values that made so many Cambodians reluctant to struggle for their "rights" under the French, Sihanouk, and Lon Nol has preserved many survivors of the 1970s from revolutionary transformations. Although the *status quo* for nearly everyone in Cambodia in the 1960s left much to be desired, what happened to everyone under Pol Pot has been difficult for anyone over fifteen or so to comprehend. In other words, Pol Pot and his "organization" (*angkar*) were entangled and defeated not only by the Vietnamese and by their own ideas but by the social behavior they set about to undermine.[31]

---

[31] See David Chandler, "Seeing Red: Perceptions of Cambodian History in Democratic Kampuchea", below, pp. 233–254. It can be argued that the excesses of the Pol Pot regime, rather than its ideology *per se*, frightened people into inactivity. In any case, the possibility of a socialist regime in Cambodia is now (1983) stronger than anyone (except members of the Communist Party) would have imagined twenty years ago. Whether or not events in Cambodia have transformed the way people think about each other, however, is less clear.

It should be clear, moreover, that the personalized character of Cambodian social behavior was what immunized most people from imported ideology and protected them from the dangers and the intricacy of change. In Valery's terms, the *chbap* held sway "toward the beginning of the end of a social system" that lasted, more or less unbroken, from the abandonment of Angkor to the abandonment of Phnom Penh.

Like the villages they served, the *chbap* themselves have been abandoned. For several centuries they celebrated the sociability, politeness and obligations of family life. These values could be used against the reality of the forest, invasions, disease, colonialism and revolution. Sanctifying a social order that had been handed down from the past (in part by the act of handing it down again), the *chbap* could be set against what was transitory, disorderly, brutal and unknown. In the 1970s, however, the protective layer provided by the poems and by many other traditions was burnt away. For nearly all Cambodians, it became impossible to hear either the "gongs" or the "royal drum".

With so much of Cambodia's history blown away, however, it is possible that many Cambodians in exile or refashioning their lives under the Vietnamese-imposed regime will return to the *chbap* from time to time in response to nostalgia, to curiosity about an earlier time, or to more compelling personal needs.

AN ANTI-VIETNAMESE REBELLION IN EARLY NINETEENTH CENTURY CAMBODIA

The "holy man's" (*nak sel*) rebellion against the Vietnamese that broke out in 1820 along the Cambodian-Vietnamese border is the best-documented one of its kind in pre-colonial Cambodia and makes a useful addition to the literature of such revolts in Buddhist Southeast Asia.[1] Its importance in Cambodian terms lies in its anti-Vietnamese character, the participation in its ranks of Buddhist monks, the collusion of Cambodian authorities and the way in which these themes foreshadow Cambodian political thinking before and after the arrival of the French.

The most detailed account of the rebellion forms part of an eloquent narrative poem in Khmer, composed at least as early as 1869.[2] The rebellion is also discussed in the Vietnamese

This paper was first published in the *Journal of Southeast Asian Studies*, Vol. VI, No. 1, March 1975, reprinted with permission. I am grateful to Nguyên van Hung for translations from Vietnamese.

[1] For a general discussion, see Kitsiri Malagoda, "Millenarianism in Relation to Buddhism", *Comparative Studies in Society and History*, (*CSSH*) XII (1970), pp. 424–441. See also Tej Bunnag, "The 1901–1902 Holy Man's Rebellion in Northeast Thailand" (in Thai), *Social Science Review*, V, 1 (June 1967) pp. 78–86; Frances Hill, "Millenarian Machines in South Vietnam", *CSSH*, XIII (1971) pp. 325–350 and John B. Murdoch, "The 1901–1902 Holy Man's Rebellion", *Journal of the Siam Society*, (*JSS*) LXII, 1 (January 1974) pp. 47–66.

[2] *Rioeng rabalkhsat sruk khmaer* (The story of the royal lineage in Cambodia) (Phnom Penh, 1958), hereafter *RRSK*, pp. 45–54. Two manuscripts dating from 1869–1870 and from 1874 are in the Buddhist Institute in Phnom Penh. The earlier one appears to be the source of the printed version. A collation of the 1874 text with *RRSK* reveals no substantive variations in the section dealing with the rebellion. According to Eng Sut (comp.) *Akkasar mahaboros khmaer*

annals,[3] a Vietnamese gazetteer from the 1850s,[4] and in one "family" of the Cambodian chronicles, or *bangsavatar*.[5] The Khmer and Vietnamese annals overlap in many respects, while the gazetteer and the 1869 poem are more idiosyncratic. The picture that emerges from all of the texts is that the rebellion posed a brief but serious threat to Vietnam's hegemony over Cambodia and that Vietnamese controls increased thereafter as a result.

Three broad themes – tributary dependency, Vietnamese migration and the forced mobilization of labor – run through accounts of Cambodia's relations with Vietnam in the early nineteenth century.[6] Although Cambodian kings had sent tributary gifts of "barbarian" products to Vietnam since the middle of the seventeenth century,[7] the practice had lapsed in the chaos that engulfed both kingdoms around 1770. By 1803–1804, however, when the Nguyên Dynasty installed itself in Hue to rule over a reunited Vietnam, Emperor Gia Long revived the custom of demanding tributary gifts, even though the Cambodian king, Chan (b. 1790, r. 1797–1835), was technically a protegé

(Documents about Cambodian heroes) (Phnom Penh, 1969), p. 1209, a third manuscript exists, but I have not been able to consult it.

[3] *Dai-nam thuc luc chinh bien* (Primary compilation of the veritable records of imperial Vietnam), trans. into modern Vietnamese by Nguyen Ngoc Thinh and Dao Duy Anh, 26 vols. (Hanoi, 1962–) hereafter *DNTL*, V, p. 125.

[4] Nguyen van Sieu, *Phuong Dinh Du Dia Chi* (The Geographical chronicles of Phuong Dinh) trans. into modern Vietnamese by Ngo Manh Nginh (Saigon, 1959), hereafter *PD*, 192. I am grateful to John Whitmore for drawing my attention to this text.

[5] For a discussion of *bansavatar* "families", see David Chandler, *Cambodia Before the French: Politics in a Tributary Kingdom*, 1794–1848 (Ann Arbor, 1974) Ch. I, which rests to a large extent on Michael Vickery's unpublished analysis of the various *bangsavatar*.

[6] See Chandler, *Cambodia Before the French*, Chs. III–V, and Thanom Anamwat, *Relations Between the Thai, the Khmer and the Vietnamese in the Early Bangkok Period* (in Thai), M.A. thesis (Prasarnmit College of Education, Bangkok, 1971).

[7] *DNTL*, I, 98, and *PD*, p. 188. See also Thai van Khieu, "La Plaine aux Cerfs et la Princesse de Jade", *Bulletin de la Societé des Etudes Indochinoises* (*BSEI*) XXXIV (1959) pp. 378–393.

of the Thai court, and had a pro-Thai first minister appointed by Bangkok acting as his regent.[8] With Thai pennission, Chan began to exchange gifts with Gia Long in 1806.

In earlier times, such exchanges had spelled out Cambodia's symbolic dependence on a distant court. By 1806, however, most of the Cambodian-speaking portions of Southern Vietnam had been peopled and administered by Vietnamese for at least fifty years, and the process of Vietnamese colonization along what are now Cambodia's coast and its eastern frontier continued throughout the early nineteenth century.[9] The advent of the Nguyên Dynasty meant, among other things, that Cambodia's eastern flank was occupied by a unified, powerful state, pressing west and south to bring additional people and rice-land under its control and into its cultural orbit.[10]

In the eighteenth century, the Thai court had often levied Cambodians for war or public works. After about 1811, however, the balance of power in Cambodia, and with it the ability to levy workers, shifted to the Vietnamese. An abortive *coup* by Chan's brothers in that year, supported by the Thai, led to a Thai invasion, Chan's flight to Saigon, a Vietnamese military riposte and, in 1813, after Chan's return to Phnom Penh, to the institutionalization of Vietnamese influence at his court personified by a military mandarin named Nguyên van Thuy.[11] Chan continued to send tributary gifts to Bangkok,[12] but the Thai no longer levied Cambodians for corvee.

[8] Chandler, Ch. III, and Anamwat, p. 51ff.

[9] See M. G. Cotter, "Toward a Social History of the Vietnamese Southward Movement", *Journal of Southeast Asian History*, (*JSEAH*) IX, 1 (March 1968), pp. 12–24; Paul Boudet, "La conquête de Cochinchine par les Nguyên et le role des emigrés chinois", *Bulletin de l'Ecole Française d'Extrême Orient*, (*BEFEO*) XLII (1942), pp. 115–132 and Emile Gaspardone, "Derniers regards sur l'expansion au sud", Collège de France, *Annuaire* LXV (1965–1966) pp. 392–394.

[10] The process was called "slowly eating silkworms" according to Alexander Woodside, *Vietnam and the Chinese Model*, (Cambridge, Mass., 1971), 247.

[11] *PD*, 191. See also G. Aubaret, (trans.) *Gia Dinh Thung Chi* (*Histoire et description de la Basse Cochinchine*) (Paris, 1863), pp. 128–129, and Chandler, op.cit., Ch. IV.

[12] Until 1830; Chandler, p. 107, based on Thai archival materials in Bangkok.

The Vietnamese were swift to do so. In 1816, Thuy was asked by his superiors in Saigon to recruit some 5,000 Cambodian laborers in Cambodia and Vietnam to excavate and restore the Vinh Te Canal.[13] The waterway when completed in 1820 ran some seventy kilometers from the newly constructed Vietnamese frontier post of Chaudoc (present-day Chau Phu) to the environs of Hatien on the Gulf of Siam.[14] The workers at the village level were recruited by the Khmer but worked under Vietnamese supervision and were paid by the Vietnamese. Conditions apparently were harsh, supervisors were corrupt, and many deaths occurred.[15] The importance of the canal for this study is that these conditions probably helped to ignite the 1820 rebellion, which broke out nearby and may have included former or prospective workers on the canal.[16]

What follows is a consolidation of accounts of the rebellion in the Vietnamese and Cambodian annals.

In 1820, a monk named Kai, perhaps originally from *wat* Sambaur in Phnom Penh,[17] and perhaps after raising followers among Cambodians living in three districts near Tay Ninh in Vietnam, declared himself king (*chieu vuong*)[18] in the vicinity of a small mountain in southeastern Cambodia known as Ba

---

[13] The workers rotated in two-month shifts. For a full discussion of the canal, see L. Malleret, *L'archeologie du delta de Mekong*, 4 vols. (Paris, 1959–1963) I, pp. 27–33. See also Tran Van Hanh, "Inscription de la montagne de Vinh Te", *BSEI*, No. 48 (1904) p. 2045; Aubaret, op.cit., pp. 148–149, and *DNTL*, VI, p. 179.

[14] Additional Cambodians worked on the canal, at Chan's insistence, in 1822, according to *DNTL*, VI, 107.

[15] *RRSK*, pp. 34–40. See also John Crawfurd, *Journal of an Embassy from the Governor General of India to the Courts of Siam and Cochinchina* (London, 1830, repr. 1967), Appendix, p. 578, which reports the summary execution in Saigon in 1822 of a foreman on the canal charged with corruption, and p. 587, which reports 10,000 deaths among laborers on the canal. *Phongsawadan Khamen* (Khmer chronicle: title in Thai, text in Khmer) in the Manuscripts Division of the Thai National Library, hereafter *PK*, p. 164, adds that "when the canal was dug, Vietnamese settled alongside it."

[16] The rebellion in *RRSK* follows the discussion of the canal.

[17] *PK*, p. 170.

[18] *DNTL*, V, p. 125. The districts were Quang Hoa, Quang Phong and Thuan Thanh, close enough to the Vinh Te Canal to have provided laborers for it.

Phnom. The Cambodian governor of the district, or *thommadejo*, sent against Kai by King Chan, was captured and probably killed. Soon afterwards, three Khmer officials, including one of considerable prestige,[19] met with Kai and went over to his cause, joining his followers in slaughtering Vietnamese as the rebels moved into east-central Cambodia. The viceroy of southern Vietnam, Le van Duyet, then assembled a Vietnamese naval force of some 3,000 men which joined a Cambodian one, led by a Moslem general,[20] and soon defeated the rebels, killing Kai on Sautin island, near the present-day city of Kompong Cham. The officials who had joined him were put on trial (it is uncertain where)[21] and executed.

Several tantalizing details emerge from this sparsely furnished account. The tradition in some *bangsavatar* that Kai was from Phnom Penh, for example, suggests that Chan knew of him at least by reputation and his fear of Kai's dynastic pretensions may have been tempered by his belief in the monk's supernatural powers.[22] As for the officials who went over to his cause, the highest ranking one, *chaophraya* Tei, was an experienced general who had a following in a region slightly north of Ba Phnom and probably was anti-Vietnamese already for he had been reprimanded and demoted by Vietnamese officials in Phnom Penh in 1818.[23] Nothing is known of the other two. Kai's choice of Tay Ninh and Ba Phnom was not fortuitous but was probably connected in his own and his followers' minds with his magic power. Hills in both places have a long history of associations

---

[19] These were, in descending importance, *chaophraya* Tei, *narin* Kol and *nai* Ke, from Preal. There are four villages of this name in modern Cambodia; one (11° 41' N, 105° 35' E) is near Ba Phnom.

[20] *Chaophraya tuan* (Pho). Many Moslems, of Cham or Malay origin, enjoyed positions of trust at Chan's court. See *DNTL*, XV, p. 114, and *RRSK*, p. 33.

[21] *PK*, 170, (Phnom Penh) de Villemereuil, p. 336, (Hue) and the Khmer text from which de Villemereuil is drawn, Bibliothèque Nationale, Paris, Fonds Indochinois 81 (Saigon). *RRSK*, p. 60 says that some were executed in Phnom Penh and others in Saigon.

[22] On Chan's superstitious nature, see *DNTL*, XV, pp. 232–233.

[23] *PK*, p. 162.

with millennial movements,[24] and Ba Phnom as late as 1877 was the site of periodic human sacrifices, sponsored by the Cambodian king, to the Indian goddess Uma Mahisāsuramardini, worshipped as a goddess of the soil under the local name of Me Sa ("white mother")[25]. These sacrifices were, among other things, expressions of the king's legitimacy in this particular region and in four others inside Cambodia where they periodically took place. It is likely that Kai's declaring himself king in Ba Phnom was associated with a sacrifice of this kind but even if it were not, his choice of the mountain as a base was probably connected with his drive for legitimate power.[26] On this hillside, as on another near Tay Ninh, it was believable, and honored by precedent, to declare that a new order was at hand. To his followers Kai was a saviour. His intrinsic merit as a Buddhist monk, enhanced perhaps by ceremonies at Ba Phnom and blending with local grievances connected with Vietnamese colonization and the Vinh Te Canal, gave the rebellion its *élan*.

The account of the rebellion in Nguyên van Sieu's gazetteer can be quoted in full.

In 1820, a Cambodian monk named Ke used superstitious means to assemble people to rebel. Bon-lich (a Khmer official?) was killed, but three Cambodians, Tham-dich (*thommadejo*?), Tay-Ke-

[24] Tay Ninh is sacred to the Cao Dai sect, founded in 1926 near Nui Ba Den ("Black Maiden Mountain"), revered by 19th century Vietnamese (Aubaret, op.cit., 178). See also A. Baudrit, "Correspondence de Simon de Larclause" *BSEI*, XIV, 3/4 (1939) p. 178ff., which describes the assassination of a French official in 1866 near Tayninh by a millennial band; the site of the assassination, according to R.B. Smith, "An Introduction to Caodaism", *Bulletin of the School of Oriental and African Studies* (*BSOAS*) XXXIII (1970), p. 342, is revered by local inhabitants. On p. 348, Smith lists several millennial sects in the region in the 1870s. On Ba Phnom, see Etienne Aymonier, *Le Cambodge*, 3 vols. (Paris, 1902–1904) I, pp. 233–235, and note 25 below.

[25] David Chandler, "Royally Sponsored Human Sacrifices in Nineteenth Century Cambodia: the Cult of *Nak tā* Me Sa (Uma Mahisāsuramardini) at Ba Phnom", below p. 118.

[26] Two Cambodian millennial leaders, Pu Kombo in 1866 and Prince Siwotha in 1877, also rallied followers and declared their legitimacy at Ba Phnom.

Luyen (?) and na Con (*narin* Kol?) surrendered to the rebels and joined them in their advance to Phnom Penh. Chan wanted to abandon the city, and sent a letter asking for help to Le van Duyet, who ordered Nguyên van Thuy and Nguyen van Chi to assemble an expeditionary force. They met more than thirty rebel ships, and killed many rebels. Ke escaped . . .but was pursued and killed at Ba-bon-lai (Babong, near Ba Phnom?) . . . Chan now regretted listening to bad advice from his officials, for this had led him to call for Nguyên van Thuy's replacement, earlier in the year, thus indirectly causing the rebellion. He sent a letter admitting his guilt, and asked that his country be protected as before.

Several details in this account amplify or contradict those in the *DNTL* and the *bangsavatar*. Two of the Cambodian officials siding with Kai for example, seem to be different, although one of them, the governor of Ba Phnom, appears in other versions in a different guise. The rebel's intention to attack Phnom Penh makes sense if Kai had proclaimed himself king, and explains the rebels' moving out of their base at Ba Phnom. Interestingly, Kai's unsuccessful escape and Chan's letter to Duyet, although absent from the *DNTL* and the *bangsavatar*, are featured in the 1869 poem. Finally, Nguyên van Sieu's statement that Chan felt responsible for the rebellion because he had effected Thuy's departure in 1819 is not supported directly in the *DNTL*, although Thuy attempted unsuccessfully to resign his post after the rebellion, citing disagreements with Chan.[27] Scandal clouded his time in Cambodia and Emperor Minh Mang unsuccessfully sought to get to the bottom of it.[28] Although Chan's letter admitting guilt does not figure in the *DNTL*, he made a rare visit

[27] *DNTL*, VI, 76. Minh Mang rejected the request, citing Chan's recently acquired "maturity".

[28] These came to the surface, in the *DNTL* at least, only after his death in 1828: See *DNTL*, IX, p. 254 and XI, pp. 8ff: There are echoes of Thuy's involvement in timber concessions in the 1820s in *RRSK*, p. 44–5.

to Saigon soon after the rebellion, bearing tributary gifts and at the same time offered three Khmer districts near Chaudoc as a gift to Nguyên van Thuy.[29] Unlike the texts discussed above, the 1869 poem was intended for public recitation. The survival of the poem in several manuscripts suggests that it was popular, and the stanzas dealing with Vietnamese tortures in this period also appear in an elegiac narrative poem dating from 1856.[30] In the strophe that deals with Kai's rebellion, the poet builds a narrative that would appeal to a rural Cambodian audience, soon after the departure of the Vietnamese, when their years of rule would be lively memories to many. The poet, an ex-official,[31] sees the many-faceted Vietnamese *mission civilisatrice* in terms of torture, corruption and corvee and as a corrosive assault on Cambodian values.[32] Whereas the other texts treat Kai's rebellion as a threat to established order, the 1869 poet sees it, as his audience probably did, as a doomed assault against a colonial master. He interprets it, also, in moral terms; Kai's defeat, he says, is less the result of Vietnamese

[29] Details of this unusual proposal and Minh Mang's ambiguous response to it are in *DNTL*, IX, pp. 328–329.

[30] *Sastra lboek rabkhsat . . . ong jan* (Document about the Reign of King Chan), MS. in the Buddhist Institute in Phnom Penh. The poem comes from the same area as *RRSK*, and has the same preamble. For a discussion of this poem, see "Songs at the Edge of the Forest", below p. 76.

[31] *RRSK*, p. 1. The poet claims to be a former official in Baray (Kompong Thom province).

[32] On Cambodian "non-Vietnameseness" in this period, see Aubaret, p. 129; *RRSK*, p. 129; and several Khmer nationalist novels, e.g. Dik Keam, Moen meas (a proper name) (Phnom Penh, 1969) and On Ram, *Sontujit, khmaer nak jat niyum* (Sontujit, a Khmer nationalist) (Phnom Penh, 1969). For an analysis of Cambodian-Vietnamese friction in the 1920s, see Pierre Brocheux, "Vietnamiens et minorités en Cochinchine pendant la periode coloniale", *Modern Asian Studies*, VI, 4 (1972) pp. 443–457. Cambodians in South Vietnam revolted against the Vietnamese in Tra Vinh in 1822 (L. Malleret, "La minorité cambodgienne de Cochin-chine", *BSEI*, XXI [1946–47], pp. 18–34), joined Khoi's revolt against Minh Mang in 1833–34, and with French encouragement massacred Vietnamese villagers in Vinh Binh and Ba Xuyen in 1945–46. (Christine White, personal communication.)

[33] There are interesting parallels here to the arguments in Benedict Anderson, "The Idea of Power in Javanese Culture" in Claire Holt (ed.), *Culture and Politics in Indonesia* (Ithaca, N.Y., 1972), p. 1–70.

skills, than of his own loss of merit, stemming from his violent acts.[33]

The 'non-Vietnameseness' of Cambodians – which in the nineteenth century took a wide variety of forms – has been treated by many Cambodians as an essential part of Khmer identity. Vietnamese differed sharply from Cambodians in language, dress, organized religion, architecture, literature, folk-lore, social structure, currency, table-manners, calligraphy and coiffures – to name only a few – even though some of these differences were blurred somewhat in border regions. Because of this, it is useful to see the 1820s and 1830s, when Vietnam's assault on Cambodia was systematic and intense, as a watershed in the development of one aspect of Cambodian nationalism. Without being accurate in all details, the 1869 poem's treatment of Kai's rebellion offers an invaluable glimpse of this process at work.

The strophe opens, without specifying time or place, by describing two men: a monk named Kai and his assistant, a novice named Kuy.[34] The two are pictured as peacefully attracting followers (characterized as "noisy") by means of sermons, cures and predictions. There is no hint of violence or agitation. When news of the monks reaches Chan in Phnom Penh and the "Vietnamese adviser who stood beside him", however, it is framed in terms of the refusal by the monks' followers to go on corvee.[35] A Khmer-Vietnamese force is immediately assembled in Phnom Penh to go and "surround" Kai and Kuy, but before reaching them, the Khmer elements in the force turn on and massacre the Vietnamese. A Moslem official from the Khmer army returns to

[34] Kuy may be a local hero, but it is more likely that he is drawn from oral tradition and has been confused with a Khmer of the same name whose anti-Vietnamese exploits in the 1820s in southeastern Vietnam are recounted in Malleret, Archéologie, IV, pp. 28–29, and in Kaev Savat, *Okya Kuy* (proper name) (Phnom Penh, 1966): see especially pp. 88–92.

[35] The official connected with the alleged corvee in *RRSK* is entitled *yuddha*. A Khmer official with this word in his title was governor of a district near Hatien in the 17th century: A. Leclère, *Codes cambodgiens*, 2 vols., (Paris, 1900), I, p. 116.

Phnom Penh with the news and a few survivors; the Vietnamese adviser orders clerks in the court to prepare a royal edict (in Khmer) asking for help from Le van Duyet, the overlord of southern Vietnam. The edict is entrusted to another Moslem functionary, who hurries with it to Saigon, where a land and naval force is raised to avenge the Vietnamese losses.[36] Kai, meanwhile, has recruited followers in Ba Phnom, Sunthor, Tboung Khmum and Prey Veng, i.e. throughout eastern Cambodia. The poem continues:

> When he heard of the expedition against him, elderly Kai washed the heads of his soldiers, reciting *sutras* to give them strength and shaking drops of water onto them to keep the Vietnamese from dispersing them in battle. If the Vietnamese fired guns, the power of the Khmer would keep the bullets from going far or coming close to them. When Kai's blessings were over, his soldiers lost their apathy, and went out to battle the Vietnamese.

The description of the battle that follows, in which the Khmer are invulnerable, tells us that the Vietnamese fell to the ground "like banana stalks". The Vietnamese soon retreat to Phnom Penh, unable to salvage their equipment and Kai leads his army off to Koh Sautin

> imagining that the Vietnamese would never fight again. He decided therefore to give a tumultuous feast, with no thoughts about misfortune and his followers agreed, saying, 'We will suffer no misfortune, for we have no guilt'.

Faced with this defeat, the Vietnamese in Phnom Penh are swift to blame Chan, telling him that

---

[36] *RRSK*, p. 46.

if the king failed to catch the hidden enemy, blame would fall on him, and he would have to report to the celestial emperor himself. When Chan heard this, he trembled – half in anger and half in fear.

The Khmer expeditionary force that now assembles, once more under Moslem leadership, includes no Khmer, but is made up of Chinese, Cham and Malay troops.[37] Shifting to Kai, the poet relates that

> although his people still saw him as a refuge, the misdeeds they all had done were inescapable. In the same way Kai, when he had become a monk, had gained a large amount of merit. After what he had done, the merit had faded away, and now he had no special powers; he had become an ordinary man. His honor was no longer great; his skills were ineffective. [When he heard of the forces approaching Koh Sautin] he performed his rituals and recitations as before, sprinkling water on his followers. But this time, when the enemy drew near, there was no merit to his blessings. His followers were unable to attack or fire their weapons. So the Vietnamese, Chams and Malays attacked them mercilessly from their boats, with axes, rifles and swords.

Kai escapes briefly to another island, where he is eventually killed because "his amulets and charms had lost their power". Many Buddhist monks, some of whom "had joined Kai's forces and killed Vietnamese", were also killed in the battle. This double sacrilege (violence to and from the monks), the poet suggests, threw nature out of balance. Floods and epidemics sweep the country:

---

[37] This polyglot army in fact probably accompanied the expeditionary force already "destroyed" in *RRSK*; the 1869 poet makes no mention of a Vietnamese component.

It was cold and rainy. Peoples' arms quivered in the cold. So much rain fell all day and all night, that it was impossible to distinguish sunrise and sunset. The weak and the strong alike ran off to hide, and the land was mournful.[38]

In the rest of the strophe, discussing the aftermath of the rebellion, the Vietnamese place blame on Chan and his officials for the revolt, and order a new set of high officials to be appointed at the court. The novice Kuy, however, escapes to live "among the Lao".[39]

Although lacunae in the texts are too wide to permit an accurate analysis of Kai's rebellion – for example, the sources say nothing about the kind of people who joined him, how many there were, or how long the rebellion lasted – several salient points should be examined. These have to do with the causes of the rebellion, its millennial content, Chan's involvement, the 1869 poet's ideas of historical causation and, finally, the consequences of the revolt.

Although anti-Vietnamese feeling in Cambodia had probably smouldered for years (or broken into rebellions not dealt with in the annals) what specifically brought on the 1820–21 rebellion, it would seem, was a combination of recent Vietnamese colonization and corvee which helped to make Cambodians at the eastern edge of their country susceptible to nativistic appeals from recognized authority figures, such as monks, ex-monks and officials. The breakdown of traditional patronage relations, the monetization and depersonalization of corvee by the Vietnamese and their insistence of fixing taxes annually in terms of particular fields, also subjected the Khmer to unfamiliar abuses,[40] but it is

---

[38] The poet may be echoing the *bangsavatar* accounts of floods and epidemics in 1818–*PK*, p. 169.

[39] *RRSK*, p. 58.

[40] These included withholding salaries from corvee workers, adjusting tax assessments and village census records, alienating land, substituting Vietnamese officials for local patrons, and breaking down traditional grievance procedures.

impossible from the sources to go further than this, or to be sure that the corvee requirements for the Vinh Te Canal, and abuses connected with them, ignited the revolt.[41]

The millennial content of Kai's leadership is clear. The sources agree that a monk (not a *former* monk) led the rebellion, and that he used "superstitious" means to raise a following. *RRSK* cites cures, amulets, and Kai's ability to make his followers invulnerable – a *cliché* in millennial movements.[42] The new world which Kai was announcing, it would seem, was to be a purer one without the Vietnamese and, parenthetically, their attempts at "modernization". The first of these themes reappears in the nation-wide anti-Vietnamese revolt, led by Khmer officials and supported by the Thai, that broke out in 1840–41,[43] and the second in an anti-French movement led by Buddhist monks in Phnom Penh a century later.[44] But to the 1869 poet, the rebellion

---

[41] In 1822, supplementing his gift to Thuy of three districts near Chaudoc, Chan spontaneously offered Minh Mang 13,000 Khmer laborers to work on the Vinh Te Canal. It is tempting to view both of these actions as specifically arising from Kai's revolt.

[42] The best introduction to the vast literature of millenarianism is Kenelm Burridge, *New Heaven New Earth* (Oxford, 1969) which includes a discussion of invulnerability. See also A. K. Seidel, "The Image of the Perfect Ruler in Early Taoist Messianism", *History of Religions*, IX, 9–10 (November 1969–February 1970), pp. 216–247, and Murdoch, op.cit., p. 63. For examples of amulets and charms, see A. Souyris Rolland, "Les pirates au Cambodge", *BSEI*, XXV, 4 (1950), pp. 427–437.

[43] The revolt is dealt with in *PK*, 187–192; *DNTL*, XX and XXII, *passim* (XXI is not yet [1974] available in Australian, British or U.S. library collections) and Chandler, *Cambodia Before the French*, Ch. VII.

[44] On this demonstration, see Bunchhan Mul, *Kuk Niyobay* (Political Prison) (Phnom Penh, 1971), pp. 44–62; V. M. Reddi, *A History of the Cambodian Independence Movement* (Tirupati, 1970), pp. 82–86 and my reviews of these books in *JSS*, LX, 1 (January 1972), pp. 437–438 and *JSEAS*, V, 1 (March 1974), pp. 136–137. The monks were objecting to French proposals that would have romanized Cambodia's alphabet and substituted a Gregorian calendar for the Buddhist one.

is not linked to these ideas as closely as it is to Kai's magical skills, without which his followers, literally, were powerless.[45]

The question of Chan's own merit, in the Buddhist sense, is an intriguing one, and connected to the question (in 1820 at least) of whether or not he supported Kai's rebellion. The 1869 poet is more ambiguous about this than the Vietnamese were at the time, and the record is contradictory, partly because Chan apparently had different amounts of influence over his officials at different times and places. If his control over all of them was tight (as the Vietnamese, perhaps wrongly referring to their own notions of accountability, assumed it was), the possibility of his complicity in the early stages of the rebellion, when at least three officials went over to Kai, is greater than if (as seems more likely) the aberrant officials were acting on their own. Chan's grasp of politics in the countryside throughout his reign appears to have been weak and intermittent; this was to be expected, given poor communications and the traditional restraints on a Buddhist monarch in Southeast Asia at this time.[46] The Vietnamese in Phnom Penh made Chan's position more precarious, for they diminished his credibility in the eyes of his officials and kept him from adjusting revenues, resources and patronage to suit himself. Chan was a hostage. Whatever he felt about the Vietnamese, he knew they were in Phnom Penh to stay, and that rebels like Kai, acting without foreign support, would never be strong enough to oust them. In this context, Chan's admission of guilt, his gifts to Thuy and his offer of workers after the rebellion probably stemmed less from his collusion in Kai's revolt (whatever the Vietnamese might have thought) than from a desire to retain Vietnamese patronage *vis-à-vis* his own subjects and the Thai.

Unlike the compilers of the *bangsavatar*, the 1869 poet made an effort to explain the failure of the rebellion, which was

---

[45] Minh Mang was contemptuous of amulets. In 1834, to disprove Thai faith in such "sacred rocks" he tied one to the neck of a duck, shot at it himself, and reported the duck's death: *DNTL*, XV, p. 353.

[46] These included but were not confined to uncertainty in naming a successor, diffusion of power among officials, the king's isolation and its effect on the information he received, and breakdowns in revenue collection.

connected in his mind with the interlocking notions of merit and power, symbolized by Kai's supernatural skills and his followers' invulnerability to attack.[47] By implication, these virtues were not available to outsiders like Malays and Vietnamese. Their efficacy rested on actions that were consonant with Buddhist teaching. The rebels could be made invulnerable to harm, in other words, and the Vietnamese could not, but they remained vulnerable to themselves. Violent actions even if successful for a time depleted their merit to the point that they succumbed inevitably and in Kai's case almost immediately to non-believers.

When the rebellion ended, Minh Mang wrote Nguyên van Thuy that "Peace has been restored, but there is much to be done in Cambodia, and little has been accomplished".[48] The sentence and others like it echo through the next twenty years of Vietnamese efforts to impose their will and their culture on Cambodia.[49] The efforts were interrupted in 1833 and 1841 by Thai invasions, and in 1840 by a Cambodian revolt. By the late 1840s, when warfare finally subsided, the Thai had been more successful in Cambodia than either the Vietnamese or the Cambodians who survived. The Vietnamese had been driven out, a Thai protegé placed on the throne, and the Cambodians had not become Vietnamese: the Cambodians, however, were still the clients of an outside power. The pattern repeated itself in the 1970s as the Vietnamese and the Thai have been replaced in Cambodia by more demanding patrons. From the vantage point of the 1869 poem and of the 1970s, Kai's revolt can be seen as an effort by rural Cambodians to break the pattern by confronting unwanted patrons, momentarily at least, with an invulnerable but tragically inoperative fund of merit.

---

[47] For a stimulating discussion of these ideas, see L.M. Hanks, "Merit and Power in the Thai Social Order", *American Anthropologist*, LXIV, 6 (December 1962), pp. 1247–1261.

[48] *DNTL*, VI, p. 77.

[49] See, for example, Minh Mang's additional exhortations in *DNTL*, XIV, p. 60, XV, pp. 77–78 and XVIII, pp. 225–226.

SONGS AT THE EDGE OF THE FOREST: PERCEPTIONS OF ORDER IN THREE CAMBODIAN TEXTS

"Mon ami, faisons toujours des contes. Tandis qu'on fait un conte, on est gai; on ne songe à rien de facheux. Le temps se passe; le conte de la vie s'achève, sans qu'on s'aperçoive."

—Diderot, *"Letter to Grimm"*

When the French imposed their protectorate on Cambodia in 1863, they took control of a society that had been pulverized by half a century of invasions and civil war. In these years, Cambodia often lacked a monarch, or had its monarch imprisoned, or closely patronized, by one of its two neighbors. In many ways, the first fifty years of the nineteenth century were "dark ages" resembling those which the country re-entered in the 1970s. I have discussed the narrative history of this period elsewhere.[1] For our purposes it is important to note that many of the pre-colonial manuscripts which have come down to us date from the 1850s when, under King Duang (r. 1847–1860) Cambodian literature,

This paper was originally prepared for a symposium on Southeast Asian Intellectual History, sponsored by the Social Science Research Council, which took place in Ithaca, New York in August 1978. In revising it, I benefitted from discussions with the late Lode Brakel, Ron and Barbara Hatley and Tony Day. I am grateful also for comments from Bob Elson, Craig Reynolds, Thong Thel, Hiram W. Woodward, Jr. and Alexander Woodside.
[1] David Chandler, *Cambodia before the French: Politics in a Tributary Kingdom, 1794–1848*. Doctoral Dissertation, University of Michigan, 1973; Ann Arbor, 1974.

benefitting from a few years of peace, enjoyed a renaissance.[2] One of the texts I will discuss is a chronicle that looks back over the century from the vantage point of 1856. The other two are folk-tales, chosen from a wide range of published work, which seem to me to heighten and exemplify some of the themes in the chronicle and the perceptions of ambiguity in the moral order which the chronicle transmits.

Before turning to the texts we might look briefly at the semantics of Cambodian concepts of order; these are as valid for most of the twentieth century as they are for the nineteenth.

The word for "order" (as in, "to put in order"), or more exactly, the phrase *robāb rap roy* means "the way things are [properly] arranged", to place them symmetrically like books and papers on a desk and also to rank them correctly, i.e. hierarchically, the way they have been ranked before. The phrase *lomdab lomdoy* implies order on a horizontal plane while another phrase for "order," *sandap thno'p* means literally "customary fingers' width measurements," where the word translated as "customary" (*sandap*) means "what has been heard" – presumably as the Buddhist Institute Cambodian Dictionary suggests over and over again.[3] This phrase is used to describe order in vertical terms, i.e. in terms of strata.

There is nothing ad hoc about these terms for "order." The contrast between wildness (*prei*, which means "forest") and what is grown, civilized, arranged, predictable, like rice or families, is common to many Southeast Asian cultures and is one which I shall emphasize in the paper.[4]

---

[2] See David Chandler, "Going Through the Motions: Ritual and Restorative Aspects of the Reign of King Duang of Cambodia,"below p. 99.

[3] Buddhist Institute, *Vanananukrama Khmera, Dictionnaire Cambodgien,* Phnom Penh, 1968.

[4] See S. Lewitz, "Les inscriptions modernes d'Ankor Wat," *Journal Asiatique* 1972, p. 116, and also Denys Lombard, "La vision de la forêt à Java" *Etudes Rurales* 53–56 (1974), pp. 479–485, and G. Martel, *Lovea* (Paris, 1978), p. 36 which points out the philosophical contrast between the Cambodian words *sruk* (cultivated and settled land) and *prei*. For a stimulating analysis of this contrast in Western thought, see Hayden White, "The Forms of Wildness: Archaeology of an Idea" in H. White, *Tropics of Discourse*, (Baltimore, 1978), pp. 150–82.

In a similar vein, the Cambodian word for "to be" (chea) also means "normal," as in the phrase, *chea vinh* "to regain one's [normal] health." The relationship between things as they are when they are properly arranged and things as they ought to be (or perhaps, the only way they can "be") is thus a close one, linguistically, as suggested by our own colloquial phrase, "That's the way it [always, repeatedly] goes."

In nineteenth century Cambodia when people were always in danger and almost always illiterate, examples of orderliness (such as an elegant ceremony, a design in silk or a properly chanted poem) were few and far between; all the same, the semantic overlappings mentioned above suggest that to many Cambodians, things, ideas and people – societies, in fact[5] – were thought to be safer and more authentic when they were ranked and in balance, arranged into the same hierarchical patterns (however ineffectual or unhappy) which they had occupied before. Wildness was to be feared, and so was innovation. "Don't avoid a winding path," says a Cambodian proverb. "And don't [automatically] take a straight one, either. Choose the path your ancestors have trod."[6]

Cambodians in the nineteenth century – at least insofar as their social ideas are reflected in their literature – were backward-looking people, but I don't mean to suggest that they were nostalgic for a verifiable golden age – at Angkor, for example. Instead, by "backward – looking" I mean only that their social

---

[5] The Cambodian word for "society" (*sangkum*) appears to be a neologism, for it does not appear in J. Guesdon, *Dictionnaire cambodgien-français*, Paris, 1930. The word itself apparently derives from a rarely used Sanskrit one *samgrama* (Pali *samgāma*) meaning "assembly," or "host": Ian Mabbett, personal communication.

[6] A. Pannetier, "Proverbes cambodgiens", *BEFEO*, XV/3 (1915), p. 71. There are several collections of proverbs in Khmer, which would be rewarding to study; see Solange Thierry, "Essai sur les proverbes cambodgiens," *Revue de psychologie des peuples*, 13 (1958) and Karen Fisher-Nguyen, "Khmer Proverbs: Images and Rules" in May Ebihara, Judy Ledgerwood and Carol Mortland (eds.) *Cambodian Culture Since 1975* (Ithaca, NY, 1994), pp. 91–104.

conduct was based on ideas, techniques and phrases which had been passed along through time and space like heirlooms with the result that people were continually reliving, repeating or "restoring" what was past – in ceremonial terms, in adages and in the agricultural cycle. Things which could not be predictably transmitted like violence, droughts and disease were linked in people's minds with what was wild and less distinctly perhaps with immoral, unremembered behavior in the past. Similarly, high rank, people thought, could be traced to meritorious, unverifiable behavior in *another life*. This dependence on the past for explanations, and the partial disassociation of people from responsibility for their actions produced tensions in people trying to construct a usable moral order in terms of the everyday world. What comfort was it, for example, to "explain" that meritorious people (i.e. those with wealth and power) monopolized exploitation and commanded violence? How could supposedly "universal monarchs" – like the Cambodian queen in the 1840s – be held prisoner by the Vietnamese? Why did meritorious people die?

The chronicle I will discuss deals with some of these questions in the context of events while the folk-tales face them metaphorically. The chronicle, after all, is firmly rooted in the nineteenth century, while the stories, probably much older than that, passed through the nineteenth century on their way to being written down. Both of them deal with crises in loyalty and culture resembling those which Cambodians as a whole endured in the 1830s and 40s; for this reason, I think, the three texts can be discussed together.

The first of the stories sets out to explain why a certain magpie-like bird in Cambodia is known by its cry *koun lok*, a phrase meaning "child of man," or "child of the world."[7]

---

[7] For the Khmer text of this story, see Buddhist Institute (comp.) *Brajum rioeñ preñ bhak ti 4* (Collected Folk Stories), Vol. 4, Phnom Penh, 1966, pp. 1–10. See also Solange Thierry, *Etude d'un corpus de contes cambodgiens traditionnels.* Paris, 1978, pp. 217–222. I have translated the story in *The Friends Who Tried to Empty the Sea: Selected Cambodian Folk Tales* (Clayton, 1976).

Three small girls are abandoned by their widowed mother who has no interest in them and plans to remarry a "good-for-nothing man". She leaves them to grow rice beside a pond in the forest, where

> She gave them each a handful of cooked rice, some uncooked rice, and a little corn. She also gave them salt, some fish-sauce, and a piece of smoldering wood with which to start a fire. She thought, "A tiger will devour them tonight, for certain. If they manage to survive, they'll be dead from hunger soon enough."

That night as the girls lie awake terrified by the noises of the forest they are protected by a local spirit (*arak thevoda*) who bellows to keep wild animals away and then goes off to plead on the children's behalf, with Indra's guardian, Varuna.

> "There's no need to bother Indra with this problem," Varuna said. "Those girls will be changed into birds soon enough. But in the meantime, you should protect them against wild animals, and be sure they get enough to eat – small fishes and snails for example."

Little by little, the girls take to eating their food raw. Upset by this, they try to go back to their mother, but she thinks they are lying to her (the conversation turns around a play on words): exasperated, she chases then back into the forest.

At the pond when they return the smoldering wood has gone out but some of the corn has begun to grow. The girls eat it raw, along with shellfish, as the guardian spirit has directed them to do. For three months, the spirit keeps wild animals away from the children and the pond, and

> After six months had passed, the girls grew downy feathers all over their bodies, and their arms turned into wings. They could fly on branches now, and their new claws could grip the branches

or pluck fruit . . . Their lips narrowed at this time into beaks, and they lost their ability to talk. In their hearts, all the same, they knew they were people, not animals, even if when they tried to talk they had animals' voices.

Meanwhile their mother's second husband has been sent to prison. The mother repents and comes to redeem her daughters. Even though they are birds, she can still recognize them, and follows them deeper and deeper into the forest, while they call out to her,

"We are released from our humanity; we have turned into animals, and we are far more beautiful. Don't come near us!"

The mother hears only the phrase *koun lok* ("child of the world," translated as "humanity"). She runs on after them, runs out of breath and dies.

The second story claims to be historical, taking place during the time when Udong was the capital of Cambodia (c. 1600–1866).[8] It concerns a crocodile named Thon who is a playmate-disciple of the abbot of a Buddhist monastery at Sambaur on the upper Mekong. The abbot

was fond of Thon and he'd often go to sit on a rock at the water's edge and call for Thon to come and play with him. Whenever the crocodile heard his voice he hurried over to pay his respects to the abbot, taking care to honor the other monks of the monastery as well.

---

[8] For the Khmer version of the story, Buddhist Institute (comp.), *Brajum rioeṅ preṅ bhak ti* 5 (Collected Folk Stories, Vol. 5), (Phnom Penh, 1969), pp. 179–188. See also Donald Lancaster, "The Decline of Prince Sihanouk's Regime" in J. J. Zasloff and A. E. Goodman (eds.), *Indochina in Conflict*. (Lexington, Mass., 1972), p. 54. For other versions of this legend, see Evéline Porée-Maspéro, *Etude sur les rites agraires des cambodgiens*. 3 vols., (Paris and The Hague, 1962–1969), pp. 92–94, 97–100, and 196–197.

One day, the abbot is called away to Udong to cure a princess who has fallen ill. After a time, the crocodile misses his master and swims off after him. On the way he encounters a wicked crocodile but manages to avoid a fight. When he reaches Udong and finds the abbot resting in a pavilion beside the river he catches him in his jaws, puts him on his back, and begins his voyage back to Sambaur.

In the first part of the journey, Thon tried to keep the abbot out of the water. He swam along carefully, skimming the surface. When he reached the territory of the wicked crocodile, however, Thon thought to himself: "If I fight this enemy, I'll have to go up and down in the water, flailing around, and my master will fall off. What can I do? Change myself into something different? Avoid a fight?"

The crocodile swallows the abbot, defeats the wicked crocodile and when he reaches Sambaur to disgorge his master, the abbott is dead. Filled with chagrin, Thon decides that the princess is responsible for his master's death (for without her illness, the abbot would never have left home), so he swims back to Udong and swallows the princess, whom he surprises bathing. This leads to a hunt for the crocodile, sponsored by the king, and the story closes with Thon's dismemberment and the construction of a stupa holding the princess's ashes at Sambaur.

These stories say interesting things, I think, about tensions in the moral order between servitude and autonomy, for example, wildness and humanity, destiny and chance. Both stories ask: What is an animal? Who is to blame? and Who is rewarded? And they give contradictory, oddly satisfying answers.

In the girls-into-birds story, we notice that not even Indra the king of the gods can halt the process of devolution. The gods, like students of Levi-Strauss, recognize an abyss between the raw and the cooked. The story is not, however, a mechanical working out of this idea. Because the girls are innocent and because a local spirit happens to be there they are protected by the spirit's beastlike roaring from predatory beasts. Their mother, on the other hand, is a wicked human being. She dies in the forest alone, which is to say, like a beast. Just before this, the girls rejoice to be free from the human condition, even though we are told that they "knew they were still people"; their mother recognizes them in spite of their appearance; she can't understand what they say.

The story, then, is in a sense "about" the frontier between the wild and the tamed, with "human" birds on one side of the border, and an "animal" woman on the other. Once the girls turn into birds, the gods are not needed to help them, for now they are "at home" in the forest. And yet the story is richer still, for it suggests that *koun lok* birds, even today, might be aware, as we are, of their past. The story closes by mentioning that the birds cry out "*koun lok*" when surprised by men in their natural habitat, which lies just at the edge of the woods, along the border of the cultivated world; and at night – perhaps at the time just after sunset which the French refer to as *entre chien et loup* – the story says that the cry "*koun lok* disturbs the stillness."

The story about Thon and the abbot also has a dreamlike quality which springs in part, I think, from the failure of the two characters to communicate with each other or to influence events. Thon, an animal, is capable of more subtlety of feeling than his master realizes. The monk plays with the crocodile and accepts his homage, but doesn't seem to tell him much about the world. The two don't understand each other's language or each other's mission in life. By his loyalty to the king, incomprehensible to Thon, for example, the abbot sets off a chain of deaths. By his humanly incomprehensible quarrel with another crocodile, Thon imperils his master. Seeking to save his master, the crocodile swallows him up; seeking to avenge the monk, he swallows the princess; he is a prisoner of his natural style, swept up inside a ruinous charade.

In both stories, an emphasis falls on the links between things as they are and things as they ought to be. Looking at the stories from this angle, several platitudes emerge, such as: girls who behave like birds will turn into birds; mothers who leave their children should be punished; crocodiles have no understanding of human affairs; kings are more powerful than beasts. But the stories themselves are not assertions of the *status quo*; they are momentarily successful assaults against it. The girls are preserved in the forest (as no one is), the crocodile is consumed with loyalty (as reptiles never are). On the whole, of course, while the stories say something about the perils of dependency, neither of them calls dependency into question. The girls, after all, try to go back to their mother; the crocodile's loyalty to his master is what eventually destroys him.

The verse chronicle from *Wat* Srolauv, in north central Cambodia, was composed in 1856, to commemorate the completion of the *wat* itself. The poem consists of twenty strophes or *bot*, averaging (in typescript) about thirty lines apiece. Four distinct metric forms – all common to nineteenth century Cambodian verse – are used. Unlike the two folk stories, the chronicle has not been published, although parts of it appear in other nineteenth century texts.[9]

The poem traces the fortunes of an elite Cambodian family – father, mother, and son – from about 1811 to 1856. In the course of the poem, which also tells of dislocations suffered by the kingdom, the father and son die, and long stretches of the text, which was sponsored by the widowed mother, consist of dirges for these men. *Wat* Srolauv itself was built in memory of the son, whom many people in the audience probably knew. The author, a monk named Pech, was a relative of the sponsor, and perhaps was serving as abbot of the *wat*. Like the audience, he knew what

[9] *Sastra lboek rabalksat (Ang Chan)* (Document concerned with the annals of Ang Chan.) Manuscript from *wat* Srolauv, Kompong Thom, 1856, recopied 1951, in the archives of the Buddhist Institute, Phnom Penh. I am grateful to the late Dik Keam (murdered as a "class enemy" under Pol Pot in 1976) for providing me with a typescript in 1971. A related, published verse chronicle, from the same region, is *Rioeñ robalksat sruk khmaer* (The Story of the Royal Lineage in Cambodia) (*RRSK*), Phnom Penh, 1958, which was composed in 1874, but contains many passages identical with ones in the *wat* Srolauv ms., and clearly draws on earlier material.

life had been like in Srolauv under the Vietnamese protectorate and during the Thai Invasions of 1833 and 1841. Theirs was not a fanciful world where girls turned into birds or monks rode crocodiles. It was a world of suffering, instability and war. The poem is about what has happened to a kingdom, a family, and an audience, all sharing a decline in merit for reasons that are difficult but necessary for the poet to explain. The poem describes two attempts by King Duang and the widowed mother to push back the wilderness and to restore and reenact the seemliness of the past by reconstituting kingship and by sponsoring a *wat*. The poem itself, in this way, is an expiatory act. As far as we know, it was recited only on the one occasion.

In the preamble the poet discusses the notions of merit and rebirth, which are central to the poem:

> Sometimes people have merit, high status, possessions, more than anyone else, for sure, and on other occasions people are small and low, their lineage and descendants insignificant, like poor orphans altogether. This is destiny (*karma*); suffering comes as a result of what we have done; merit and demerit are all mixed up together.

The reversals of fortune suffered by the family are then made more specific:

> This poem has been composed for Lady Prak, deprived of her husband, so that all of you, men and women alike, can listen and understand. . . Once she had merit, riches, possessions. Now all that has been reversed, has changed, and she is poor and bereft.

"Misfortune," continues the poet, "is the essence of this poem":

> and as for fate, it's like being in the middle of the sea, with no islands and no shore in sight, with no one to help, with none of the images of life.

The narrative then begins, with the marriage of Lady Prak around 1800 to a high official named Narin. Her own background is not recorded. The poet gives a lavish description of their horses, elephants, carts, food, servants and slaves, commenting that "in those days, officials were better equipped than they are now." Soon both receive titles and emblems of rank from the king (Chan, r. 1796–1835) for it is the king who bestows identities and when he dies – as we shall see – these identities (and the merit they imply) become less efficacious.

In the second strophe, the couple's only child, a son named Meas, is born. Nourished by loving parents, he becomes "more beautiful than his father, "neither short nor tall," with a "round, lovable face." His childhood passes peacefully, for King Chan, still meritorious, "watched over the border markers (*seima*) of the kingdom of Cambodia, "presumably from his "sacred center" in Phnom Penh.[10]

Then, in the year of the snake (i.e. AD 1833, the correct date) Siam launches an unexplained attack. Some officials flee into the fortress of Phnom Penh; others hurry off by boat to warn the "celestial king," i.e. the emperor of Vietnam, allegedly in Saigon. Chan himself, however, offers no resistance to the invasion and flees instead to seek refuge at the Vietnamese court, at Hue where he tells the emperor, Minh Mang, of the attack. Minh Mang orders a military expedition into Cambodia. This part of the poem plays tricks with the historical record. Two important issues are played down. The first is that the Vietnamese had in fact exercised informal control over the Cambodian capital since a Thai invasion of 1811–1812; therefore, Meas and his parents

---

[10] For discussions of this notion, see Clifford Geertz, "Centres, Kings, and Charisma" in J. Ben-David and T. C. Clark (eds.) *Culture and its Creators. Essays in Honor of Edward Shils*, Chicago, 1977, 172–146; Paul Mus, "Angkor in the time of Javavarman VII," *Indian Art and Letters*, XI/2 (1937), pp. 65–75, and H. L. Shorto, "The planets, the days of the week and the points of the compass: orientation symbols in 'Burma'" in G. B. Milner (ed.) *Natural symbols in Southeast Asia*, London, 1978, pp. 152–164.

would have had to acquiesce, at least once before, to Vietnamese protection.[11] Moreover, the Thai attack of 1833 is made to seem unprovoked, perhaps to throw people's sufferings (and their innocence) into relief, or to allow the poet to disapprove of an attack that did not include (as the 1841 invasion was to do) the restoration of a rightful king. In other chronicles, Chan orders resistance to the Thai before fleeing, but his ministers are unable to recruit any troops. Chan's flight into the Mekong Delta is confirmed in these sources, but his visit to Minh Mang is fictional and meant as a way of pointing to a culpable collaboration with the Vietnamese, who succeeded, in 1834, in driving a Thai army out of eastern Cambodia, as well as suggesting that Chan could speak as an equal with the emperor of Vietnam. The poet describes the sacking of Phnom Penh by this retreating Siamese army:

> They took everything away, and burned what had been people's houses, until not one of them remained; they took off everyone's possessions, masters' and slaves' alike, and they carried off all the people until not a man was left.[12]

When Chan returned to the devastated city in 1834, he asked the Vietnamese to rebuild it. The poem relates that the Vietnamese then despatched middle-echelon officials like Narin to the country side to build fortifications at "the doors of the country," using locally recruited labor.

Narin is sent to north-central Cambodia, to the region of Barai, astride a potential invasion route, and rather near Srolauv. Under the Vietnamese the population there is mobilized to dig wells, ponds "moats, and canals, to raise fortifications, and to build granaries and gun emplacements:

---

[11] Interestingly, Narin appears in a manuscript chronicle (P-30, Fonds EFEO, Phnom Penh) as leading an anti-Thai expeditionary force in 1815.

[12] See also K. S. R. Kulap (pseud.) *Anam Sayam yut* (*Annam's war with Siam*), Bangkok, 1970, pp. 658–660.

And all the officials, high and low, stayed close together. None of them resisted the Vietnamese – for they were afraid of them, and tried not to displease them. They ordered workers to build fortifications the way the Vietnamese wanted them, with pointed stockades around them.

The poet adds that the Vietnamese also "taught the people how to fight, how to make rifles, and how to use their knives in combat." All this, he says, was like a "meaningless game," and when workers were slow, the Vietnamese beat them "like cats, dogs, cows or buffaloes."

After mentioning Chan's death in 1835 and the succession to the throne of his three daughters under Vietnamese control the poet relates that the governor of Kompong Svay, who was probably Narin's patron, flees to Siam to be replaced by an official friendlier to the Vietnamese who soon decides to

capture all the Cambodian officials, high and low, and charge them with crimes. When the ordinary people heard this, they gathered together and said, "If they capture our leaders, we will have no one to honor and respect," but they were terrified of the Vietnamese, and far too scared to say anything in public.

In these lines, the necessity of hierarchy, as seen by underlings, is nicely put; it is echoed in other contemporary texts.[13] Another point to stress about the poet's description of events in Barai in the 1830s is that his statements and chronology could be verified by older members of his audience, who had lived through this period of Vietnamese control.

Although ordinary people are too frightened to act, the Vietnamese threat to capture the officials pushes some Cambodian officials into revolt.

[13] See, for example, those cited in Chandler, Cambodia before the French, p. 144.

They did not wait to be told to do so, but raised a military force, rapidly, crying out to their troops: "Kill all the Vietnamese. From Kandal to Stoung, kill them in their fortresses, until not one of them is left alive!"

To be effectively *recited*, a poem in Narin's memory, sponsored by his widow, and confined largely to a Buddhist frame of reference, must strike a balance between Narin's "correct" anti-Vietnamese feelings (the Vietnamese, after all, were thought of as unbelievers) and playing down his violent unmeritorious acts. There is the problem of transmission, also, for the text was passed along, in the first instance, by being chanted at participants in some of the events which it relates. For this reason, the poet – himself a Buddhist monk – had to walk a fine line between accuracy and prettiness. Although we know from other sources, for example, that massacres of Vietnamese took place all over Cambodia in the late 1830s, the poet makes sure that the Vietnamese attack before the Cambodians are provoked. When Narin hears of this attack, he

> was unable to stay until the army came. He lost his head with fright; and so he ordered his (extended) family (*jat kruo*), many of whom were elderly, to fill their ox-carts with possessions and to leave at once.

In the scramble to leave, several carts are broken, and the family's possessions, including such manifestations of high status as gold and silver trays, spill out onto the ground:

> That was the year of the cock (1837); in the year of the cock, everyone was frightened, and many possessions were lost forever, scattered along the roads and in the forest.

The possessions are like the smoldering stick in the story about the birds. They are symbols of civilization, ways of expressing a frontier between the wild, undifferentiated world, and the world of hierarchies anchored in ritual and in the past. As the exiles move north-westward through unfamiliar, uncultivated land, they encounter many hardships. Food is scarce. After several days on the edge of death, they push on, convinced that the Vietnamese are in pursuit:

> Their misery was great. There was no food at all, no fish, no rice, nothing normal to stave off their hunger; instead, they dug for lizards, without pausing to think, or be guilty about it; they simply did it together. They hunted *saom* roots in the depths of the forest, and other roots as well to make into a kind of soup; there was no fish – no fish-paste, nothing to make food palatable. They ate like this until their hunger went away, but it was hard to swallow the food; they sat silently beside the road, intensely poor, and miserable.

This passage reiterates the themes of brutalization and reversal which permeate the poem, but softens and ennobles them somewhat by casting them into metered verse that links these hardships and wanderings in the forest to those of characters *in other poems*, like Prince Rama, for example.[14]

On the frontier of Siam, the caravan encounters some Thai officials (*kha luong*) who "take pity" on them, and give them some provisions. Narin goes alone to Bangkok to pay homage to King Rama III (r. 1824–1851), the patron of Chan's self-exiled brother, Prince Duang, who has lived in Bangkok under Thai protection since 1812. Rama III questions Narin about his voyage and restores his rank (while perhaps deflecting his loyalties somewhat) by presenting him with gold and silver trays, bowls, goblets, and lengths of patterned silk.

---

[14] See Saveros Pou (tr.) *Ramakerti*, Paris, 1977, and Pou, *Etude sur Ramakerti*, Paris, 1977. Wandering in the forest is a feature of many Cambodian folk-tales and of Javanese *wayang* theatre. The family's peregrinations, then, might be seen as an example of life imitating art.

Interestingly, many of these emblems of rank are connected with ceremonial consumption of food or betel. Emblems of rank in Vietnam, on the other hand, were often such things as seals of office and paper on which to write decrees.[15] By paying homage to the only Buddhist monarch accessible to him Narin regains his "rightful" position in the world; however, in another reversal still he dies as soon as he gets back to his family, in the forest, far from home, as if lacking merit in some way.

In a strophe given over to Lady Prak's mourning for him, she regrets that she is so far from home "where possessions, riches and rank would make it easy to celebrate [a funeral] while it is so difficult here." And she continues:

Now all families, as they live out their lives, grow sick, die and disappear, losing to misfortune, as if on the slope of a hill. Some die as children, some as brothers and sisters, and indeed all of us must die, husbands and wives as well, weakened with suffering and fever.

The linking of propriety/property recurs often in the poem; part of the widow's sadness on the frontier is that her husband's merit has become so ineffectual so soon. Nonetheless, a suitable funeral ceremony takes place, with brahmins (*youki*) on hand to officiate, as well as Buddhist monks. Hearing of the family's plight from officials in the region, Rama III allows them to "settle and grow rice" (or, presumably, have rice grown for them) along the frontier.

The poet then shifts his focus to the Vietnamese zone of occupation which, "after the family had left, (became) unhappy "Vietnamese and Vietnamese-sponsored Cambodian armies, he tells us, scour the countryside, hunting down the people who

---

[15] *Cambodia before the French*, 81. For Thai parallels, see Lorraine Gesick, *Kingship and Political Integration in Traditional Siam 1767–1824*, (Ann Arbor, 1976), especially pp. 48 and 112 ff. Some of the emblems of office were in use as early as the tenth century AD: cf. G. Cœdès (ed.) *Les Inscriptions du Cambodge*, Vol. 4, (Paris, 1957), p. 181.

had been killing Vietnamese. Reaching north-central Cambodia, the troops find only "people cowering in the forest"– a chilling premonition of events in 1979 and 1980. Many of these are brought back and imprisoned presumably in villages, to the number of "one hundred thousand men." The poet goes on to describe Vietnamese punishments and tortures in detail.[16] At precisely this point, the Vietnamese (1841, according to other sources) arrest the princesses and the highest-ranking Cambodian officials in Phnom Penh:

> The officials (who remained at liberty) and the people pondered together, and decided to raise troops and kill the Vietnamese, so that the Vietnamese wouldn't be able to capture and kill them first; for if they did, Cambodia would no longer exist.

The phrase "pondered together" (*kut knea*) in the presage should not suggest democratic procedures so much as a community of interest and a sense of oppression shared between "high" and "low" members of society, especially at this time.

Once again, what pulls Cambodians into concerted action is the fear that upper ranks in the society, which defined the others, had been eliminated by unbelievers and that, therefore, Cambodia – as set of hierarchical arrangements – "would no longer exist." Being "wild" meant having no one to respect, or to look down on; orderliness had been destroyed by foreigners and violence, perhaps, was at last permissible, to restore it.

In forming a notion of what Cambodia "was," regalia, and especially the king's sword (*preah khan*) always played an important part, right up to 1975. Similarly, possessions indicative of status – such as umbrellas, betel-boxes, or gold and silver

---

[16] These include salting open wounds, burying alive, eye-gouging, and so on. The ensemble of these tortures passed into Cambodian folk-lore and history; see Eng Sut, *Akkasar mahaboros khmaer* (Documents about Cambodian heroes), Phnom Penh, 1969, pp. 1214–1216. Interestingly, the passage describing the torture is one which this version shares with the published verse chronicle about this period (see note 9 above).

trays – play an important part in the poem. In some ways, they seem to have been more important than any duties an official was expected to perform. Duties, in fact, aren't mentioned in the poem, which focuses instead on shifts in status, fortune and patronage, which is to say, in *merit* as observed by others. The poet suggests, indeed, that there is a close connection between power and possessions, which aren't merely symbols of merit, but proofs or manifestations of it. A linkage like this is not unusual in a society which places such emphasis on rank differentials and the difference between haves and have-nots; the Cambodian word for "rich," indeed, means primarily "have." The haves, in other words, had to be seen (by the have-nots) amidst their numerous possessions.[17]

The poet skims over the war that raged in Cambodia in the early 1840s, choosing instead to stress the restorative aspects of the reign of King Duang, who returned to the former capital of Udong with a Thai army in 1841 and was crowned king after protracted Thai-Vietnamese fighting and negotiations in 1847.

What Rama III had done for Narin, by presenting him with regalia, Duang now performs for Cambodia as a whole. Reimposing propriety, he brings the kingdom back to life – blotting out the troubles that had occurred. Like the Thai monarch Rama I's refashioning Ayudhya in the new city of Bangkok in the 1780s, Duang fastidiously restores his father's capital in Udong. The passage in the poem describing the restoration resembles one in the chronicles that describes similar work, by Duang's father, coming back from exile in Siam in 1794.[18] Duang's own return, of course, was vivid to listeners to the poem.[19] A point to stress is the contrast between the harmony,

---

[17] This notion of visible merit (*bun*) leads us back to the idea of regalia (including chronicles) which are hidden away, polished, added to and passed along, through time. Chronicles, like merit, are additive; the notion of personal transformation is lacking from them. See Shelly Errington, "Some comments on style in the meanings of the past," *Journal of Asian Studies*, XXXVIII/2 (February, 1979), pp. 231–44.

[18] Eng Sut, *Akkasar*, pp. 1012–1013.

[19] Inscription K. 142 (Cœdès' classification). See E. Aymonier, *Le Cambodge*,

propriety and elegance of his actions and the homelessness, barbarism, and the loss of status described in earlier strophes. After Duang's coronation, the refugees along the frontier gradually drift home. Meas, his mother and their followers hurry to Srolauv with their possessions, their ox-carts making the noise *kokik kokok*. They are welcomed back by local people. Meas orders them to build him a new house. When this is finished, he frets about his lack of rank:

"I am destitute," he thought. "I am too poor; and as this is true, I should consider offering myself [to the king] as a slave. My father used to be important; he had honor and high rank, but that has vanished. I must go and become a slave to the king."

The audience would not take Meas' allegation of poverty very seriously, sitting outside a gilded *wat* constructed by his mother. But to Meas himself, the fact that he lacked an identity bestowed by the king meant that he was impoverished, in terms of merit, and perhaps in terms of an entourage, or at least entitlement to it, as well.[20]

His departure gives the poet, *via* Lady Prak, the opportunity for an aria about the perils of living in the city (which few in the audience would have visited); but Meas persists, and sets off by boat for Udong.

He soon attracts the attention of the king, because he acts like a "true servant, who never does anything improper," probably – although the text is unclear about it – as some sort of a page at court.

Vol. I, Paris, 1900, 349–51. See also Lunet de Lajonquire, *Inventaire . . . du Cambodge*, Vol. I, Paris, 1910, pp. 208.

[20] Cf. the words of the Sunan of Surakarta (1788–1820), quoted in Soemarsaid Moertono, *State and Statecraft in Old Java*, (Ithaca, N.Y.), 1968 (repr. 1974), p. 94: "There is nothing to be compared with serving the king; he will see the king's courtyard and will be respected and have a name (in society) . . .; serving can be likened to debris drifting in the ocean, going wherever it is commanded to."

Returning to Srolauv, he courts the daughter of a governor, impressing her parents with his "ancient pedigree," his merit and his ability to arrange ceremonies "according to old traditions." His brief separation from his bride-to-be (who was probably in view during the recitation of the poem) allows the poet to spin and embroider stanzas of advice to her, stressing the importance of obedience to her husband. When she joins Meas in Srolauv, she finds him "worried sick" that he might be recalled to Udong, away from his village, his mother and his wife. Satisfied with his new rank, he has become fearful of Duang; for the main purpose of his visit, it seems, had been to have a rank bestowed on him with which he can lead his easy life.

Soon after he returns home with his wife, i.e. just as his merit is established, Lady Prak complains to him that she lacks proper offerings (*borikkha*) to present to local monks. Meas, "intelligent and understanding his mother's heart," offers to go back to Udong to procure them for her. His mother tries to dissuade him but she fails and he leaves for the capital by canoe. After buying the offerings, he sets off for Srolauv. However,

> when they reached Thkoub Island, he was stricken ill, and then got worse. He tried to stay conscious, and the servants in the canoe tried to row faster; but his fate was very near, his illness was too heavy. He tried to think of life; then he couldn't think of life; his life was over.

Meas dies as his father had done, on his way home from performing what seems to have been a meritorious act. Why, asks the poet, was it his fate to "die in the middle of the forest, like a poor man in a far-off land?"

Here again we encounter the contrast between wilderness, animality, poverty, anonymity and loneliness on the one hand, and villages, cultivation, sociability and bestowed identities on the other. Just as girls are not supposed to turn into birds, meritorious people are not supposed to die like ordinary men –

i.e. unexpectedly, like the people listening to the poem – although they often do. In nineteenth century Cambodia, the frontier between the two was not especially sharp; people in the audience had crossed it, and come back, more than once, just as the *koun lok* do.

The strophes that follow are given over to laments of Lady Prak and her daughter-in-law, who feels as if "life has been beaten from her body." Lady Prak declares:

> O favorite son, when you were born I nourished you, gently, gently, and lay beside you, and embraced you, so that no powdery dust could touch you; no one allowed you to be sad or to cry from hunger. Oh why did you die in the forest, while you were still so young?

The remainder of the poem, perhaps a hundred and fifty lines, deals with Meas' cremation, his mother's mourning, and the construction of *wat* Srolauv. The poet recounts that work began on the construction in 1851, and continued, on a part-time basis, alternating with work in the fields, until 1855. One problem mentioned by the poet is the shortage of able-bodied men; another is the scarcity of decorations, like gilded mirrors and gold leaf. At each stage of the construction, festivals take place; at the most recent of these Lady Prak recites a long prayer, addressed to the Buddha-image of the *wat*, offering up the *wat* itself in exchange for assurances of salvation. The poet describes the levels of hell to which people are consigned when they lack merit and "act like crazy pigs," comparing this to the behavior of the patrons of the poem who, by constructing a *wat* (and perhaps, by allowing history to be recited) have a meritorious future, for themselves.

The recitation of the poem, in fact, like the construction of the *wat*, is at once a celebration of hierarchy and sociability: hierarchy by means of the values expressed, and the elegance which expresses them, and sociability because the people listening to the poem are also the ones who built the *wat*, and thus partake of these two kinds of elegance. Similarly, the recitation of tales that are "about" the boundary between the forest and the field is, in a sense, to *mark off* the boundary, as we listen together to the stories.

The three texts that I have discussed suggest that there were two contrasting perceptions of moral order in early nineteenth century Cambodia. They were not, as one might expect, perceptions on the part of those in power *versus* perceptions of the powerless, or perceptions of people who could read *versus* those of people who could not.[21] Rather, there was a moral order for everyone – or at least those reachable by texts of this kind – based on prescription, memorization, and teaching, largely Buddhist in orientation on the one hand, and perceptions rooted in the real world on the other. The first was a celebration of hierarchical arrangements, operating, ideally, in the common good. The second was an attempt to survive inside the framework of what was going on.

Some Cambodian literature, like epic poetry or the Tmenh Chey cycle (a picaresque novel about a rogue) can be seen as primarily idealistic, or primarily profane, either sanctifying or overturning the meritoriousness of power. People called on these forms of discourse not only when they were told to, by the elite, but also on their own, to relieve the pain that came from living in the world. They could escape the world for an evening by following Rama into an enchanted forest, or they could overturn it, momentarily, by hearing how Tmenh Chey outwitted kings, ministers, and even the Chinese. But there was no real escape

---

[21] For a discussion of this issue, see Jack Goody, *The Domestication of the Savage Mind*, (Cambridge, 1977), especially Chapters 1–3. See also Kathleen Gough, "Implication of Literacy in Traditional China and India," and Jack Goody and Ian Watt, "The Consequences of Literacy" in Jack Goody (ed.), *Literacy in Traditional Societies*, (Cambridge 1968), For Asian references to this general theme, see Biardeau, "Théories du langage en Inde" in Julia Kristeva, et al., *La traversée des signes*, (Paris, 1975), and also S. J. Tambiah, "Literacy in a Buddhist Village in Northeast Thailand" in Goody, *Literacy*, pp. 85–131.

from the world outside the stories, a world which, in many ways, these two extreme forms of literature failed to address.

The texts I have chosen, on the other hand, exemplify tensions and overlappings between these two extremes, and between two ways of looking at the question of moral order. They describe the gaps that open between what ought to happen in the world, what often happens, and the "normal." Thus the girls, although good, change into animals; the crocodile, although loyal, is destroyed. Narin honors a monarch, and Meas his mother. In the course of doing so both of them are stricken dead. Similarly, people listening to the poem, who had hidden in the forest like animals in the 1830s, are now celebrating around a new *wat*, glittering with mirrors and shimmering gold leaf. There is poetic justice here, as there is for the girls, who as birds remember their humanity, and for Lady Prak, who asks for merit on a bereaved occasion, and is granted it, if not perceptibly by "heaven," by the people who have worked on her behalf and have now gathered to celebrate their work with her.

In spite of momentary triumphs, poetic justice or moments of shared intensity (as when listening, together, to poems and music), the world of nineteenth century Cambodia was a desperate, cacophonous place. People had no explanations for suffering that would allow any but the magically endowed to overcome it; they had no explanation for justice that led them to question the propriety of exploitation. They had practical explanations for injustice, and Buddhist ones as well: a tiger is bigger than a frog; King Chan's lack of merit brought misery to

---

[22] I have borrowed this image from a lovely passage in Fredrik Barth, *Ritual and Knowledge among the Baktaman of New Guinea*, (Oslo, 1975, p. 267:)

. . . My own image for the achievements of Baktaman understanding and codification is provided by the concrete symbol of their own dance evenings. Occasionally, a score or two of adults and youths will come together at night, aided by torches and a partly overcast moon. They dress in their finery, including cassowary-feathers for the seniors, dance to their sacred drums, and sing their songs of love and violence, thereby shaping the whole scene in complex cultural imagery positively intoxicating themselves with the force and vitality of their own expression. But if you move a hundred metres along one of

his people. These explanations fitted some of the facts but not as many as the texts I have discussed. In a sense, the texts "answer" questions that no one dared to ask, but in the end, what do they *explain*? No more, and of course no less, than songs at the edge of the forest, as night comes on,[22] the time *entre chien et loup*. Certainly neither the poet nor the characters in the poem saw themselves as acting out roles in an historical process; for at this time, as George Steiner suggests in another context, "All human beings were subject to general disorder or exploitation as they were to disease. But these swept over them with tidal mystery."[23]

Hierarchies and those who inhabit them – like the characters in the poem – are oriented to the past, when things were not so bad, and so are perceptions of the moral order that hesitate, as these perceptions do, in the presence of revolutionary change. The idea that bestowed identities as an official, for example, or a Buddhist monk kept the wilderness at bay for the "haves" at least was widely held in nineteenth century Cambodia. But when hierarchies break down, spilling onto the roads of the forest like gold and silver trays, and when a society, like Cambodia's in the 1830s, 1840s, and 1970s, appears to have come to an end, where does one look for explanations?

their paths you find yourself outside this circle of cultural imagery; and through the trees you glimpse a panorama of immense, untouched forest-covered landscape, dwarfing man's tiny village clearing and muting his tiny noise. The command which the Baktaman achieve over their situation is, as for all of us, at best a subjective command only, asserted in those limited sectors where their awareness asserts itself. And in creating this awareness, the symbols fashioned in their rites are both their main beacons and their tools.

[23] George Steiner, *In Bluebeard's Castle* (London, 1971), p. 19.

It is illuminating to note, in closing, that the Javanese word for "chronicle" (babad) derives from a verb that means "to clear a wilderness": Peter Carey, *The Cultural Ecology of Early Nineteenth Century Java* (Singapore, 1974), p. 4.

GOING THROUGH THE MOTIONS: RITUAL ASPECTS OF THE REIGN OF KING DUANG OF CAMBODIA (1848–1860)

Frazer says it is very difficult to discover the error in magic and this is why it persists for so long – because, for example, a ceremony which is supposed to bring rain is sure to be effective sooner or later. But then it is queer that people do not notice sooner that it does rain sooner or later anyway.

Wittgenstein, "Remarks on Frazer's *Golden Bough*"

King Duang's reign over Cambodia began after a daunting period of kinglessness and ended in confusion and disorder. The reign is interesting to study, I think, because of the contrast we can discern between its story insofar as we can reconstruct it from a range of sources and the way it is treated in Cambodian chronicle texts. Using all the sources, we can lay out and evaluate Duang's reign in terms of nineteenth century Cambodian history. By studying what the chronicles stress, play down and leave out, however, we can go a step further and uncover some nineteenth century Cambodian ideas about kingship and historiography, so as to determine the meaning of the reign as Cambodians at the time, and chroniclers later on, perceived it.

This paper was first published in Monograph Series No. 26 Yale University Southeast Asia Studies, reprinted with permission.

I came to favor this dual approach when in comparing the two most detailed chronicle accounts I was struck by the amount of space – more than half the total in both manuscripts – which was devoted to the enumeration of ceremonies, decrees and political acts that took place at the beginning of the reign, and described in detail the moment when Cambodian kingship was restored.[1] In the chronicles, this enumeration of rituals follows a sentence telling us that Duang had received his royal name and his regalia from his patron, the King of Siam, on a certain date, at a certain time, and when he was a certain age. The enumeration of ceremonies is sandwiched between stretches of narrative "political" history. Now Cambodian chronicles as a *genre*, especially in the nineteenth and twentieth centuries, tend to emphasize actions on a king's part, places where he travels and things that happen to him, rather than his policies or conversations. Even so, the material which overshadows Duang's chronicle takes up what *looks like* too much space.

Before turning to this material, I should mention that the chronicles in question were not intended for recital, like Malay *hikayat* or Javanese *babad*, but rather were for perusal, recopying and storage inside the palace and in Buddhist *wats*. Chronicles were also occasionally sent abroad as tributary gifts. In other words, they were part of a monarch's wealth.[2] They do not necessarily impart what ordinary people knew from other sources

---

[1] The manuscripts I have used are the chronicle "P-63" in the library of the École Française d'Extrême Orient (EFEO), in Paris, which dates from 1904, and the palace chronicle from the Institut Bouddhique in Phnom Penh, microfilmed in 1969 under the auspices of the Toyo Bunko, and dating from 1933–1934. For a discussion of Cambodian manuscript "families," see David Chandler, "Cambodian Royal Chronicles [*Rajabangsavatar*] 1927–1949: Kingship and Historiography at the End of the Colonial Era," below p. 187. For a helpful political history of Duang's reign, see Bun Srun Theam, "Cambodia in the Mid-nineteenth Century: A Quest for Survival, 1840–1863" (M.A. diss., Australian National University, 1981), pp. 104–68.

[2] See Thailand, National Library, *Chotmaihet ratchakan thi 4* [Documents relating to the fourth reign] 1219/21 (hereafter cited as e.g. *Cmh*/4), which records Duang's presentation of a chronicle to Rama IV in 1858.

or their own recollections about a given monarch or a given reign. In Duang's case, however, there seems to have been an overlap between the chronicles' emphasis on the redemptive restoration of kingship and what Cambodians came to believe about Duang's reign, especially after his death and the imposition a few years later of the French protectorate.

In relation to the stretches of narrative history which they interrupt, the beginnings of the two reign chronicles and the ceremonies they describe resemble the winding of a clock. The ceremonies set in motion a narrative performance – Duang's reign – which, to maintain the metaphor, gradually ran down.

Duang was over fifty when he reached the throne. Like his father, Eng (r. 1794–1796), he had spent nearly all his grown life in Bangkok as a client and hostage of successive Siamese kings. Born during the reign of the Thai monarch King Rama I, he shared that king's personal name.[3] Like his father, who had been Rama I's client-hostage, Duang was allowed back into Cambodia on sufferance in the early 1840s by Rama III; he was maintained in power under the patronage of Rama III's half-brother, Rama IV.

The years between his birth and his coming to power can be seen – leaving aside the 1970s – as Cambodia's dark ages and I would stress the weakening and fragmentation of the institution of kingship as well as other institutions, such as monasticism and literacy which took place in the 1820s and 1830s, when the country fell to a large degree under Vietnamese control.[4] Duang's elder brother, King Chan (r. 1806–1835) had no sons and when he died was succeeded by a daughter, Mei, who reigned under Vietnamese supervision until 1841, when she was taken with Cambodia's regalia (a sword, some weapons, statues of Siva

---

[3] See G. Cœdès' review of H.G.Q. Wales' "Siamese State Ceremonies", *Bulletin de l'École Française d'Extrême Orient* (*BEFEO*), XXXII (1932), p. 532.

[4] Thailand, Department of Fine Arts (comp.) *Prachum phongsawadan* phak ti 56 [Collected Chronicies, Volume 56] (Bangkok, 1968), pp. 161–74, and also David Chandler, *Cambodia Before the French*: Politics in a Tributary Kingdom 1794–1847 (Ann Arbor, Mich.: University Microfilms, 1974), especially pp. 126–75.

and Vishnu, and other paraphernalia) into Vietnam to escape a Siamese invasion. During her reign many Cambodian institutions such as monastic Buddhism and royal patronage were battered, forgotten, or reduced in scope. And yet, as long as titles were awarded officials by a Cambodian ruler, such as Mei, the officials were quiescent *vis-à-vis* Vietnamese political demands. It was only when Mei was physically removed from the kingdom (and sources suggest that many of her subjects thought she was dead) that the officials were prepared to lead their followers into revolt. This is because, as one of them wrote, their identity as "superior people" was now at stake.

Duang returned to Cambodia in 1841 alongside a military expedition under Siamese command. Without regalia and a royal name, he was still unable to reign, even though his messengers fanned out into the countryside to tell people that he had returned after thirty years of exile.[5] An inscription carved in the 1850s, when Duang was already king, recaptures the popular enthusiasm that greeted him on his arrival ten years before:

In that year [1841], there was a mighty ruler, whose name was Duang; he came from the royal city [Bangkok] to the region [*mondol* – i.e. 'mandala') of Cambodia, where he took up residence in the fortified city of Udong the Victorious. Using merit, skill, and masterly intelligence, the king scattered his enemies in terror; and soon the three warring states were friends again.[6]

The passage enhances Duang's status by making no mention of the Thai, except as one of three apparently equal "warring states." In reoccupying his father's city (Udong) in 1841, Duang paid

---

[5] See K.S.R Kulap (pseud.), *Sayam-Anam yut* [Wars between Siam and Annam] (1905, reprint Bangkok 1970) II, p. 952, which adds that Duang distributed seals of office to provincial officials at this time.

[6] Inscription K.142, translated in E. Aymonier, *Le Cambodge* (Paris: E. Leroux, 1900), pp. 349–51. I am grateful to Michael Vickery for transcribing the Cambodian text for me from the *estampage* in the Bibliothèque Nationale in Paris.

homage to him, refurbishing the *chedi* that contained his ashes. Like his father a half century before, he came back to a forlorn city, and, like him, he marked his return by building a palace for himself and by redecorating and repopulating the city's Buddhist *wats*, several of which are listed in the chronicle by name. A verse chronicle from the 1850s emphasizes how necessary this process of restoration was:

> In the years of war, people had fled into the forest, and no one knew any longer how *wats* were supposed to be built, until the king returned to Udong and restored them, placing Buddha-images where they belonged.[7]

The reimposed patronage of Buddhism and the arts in a reconstituted royal city were things that Cambodians expected from a king. Before his coronation, Duang performed other kingly acts as well, such as distributing symbols of rank to an assembly of Cambodian officials who had promised him military help and prescribing the forms of address and response which laymen were to use in talking with Buddhist monks.

Indeed, in the six years which passed between his return to Udong and his coronation, we can see that Duang's career progressed along two tracks which were proper for a king to follow. One was practical, vigorous and warlike. Duang sought alliances, engaged the Vietnamese in battle, parlayed with them, travelled to different places, and rewarded his officials. The other track was private, ceremonial, religious. Kingly actions of the latter sort included *wat* restoration, palace decoration, and linguistic reforms. In living through these years, when he was still a hostage of the Thai, Duang was concerned with amplifying his fund of merit along both lines of kingship – i.e. as a warrior,

---

[7] *Sastra lbaok rbalkhsat . . . ong chan* [Chronicle Concerning the Reign of King Chan], a manuscript composed in 1856 and recopied in 1951 and 1971 at the Institute Bouddhique in Phnom Penh.

and as a Buddhist to the point where the lines converged and he had the merit, or *bun*, appropriate for a king – that is, more than anyone else nearby. It was at this point, in 1848, that he actually *became* a king following the departure of the Vietnamese, the return of the regalia, and the receipt of a royal name, incised on a sheet of gold foil which had been brought with great ceremony from Siam.[8]

The chronicles do not describe Duang's coronation in detail. They say merely that the ceremony occurred and then transcribe his royal name which occupies ten lines of text. Parts of this name match those bestowed by the Thai on his father, King Eng, and on his brother, King Chan. Perhaps traditional to Cambodian royal names, other parts link Duang with his predecessors at Angkor and with Hindu deities, in an apparent hodge-podge of Sanskrit-Pali honorifics. The name by which he is known in the remainder of the chronicle translates, in part, as "Lord Rama-Isvara protected by Hari" – i.e. a blending of Vishnu and Siva (protected by a manifestation of Vishnu) as in statues, popular in Angkorean times, of the composite deity Harihara (Vishnu/Siva).[9] If ceremonies by later Cambodian kings can serve as a guide, Duang received these names while holding a statue of Siva in his right hand and one of Vishnu in his left.[10] To him and to his people (if they ran across this name at all), the blending and acceptance of the names would mean that he had absorbed contrary kinds of power, for in Cambodian thinking, Vishnu was associated with the sun and Siva with the moon. Other dichotomies, such as those between male and female,

---

[8] For the title, see also Thailand, National Archives, *Cmh* 3/1209/15.

[9] Adhemard Leclère, *Cambodge. Fêtes civiles* (Paris, 1961), pp. 30–31, which describes the coronation of Duang's son, Sisowath, in 1904.

[10] Paul Mus, "Barabudur," *BEFEO* 33 (1933): 701–702 provides an explanation of the Cambodian regalia offered him by a Cambodian official, associating Shiva with the king's left eye, and Vishnu with his right. See also K. Bhattacharya, *Les religions brahmaniques dans l'ancien Cambodge* (Paris, 1961), p. 76, which notes the contrast between *devayana* (the way of the gods) associated with Vishnu, and the *pitrayana* (the way of the fathers) associated with Shiva. The way of the fathers, in Cambodian terms would link Siva with the ancestors.

right and left, sky and earth and fire and water are also present in the interplay between them. Duang's royal name, then, drew together and synthesized complementary oppositions, just as a king by resolving problems was uniquely equipped to do.

Immediately after accepting his royal name, Duang accepted the kingdom itself from his brahmins, or *baku*. An eyewitness to a later Cambodian coronation recorded that as he accepted the kingdom, the monarch recited a formula which authorized, in keeping with practices in the past, people to work the soil, inhabit it, and take from it what was necessary for existence.[11]

The king's acceptance of the kingdom and his authorization of the people to use it does not mean that he, the brahmins, or the people could be said to "own" it in a juridical sense. If the land belonged to anyone, it would seem to belong to the dead (the *nak tā*, or ancestor people) who carried on inside it. Instead of owning the land, the king "consumed" it, (*saoyreach* in so-called royal language), much as he was said to consume his subjects. By his brahmins, his ancestors, his names, by his regalia, his subjects and by his behavior in various ways, the king was now *authorized* to reign. In setting out to do so, he was expected to mediate among his subjects; among sky, earth, and underworld; Vishnu, man, and Siva; gods, people and ancestors. But the authorization *per se* was no guarantee for success; this depended on his merit, his performance, and on his exemplary re-enactment of ceremonies over a length of time.

In other words, the king's efficacy – like that of any politician – was judged in terms of what he could *produce* – in terms of general welfare, and in terms of weather, peace (or victories), good harvests, and the absence of disease. His performance did not arise, officially at least, from his dealings with other people, but from his pre-arranged, repeated dealings with moments of the agricultural year, with ceremonies involving the placement and

[11] Leclère, *Fêtes civiles*, p. 36. See also Aymonier, *Le Cambodge*, pp. 58–59 and Leclère, *Les Codes cambodgiens*, 2 vols. (Paris, 1900) 1, p. 42, for a similarly worded coronation oath allegedly from the seventeenth century.

status of his officials, and with rites directed toward Hindu gods, local spirits, or the Buddhist church. In the chronicles, Duang's rule was *acted out* and the world we are witnessing in the tests is one which Clifford Geertz has called the "theatre state,"[12] a term that is useful for many Southeast Asian kingdoms.

The chronicles relate that Duang's first act after being crowned was to set the proper forms of discourse between the king and his ministers, and the proper forms of promulgating and responding to decrees. Because kingship at this stage of its enactment had to do with the imposition of propriety, it is interesting that this particular act, rather than one we might find more significant, was selected by the chroniclers or by Duang to begin his reign. Setting proper responses and forms of address between people with different status was important in nineteenth century Cambodia because it imposed propriety on conversations which might have been thought otherwise to contain elements of conflict and disorder. Here we encounter the notion of "linguistic etiquette" familiar to students of Java and Javanese as well as other "Indianized" Southeast Asian languages. Freshly instituted forms of address renewed recognized aspects of social distance and allowed conversation to proceed along familiar if redecorated lines.[13]

The next part of the chronicle has, by contrast a distinctly Buddhist tinge:

He forbade all of his ministers to drink alcohol. Likewise, he forbade people to fish by emptying out ponds and creek beds. On royal tours, no shooting of animals was allowed. In quarrels among the people, if local officials couldn't solve the problem, the king could be consulted. He asked monks to give shelter to the poor

---

[12] See Clifford Geertz, *Islam Observed* (New Haven, 1968), p. 38ff.
[13] See Clifford Geertz, *The Religion of Java* (Glencoe, Ill., 1960). pp. 248–60.

and homeless; and he drew on the resources of his treasury to pay for this.[14]

Following this passage, the 1934 recension of the chronicle inserts some narrative history, recording that the general who had led the Siamese army into Cambodia in 1841 departed at this point for Bangkok. Perhaps the placement of this event in the chronicle can be seen as a coded way of saying that Duang had assumed control when, in fact, he still owed much to the Siamese king. But it is dangerous to overload Cambodian chronicles, from this period at least, with structure and authorial intent; the inclusion of this material at this point probably reflects the fact that the general departed for reasons of his own after some of Duang's ceremonial actions had taken place.

It is possible to set out some contrasts in Duang's ceremonial actions before and after he was crowned.

Before his coronation, as we have seen, he had honored his ancestors, built a palace, gathered support, and restored the Buddhism in the region close to the place where his ancestors were buried. Interestingly, the sequence follows one described for Angkorean kings by the French scholar Phillipe Stern in the 1930s.[15] In his coronation he had accepted a name from Siam, and, locally the patronage of complementary Hindu gods, regalia, and the kingdom itself from his brahmins, on behalf of the spirits of the dead. After that he had set patterns of speech and conduct for his entourage. His actions moved, therefore, from honoring, building and gathering, through accepting, to imposing. And the pattern of imposing continued in the next sequence of actions, in which people and places were *renamed*.[16]

The first people to be renamed or ennobled were his mother and his children. After that, his consorts and concubines were

---

[14] Chronicle P-63, pp. 239–40.

[15] See Philippe Stern, "Diversité et rhythmes des fondations royales khmères," *BEFEO*, XLIV (1954), pp. 649–85.

[16] Receiving new names and changing old ones was until recently a recurrent feature of Cambodian peasant life. See Gabrielle Martel, *Lovea: village des environs d'Angkor* (Paris, 1975), p. 211.

renamed; then other palace women grouped in clusters of four; and then the wives of high officials whose new titles were keyed to their husbands' newly awarded ranks. The order "descends," therefore, from females connected to the king by blood, through those connected by marriage down to those enjoying more tangential associations.

The next group to be put in order were the male officials. Fifty-three of these are listed in terms of their position (i.e. on the "right" or "left") and in terms of their specific royal patrons. Four officials with "dignity marks" (*sakdi na*) respectively, of 6,000, 7,000, 8,000, with a 9,000 *sakdi na* chief are attributed to the queen mother, who alone, besides Duang (according to the chronicle) was equipped with a royal seal (*tra*).[17]

An official's title in actual use was made up of several parts. First came a hierarchical title, common to a class of officials – e.g. *preah* (cf. Thai *prah*), "lord"; then followed a personal title bestowed by the king, made up of Sanskrit and Pali honorific (e.g. *vongsa sarapech*); and finally came the distribution to the left or the right, to the patronage of one member of the royal family or another and also, according to other sources, to high-ranking palace officials as well.

To someone outside the system, this arranging of men and women into overlapping, complementary patterns and assigning them, in some cases, to nonexistent patrons (i.e. to posts that remained unfilled) might seem to be a kind of doodling, or protocol, devoid of political meaning. But from the Cambodians' angle of vision in 1848, and especially of those at court, these positionings and entitlements were the essence of politics, because they explained and amplified propriety, putting each person "in his place," and thus setting him "above" or "below" other people. The naming itself, particularly of provincial officials, had precise

---

[17] See A. Foures, "Royaume du Cambodge. Organisation politique," *Excursions and reconnaissances* 13 (1882), pp. 169–211. Interestingly, in recent times the term *sakdi na*, in both Thai and Cambodian radical writing, has been used to mean "feudalism," in a Marxian sense.

political importance too. This was because in nineteenth-century Cambodia, kingship was the only institution, and a king the only man who could legitimately assign and distribute rank and status. Under Queen Mei, the absence of such authority threw the country into chaos. Only the king could grant authority for certain people, like provincial governors, to demand the services of others. He did this in the first instance *by giving people names*. To Cambodian officials, the distribution of their titles in exchange for their loyalty (expressed by periodic gifts) was the essence of kingship. This exchange entitled the officials literally to consume the people under their control. Similarly, from the people's vantage point, the titles limited the service an individual had to perform to the men who were entitled to it.

The overlapping, additional ways by which the officials are referred to in the texts resembles the way in which the chronicles themselves, like so much of Southeast Asian writing, anchor an event simultaneously in different kinds of calendrical time.[18] The names, like the dates, are different ways of saying the same thing ("who" as opposed to "when"), isolating someone in the hierarchy-continuum in the same way that an event is isolated and then embroidered into calendrical time. For those with high rank in nineteenth-century Cambodia, identity was successively acquired in a process of encrustation and embellishment stretching away in time and in terms of complication from one's (usually monosyllabic) personal name – a process resembling in some ways a literary composition.[19]

The chronicles assert that officials' ranks were visible to the people as well, not only in terms of the regalia that went with them (tiered umbrellas, gilded tables, betel paraphernalia and the like) but in terms of the colors they were allowed to wear and the

[18] See Clifford Geertz, Person, Time and Conduct in Bali: An Essay in Cultural Analysis (New Haven: Yale University Southeast Asia Studies Cultural Report Series No. 14), 1966.
[19] On embellishment, see Karnchana Nacaskul, "Types of Elaboration in Some Southeast Asian Languages," in Philip Jenner et al., eds., Austroastic Studies II (Honolulu: University of Hawaii, 1976), pp. 873–90.

weapons they were authorized to carry when travelling with the king. Three colors mentioned in descending order are: grassy-green (*bay-tong*), purple (*svai*) and blue-green (*khieu*).

A French writer in the 1860s, quoting an eyewitness, confirmed that these orders were carried out:

> [Duang] ordered all his courtiers to wear a series of uniforms – violet, red, etc. – whose striking colors, *grouped symmetrically in the throne room*, gave his audiences the appearance of a bouquet of flowers.[20]

The visibility of differential aspects of rank, like the names which they bore as gifts from the king, had the effect of playing officials off against each other while at the same time fastening them within a continuity of rank. In other words, the officials are depicted less as a collection of individuals than as occupying places on a map, as a *yantra*, a *mandala*, or a parade.[21]

Interestingly, the patterned list of fifty-three officials just described is followed in the chronicles by a patterned listing of Cambodia's fifty-six provinces, divided again in terms of "right" and "left," royal and official patrons and by the titles of governors placed in office by the king. The provinces are listed very roughly if one were to travel in a clockwise direction, beginning with provinces to the east of the capital – a familiar itinerary in Indianized Southeast Asia – and gradually encircle the kingdom's center which contained the king, his ancestor's tombs and his regalia.[22]

---

[20] C. Janneau, "Le Cambodge d'autrefois," *Revue indochinoise* (hereafter cited as *RI*) (1914), pp. 272. See also A. Cabaton, "Le Changement de Costume sous Vo-Vuong," *Bulletin des Amis de Vieux Hue II* (1915), pp. 417–24.

[21] See, for example, microfilmed chronicle 1190 which describes the parade offered in Phnom Penh in 1921 in honor of Marshall Joffre.

[22] For a detailed discussion of this form of mapping, see David Chandler, "Maps for the Ancestors: Sacralized Topography and Echoes of Angkor in Two Cambodian Texts," above p. 25.

The naming of the kingdom came to an end with the statement that people of Chinese, Cham, and "Javanese" origin inside it would be looked after by officials named by the king and belonging to these minorities.

The ceremonial emphasis in the chronicles up to this point can be traced, perhaps, to the ceremonial opening of Duang's reign – a time taken up as it were with opening prayers and, as we have seen, with naming the king himself, his relatives, his officials, and his provinces. As Shelly Errington has shown in the case of Malay *hikayat*,[23] Cambodian chroniclers, even when writing or re-copying in the 1930s, never exhibit a recognizable *style*, or a personal point of view. They fail to highlight what they are taking down. At the same time the relatively large space occupied by these opening prayers may indicate that the chroniclers, at least, saw them as forming an important aspect of Duang's reign which their account, compiled after his death, was intended in some manner to convey. Only after everything is named and put into its place, therefore, could Duang himself – heavy, short, good-natured, scarred by small-pox, as we learn from visitors' accounts – enter the text as a man, which is to say in motion in a narrative, as well as in a ceremonial role.[24]

At this point, the texts resume a narrative treatment of events, remarking that in the same year, 1848, certain officials left Udong with tributary gifts for the Siamese court. This implies that the historical fact of Duang's dependence played against the perhaps fictive autonomy that was his to enjoy, in a sense, while he was giving his kingdom and his officials the names with which they came alive.

For the remainder of the reign, the chronicles pay little attention to royal ceremonies or decrees, failing to mention

---

[23] Shelly Errington, "Some Comments on Style in the Meanings of the Past" *Journal of Asian Studies*, IIIVIII (February 1979), pp. 231–44.

[24] See for example L.V. Helms, "Narrative of an Overland Journey from Kampot to the Royal Residence" *Journal of the Indian Archipelago and Eastern Asia* (1851) and Christopher Pym, ed., *Henri Mouhot's Diary* (London: Oxford University Press, 1960).

Duang's promulgation of several new laws in 1853,[25] various European visits we know about from other sources, and his sponsorship of a national ceremony to pray for rain in 1859.[26] Instead, they concentrate on his travels within the kingdom, on his abortive diplomatic initiatives toward the French to stave off the Vietnamese as well as on public works completed during his reign. These included a new royal residence at Udong and a new road linking the capital with Phnom Penh and the coastal village of Kampot, undoubtedly to give the capital access to the sea for water-borne trade with Siam. The chronicles also mention two rebellions. One, easily subdued, was led by a millenarian fanatic; the other, in 1858, was crushed by an army under Duang's command. As part of making peace, interest-ingly, the king gave the rebels' village a new name.[27]

In the summer of 1860, Duang fell seriously ill.[28] Sensing the end, the chronicles tell us that he bought liberty for three hundred and fifty slaves and requested that his body, instead of being cremated, be exposed "to be the food of crows, vultures, and other beasts." There is no evidence in the chronicles that his order was carried out, and indeed there is evidence from other sources that Duang was cremated in a normal way. What are we to make, therefore, of his request? Perhaps Duang was calling himself a failure as a king and sought in this way to

[25] See Adhemard Leclère, *Les Codes cambodgiens.*

[26] See note 21 above, and Adhemard Leclère, "Un pithi polikar plieng" [The Rainmaking], *RI* (1906), pp. 90–99. See also G. Cœdès, ed., *Inscriptions du Cambodge,* Vol. 7 (Paris, 1962), p. 173.

[27] Similarly, in 1925, following an incident in which a French provincial official was killed by villagers in Kompong Chhnang, the village was renamed by the king himself. See Dik Keam, *Phum Tirichan* (Phnom Penh: n.p., 1971), pp. 182–83, and also David Chandler, "The Assassination of Résident Bardez (1925)," below p. 139.

[28] See Thailand, Office of the Prime Minister (comp.) *Thai sathapana kasat khamen* [The Thai Establish the Khmer Kingdom] (Bangkok, 1961), 4952, pp. 60–65. The references are to letters from Duang to Rama IV, complaining about his final illness (a Thai doctor was sent to Udong to help) and letters from Thai officials attached to Duang's court describing uncertain conditions along the frontier with Vietnam. I'm grateful to David Wyatt for providing me with translations of these fascinating letters.

expiate his guilt. It is hard to say exactly why he had reached such a conclusion. The next few years of Cambodian history were turbulent ones, to be sure, and Duang's eldest son, Norodom, was not to be crowned as king (by the French, as things turned out) until 1864. But Duang's own life and reign, as far as we can tell, drew to a peaceful close. Perhaps he saw his life-long dependence on Siam as evidence of his weakness as a Cambodian king; perhaps he sought by this bizarre request to protect his kingdom from the possibility of an invasion from Vietnam, considered a possibility at the time. Perhaps he saw his debilitating illness as a "sign." Perhaps he blamed himself for the rebellions of the previous two years, or for the drought of 1859, or for his anger against his son (for an unspecified offense) mentioned by the chronicle in this same year. There is no way of finding out for sure.

The 1904 recension of the chronicle closes its account of Duang's reign with the king's macabre request. The 1934 version, however, has him asking his sons "not to allow quarrels to arise in the country" – even though, as the chroniclers would have been aware, Duang's three sons themselves began quarrelling almost at once. In both versions, Duang departed his reign as he came into it, almost anonymously; his death is recorded only in terms of the exact time and date when it occurred.

In closing, we must ask what had been resolved in 1848 from the point of view of the Cambodian people? For this reign at last, what did kingship mean? How can we *evaluate* Duang's reign?

There is danger, of course, in using royally-oriented texts, written in the palace, to evaluate a king. Happily for Duang's reign there are some secular ones, written at the time as well as later, which support the view that he was widely seen as a pious and competent monarch. There is a sharp, implicit contrast in these texts between Duang and his predecessors, as well as between conditions in Cambodia before and after his return. The price of Thai political influence at his court was not especially high, in people's eyes, to pay for the reimposition of propriety in Udong, the departure of the Vietnamese, and, more importantly, the reappearance of monastic Buddhism which had languished without a monarch to sponsor it in the years of Vietnamese control. Similarly, before the colonial era, the taxes levied by the king as opposed to the exaction of local officials appear to have been light enough so that the monarch was not connected in most people's minds with exploitation. In many ways, and despite his almost abject subservience to the Siamese, Duang was Cambodia's last independent king, "remembered" with pleasure in colonial times and after independence.

The relationship between Duang and the people who grew rice was a reasonably pleasant one also, in part because communications were so poor and Duang was increasingly weak, *vis-à-vis* the regional elite. In any case, he made fewer demands on the people than the elite did; he was relatively far away, and all this made him innocent and friendly in the eyes of the people.

Kingship under such a king was not a burdensome institution. Twice a year, tax-collectors were sent out from the palace to collect taxes paid largely in rice – and bring them to the king.[29] Twice a year also, provincial authorities were summoned to Udong to swear their loyalty to the king (in the form of an oath and gifts at the *tang tok* or birthday ceremony) and to collect his approbation. As he inhaled his gifts, the king exhaled his protection. In exchange for their reverence he gave officials their names. While collecting surplus food he distributed his merit as largesse. And he did this in the 1850s, after a gruesome period of kinglessness, famine, and Vietnamese control. In 1848, verse chronicles inform us, people came out of the forest where they had been hiding. They started growing rice and went to *wats* again. They were no longer "wild." Collectively, of course, their

---

[29] On the tax system, see *Leclère, Recherches*, pp. 234–49, and Janneau, "*Le Cambodge* d'autrefois," pp. 409–11.

behavior rather than anything Duang did is what brought the kingdom back to life, but before 1848 Cambodians, longing for deliverance, would not have thought themselves capable of such a transformation; for one thing, they had no word for "society" at this time.[30] Propriety – and liberation – had to come from somewhere else, "above" them, as Maurice Godelier has suggested in another context.[31] While people in villages would probably not have known about or recognized the ceremonies I have discussed, they would not have been surprised by them either, because they assumed that royal ceremonies of some sort, probably resembling the ones they periodically performed themselves to punctuate the year, were what enabled them to grow their rice in healthiness and peace. In a time of minimal kingship like the 1840s, this is what kings were for, and in popular literature, interestingly, the institution of kingship is almost never attacked because its effects on people's lives were imaginary and beneficent, insofar as they were thought of as appropriate to a king.[32] A bad king, in other words, was a bad man; a good king was a king.

But the king was almost always far away and it would be a mistake to make the relationship between a king and his people in nineteenth-century Cambodia too formal, deep-dyed, or schematic – however formally, in metaphorical terms, it is expressed in chronicles, royal edicts, or the panoply of coronations, funerals, language, and the like. People in the

---

[30] The word for "society" (*sangkum*) is shared nowadays by Cambodian and Thai, but does not figure in nineteenth-century Thai dictionaries or in Joseph Guesdon, *Dictionnaire cambodgien-français* (Paris, 1930).

[31] Maurice Godelier, "Myth and History," in his *Perspectives in Marxist Anthropology* (Cambridge, 1977), pp. 204–20.

[32] See Solange Thierry, "La personne sacrée du roi dans la litterature cambodgienne traditionelle," *Studies in the History of Religion* (supplement to Numen, IV) (Leiden, 1959), pp. 219–30. See also Masao Yamaguchi, "La royauté comme système de mythe," *Diogène* 77 (January-March 1972), pp. 48–74, and S. Thierry, *Étude d'un corpus de contes cambodgiens traditionnels* (Paris, 1978), especiallly 485–97, and P. van Esterick, "Royal Style and Village Context," in C. Wilson et al., eds., *Royalty and Commoners: Essays in Thai History. Contributions to Asian Studies* 15 (Leiden, 1980), pp. 102–17.

countryside had their own lives to live as well as kings to honor and the king was far away. This point is eloquently put in a popular history collected in the 1940s in a Cambodian-speaking area of southern Vietnam, where an old man speaks of "former times" in this way:

In former times, there was little dry land here, and people would go everywhere in boats, but never farther than the sounds of dogs barking in their village could be heard. There were no canals then, and no paths; there were only forests with tigers, and elephants, and wild buffaloes; no people dared leave their villages.

For this reason, hardly anyone ever went to the royal city [*krung sdach*]. If anyone ever reached it, by poling his canoe, the others would ask him about it. 'What is the king's appearance like? Is he like an ordinary man?" And the traveller, seeing all these frightened, ignorant people asking questions, would say: 'The king has an elegant beautiful appearance, unstained by dust, or sweat, and he has no scars. He's neither short nor tall, neither too young nor too old.' Now dishonest travellers would tell lies about the king, and would exaggerate. . .

People would ask what the realm was like, the older people would say that being there meant that there was always plenty to eat – soup, rice, and meat, and that everyone was happy. Others would ask, 'What does the king do?' Some people would say they had seen the king, when they hadn't. And the children . . . the children would ask questions and more questions.[33]

And so should we, as we watch official history unfold with courtiers, relatives, and insignia forming themselves ornately into visible and linguistic patterns, acting out (which is to say, repeating) their relations to the king and to each other. Duang's

---

[33] MCC 94.004, "Bangsavatar Basak" [Chronicle of Bassac].

humility at the end of his life suggests that he believed that the ceremonies which had begun his reign had somehow failed. In some sense the kingdom had come undone; the king's solution was to debase himself in the hope that the proprieties imposed in 1848 could be restored by abnegation.

In making this ceremonial gesture, it looks as if Duang believed in what he was doing, that he was acting out a part rather than going through the motions. This differentiates him, perhaps, from the chroniclers of 1904 and the 1930s who probably never paused to think if they believed what they were setting down – that is, as verifiable "history." What they were doing, however, did resemble what Duang did as king in the sense that their action was sanctified by repetition: the chronicle had been set down before in a similar order using similar words. There was no room for their opinions, or for hindsight. What had happened to kingship, historiography and opinions of Duang's reign between his death and the 1930s made no difference to these historians for whom the writing itself, like the ceremonies themselves, was what they were called upon to do. In this way, Duang's chronicles lead us immediately into the past, as if they were written in the 1890s or the 1850s and show us how kingship was regarded at court at a time when a king thought he could save all of his people by renaming some of them and then, when he had failed, by offering up his body to predatory birds.

ROYALLY SPONSORED HUMAN SACRIFICES IN NINETEENTH CENTURY CAMBODIA: THE CULT OF *NAK TĀ* ME SA (MAHISĀSURAMARDINI) AT BA PHNOM

Toward the end of February, 1877, four columns of troops, including French, Cambodian and pro-French Vietnamese elements, converged on a low range of hills called Ba Phnom, approximately sixty kilometers southeast of Phnom Penh.[1] Their objective was an earth and timber stockade, measuring roughly a hundred meters by seventy-five, where a rebellious prince named Siwotha had installed himself with an entourage and had begun recruiting an army at the beginning of the month.[2] As the columns approached the enclosure, Siwotha slipped away to the

In slightly different form, this paper was read at the XXIX Congress of Orientalists in Paris in July, 1973. For their comments and assistance, I am grateful to Charles F. Keyes, I.W. Mabbett, Uk Muntha, the late Eveline Porée-Maspéro, Mak Phoeun, Craig Reynolds, Pech Thinh, Michael Vickery and Hiram W. Woodward, Jr.

The paper was first published in the *Journal of the Siam Society* Vol. 2, Part 2, July 1974, reprinted with permission.

1. For descriptions of the region in the late nineteenth century, see Etienne Aymonier, *Le Cambodge*, Paris, 1902, Vol. I, 283 and P. Peyrusset, 'Le chemin de fer de Saigon à Phnom Penh' Cochinchine Francaise, *Excursions et Reconnaissances* (E & R) I (1880) pp. 186–187. The best description of the campaign is France, Archives d'Outremer (FOM) Indochine A-30 (26), Despatch from Duperre dated March 24, 1877. See also Jean Moura, *Le royaume du Cambodge*, Paris, 1883, Vol. I, pp. 182–183.

2. Moura, p. 183. Siwotha, a half-brother of the Cambodian king, Norodom, had family connections in the area. His mother's father had served there as a royal delegate. See Adhemard Leclère, *Histoire du Cambodge*, Paris, 1914, p. 449, and Eng Sut, *Akkasar Mahaboros khmaer* (Documents about Cambodian heroes), Phnom Penh, 1969, p. 1155.

north, on elephant-back, with a few men. His 'army' surrendered soon afterwards without firing a shot,[3] and for the moment the revolt was over. The Cambodian king, Norodom, declared a general amnesty and on February 26, appointed a new royal delegate, or *sdach trān*, to Ba Phnom,[4] at about this time, also, according to the printed version of the Cambodian chronicle, two prisoners-of-war were 'offered up' nearby.[5]

The reference is obscure. It comes in a speech by the Cambodian commander, Prince Sisowath, to his followers at the end of the campaign.

'I have fought with Prince Siwotha's troops [he said] for a day and a night. Many have fled, many have been killed, and many have been wounded. Two ordinary soldiers have been taken prisoner. One is named A Prak and one is named A Som. I have ordered . . . [an official] . . . to put them in a boat and take them to be offered up in the province of Ba Phnom.'[6]

The chronicle says no more about the matter. One purpose of this paper will be to suggest that the men were beheaded on Ba Phnom in April or May, 1877 in the course of a royally-sponsored ceremony known as *loeñ nak tā* ("raising up the ancestors") that honored the new *sdach trān*, the agricultural year, and a local ancestor spirit (*nak tā*) known as Me Sa, the 'white mother'.

---

[3] FOM Indochine A-30 (26) refers to 'quelques serviteurs et cinq éléphants' and says that the rebels were 'saisi de frayeur'. In the course of the campaign, six French soldiers died of fever.

[4] There were five 'royal delegates' in nineteenth century Cambodia. Their largely ritual responsibilities connected them with the areas, or *dei*, of Ba Phnom, Kompong Svai, Pursat, Treang, and Thboung Khmum. See Etienne Aymonier, *Cours de Cambodgien*, Saigon, 1875, pp. 124–125; Adhémard Leclère, '*Sdach meakh*', *Revue Indochinois* VIII (1905), pp. 1378–1384, and also Institut Bouddhique (ed.) *Bram racbidhi dvad samas* (Royal Festivals in the Twelve Months), Phnom Penh, 1969, pp. 86–88.

[5] Eng Sut, p. 1157.

[6] The boat voyage suggests that the prisoners were not native to Ba Phnom.

The evidence comes largely from a Cambodian text, composed in 1944 and printed in 1971 by the Buddhist Institute in Phnom Penh as part of a collection of documents dealing with the cult of *nak tā* throughout Cambodia.[7] The central portion of this text[**] quotes an elderly resident of Ba Phnom, Dok Than, as saying that human sacrifices took place on the northeastern slopes of the mountain when he was a boy, and he describes one of these – perhaps the last, and perhaps the one in 1877 involving A Prak and A Som – which he attended.[8]

The text begins by describing a small 'Chinese-style' cement temple that had recently been built against the northeastern slope of the hill. In 1944, the temple housed broken statues of several Hindu gods, including a damaged one of a female divinity identified by Dok Than as 'Me Sa'. Perhaps a hundred meters to the east he said, in what was by then 'an ordinary rice-field', human sacrifices had once been carried out. The statue is described as follows:

'. . . an upright human female, approximately sixty centimeters tall, with her hair tucked up inside a diadem. The face is well-rounded, even plump; the breasts are globular and firm. The image [once had] four arms. The lower arm on the right . . . bears a rectangular object . . . The upraised left arm bears a wheel, while the lower one catches hold of the tail of [an animal that resembles] a tiger or a lion. The female presses against this animal with her feet . . . [as if to] lift it up . . . and has a boastful expression.'

No photograph of the statue has been published, but this description matches earlier ones by Aymonier, who visited the

---

[7] Institut Bouddhique, *Brajum rioen bren* (Collected Old Stories), (Phnom Penh, 1962), Vol. VIII, pp. 81–88.

[**] A translation of this text appears on pp. 130–134, below.

[8] Dok Than dates the ceremonies from the regime of Siwotha's grandfather, who had died by 1877; Eng Sut, p. 1155.

site in the 1880s,[9] Parmentier (1934) and Mme. Porée-Maspéro, who saw the statue in 1941 and is clearly right when she says that it represents Siva's consort, Uma Mahisāsuramardini, in the act of subduing the demon-buffalo Mahisā. Dok Than's identification of the statue as 'Me Sa' moreover, supports Mme. Porée-Maspéro's additional assertion that the short name is a corruption of the longer one.[10]

Uma (or Durga) Mahisāsuramardini appears to have entered the Indian pantheon along with other consorts of Siva toward the beginning of the Christian era as part of the exchange of religious ideas that took place in India between its Aryan and non-Aryan populations.[11] Images of the goddess were widespread in eastern and southern India during the Pallava period in the second half of the first millenium AD.[12] A temple at Mahaballipuram near Madras is dedicated to her.[13] This was the era, too, of the most intensive 'Indianization' of much of Southeast Asia, and it is not surprising that images of the goddess are plentiful in the art of early Java.[14]

[9] Aymonier, *Le Cambodge*, 1, p. 235.

[10] Eveline Porée-Maspéro, *Les rites agraires des cambodgiens*. Paris and the Hague: 1962, pp. 8–9.

[11] See R.C. Agrawala, 'The goddess *Mahisa*suramardini in early Indian Art', *Artibus Asiae*, XXI (1958), pp. 123–130; Sukimi Bhattacharji, *The Indian Theogny*, Cambridge University Press, 1970, 167 and B.C. Mazumdar, 'Durga: her origin and history', *Journal of the Royal Asiatic Society* 1906, pp. 355–362. Regarding Indianization, I am using the arguments advanced by Paul Mus, 'Cultes indiens et indigènes au Champa', *Bulletin de l'Éole Francase d'Extrême Orient (BEFEO)*, XXXIII (1933), pp. 367–410. For Indian myths surrounding *Mahisa*uramardini, see P.V. Kane, *History of the Dharmasastra Purana 1958–1969*, Vol. V, pp. 157–163; F.E. Pargiter (trans.) *Markandeya Purana*, Calcutta, 1904, pp. 473–488; K. van Kooij, *Worship of the Goddess according to the Kalikapurana: Part I*, Leyden: 1971, p. 94ff. and W.C. Blaquiere, 'The Rudiradaya, or sanguinary chapter, translated from the Calica Puran', *Asiatick Researches*, V (1799), pp. 369–391.

[12] See A. Coomaraswami, *The Art of India and Indonesia*, New York, 1965, 103 and Odette Viennot, 'The goddess *Mahisa*suramardini in Kushana art', *Artibus Asiae*, XIX (1956), pp. 360–373.

[13] See Heinrich Zimmer, *The Art of Indin Asia*, New York, 1954, Plates 210, 234, 284 and 288.

[14] J. Knebel, "De Dorga-vorstelling in de Beeldebouwkunst en Literatur der Hindoes", *Tijdscrift voor Indische Taal-, Land-en Volkenkunde (TBG)*, XLIV (1903), pp. 213–240 lists over thirty Javanese images of the goddess. See also P.

During this same period, Uma Mahisāsuramardini was a popular subject of Cambodian sculpture. Over twenty free-standing statues, and half a dozen bas-reliefs of her have been noted,[15] ranging in time from the seventh to the tenth centuries AD and over space from the Camau peninsula in southernmost Vietnam (then probably populated by Khmer-speakers) to a brick temple about thirty kilometers north of Angkor. By and large, the statues are of an earlier date than the bas-reliefs,[16] and all but two of them come from southern and southeastern Cambodia and Vietnam, rather than from the neighborhood of Angkor, where all but two of the bas-reliefs have been found.

The statue at Ba Phnom seems to be in a transitional style, and resembles another image of the goddess discovered in Kompong Cham province in 1934 by R. Dalet.[17] Both depict the goddess mounted on an unrecognizable animal carved in the round while other statues show her standing on a square base where the head of a buffalo has been carved in bas-relief. The livelier pose is popular in the generally later bas-reliefs, like those from the temples of Bakong and Banteai Srei. Tentatively, the statue of "Me Sa" can be dated from the second half of the eighth century

Pott, *Yoga and Yantra*, The Hague, 1966, 86: "The number of representations of Durga *Mahisa*suramardini in Javanese sculpture is incredibly large. In Java, this is the form *par exellence* of Devi."

[15] For a description of the cult in pre-Angkorean Cambodia, see Kamalswar Bhattacharya, *Les religions brahmaniques dans l'ancien Cambodge*, Paris, 1961, pp. 91–92 and 155–156. Pierre Dupont, *La statuaire pre-angkorienne*, Ascona, 1955, pp. 139–140 argues that the cult developed among the Khmer in the seventh century AD, and Jean Boisselier, *Le Cambodge*, Paris, 1966, p. 293, agrees. For notices or plates of the free-standing representations of the goddess, see Aymonier, *Le Cambodge*, II, p. 359; *BEFEO*, XXXIV (1934), p. 746 and XXXVII (1937) p. 627; Boisselier, loc. cit.; R. Dalet,'Quelques nouvelles sculptures khmères,' *BEFEO*, XXXV, (1935), p. 158; Dupont, *Le statuaire*, Plates 25B, 28B, 31B, 32, 38A, 38D, 39, 43 A-C; Sherman Lee, *Ancient Cambodian Art*, New York, 1970, Plate 15; Louis Malleret, *L'achéologie du delta du Mekong*, Paris, 1959–1963, I, p. 67. 159, 432–433 and figure 96; IV, 39, 56, 84 and plate 12; Henri Parmentier, *L'art khmer primitif*, Paris, 1927, 313 and H. Parmentier, 'Complément à l'art khmer primitif' *BEFEO*, XXXV (1935), p. 35.

[16] For bas-reliefs, see Bhattacharya, *Les religions*, Plates 9–11 and Parmentier, 'Complément', p. 35.

[17] Dalet, 'Quelques nouvelles sculptures', loc. cit.

AD. There is no written evidence that the statue was *in situ* earlier than the 1880s, when it was described by Aymonier. However, the statue may well have been on Ba Phnom for hundreds of years. The mountain is an ancient inhabited site[18] and George Cœdès argued in 1928 that the capital of the early kingdom known to Chinese travellers as 'Funan' was located at its base.[19] Although this view was later modified[20] a city was nearby in the tenth century AD.[21] The earliest inscription found on the mountain mentions a devotion to Siva, and dates from 629 AD.[22] In the tenth century, another inscription refers to Ba Phnom as a 'holy mountain'.[23] The latest inscription there was carved toward the end of 1877; this inscription celebrates Buddhist ceremonies sponsored in a local *wat* by the newly installed *sdach trān*, and mentions the reassertion of Norodom's control over the region.[24]

The phrase *me sa*, with the meaning of guardian spirits in general, occurs in two nineteenth century Cambodian texts preserved by the Buddhist Institute in Phnom Penh. One describes a purification ceremony, sponsored by King Ang Duang, which was held at the royal capital of Udong in July-

[18] For a discussion of the terms *ba* and *me*, see Francois Martini, 'De la signification de BA et ME affixé aux noms des monuments khmers', *BEFEO*, XLIV/1 (1954), pp. 201–210 and L. Malleret, *L'archéologie*, I, p. 156 ff.

[19] G. Cœdès, 'La tradition généologique des premiers rois d'Angkor', *BEFEO*, XXVIII (1928), pp. 124–144.

[20] G. Cœdès, 'Quelques précisions sur le fin du Funan', *BEFEO*, XLIII (1943 1946), p. 4; Malleret, *L'archéologiie*, I, pp. 423–425. On the absence of archeological sites on Ba Phnom, see Dupont, *Le statuaire*, pp. 17–18 and the plates in P. Paris, 'Anciens canaux reconnus sur photographes aeriennes', *BEFEO*, XLI (1941), pp. 365–373.

[21] G. Cœdès (ed.) *Les Inscriptions du Cambodge*, Hanoi and Paris, 1937–1966, VI, 115.

[22] R.C. Majumdar, *Inscriptions of Kambuja*, Calcutta, 1953, inscription 25 (classified by Coedès, *Inscriptions*, VIII, 84 as K. 60).

[23] Aymonier, *Le Cambodge*, I, p. 283.

[24] Aymonier, *Le Cambodge* I, p. 234; numbered by Cœdès as K. 59. In the rubbing of K. 59 in the Bibliothèque Nationale in Paris, the personal name of the *sdach trān* is illegible.

August 1859.[25] The other is an oath used in Cambodian civil trials, known as the *Pranidhan*.[26] Both texts contain long lists of *me sa*, associating each one with a particular site. The text from 1859 begins its list with the *me sa* of Udong. The *me sa* of Ba Phnom is not mentioned in this text, but the *Pranidhan* opens its list with the *me sa* of Ba Phnom, putting the guardian spirit of Udong in second place.[27] Since Udong was abandoned as Cambodia's royal capital in favor of Phnom Penh in 1866, the *Pranidhan* (which makes no mention of Phnom Penh) is probably at least as old as that.[28] What is important for our purposes is that the phrase *me sa* meant something like 'guardian spirit of Udong', if not of the whole kingdom, as Guesdon suggests,[29] less than twenty years before the sacrifices recalled by Dok Than in 1944 allegedly took place. The importance of Ba Phnom as the central locus of the cult can be inferred from the fact that only two small villages (and not hundreds) in Cambodia are called 'Me Sa' and there is no evidence, from the printed *corpus* of Cambodian legends, that a *nak tā* of this name was worshipped anywhere but on Ba Phnom.[30]

---

[25] Institut Bouddhique (ed.) *Bram rac pidhi dvad samas II*, pp. 172–179. For an incomplete and often inaccurate translation, see Adhémard Leclère, *Cambodge: Fêtes civiles et religieuses*, Paris, 1916, pp. 81–95.

[26] See "Maps for the Ancestors", above p. 25.

[27] In the list translated by Leclère (note 26, above), the first *me sa* is associated with 'Phnom Bat'.

[28] The toponyms in the 1859 text, many of which were identified by Leclère in his translation, include archaeological sites like Phnom Krom and Phnom Bakheng near Angkor which, in 1859, had not yet been 'discovered' by the French. as well as places like Nakorn Ratchasima (Korat) which had not been under Khmer control for a century at least. The toponyms in the *Pranidhan* seldom overlap with those in the document from 1859, and seem to have been chosen in many cases to meet the exigencies of rhyme.

[29] Joseph Guesdon, *Dictionaire Cambodgien-Français*, Paris, 1930, p. 1380. See also Institut Bouddhique (comp.) *Vajananukrom Khmaer* (Khmer Dictionary), Phnom Penh, 1967, p. 912, where this meaning of '*me sa*' does not occur.

[30] Aymonier, *Le Cambodge*, I, 235 asserts that 'Me Sa' is a frequent toponym in Cambodia but there are no references to places of this name in the index to *Le Cambodge* prepared in 1916 by G. Cœdès. For two current toponyms containing the phrase, see United States Army Topographical Command, *Cambodia*, Washington, D.C. 1971, pp. 185, 330.

To this cluster of associations between Uma (Durga) Mahisāsuramardini, human sacrifice, royal patronage, purification, Ba Phnom and a species of guardian spirit known in the nineteenth century as *me sa*, a few supplementary points can be made. One is that the goddess Mahisāsuramardini was sometimes associated with ritual suicide, and perhaps with human sacrifices in Pallava India-that is, at the time when Indianization was most extensive in Cambodia and when images of this goddess were most popular there.[31] Another point, reinforcing the links between royal patronage, mountains, and human sacrifice comes from *Wat* Ph'u in southern Laos, where a twelfth century inscription incidentally refers to an image of Mahi-sāisuramardini.[32] The site was the center of a cult honoring Siva in very early times, and a Chinese visitor around 600 AD reported that

'On the summit of the hill there is a temple, guarded at all times by a thousand soldiers. This is dedicated to [Siva] and human beings are sacrificed there. Each year the king goes to the temple and makes a human sacrifice at night.'[33]

Charles Archaimbault records that memories of this custom were embedded in Lao oral traditions in the 1950s.[34] Oral tradition from the eleventh century Sivaite site of Phnom Chisor in southern Cambodia, likewise, associates the temple with living, disembodied heads.[35]

---

[31] J. Ph. Vogel, 'The Head Offering to the Goddess in Pallava Sculpture', *Bulletin of the School of Oriental and African Studies (BSOAS)*, VI (1930–1932), pp. 533–544.

[32] Cœdès, Inscriptions V, 288–293 (Inscription K. 366). See also G. Cœdès, 'Nouvelles données sur les origines du royaume khmèr' *BEFEO*, XLVIII (1957), pp. 209–220.

[33] Ma Tuan Lin (trans. Marquis d'Hervey de St-Denis) *Ethnographie des peuples étranger à la Chine*, Geneva, 1876, p. 483.

[34] Charles Archaimbault,'Le sacrifice du buffle à W'at P'ou' *France-Asie (F-A)* 118–120 (1956), p. 840. See also Pierre Lintingre, 'Légendes du Sud-Laos', *Bulletin des Amis du Royaume Lao* Nos 7–8 (1972) p. 213ff.

[35] Institut Bouddhique, *Brajum rioeñ preñ* VI, p. 56ff.

The beheadings witnessed by Dok Than and mentioned obliquely in the Cambodian chronicle are examples of an ancient and at one time nearly universal tradition studied in many cultures by many authors whereby human beings are beheaded at planting time often in honor of a goddess of the soil.[36] Annual imperial sacrifices in pre-revolutionary China and Vietnam are muted examples of this tradition and so are the yearly buffalo-sacrifices that have been attested in so much of modern Southeast Asia.[37] What is unique about the nineteenth century sacrifices in Cambodia is that they took place in a Theravada Buddhist nation and enjoyed royal patronage. In tribal parts of Cambodia, in the mountains of Vietnam and in southern Laos there is evidence that human sacrifices of this general kind occurred from time to time in

[36] For general surveys of the phenomenon, see J.G. Frazer, The Golden Bough, (12 vols.) London, 1955 and E. Hogg, *Cannibalism and Human Sacrifice*, London 1958. More specialized studies, dealing with eastern and southern Asia include M.N. Das, 'Suppression of human sacrifice among hill-tribes of Orissa' *Man in India (MI)*, XXXVI (1956), pp. 21–48; W. Eberhard, *Cultures of South and East Asia*, Leyden, 1969; E. Erkes, 'Menschenopfer und kannibalismus in alten China' Der Erdball I/1 (1926), pp. 1–6; Christoph von Furer-Haimendorf, 'Beliefs concerning human sacrifice among the Hill Reddis', MI, XXIV (1944), pp. 11–28; E.A. Gait, 'Human sacrifices in ancient Assam' *Journal of the Royal Asiatic Society* of Bengal (*JRASB*), LXVIII (1898), pp. 56–65; R. Heine Geldern, 'Kopfjagd und menschenopfer in Assam und Burma. . .' *Mittelllngen der anthropologische Gesselschaft in Wien*, XLVII (1917), pp. 1–65; R. Mitra, 'Human sacrifices in ancient India', *JRASB*, XLV (1876), pp. 76–118; Severine Silva, 'Traces of human sacrifice in Kanara', Anthropos L (1955), pp. 577–592 and H. G. Quaritch Wales, *Religion and Prehistory in Southeast Asia*, London 1957.

[37] See, for example, Charles Archaimbault, 'Religious Structures in Laos', *Journal of the Siam Society (JSS)* LII/1 (January 1964), pp. 57–74; E. Aymonier, 'Notes sur les coûtûmes at croyances superstitieuses des cambodgiens' *E&R* XVI (1883), p. 178; Georges Condominas, 'Notes sur le *tam bo mae baap aa kuon*', *International Archives of Ethnography*, XLVII, pp. 127–159 and G. Condominas, *L'exotique est quotidien*, Paris, 1965, p. 168ff; P. Guillemenet, 'Le sacrifice du buffle chez les Bahnar de la province de Kontum', *Bulletin des Amis de Vieux Hue (BAVH)*, XXIX-XXX (1942), pp. 118–154; R. Hoffet, 'Les Mois de la chaîne annamitique', *La Geographie*, LIX/1 (1933), pp. 1–43, A. Leclère, *Cambodge: Fêtes civiles*, p. 577ff; Paul Levy, 'Le sacrifice du buffle et le prédiction de temps à Vientiane', *Institut Indochinois pour l'Etude de l'Homme (IIEH)*, VI (1943) pp. 69–91, and Andre Souyris Rolland, 'Contribution à l'étude du culte des Génies ou *Neak ta* chez les cambodgiens du Sud', *Bulletin de La Societé des Etudes Indochinoises (BSEI)*, XXVI (1951), pp. 162–173.

the nineteenth century.[38] But these sacrifices were among people not yet converted to Theravada Buddhism (in Cambodia and Laos) or to any of the religions with official standing in Vietnam.

The explanation for this anomaly does not lie necessarily in nineteenth century Cambodia (or the region around Ba Phnom) being 'more primitive' or 'less Buddhist' than other places on the mainland of Southeast Asia. Instead, as the two texts and other pieces of evidence reveal, there seems to have been a royal association with the mountain, carried out in the person of the institutionally Hindu *sdach trān*, who were the figures linking the king's ceremonial power with the surrounding regions of Cambodia.[39] Indeed, only three sites are associated with ritual beheadings in nineteenth century Cambodia: Ba Phnom, Thboung Khmum, and Kompong Svai;[40] each was the seat of power of one of the five *sdach trān*.

---

[38] Citations include R. Baradat, 'Les Samre ou Pear' *BEFEO* XLI (1941), p. 76; Brengues, 'Notes sur les populations de la région des montagnes des cardamomes' *JSS* II (1905), p. 32; Claeys, 'A propos d'un sacrifice rituel . . .', Far Eastern Association of Tropical Medicine, Tenth Congress, Hanoi, p. 1938, *Transactions*, p. 848; Guillemenet, 'Le sacrifice du buffle . . .', p. 131; P. Guillemenet, *Coutumier de la Tribu Bahnar*, Paris, 1952, p. 58 n.; Hoffet, 'Les Mois . . .' p. 42 and Erik Seidenfaden, 'Appreciation of the *Cahier* of *BEFEO*' *JSS* XXXIII/1 (January, 1931), p. 45.

[39] On the connections between *sdach trān* and the court 'brahmans' or *baku*, see Leclère, *Cambodge: Fêtes civiles*, p. 610. Aymonier, *Cours de cambodgien*, p. 125 states that the *sdach trān* shared with the king (and with no one else) the power to order capital punishment. In *Le Cambodge* I, p. 235, Aymonier writes that the annual sacrifices to Me Sa at Ba Phnom took place in the month of *pisakh* (April-May) which, according to Leclère, Cambodge: *Fêtes civiles*, p. 575, is sacred to Kali – a statement echoed by a nineteenth century Khmer manuscript (Fonds Indochinois 129 E) in the Bibliothèque Nationale in Paris.

[40] Porée-Maspéro, *Rites agraires*, pp. 246, 248. See also Adhémard Leclère, *Recherche sur le Droit Public des Cambodgiens*, Paris 1894, p. 189, which associates *sdach trān* with human sacrifices, as they took office, in the early nineteenth century. Conducting research in Tboung Khmum in 1995, the Australian-based scholar Penny Edwards interviewed a 57 year old Sino-Khmer who had heard from his father-in-law (who in turn had heard from "older residents") that a prisoner was ritually beheaded "in Ang Duang's time" (i.e. before the French) whenever a new official took charge of Tboung Khmum. The blood from the beheading was offered "to the Chinese nak ta". I'm grateful to Ms Edwards for this evidence, fifty years after the evidence assembled by Mme Porée-Maspéro.

Another reason for the persistence of human sacrifices at Ba Phnom may have been the coexistence, at the popular level, of Indian religions there long after the conversion of the people to Theravada Buddhism. Jean Moura, writing of the 1870s, calls the region the 'most Hinduized' in Cambodia;[41] in the 1860s, a German visitor, Bastian, had noticed 'local Brahmans wandering about or begging alms',[42] and prayers invoking Siva and Kali by name were still being recited at village festivals (especially ones associated with the *nak tā*) in this part of Cambodia in the 1950s.[43]

The sacrifices at Ba Phnom came at the end of an annual ceremony known as *loeñ nak tā* ('raising up the ancestors'). This festival still occurs throughout Cambodia at the beginning of the growing season, and its extensive regional variations have been studied by French and Cambodian scholars.[44] Dok Than recalls that

'In former times the festival of *loeñ nak tā* [at Ba Phnom] occupied three, five or even seven days. All the officials who were dependent on [the *sdach trān* of] Ba Phnom assembled and made their shelter on the grounds of *wat* Vihear Thom, about a kilometer northwest of Me Sa.'

Buddhist monks were called in, he continues, to recite unspecified prayers at the *wat* in the early days of the festival, and also to pray for the dead (*dār*)[45] at the cult sites of 'Me Sa' and at those of three other *nak tā*, located respectively to the north,

[41] Moura, Royaume du Cambodge, I, p. 173. See also Aymonier, *Le Cambodge*, I, pp. 174, 231 and 256.

[42] A Bastian, 'Remarks on the Indo-Chinese Alphabets', *JRAS*, III (1868), pp. 69. 43)

[43] Institut Bouddhique, *Brah racpidhi* II, 183–184; Institut Bouddhique, *Brajum rioeñ preñ*, VIII, pp. 39–40, 56, 138 and 182. See also Souyris Rolland, 'Contribution', pp. 171–172.

[44] For a general analysis, see Institut Bouddhique *Brah racpidhi* II, pp. 1–36 and my review of Institut Bouddhique *Brajum rioeñ preñ* VIII, *JSS*, LXI/2 (July 1973), pp. 218–221.

[45] Guesdon, *Dictionnaire*, pp. 46–47, 614.

south and west. There was Buddhist clerical participation, then, in the non-violent aspects of the cult of *nak tā*.[46] Interestingly, too, the sites of the *nak tā* mentioned in the passage stand at the corners of a roughly rectangular line, taking in at least the eastern slopes of the Ba Phnom,[47] just as the four other regions governed by *sdach trān* were located to the southeast, north, northwest and northeast of Ba Phnom-that is, at the corners of a massive rectangle surrounding the hill itself, suggesting that it was thought of at one time as the central district of the five and, *via* the cult of 'Me Sa', the holiest and most important.[48]

The sacrifices at Ba Phnom that seem to have taken place in 1877 were political ones, in a sense, which is perhaps why they are mentioned in the chronicle. Prince Siwotha had been linked through his mother's family with Ba Phnom; he had a following there;[49] and his rebellion against King Norodom might have succeeded had the king not benefited from timely and extensive French assistance.[50] Several millenarian rebels earlier in the century had rallied forces around Ba Phnom.[51] Perhaps possession of the cult-site, or sponsoring a sacrifice there, was synomomous with legitimization. In any case, the rapidity with which Norodom named a new royal delegate to the region, and

---

[46] Cf. Leclère, Cambodge: *Fêtes civiles*, p. 576, where monks retire before a buffalo is sacrificed to a *nak tā* .

[47] See below, and Aymonier, *Le Cambodge* I, p. 161.

[48] By the mid nineteenth century, the *dei* of Treang, greatly reduced in size, was located west of Ba Phnom, rather than to the south near the southern Vietnamese province of Soc Trang; see Malleret, *Archeologie*, I, p. 139; at one time, however, this *dei* probably included most of the Mekong Delta. The map enclosed with G. Aubaret's translation of the *Gia-Dinh Thung Chi* (Histoire et Description de la Basse Cochinchine.) Paris, 1863 lists the royal capital, Udong, as the capital of Treang, located on the map to its southwest.

[49] M. de Villemereuil (ed.) *Explorations et Missions de Doudart de Lagrée*, Paris, 1883, p. 344.

[50] Archival sources indicate that French support in putting down the rebellion was a *quid pro quo* for Norodom's accepting a French-sponsored programme of reforms in February, 1877. See FOM Indochine A-30 (26), letter from Duperre to Minister of Colonies, 12 February 1877.

[51] For some examples, see Leclère, *Histoire*, pp. 252, 287, 334, 376, 415 and 457; Eng Sut, p. 1125, and Moura, *Royaume*, pp. 143, 162 and 183.

the way that this reassertion of political control is celebrated in the 1877 inscription, strongly suggest that the cult site was politically important to him and to his regime.

In closing, the persistence of a royally-sponsored cult honoring a consort of Siva with human victims in the late nineteenth century would indicate that Indian religion was less vestigial outside the confines of the court than has been thought. Likewise, the location of the cult-site of 'Me Sa' at the rough center of a rectangle marked out by the four other locii governed by *sdach trān*, and the occurrence of the words *me sa* in at least two nineteenth century texts to mean 'patroness of the capital city' all indicate that the cult of the goddess Mahisāsuramardini at Ba Phnom may have extended back for several hundred years and perhaps, under a different name, to an era preceding 'Funan' and the introduction in Cambodia of a recognizably Indian religion.

TRANSLATION

NAK TĀ ME SA (BA PHNOM)

About 1,500 meters to the east of the summit of Ba Phnom mountain, and about 500 meters southeast of the district offices of Ba Phnom, there is a small hillock, approximately 10 meters high, located at the edge of the forest. On the top of the hillock, in the space between large rocks lying helter-skelter against each other, there is a small shrine, nicely made of cement, measuring approximately two meters on each side. The building opens onto a field to the east, across which a cement walkway has been laid, culminating in a stairway that zig-zags up the hillock to the shrine. Inside the shrine the rear half is raised up approximately a meter off the ground, flush against the stones of the hill, and these stones have drawings of animals on them. Along this shelf there are 'Brahmanical' images – some large, some handsome, but all stuck together with cement to form heads, arms and feet as the case may be. On the ground in front of them is a jar for incense sticks, and two small statues of elephants, carved out of marble. On either side of the statues are vases offered to the shrine by the Chinese. In front of them there is an open space, paved with brick, wide enough for two people to kneel side by side and make their offerings.

The shrine and its furnishings are in a Chinese style, because the Chinese are the ones who most recently rebuilt the shrine. In former times, the *nak tā* had a (wooden) shelter (asram) but it disappeared, and was replaced.

In the second of the three rows of statues at the back of the temple, exactly in the middle, is the upright statue of a female, approximately sixty centimeters tall, with her hair tucked up inside a diadem. The face is well-rounded, even plump; the breasts are globular and firm. The image [once had] four arms. The lower arm on the right side, thrust forward, bears a rectangular object, slightly indented . . . the upraised left arm bears a wheel. The lower one, reaching down, catches hold of the tail of [an animal that resembles] a tiger or a lion. The female presses down with her feet as if to lift the animal up. The statue stoops a little to the right, giving the impression that it is trying hard to lift up the beast; and has a boastful expression . . .

An old man named Dok Than, seventy years old, from the village of Rong Damrei, near the northern slopes of Ba Phnom, who showed us around the shrine, said, 'This is the statue of *nak tā* Me Sa, the most important of all the *nak tā* in Ba Phnom. Her cult site is the one most honored by the people of the district. This has been true since ancient times, and it is true today.'

There are fourteen other statues of *nak tā* there, of secondary importance. About fifty centimeters in front of the statue of Me Sa, there are two (statues of) *nak tā*, on either side of a space opening in front of her. These are [sometimes] called the *nak tā* of the gates; others call them the *nak tā* of right and left.

Approximately ten meters in front of them (at the foot of the stairs?) is the place where buffaloes are sacrificed to the *nak tā*. A hundred meters further east is the place where human beings were sacrificed in former times. Nowadays, this is an ordinary rice-field.

In former times – I have no idea of the date, for people's memories are imprecise-tradition asserts that a man was beheaded every year as an offering to *nak tā* Me Sa. Sacrifices were still being made (as recently as the 1860s and 1870s) in the era of *kralahom* Pang, *thommadechou* Haen and *thommadechou* Tei,[*] who succeeded each other as governors of Ba Phnom

An elderly man, Dok Than, related that approximately sixty years ago, during the administration of Tei (sic) he had twice been present at sacrifices at Ba Phnom. According to him, men or animals were killed and offered to the *nak tā* on a Saturday in the month of *ches*, (May-June) either during the waxing or the waning phases of the moon. According to . . . the governing official [nearby] at Kompong Trabek, the sacrifices took place on a Wednesday, during the waxing phase of the moon in the month of *ches*; an old man named In Va, aged seventy-three, however, who works as an adviser (*ajar*) at *wat* Prasat in the district of Kompong Trabek, said that the festival occurred on either Tuesday or Saturday in the waxing phase of the moon in the month of *pissakh* (April-May) or *ches*.

In former times, the festival of *loeñ nak tā* used to occupy three, five or even seven days. All the officials dependent on Ba Phnom assembled and made their shelters on the grounds of *wat* Vihear Thom, about a kilometer northwest of Me Sa. To this place monks were invited to recite prayers. In the mornings, they would [perform the Buddhist ritual known as] dar[**] at various places, including the cult-site of *nak tā* Me Sa, the cult site of *nak tā krohom ko* ('Red Neck') to the north of the hillock; the cult site of *nak tā sap than* ('Everyplace') on the slopes of the large mountain, to the west, and *nak tā tuol chhneañ* ('Fishing-Basket Mound') to the south. These prayers were recited every day until Saturday, the day of the festival of *loeñ nak tā*.

---

[*] that is, in the 1860s and 1870s. See Eng Sut, *Akkasar*, pp. 1155–1156.
[**] prayer for the dead

As for the victims, only a man under sentence of death for a serious crime was chosen. He was informed of the choice beforehand, and was allowed to go and watch the activities [at the *wat*] just as if he were an ordinary man.

On the execution day, the victim was put into a neck-stock and led off to the sacrifice-site. The file of people behind him made a clamorous noise as they moved; in front and behind him were soldiers carrying swords, spears and fire-arms, followed by about a thousand people. The file moved off [first] to the cult site of *nak tā prah sruk* (Lord of the district), about five hundred meters east of *wat* Vihear Thom. The people paused there to honor the *nak tā* by setting off firecrackers and rifles. When this was over, the victim was led off to Me Sa, approximately 800 meters to the south. Here the site was properly prepared for the sacrifice, and the people humbly asked the *nak tā* to help them to be healthy and fortunate, to help the governing officials and all their assistants, and also the ordinary people. They joined together, too, in asking that enough rain fall, and at the proper times.

When the prayers were finished, the crowd shouted *yak oieu* three times, and then the executioner, who was entitled *monu* ('intelligence') and whose given name was In, holding a sword, danced hesitantly around the victim and then cut off his head with one stroke. The people looked to see what direction the victim's blood fell. If it fell evenly, or spurted up, then rain would fall evenly over the entire district. But if the blood fell to one side, rain would fall only on that side of the district.

At this point, rifles were fired off, and firecrackers lit, and there were all kinds of loud explosions. When people who had assembled at other cult sites-that is, those of *nak tā krohom ko*, *nak tā sap than* and *nak tā tuol chhnean* heard the explosions from the cult site of Me Sa, they fired off rifles and set off firecrackers, too, in honor of these *nak tā*.

In the meantime, the victim's head was impaled and offered up (*thvar*) to *nak tā* Me Sa, and so were a hundred pieces of his flesh.

Fifty pieces were impaled on a stick and offered to *nak tā sap than* and fifty others were offered to *nak tā tuol chhneañ*.

In the era of *thommadejou* Tei, people gave up killing men, and sacrificed buffaloes instead. Only rutting buffaloes were chosen, which were valued at more than 50 *riels*.

The character of the festival, however, was unchanged, and people made the same predictions about rainfall from a buffalo's falling blood as from a man's. When the buffalo was killed, its flesh, too, was divided up; one hundred pieces went to Me Sa; one leg was offered to *nak tā krohom ko* and another was offered to *nak tā sap than* but *nak tā tuol chhneañ*, it seems, was no longer honored. Perhaps the cult of this *nak tā* had been abandoned for a long time, since his cult site was far away.

There was one innovation in these buffalo-sacrifices. If at the time it was being prepared for execution the buffalo ran off, this was a sign that the *nak tā* would not accept it, and another buffalo was purchased to be sacrificed in its place.

In the years of *thommadechou* Plun, the sacrifice of buffaloes was abandoned, and live ones were offered (symbolically) instead. About twenty years ago (c. 1924) people began to sacrifice a pig instead of a buffalo, but afterwards even this stopped, and now (1944) the sacrifice takes the form of an offering of cooked pork, purchased at the market . . .

—from Institut Bouddhique (comp.) *Brajum Rioeñ Breñ* (Collected old stories) Phnom Penh, 1971–Vol. VIII, 81–88.

PART III

THE COLONIAL ERA

Two essays in this section reflect my ongoing interest in Cambodian historiography. One of them, "The Duties of the Corps of Royal Scribes" is a translation of a primary source photographed for me by Ben Kiernan in the Institut Bouddhique in early 1975. A related paper, "Cambodian Royal Chronicles" was prepared for a conference on Southeast Asian historio-graphy convened at the Australian National University in January 1976.

The other essays reflect my gaining access unexpectedly to some valuable primary sources. "The Assassination of Résident Bardez" uses archival material from Aix en Provence, and also benefits from Ben Kiernan's fieldwork in Cambodia in 1980, when he met and interviewed a man who had been involved in Bardez' assassination over half a century before. The paper dealing with Cambodia's brief independence in 1945 draws on the Son Ngoc Thanh papers, kindly presented to Monash University by General Channa Samudvijana in 1981 and on the wartime journals of the late Evéline Porée-Maspéro, who let me consult them when I visited her and her late husband, Guy Porée, in Mormoiron (Vaucluse) in 1983.

THE ASSASSINATION OF RÉSIDENT BARDEZ (1925): A PREMONITION OF REVOLT IN COLONIAL CAMBODIA

On Saturday April 18, 1925, at about one in the afternoon, Felix Louis Bardez, the French *résident* in the Cambodian province of Kompong Chhnang, about a hundred kilometers north of Phnom Penh, was beaten to death by the villagers of Kraang Laev where he had been attempting to collect delinquent taxes. Bardez was an experienced administrator with over ten years of service in the Protectorate. He was forty-two years old. Two Cambodians who had accompanied him to the village, a militiaman and an interpreter, were killed at the same time.

Over the next few weeks, nineteen suspects were rounded up. All were men, ranging in age from seventeen to forty-five; thirteen of them were in their twenties. All but two were natives of the village. After what the French picturesquely refer to as a *passage à tabac*, or roughing up, the prisoners admitted they were guilty, but they withdrew their confessions, and pleaded not guilty, when the trial opened in Phnom Penh at the end of 1925. By then, one of them had died in prison. There were many witnesses to the killings, well-briefed by the prosecution, and

This paper was originally prepared for a staff colloquium in the Department of History, Monash University. I'm grateful to my colleagues for their comments on that occasion and also for those of Anthony Barnett, Ben Kiernan and J.D. Legge.

This paper was first published in *Journal of the Siam Society*, Summer 1982, reprinted with permission.

the defense lawyers made little effort to prove the innocence of most of the defendants. They pleaded instead that the crime was a political one, a collective response to unbearable economic pressure. The explanation, of course, did not excuse the murders, and the presiding judge sentenced one defendant to death, four to life imprisonment, three to fifteen years and one to five; the other nine were released.

Soon after the killings, and long before the trial, the name of the village was changed, by royal decree, to *Direchan* ("Bestial"); the decree required villagers to conduct expiatory Buddhist ceremonies, on the anniversary of the killings, for the next ten years.[1] It is unclear if the ordinance originated in the royal palace, or responded to French pressure; in any case the ordinance comformed to precedents from precolonial times, and probably reflected King Sisowath's own response to the events, as the manuscript chronicle of his reign suggests.

L'affaire Bardez deserves our attention for several reasons. One is its uniqueness. As far as I know, it was the only occasion when a French official was killed by ethnic Khmer while carrying out his offical duties. Its uniqueness leads us to two questions, or even three. Why did the killings happen when and where they did? If conditions were as bad throughout Cambodia as the defense lawyers and anti-colonial journalists at the time maintained, why had no Frenchmen been assassinated before? To this we may add, why were none killed thereafter?

Another approach to the affair is to place it inside the framework of French economic policies toward Cambodia in 1925. Were these so severe as to explain the killings? A third is to see the incident in an even broader context, namely the enactment of French colonialism in Indo-China. This is the view taken by some anti-colonial journalists, like André Malraux, who covered the trial in Phnom Penh.[2]

---

[1] This text of the decree is printed as an appendix to Dik Keam, *Phum Direchan/*("Bestial Village") Phnom Penh, 1971.

[2] See Walter Langlois, *André Malraux: the Indo-China Adventure*. New York, 1966, pp. 190–196.

Approaching the Bardez affair in terms of its uniqueness, in terms of the *zeitgeist* of 1925, or in terms of French policy are ways of looking back at the killings, while trying to reduce our dependency on what has happened since. Another approach, leading away from them, is to assess them in terms of the iconography of Cambodian nationalism which we can date in recognizable form from the 1940s. In 1945 a nationalist orator placed the killings in a long list of heroic anti-French (and anti-dynastic) uprisings, going back to the 1860s.[3] Five years later, a Communist guerilla leader referred to the assailants in a radio interview as "heroes".[4] They were cast in a similar light in a fictionalized treatment of the affair, written by a republican nationalist in 1971.[5] These judgments are interpretations of the killings. In the context of 1925, however, they are not descriptive because as we shall see the killings were not considered patriotic or progressive by many Cambodians at the time.

The sources we can use include the French-language press of Saigon and Phnom Penh. The Saigon papers that are available in Australia from this period cover a wide range of views but I was unable to consult the most pro-goverment of them, ironically entitled *L'Impartial*.[6] The Phnom Penh paper at the time, *l'Echo*

---

[3] Manuscript chronicle of Norodom Sihanouk (microfilm available from the Centre of East Asian Studies in Tokyo), pp. 546–547.

[4] *United States Foreign Broadcasting Service* (*FBIS*) Daily Report 2 March 1951.

[5] Dik Keam *Direchan*, op. cit.; see aleo *Republique Populaire du Kampuchea*. "Rapport politique du comité central du Parti Populaire Revolutionnaire du Kampuchea (26–31 Mai, 1981)", p. 3, where the First Secretary of the Party, Pen Sovan, dating the incident to 15 November (*sic*) 1925. writes in the official French translation of his Cambodian speech that "la *résident* Bardez ainsi que ses subordonnés adulateurs, responsables de la tentative de repression des paysans, et contre les tentatives de revolte hostiles au systéme d'augmentation des impots, furent exterminés".

[6] These newspapers include *La presse Indochinoise*, *L'Echo annamite*, *L'Echo du Cambodge*, *Indochine Enchaînée*, *La Cloche Felée*, *Le voix libre*. Archival materials on the incident were impossible to locate in Phnom Penh (Ben Kiernan, personal communication), while the archives in Aix-en-Provence apparently contain only funeral orations (Archives d'outremer, Cambodge, F-69, Attenats politiques). Other archival sources are cited below.

du Cambodge, however, is unblinkingly pro-colonial in its coverage of the killings and the trial.

A second contemporary source is the manuscript chronicle prepared by scribes in the royal palace for Cambodia's octagenarian king. Its brief references to the affair are interesting because they imply collective, communal guilt, rather than supporting the prosecution's contention that the killings had been the work of outsiders to the village, eager to rob Bardez.[7] In fact, all but two of the defendants came from Kraang Laev, and Bardez's wallet was found on his body, untouched.

I have also consulted Bardez's own quarterly reports from Kompong Chhnang and from his previous post as *résident* in the southeastern province of Prey Veng. These are available in the French colonial archives in Aix-en-Provence. They tell us something about his working style and help to explain why as an *administrateur de 3e classe* in 1924 he had been sent to replace a person two ranks higher in assuming his position at Kompong Chhnang. Happily, too, the Monash Library has a complete run of an administrative yearbook from Indo-China, which allowed me to trace Bardez' colonial career.[8]

This combination of more or less contemporary sources enabled me in 1979 to assemble two or three pages about the affair in a chapter I was writing about French colonialism in Cambodia. What convinced me to go further was an extraordinary piece of luck. When Ben Kiernan was in Cambodia in September 1980, doing research for his dissertation on the Pol Pot period, he inquired locally and learned that one of Bardez' assailants, an eighty-year old farmer named Sok Bith, was still alive. Bith, alert and active in Kraang Laev, had served a fifteen-year sentence for the crime and he recalled it vividly to Kiernan, in a half-

---

[7] The manuscript chronicle from Sisowath's reign, 1207, uses a collective noun (*bandaras*) to describe the assassins, as wall as the verb *no'm knea* (literally, to "lead together" or "join"), to describe the action.

[8] Indochine Française. *Annuaire générale de l'Indochine*, Hanoi, p. 1877ff. I have consulted the volume for 1907–1925.

hour interview, preserved on tape. The interview is useful in confirming or contradicting other sources which Bith, illiterate and knowing no French, cannot be expected to have seen. Its value also lies in providing a participant's assessment, however blurred or tinted by the passage of time, of the important issues of sequence, coincidence, guilt and motivation.

In reconstructing the story we can begin with *résident* Bardez. He was born in Paris in 1882. When he died, he left a widowed mother, a widow of his own, a brother old enough to have a married son and a brother-in-law employed elsewhere in Indo-China. Another Bardez, possibly a relative, had worked in the Saigon post office at the beginning of the century. We know nothing about Bardez' schooling, appearance or hobbies. Witnesses agreed that he was fearless – perhaps a euphemism covering an aggressive personality – and a Cambodian colleague testified at the trial that for all his kindness to Cambodians he "shouted a bit".

Bardez entered the colonial service in 1907 and reached Indo-China the following year. Until 1912 he served in Cochin-China, the French name for their colony in southern Vietnam. In 1913 he was transferred to an adjoining Cambodian province, Svay Rieng, as a junior administrator, before being shifted to Phnom Penh, in 1915, as the *sécretaire particulier of the chef du cabinet of the résident supérieur*, a politically sensitive position, where he came to the attention of the long-serving *résident supérieur*, Baudouin who later played a role in shepherding his career.

In 1917 Bardez enlisted in the French Army. He saw service on the Western Front where he was slightly wounded and was mentioned in a regimental despatch for bravery, during the final offensive of August 1918. Two years later, he was back in Phnom Penh in charge of the Protectorate's personnel section, presumably another favored post. He became the acting *résident* in Prey Veng in 1923 while still an *administrateur de 3e classe*, two ranks lower than the majority of residents at the time. He seems to have seen his first posting to the field in five years as an opportunity for advancement or perhaps as an opportunity to give vent to his energies and his fondness for command. He saw the job, his reports to the capital suggest, as centering on the steadfast and unrelenting collection of taxes.

We should look for a moment at the taxes he was empowered to collect.

Some of these like those on opium, alcohol and salt were paid directly into the budget for all of Indo-China and were collected by customs officials. Others were levied on fishermen and merchants; still others, in lieu of corvee, and in exchange for identity cards, which functioned as receipts. Finally, taxes were levied on all the crops that were grown in the province. In most of Cambodia the crop most heavily taxed was harvested rice, or *padi*. The *padi* tax affected nearly all Cambodian families. Bardez was collecting it when he was killed.

Before 1920, taxes on *padi* had been collected by delegates sent out from the capital on the king's behalf. These men, known as oknha luang, negotiated with local officials for a cash payment in lieu of a fixed percentage – generally 10% – of the year's rice harvest, taking into account such matters as the amount of land under cultivation, meteorological conditions during the year just past, soil quality, the availability of water, and so on.[9] In fact, it's doubtful if their conversations ever covered these matters in much detail. The system flourished on abuse. Cultivators and local officials tended to under-report land under cultivation and the size of harvests; they also exaggerated catastrophes. The delegates, in turn, were happy to be paid off, so long as an appropriate amount of cash went forward to Phnom Penh. After 1920, the French "modernized" the collection of *padi* taxes, authorizing local officials, rather than visitors from Phnom Penh, to negotiate with landowners. Naturally enough, the removal of one layer of officials did little to reduce malpractice on the part

---

[9] For a run-down of the tax system, see A. Silvestre, *Le Cambodge administratif*, Phnom Penh, 1924. The disparity between taxes paid by Frenchmen and Cambodians was very wide. A Frenchman earning 12,000 piastres per year paid only 30 piastres tax. A rural Cambodian, out of whatever earnings he could accumulate, often paid as much as 9 piastres *per annum* in various forms of tax.

of the remaining parties. In several provinces, in fact, *padi*-tax revenues actually declined under the new arrangements.[10]

Most *résidents*, apparently, were content to let the system run its course, so long as a steady amount of revenue, roughly consistent from year to year, could be applied to meet the exigencies of their local budget, as well as the demands placed on them by Phnom Penh. Bardez was cut from different cloth. One of his first reports from Prey Veng analyzed economic conditions in the province between 1914 and 1923.[11] Head taxes, he observed, had kept pace with gains in population and had risen from 150,000 piasters to 248,000. Taxes on *padi*, on the other hand, had dropped from a quarter of a million piasters in 1914 (admittedly an excellent year) to barely 102,000 piasters in 1923. Commenting on the decline, Bardez wrote:

> It's not hard to find the reasons: complete inactivity on the part of Cambodian authorities, complete lack of supervision over local officials [i.e. those empowered since 1920 to collect the taxes] and a lack of systematic collection procedures.

Eager to correct abuses, and to make an impression on his superiors Bardez was able to collect an additional 100,000 piasters (including 25,000 new piasters of revenues from *padi* taxes) by the middle of 1924.[12]

Results like these probably shamed his French colleagues, fatigued his Cambodian associates and pleased the powers that were. Bardez' effect on local inhabitants is ambiguous. He acted promptly, for instance, when 100 peasants petitioned him to remove a corrupt village headman.[13] A month or so later, on the

---

[10] Silvestre, *Le Cambodge*, op.cit., pp. 524–525. See also A. Pompei, "La notion de proprieté foncière au Cambodge" *Revue Indochinoise Juridique et Economique* 19/20 (1943), p. 438n.

[11] AOM 3 E 8 (3) Report on period 1914–1923, Prey Veng

[12] AOM 3 E 8b (3) Second trimester report, 1924, Prey Veng.

[13] AOM 3 E 8 (3) Third trimester report, 1924, Prey Veng.

other hand, he admitted in an official report that he enjoyed being feted as a *luc thom* (i.e. "big master") in his *tournées en province*.[14] According to Sok Bith, his spoken Cambodian was rudimentary, after more than a decade in the country.

Turning from Bardez' achievements in Prey Veng we should look for a moment at the destination of the funds he was so eager to collect. Throughout the immediate post-war period, Baudouin's government had been attempting to increase tax revenues, primarily to underwrite an ever more extensive program of public works. To a large extent these took the form of roads. Between 1922 and 1924, 400 kilometers of hard-surfaced roads were built in Cambodia.[15] In 1912 there had been only 430 kilometers of such roads in the entire Protectorate. Labor for the roads was drawn from Cambodia's convict population, from people unable to meet their tax obligations in cash and from impoverished rice-farmers in the off-season. An even more impressive and expensive project was the newly completed resort complex at Bokor atop a windswept plateau overlooking the Gulf of Siam.[16] Anti-Baudouin newspapers in Saigon and Hanoi referred to the complex as "Baudouin's Folly". The road to the hill-station wound through a malarial forest. In the nine months it took to build it, nearly 900 convicts and coolie labourers died from the disease. A speaker at the Bardez trial went so far as to suggest that the hotels at the resort should fly the skull and crossbones rather than the *tricolore*.[17]

Partly to pay for Bokor and perhaps also to meet such additional expenses as a new yacht for the Cambodian king launched in May 1925 and a new *palais de justice* inaugurated later in the year, French administrators and their rubber-stamp Cambodian advisors drawn from the royal family and the Phnom

---

[14] AOM 3 E 8 (3) Second trimester report, 1924, Pray Veng.

[15] See *La Presse Indochinoise*, 22 April 1925 and *La voix libre*, 7 January 1926.

[16] *Echo du Cambodge*, 18 April 1925, and *La voix libre*, 9 January 1926, quoting from *Le libre Cochinchine*, 9 January 1926. Marguerite Duras, *Un barrage contre la Pacifique* (Paris, 1950) is a thinly fictionalised account of life among less privileged Frenchmen near Bokor in the 1920s.

[17] *La clôche felée*, 24 January 1926.

Penh commercial elite proclaimed a new tax at the end of 1924, that increased charges levied on uncultivated land.[18] They did so to close the loop-hole of under-reported land-holdings and harvests. The regulation tempted people to pay the new tax by promising that receipts would be taken as proof of ownership when and if a full-scale cadastral survey was carried out. As the regulation was coming into effect in November 1924 Bardez was transferred to a more "difficult" province, Kompong Chhnang, on the southern shore of the Tonle Sap. The province had a reputation for banditry. One bandit in particular, a Vietnamese named Tinh, was at large there in 1923–1924 and Bardez was active in driving him and his followers out of the province in early 1925. Because so many of its people were engaged in fishing Kompong Chhnang was a rice-deficit area. Most of its primarily agricultural districts, however, were prosperous enough.

Kraang Laev was one of these. Its name appears three times in French reports from the early 1920s. In 1922 it had been visited by a charlatan who claimed royal descent and had been arrested for selling charms and potions.[19] A year later a Cambodian accused of murder was found hiding in the village *wat*.[20] In early 1925, a Cambodian official, sent to collect delinquent taxes in a nearby commune was set upon and beaten by what he called "fifty or sixty" local people.[21] Interestingly, Bardez refused to press charges against the assailants, blaming the official for tactless and bullying behavior. Allegedly the official had harangued the people, saying the taxes must be paid and suggested that village women could prostitute themselves, if necessary, to raise the money. In one account at the Bardez trial this suggestion had drawn an astute reply from one of the women:

---

[18] *Echo annamite*, 12 December 1925.
[19] AOM 3 E 11 (4) Second trimester report, 1922, Kampong Chhnang.
[20] AOM 3 E (4) First trimester report, 1923, Kompong Chhnang.
[21] AOM 3 E (4) First trimester report, 1925, Kompong Chhnang.

No one would want us. We are ugly and dirty. But your wife who's beautiful and wears jewelry and perfumes herself, could easily do what you suggest.[22]

With hindsight, another premonition of the killings occurred in January, 1925 when a delegation of about a hundred peasants from the region visited Bardez in Kompong Chhnang to complain that taxes were too heavy and that they had no cash.[23] On this occasion, Bardez promised to give them extra time to pay. The petitioners went home.

It is unclear why Bardez decided to tour the province himself in April, 1925. Baudouin, disturbed by the two incidents just mentioned, may have ordered his protege to take a firmer stand. For at least two reasons it seems unlikely that the fatal *tournée* was Bardez' own idea. The timing was unfortunate, for one thing, because it coincided with the week-long celebrations taking place throughout the kingdom of Buddhist New Year. Moreover, Bardez does not seem to have been certain of success. Testifying at the trial, a colleague said that Bardez had told him, shortly before setting out:

The situation is serious. I'm harrassed with the Tinh affair and there's no money. . . What's to be done? Can the Governor General help us?[24]

Whatever had impelled him to visit the countryside when he got there he behaved with his customary doggedess and flair. In each *khum*, or group of villages, he followed a set routine. People from outlying villages had been summoned several days before by messages from the *mekhum*, or communal headman. Many would have been planning to visit each *khum* in any case, for the new year celebrations; in two visits preceding the fatal one, Bardez

---

[22] *La voix libre*, 16 December 1925.
[23] *Echo annamite*, 14 December 1925.
[24] *Echo du Cambodge*, 23 December 1925.

had consulted with local elite figures – particularly the *mekhum* and the monks of the local *wat* – before asking delinquent taxes be paid in the open-sided communal meeting hall, or *sala*, usually located along-side the *wat*. These visits appear to have gone smoothly enough, but after visiting these other villages, Bardez sent a note to his assistant in Kompong Chhnang, asking that a detachment of militia be readied to accompany him on the rest of the tour, in view of the difficulties he expected to encounter. He made notes of the tour, to be included in a subsequent report, that probably stressed his pessimism and the stubborn response of local people, for the notebook was impounded by the prosecution, and denied to the defense on the grounds that it was "confidential" and "political".[25] As far as I can tell, no one has consulted it since the trial and it may well have disappeared.

Bardez arrived at Kraang Laev at around 8:00 a.m. on April 18.[26] He was accompanied by an interpreter, Suon, a militiaman, Lach and a Vietnamese cook. The village headman, Phal, had already assembled between fifty and sixty village elders in the *sala*; a crowd estimated by several witnesses as 500, summoned for the occasion were seated outside in the sun.

When he arrived, Bardez told the headman that the village had paid few of its taxes for several years. When Phal and the abbot of the *wat* pleaded that this was because no one had any money, Bardez pointed ironically at the newly redecorated *wat*, which had been paid for by public subscription. He then made the *mekhum* read out the royal ordinance of November 1924 to the assembled crowd. The *mekhum* was followed by the abbot, who told the crowd that the taxes should he paid because people should always honor their parents and the French were now playing this role.

---

[25] *Echo du Cambodge*, 18 December 1925.

[26] The following account is drawn from stenographic accounts of the trial; these have been checked against the remarkably similar memories of Sok Bith.

No money was forthcoming. Bardez ordered that three men in the *sala*, picked at random be tied up as hostages until all the outstanding taxes had been paid. At around 10:00 a.m., he sent a message to Kampong Chhnang, some 14 kilometers away requesting a detachment of militia. These reinforcements left Kompong Chhnang around noon but were too late to avert the killings.

Toward 11:00 a.m., the situation in the *sala* was calm enough for Bardez to eat a meal prepared for him by his cook. The hostages were not released. Soon after Bardez returned, however, the wife of one of them approached the *mekhum* with the money for her husband's taxes. She had borrowed the sum from the *mekhum*'s wife and begged that her husband be released so he could go home for lunch. According to the defense, Bardez told her rudely to *fouter le camp*; the prosecution alleged that he asked her politely to wait; Bith insists that Bardez told her that none of the hostages would be released until all the taxes owing had been paid. In any case, no one was released. At this point, Bith says:

> I told her . . . the table was there; and the French . . . we were over here, on this side . . . I told her, "Take your husband away", and she touched her husband on the arm. When I said this the soldier raised his rifle, and pointed it at me, and cocked it, *pruk pruk*, so we pushed the rifle away and punched him. Soon everyone was punching *plup plup* and fighting; the three had fallen to the ground [i.e. outside the *sala*], and people came up and beat them some more, until the three were dead on the ground.

None of the three died instantly. The militiaman, disarmed, injured and attempting to escape, was beaten to death a hundred meters from the *sala*, while Bardez, severely hurt, was being nursed in the *wat* by the abbot and the *mekhum*. The people who had killed the militiaman returned and beat Bardez to death.

Twenty-four wounds were later found on his body, although no formal autopsy was performed. The interpreter was killed last. The weapons used against the three included the miltiaman's rifle-butt, staves from the fence around the *sala*, and (in two cases) knives.

When the three men were dead the villagers streamed out of Kraang Laev apparently leaving only the monks behind. According to Sok Bith they were headed for Kompong Chhnang on foot and using "over a hundred" ox carts, with the vague idea of attacking the *résidence*. They were intercepted *en route* by the militiamen summoned earlier by Bardez. When shots were fired into the air they scattered and returned to Kraang Laev. Bith took advantage of the confusion to flee to Pursat where he was arrested about a month later. The militiamen proceeded to Kraang Laev where the three bodies were recovered and taken to Kampong Chhnang.

The defense lawyers at the trial, and Bith fifty-five years later, stressed that the murders were communal actions. Bith says that "the whole village" took part; he blames the affair specifically on the *contretemps* involving the hostage's wife, and more generally on the hardship imposed by the *padi* taxes.

The French and their proteges in Phnom Penh moved swiftly to defuse and take control of the situation. The royal ordinance condemning the village was promulgated five days later, on the 23rd. By then the French official in charge of political affairs in Cambodia, Chassang, had visited the region, accompanied by the king's eldest son, Prince Monivong, who was himself to be crowned king two years later. Within two weeks over two hundred villagers were rounded up for questioning. In an obscure incident, in June, the prime suspect, Neou, was shot and then beheaded by local offcials while resisting arrest.[27] For the prosecution, he soon became the mastermind of the incident

---

[27] *Echo annamite*, 12 December 1925. The event had occurred in June 1925. Neou had served a jail sentence for robbery and was a fugitive from another, imposed for walking away from corvee labor engaged in building a landing strip near Kompong Chhnang .

and the lynchpin of their case that lawless outsiders eager to rob Bardez had committed the crime, rather than local people disrurbed by his conduct and by excessive taxes.

It is not clear how Neou and his accomplice, Chuon, both wanted by the police, had been able to obtain asylum in Kraang Laev. Similarly, their presence at the incident (when they could have stayed concealed) suggests bravado on their part, although this is not the same as premeditation. Charged with using a lethal weapon in the attack (a charge substantiated by Sok Bith), Chuon was in due course condemned to death.

Eighteen suspects came to trial in Phnom Penh in December 1925. The proceedings attracted wide attention. A pro-government *claque* attended every day, applauding prosecution statements and ridiculing the defense. The trial was also attended by journalists from Saigon, including the author André Malraux, who was awaiting trial himself, and others who were hostile to Baudouin and interested in colonial reform.

Just as these people opposed to French colonial injustice sought to expand the focus of the Bardez trial, the French administrators, battling against intensifying nationalist pressures particularly in the components of Vietnam, took a narrow view of the resident's assassination. In addition, they were nervous about the intentions of the recently appointed socialist governor-general of Indo-China Alexandre Varenne;[28] the trial of the Vietnamese patriot, Phan Boi Chau, was taking place at the same time as the trial in Phnom Penh;[29] and another Vietnamese nationalist, Phan Chu Trinh recently returned from France, was agitating for extensive colonial reforms.[30] The French saw no point in allowing the

[28] See William Frederick, "Alexandre Varenne and Politics in Indochina 1925–1926", in Walter Vella (ed.) *Aspects of Vietnamese History*, Honolulu 1973, pp. 95–159. See also Langlois, *Andre Malraux*. op. cit., pp. 163–180.

[29] Sea David Marr, Vietnamese Anti-Colonialsm, Berkeley, 1971, pp. 265–268.

[30] Marr, *Vietnamese Anti-Colonialsm*, op. cit., pp. 269–271. The year 1925 was also the high water mark of the Constitutionalist Party, which urged co-operation with the French authorities. See R.B. Smith, "Bui Quang Chieu and the Constitutionalist Party in Indo-China" *Modern Asian Studies*, III/2 (1969), pp. 131–150.

Bardez trial to become a political forum. The defense found conditions ideal to make it one.

Although the guilt of most of the defendants was never seriously in doubt (and was admitted in 1980 by Sok Bith) the tactics of the prosecution at the trial were heavy-handed and often farcical as they tried to head off any discussion of French taxation policies, any criticism of Bardez, or any evidence which contradicted their argument that the culprits were outsiders who had wanted to rob the *résident*. There was even a clumsy attempt by someone to poison the principal lawyer for the defense, Gallet, and a stenographer hired by the defense was forced to return to her former employer while the trial was still going on, probably to prevent further transcripts of testimony appearing in the anti-government Saigon press.

André Malraux, for one, was infuriated by the procedures followed by the court. When the trial was over, he parodied it in the pages of his Saigon journal, *Indochine Enchaînée*:

1. Every defendent will have his head cut off.
2. Then he will be defended by a a lawyer.
3. The lawyer will have his head cut off.
4. And so on.[31]

Another observer was the late Nhek Tioulong, then a student at the Collège Sisowath, and in later life a provincial governor, commander of the Cambodian army and a trusted confidante of Sihanouk's throughout the Sihanouk era. In 1981, Tioulong asserted that the defense lawyer, Gallet, was especially eloquent, "flapping his sleeves dramatically" when he made his points.[32]

Sok Bith now feels that his trial was fair. One revelation in his testimony is that prosperous businessmen in Phnom Penh and Saigon (he uses the word *taokay*, suggesting that they were

---

[31] Quoted in Langlois, op. cit., p. 197.
[32] Author's interview with Nhek Tioulong, Bangkok, 29 August 1981.

Chinese) anonymously aided the defense, providing "baskets of money" for the lawyers and presents of food and cigarettes to the prisoners. A crippled Cambodian lawyer named Nuon was also helpful to the defendants. Bith recalls Nuon's remark that it wasn't the village which was *direchhan* ("bestial"), but the king himself, a *mot* that still made him chuckle more than half a century after it had been made. Nhek Tioulong contended that Nuon's partisan behavior led to his being demoted by the French soon after the trial was over.

When Bith returned home after serving fifteen years for what he calls "a single punch in the face" (this was the charge made against him) he resumed work in Kraang Laev as a rice-farmer and a tapper of sugar-palms. Anti-French guerillas in the late 1940s, knowing of his implication in the affair, sought him out and tried unsuccessfully to recruit him. Apparently he has never been happy with being known as a revolutionary, preferring to view his conduct in the context of the day Bardez was killed. During the Pol Pot years, he told Kiernan, he was "an old man . . . concerned to stay alive, that's all".

In a 1971 novel about the killings, *Phum Direchhan*, the republican writer Dik Keam argued that Neou and Chuon planned to kill Bardez with the knowledge that they would be executed for the crime.[33] No evidence from 1925 or in Bith's recollections can be cited in support of this contention although Bith agreed that both of them used knives in the attack. And yet, rebellious peasants are a fixture in most post-colonial ideologies especially those which contain an antimonarchic component. In a sense, premeditation and heros are essential for such an iconographic incident to be valuable for nationalists later on, when events and memories are often transformed by the need for precedents and heroes.

---

[33] Dik Keam, *Phum Direchan*, op.cit., pp. 68–69. Although the book takes the form of a novel, Dik Keam claims to have interviewed survivors of the incident. Dik Keam was murdered as a "class enemy" in northeastern Cambodia in 1977. During my research in Cambodia in 1970–1971, he was unfailingly kind to me and to other scholars interested in Cambodia's past.

Little can be said in defence of the French taxation system in Cambodia. Testimony at the trial and information in contemporary sources reveal that it placed heavy burdens on ordinary people. Moreover, funds collected in Cambodia were often funnelled elsewhere in the Federation. Indeed, writing in 1935, a French *résident* suggested that anyone interested in stirring up trouble among Cambodians might do well to emphasize the inequities of the taxation system, *vis-à-vis* the other components of Indo-China.[34] Certainly they were outrageously heavy in comparison to what French citizens were asked to pay, and they were heavy in terms of any benefits from them returning to the peasants. At the same time, the persistence of abuse and of short-falls between what was asked for and what was paid meant that some people paid less taxes than they were supposed to pay, or none at all. As Sok Bith remarked, people were poor and uncomfortable about paying so many taxes but they had enough to eat.

Why was the affair unique? One answer is that Bardez, stepping out of character and behaving like a Cambodian official, was treated like one by the villagers of Kraang Laev. Very few *résident*s made the same mistake. The lesson of the incident, in fact, was that villagers were better off left, if not to their own devices, then to the types of indigenous "control" to which they were accustomed. Bardez insisted recklessly on removing some of the flexibility from the tax-collection system by collecting taxes himself. His presence in the village offended the large and restless crowd. Perhaps he was banking on their proverbial peaceability. He made no allowance for the likelihood that many of the men in the crowd would have been drinking sugar palm-wine in the sun as the day wore on. He made things worse for himself by taking hostages at random without sufficient force to back up his decision.

Bardez' error, in other words, was his decision, which may have been wrung from him by officials in Phnom Penh, to go into

---

[34] AOM 3 E 15 (8): Annual report from Kampot, 1935.

the village himself. Something about the village or the crowd made this experienced officer sufficiently nervous to summon reinforcements from Kompong Chhnang; at the same time, his conduct in Kraang Laev appears to have been edgier and more exasperated than it had been in the villages he had visited earlier.

To make an assessment of the affair we can easily dismiss it as the *Echo du Cambodge* did in an early report as a "crapulous crime".[35] In the prosecution's words, we can see it as not "a Cambodian crime, but only a crime of a few individuals who in no way resemble the Cambodian". This assessment begs the question of what "proper" Cambodian behavior is, and archival records reveal a different picture about rural violence in the 1920s and 1930s than is purveyed by French mythology. Another view taken by the defense was that the village was collectively at fault and that the "crowd had been its own leader", provoked by an unjust system and Bardez' extreme behavior. *Maitre* Gallet pointed out that several hundred people had been arrested for the crime at first, and noted that the palace itself had already collectivized the guilt by stigmatizing the village as a whole before anyone had come to trial.

This was also Sok Bith's view. Talking to Kiernan, he linked the village's behavior to the heaviness of taxes as well as to Bardez' behavior on the 18th.

This interpretation suggests that in the 1920s Cambodians were politically astute enough to organize themselves and take action in what they perceived as a just cause. This notion fitted poorly with patronizing French conceptions prevalent in the 1920s about the "Cambodian race" and France's obligation towards it. Perhaps part of this misperception had to do with the nature of France's colonial mission. If the Cambodians could look after themselves, in other words, were French days in Cambodia

---

[35] *Echo du Cambodge*, 9 December 1925.

numbered? And if Cambodians could make up their minds, acting together, how could they be governed by other people?

The answer, for a time, was that they could be governed by dissolving their solidarity, by *passages à tabac*, and by forcing them to testify against themselves. They could be governed by being detached from the Cambodian state and being renamed "Bestial". And they could be governed in the old way by their own officials because no other way had yet occurred to anyone. It's clear that the royal family saw the incident in part in terms of *lèse majeste*. Government in the kingdom had always been "royal business" (*rajakar*); in the provinces, the word for "govern" also meant "consume". These arrangements had been in effect in Cambodia for centuries; the French had found them easy to use once they had bought off the Cambodian elite. In traditional Cambodia, when a village or a group of people refused to be "consumed" they were defying the structure of the state and had to be removed from it. This is the rationale behind the "bestial" decree.

To Cambodian thinkers of the 1940s, or to historians of Indo-China later on in search of trends, watersheds and turning-points, the Bardez incident offers a rare example of rural Cambodians uniting in an anti-colonial cause. For this reason, Bardez' assassins have been made heroic. Heroes are needed for a self-respecting "national" history. In examining this particular case, however, it is legitimate to ask how much further beyond Kraang Laev its significance can really be extended. Certainly the incident reveals a reservoir of indigenous violence which normally worked itself out on other villagers, or on Cambodian officials; similarly, it shows that the French had no clear reason to count on much good will when they stepped down from the heights of the *résidence* and began to push rural Cambodians around. But whether it can be

---

[36]A French official writing in 1916 observed that "French residents lack sufficient influence in their provinces. The population appears to ignore them completely": quoted in L. Vignon, *Un programme de politique coloniale. Les questions indigènes.* Paris, 1919, p. 289 n.

treated as a prologue to nationalism is less clear. The villagers killed Bardez and his assistants because the three had no business being there at that time and because Bardez was unfair not to release the hostage who had paid his taxes. The villagers' gesture, then, was neither an heroic premonition of nationalist struggle nor the squalid plot alleged by the prosecution. Instead, it was a gesture of some exasperated men whom the crowd, palm wine, and Bardez' outrageous conduct had encouraged to behave as if they were in charge of Kraang Laev and not the French. Evidence at the trial suggests that when their fervor waned and the crowd moving on Kompong Chhnang had been dispersed they returned, ashamed, to the village, and before long were turning one another in to the police. The villagers were not habitual killers. At the same time, if Sok Bith's recollections are any indication, as time went on they took a kind of collective responsibility for their momentary liberating gesture and harbored few regrets.[37]

[37]According to Dik Keam, op. cit., p. 119, Bardez' body was exhumed in 1970 and removed to France.

THE DUTIES OF THE CORPS OF ROYAL SCRIBES: AN UNDATED KHMER MANUSCRIPT FROM THE COLONIAL ERA

Manuscript 74.002 in the archives of the Buddhist Institute in Phnom Penh consists of six sheets of foolscap paper in Khmer, signed by a Cambodian official named Yim who was in charge at the time of the corps of royal scribes.[1] The manuscript is undated, but internal evidence suggests that it was composed between 1928 and 1932, i.e. in the reign of King Sisowath Monivong (r. 1927–1941).[2]

The text lists eighteen duties of the corps of scribes. Some of these are linked to the colonial era, but most appear to have been

I am grateful to Mme Pech Sal of the Buddhist Institute for allowing me to consult this manuscript in 1971, to David Wyatt for suggesting that I present it in this form, and to Ben Kiernan for photographing it, with Mme Pech Sal's permission, in early 1975.

This paper was first published on *Journal of the Siam Society*, July 1975, Vol. 63, Part 2, reprinted with permission.

[1] In the early nineteenth century, the official's title (*ukya prannathipodei*) was borne by the ukya in charge of the 'right hand' contingent of royal clerks. See Prince Damrong Ratchanuphab, *Tamra tamniap, bandasakdi krung kamputcha* (Royal rankings at the Cambodian court), (Bangkok, 1921), p. 5, and A. de Villemereuil, Explorations et Missions de Doudart de Lagrée (Paris, 1884), p. 69. In the 1870s, the royal clerks (*krom alak*) included thirty men, of whom eleven were "Siamese": Foures, "Royaume du Cambodge. Organisation Politique" Cochinchine Francaise, *Excursions & Reconnaissances* No. 8 (1880), p. 191.

[2] The eleventh paragraph of the text mentions the railroad between Phnom Penh and Battambang as incomplete. The line was begun in 1928 and finished in 1932. See René Morizon, *Monographie du Cambodge* (Hanoi, 1931), p. 233, and the plate at 254 for the unfinished bridge also mentioned in paragraph eleven of the text.

passed down from earlier times. Their interest to an historian lies in the boundaries they place on the scribes' activities, in the world-picture and historiographical notions that these boundaries imply and in the comparisons that might be made with similar documents, when they come to light, composed at other Southeast Asian courts.

The rules themselves have several points of interest. One is that the scribes' duties apparently did not include recording and preserving a monarch's spoken words or writings. This fact may explain the absence of this kind of material in Cambodian official histories, or *bangsavatar* – an absence that contrasts sharply with the abundance of such documents in the Vietnamese imperial annals.[3] Another point is that most of the scribes' duties are linked to the king's life-cycle and his ceremonial activities and little is said about the way Cambodia was actually ruled. To the scribes, it was enough to note the arrival of a new French *résident supérieur* (rule nine) or the status of certain French-sponsored public works (rule eleven).[4] The time and place in which events occur is of more significant, it seems, than their significance. What emerges from the rules and the views which they suggest is the isolation of the palace and the king from everyday life in the kingdom. This isolation had been encouraged by the French at least since the beginning of the century, but it was also accepted willingly enough, it would seem, by the king and his entourage.[5]

---

[3] On Cambodian chronicles. see G. Cœdès, '*Etudes* cambodgiennes XVI. Essai du classification des documents historiques cambodgiens conservés à la bibliothèque de l'EFEO', *Bulletin de l'Ecole Française d'Extrême Orient* XVIII/9 (September 1918), pp. 15–28. The nineteenth century Vietnamese annals are discussed in A.B. Woodside. *Vietnam and the Chinese Model* (Cambridge, Mass.: 1971), pp. 323–325.

[4] Two of the rules, however-the tenth and the sixteenth-are of more general interest.

[5] Monivong's grandson, Norodom Sihanouk, recalled in 1971 that the king 'n'avait rien à faire en ce qui concernait le travail de bureau. Il vivait entouré de ses favorites, de sa nombreuse progeniture. Il parassait heureux. . .' Norodom Sihanouk, *Indochine vu de Pékin* (Paris, 1972), p. 27.

It should be noted, incidentally, that the archival materials (Khmer *jotmay haet*, cf. Thai *chotmai het*) referred to in the text no longer existed, in 1970–1971, either in the former royal palace or in the national library in Phnom Penh, although the palace, like the Buddhist Institute, then housed a large collection of manuscript *bangsavatar*. Finally, students seeking details of the royal ceremonies that until 1970 punctuated the Cambodian year in Phnom Penh at least and took up so much of the scribes' time (rules twelve through sixteen) should refer to the work of Mme. Porée-Maspéro and other French and Cambodian scholars.[6]

TRANSLATION

1. The scribes must look after the sacred chronicles of Cambodia's kings, who reigned at various times. They must make sure the dates of the reigns are accurate, and they must verify the narrative portions of the text.

2. The scribes must write down the king's royal titles as these are inscribed on the strip of gold foil [that forms part of his coronation regalia]. They must also record the titles of his parents, of the heir apparent, and those of the queen and the king's other consorts. All these titles must be properly recorded.

3. From archival documents, the exact hour, day, month and year when the king took office should be recorded, as well as his birthday, his given names, and the location of his palace. Details

---

[6] See Evéline Porée-Maspéro et al. *Ceremonies des douze mois* (Phnom Penh. n.d. but c. 1954), translated into Khmer, and revised, as Pech Sal and Nhun Soeun, *Pithi brajam dop pi khae* (Festivals of the twelve months) (Phnom Penh, 1966). Both books draw on Chap Pin (ed.) *Brah rajpithi tvas somas* (Royal festivals of the twelve months) 3 vols. (Phnom Penh, 1952–1960). For the *tang tok* ceremony discussed in rules fourteen and fifteen, see A. Mennetrier, 'Les fêtes de Tang Tok à Phnom Penh', *Revue Indochinoise* XV/10 (October 1912), pp. 334–345. It would be interesting to compare these festivals with their counterparts in Siam, discussed by King Rama V in *Phra ratchapithi sip song duan* (Royal festivals of the twelve months), (Bangkok, various editions) and in H.G. Quaritch Wales, *Siamese State Cerenonies* (London, 1932).

of royal journeys should also be set down, and details of feasts and ceremonies held by the monarch in the palace.

4. If the queen or any of the king's consorts gives birth to a child, the scribes should set down the month, day and hour of the birth, as well as the names given to the child.

5. The scribes should record the circumstances whereby honorific titles are given to ministers, and to male and female civil servants, as well as to important councillors and ladies-in-waiting.

6. If a king dies, the scribes must compute and set down the exact hour, day, month and year of the occurrence, as well as the king's age at his death, and the number of years he had reigned.

7. The scribes must write the poetry recited at performances' of the royal troupe . . .[**] When there are ceremonies at the palace associated with the king's children, the scribes must write appropriate songs for the troupe to sing, and the chief scribe himself should recite the titles given to the king's children [as a result of the particular ceremonyl.

8. If there is a royally-sponsored festival honoring a white elephant, the elephant's name and titles should be recorded, as well as the hymns intoned in its honor by the royal troupe. The chief scribe, in accordance with tradition should choose the titles and bestow them on the elephant.

9. If a new *gouverneur*[***] comes to look after Prey Nokor [the Khmer name for Saigon], or a new *résident supérieur*[***] comes to look after the kingdom of Cambodia, or if a new *comptolleur*[***] comes to look after the king's possessions, the scribes must record the exact day, month and year [of the official's arrival] and must write his name clearly in the palace archives.

10. If a high official commits a serious offence, and has to leave royal service, or be confined to prison, or be executed, the scribes must record the details of the event as clearly as possible.

[**] and assign costumes? three words illegible.
[***] French word appears transliterated in Khmer.

11. The scribes should record all the royal business that is transacted in the palace compound. They should also record progress on the steel bridge [across the Bassac] at Chroi Ambok, the railroad between Phnom Penh and Battambang, and the king's pavilion being built [by the French] at Phnom Prey Khieu, sometimes called Phnom Kotop, in the district of Thnol Totung in Kandal province. In recording these enterprises, the month and date [of their completion?] must be clearly stated, using French and Khmer systems of notation, so that they can be put in the royal chronicles.

12. Members of the corps of scribes should each have [proper writing equipment, viz] a metal stylus, thumb-guard, and chalk [on hand] at royal coronations and also during the festival in honor of the dead that takes place in the palace on the 14 and 15 waxing days of the month of *phatrobot* [August-September], in accordance with tradition.

13. The scribes must compose the prayers recited at the royal festivals associated with the water festival [in November], and those associated with the ceremonies honoring the moon that take place on the 14 and 15 waxing days of the same month. The scribes must also assemble the [court brahmins?] so that they can recite prayers for three nights until dawn, at this time of year, according to tradition.

14. The scribes must ask the royal guards to bring the golden foil [inscribed with the king's titles] and place it on the throne in the great hall of the palace during the feast of Tang Tok [when officials offer gifts] in honor of the prosperity of the king, the lord of life, in the month of *ched* [May-June]. Indeed, the scribes should regulate the performance of this festival each year in accordance with tradition.

15. The scribes must recite the oath [repeated by all high officials] sworn to the king in the Temple of the Emerald Buddha [to the south of the royal palace] on the occasion of Tang Tok.

16. The scribes must supervise the manufacture of the sugarcane sticks used to expel evil spirits, and the cotton cords

beaded with bits of paper inscribed with sacred texts [that are handed out] on the 13, 14, and 15 days of the waxing moon in the month of *phalkun* [February-March] At this time, the royal titles are [again] brought into the great hall of the palace. The corps of scribes regulates the performance of this festival each year according to tradition.

17. If violent disorder breaks out during a king's reign, the day, month and year of the occurrence, and the outcome, must be written down and kept in the palace archives.

18. From time to time, the scribes should collect and write down traditional tales and poems. They should also perform tasks in the *bureau*.*

[signed] YIM

(Manuscript 74.002 in the archives of the Buddhist Institute in Phnom Penh)

---

* French word appears transliterated in Khmer.

THE KINGDOM OF KAMPUCHEA, MARCH–OCTOBER 1945

On 12 March 1945, three days after Japanese forces had swept the French from power in Indo-China, Cambodia's young king, Norodom Sihanouk, declared his country's independence, noting as he did so that it would now be known in French as "Kampuchea" rather than as "Cambodge".[1] The proclamation ushered in a seven-month interregnum between periods of French control.

The interval has not been studied in detail. It is interesting for several reasons. For one thing, it forms a piece that can be fitted into the mosaic of Southeast Asian history in the closing phases of World War II. In Cambodia, as in so much of the region, the second half of 1945 was a testing ground for nationalism. Political alignments in this period foreshadow those in evidence when the French returned to power, and even after Cambodia gained its independence in 1953. During the last six months of 1945, for example, a rift opened up between the king and some of his advisors, culminating in an anti-royalist *coup d'etat* in August, where Sihanouk's secretary was shot and wounded.

This paper was first published in *Journal of Southeast Asian Studies*, Vol. XVII, No. 1, March 1986, reprinted with permission.
[1] R. Ollivier, "Le protectorat francais au Cambodge" (unpublished essay, 1969), p. 198.

The king's distrust of serious politicians, which characterized the rest of his years in power, may well have sprung from this event. It is likely, moreover, as Ben Kiernan has argued, that the roots of Cambodia's own Communist movement can also be found in these tumultuous months.[2] Finally, the period is rewarding to study because of a range of unpublished sources, not previously consulted by students of Cambodian history. These include a manuscript chronicle of the early years of Sihanouk's reign, prepared in 1949;[3] a journal kept in 1945 by a long-term resident of Cambodia, the French ethnographer Eveline Porée-Maspéro;[4] and papers relating to the career of the Cambodian nationalist, Son Ngoc Thanh (1908–1976?), which were donated to Monash University in 1981.[5] While preparing the paper, I also profitted from an interview with Laau Thouk, who had been a young police officer in Phnom Penh during the summer of 1945.[6] Taken together, and corroborated with secondary material, such as V.M. Reddi's monograph on Cambodian nationalism,[7]

[2] Ben Kiernan, "Origins of Khmer Communism", *Southeast Asian Affairs* 1981 (Singapore, 1982), pp. 161–80.

[3] *Rajabangsavarar brah norodom sihanouk* 'Royal chronicle of Norodom Sihanouk' (hereafter *RNS*), microfilm available from the Centre for East Asian Studies in Tokyo. For a general discussion of this text, see David Chandler, "Cambodian Royal Chronicles, 1927–1949: Kingship and Historiography at the End of the Colonial Era"below p. 189. For the interregnum period, the chronicle takes the form of documents copied successively, without comment, and often out of chronological order. For example, events of October 1945 appear ten pages ahead of events in August (*RNS*, pp. 551 and 561). This disorder, and the lack of commentary, strongly suggests that the texts themselves, e.g., of speeches or proclamations, have been accurately set down.

[4] I am grateful to the late Mme Porée-Maspéro for allowing me to consult this document while visiting her and her husband in Mormoiron, Vaucluse, in November 1983. I am also grateful to her for comments about the period at that time, and in private correspondence.

[5] In August 1981, Major General Channa Samudvijana kindly donated his collection of the papers of Son Ngoc Thanh to the Centre of Southeast Asian Studies, Monash University.

[6] Interview with Laau Touk, North Melbourne, 20 September 1984.

[7] V. M. Reddi, *A History of the Cambodian Independence Movement*, 1863–1955 (Tirupati, 1971).

these sources provide the elements of a detailed picture, contrasting sharply with the laconic, Eurocentric paragraphs that deal with Cambodia in official histories of World War II.[8]

A good deal has been written, particularly by French authors, about the Japanese *coup* de force of 9 March 1945.[9] In Cambodia, and nearly everywhere else in Indo-China, the French were taken by surprise. There is little evidence that pro-Japanese Cambodians had been told of the move in advance. In Phnom Penh, it seems, the Japanese set off air-raid sirens in order to draw French residents, unarmed, from their quarters.[10] In the process of rounding up and disarming them (as well as locally-recruited policemen and members of the militia) the Japanese encountered scattered resistance. Laau Thouk recalls seeing "four or five" corpses of Khmer militiamen outside the French *résidence supérieure*,[11] and Mme Porée-Maspéro recorded hearing "the rattle of machine guns, rifle shots, and deep explosions that must have been grenades, coming from every direction".[12]

A royal proclamation, issued on the following day, announced the Japanese action, and on 12 March another, noted above, declared that the French Protectorate was officially at an end. According to Laau Thouk this proclamation coincided with a Japanese decision to release Cambodian and Vietnamese members of the police force from custody.[13]

Aside from changing the French spelling of the kingdom's name, the first substantive moves by the new government

[8] See Earl Mountbatten of Burma, *Post Surrender Tasks: Section E of Report to the Combined Chiefs of Staff* (London, 1969), p. 289; and S. Woodburn Kirby, *The War Against Japan*, Vol. 5 (London, 1969), pp. 303–304.

[9] See particularly Paul Isoart (ed.). Indochine 1940–1945 (Paris, 1982), pp. 41–53; Claude Fillieux, *Merveilleux Cambodge* (Paris, 1962), pp. 33–40; and R.B. Smith, "The Japanese Period in Indo-China and the Coup of 9th March 1945", *Journal of Southeast Asian Studies*, IX.2 (1978), 268–301. See also Paul Tramonis' perceptive memoir of this period, *Camille* (Bainville sur Mer, 1966), p. 125ff.

[10] Porée-Maspéro, "Journal", 10 March 1945.

[11] Interview with Laau Thouk, 20 September 1984.

[12] Porée-Maspéro, "Journal", 10 March 1945; and Tramoni, op. cit., p. 134.

[13] Interview with Laau Thouk.

occurred on 13 March, when a proclamation declared null and void a pair of laws which had made the romanization of Cambodian script compulsory in official correspondence, and had shifted Cambodia's calendar from a Buddhist system of reckoning to a Gregorian one.[14] Both moves, which the French had seen as modernizing and inoffensive, had already aroused strong opposition, particularly from the Buddhist *sangha*, which saw itself as the curator of Cambodian culture, itself enshrined in part in Cambodian script and in the Buddhist calendar. Discussing the abrogation in a speech in April 1945, Sihanouk declared that

> We are a people known for honoring old laws and customs from ancient times . . . The French laws would make us devoid of customs, and devoid of history. Anyone who thinks he can force the Cambodian people to abandon their calendar or adopt French script is incorrect . . . [such] declarations would make people forget their moral training. [15]

According to Sihanouk's memoirs, the royal family opposed the two reforms, and the young king, earlier in the year, had even had to be dissuaded from abdicating over the issue.[16]

On 21 March the Japanese posted a notice in Phnom Penh to the effect that "8,000 Indo-chinese had been shot to death in France". The notice was removed later in the day, perhaps when the Japanese discovered it to be untrue, but in the meantime, several French civilians – few of whom had yet been interned by the Japanese – were roughed up in the streets. At least three received knife wounds. In Sihanouk's chronicle, this "merciless" behavior is blamed on Vietnamese, a view shared by Laau Thouk in 1984, and by Mme Porée-Maspéro's informants

---

[14] Ollivier, "Le protectorat", p. 213. See G. *Gautier, Jeune Cambodge* (Phnom Penh, 1943), *passim.*, for a defense of the proposals.

[15] *RNS*, p. 507.

[16] Norodom Sihanouk, *Souvenirs doux et amers* (Paris, 1981), p. 86.

at the time.[17] As a result of the incident, French civilians in Cambodia, with rare exceptions, were interned until the end of the war. In March 1945, then, the French in Indo-China began to suffer the hardships which their European and American colleagues elsewhere in Southeast Asia had been confronting since the early days of 1942.[18] These hardships, the flowering of "independence", the declining fortunes of Japan, and hopes of deliverance by France went hand in hand.

It is against this background that we should examine the tentative development of Cambodia's independent politics in the last part of 1945. The cabinet that took office following 9 March was composed of bureaucrats loyal to the king, and until very recently, to France as well. Many of them had been picked for promotion in 1942–43 by the energetic French *résident supérieur*, Georges Gautier, who had also been behind the unpopular modernization laws.[19] A confidential report about the Cambodian cabinet, received in Paris in June 1945, described the Finance Minister, Ung Hy, as "a former opium addict, foxy, somewhat slack, without much character". One of his colleagues was dismissed as "ambitious and pretentious" and a third, Var Kamel, was listed as "an excellent boy (*garçon*) fond of the French".[20]

For several months, the Cambodian government, unsure of how much power the Japanese would grant it, moved with caution. Khmer political prisoners, released by the Japanese at the end of March, were not given government positions,[21] and Cambodia's most vehement nationalist, the journalist Son Ngoc

---

[17] *RNS*, pp. 504–505; Ollivier, p. 209; Porée-Maspéro, "Journal", 20 March 1945, and interview with Laau Thouk, 20 September 1984.

[18] For a description of this period in Indo-China, see André Angladeete, "La vie quotidienne en Indochine de 1939 à 1946". *Mondes et cultures 30* (March, 1979), pp. 467–98.

[19] "See Gautier, *Jeune Cambodge*, op. cit.; and G. Gautier, *Le Fin de l'Indochine française* (Paris, 1978).

[20] France. Archives d'outremer (Rue Oudinot. Paris; hereafter AOM/P), 121/1101 (undated), "Renseignements sur les gouvernements pro-japonais".

Thanh, did not return to Cambodia from Japan until the end of May, when he joined the cabinet as Minister of Foreign Affairs.

Son Ngoc Thanh was born in southern Vietnam, then known as Cochinchina, in 1908.[22] His father was ethnically Khmer, his mother Vietnamese. They were apparently prosperous, for Thanh, after some schooling in Saigon and Phnom Penh, completed his education in France, attending *Lycée* in Montpellier and Paris; he earned his *baccalauréat* in 1933. Soon after, he returned to Indo-China, and became a civil servant, first in Cochinchina and in 1935 in Phnom Penh where, except for a brief interval as a magistrate in Pursat, he remained until 1942. In 1937, he came in contact with a group of young intellectuals, concentrated in the French-sponsored Institut Bouddhique, as well as with a somewhat older group of men associated with the Khmer-language newspaper, *Nagara Vatta* ("Angkor Wat") edited by Pach Chhoeun.[23] The paper was not particularly militant. Editorials in the l930s urged Cambodians to "wake up" and to compete with the Chinese and Vietnamese in Cambodia's commercial life. The paper also reported on the activities of Cambodia's small educated elite, which comprised its readership as well as the middle ranks of the bureaucracy. It is difficult to gauge the influence of the paper, but its weekly circulation of 5,000 copies suggests that it was widely read. Following French defeats in Europe in 1940 and at the hands of Thailand in 1941, several editorials were censored by the French authorities, but *Nagara Vatta* appeared regularly until July 1942, when its editor, Pach Chhoeun, was arrested for his role in an anti-French demonstration.

---

[21] See Bunchhan Mul, *Kuk Niyobay* (Political Prison) (Phnom Penh, 1971), pp. 257–58.

[22] Son Ngoc Thanh papers, "Etat civil", in Thanh's hand, can be proved to be dating from 1944 (with later additions in pencil), corroborated with other sources.

[23] An analysis of the content of *Nagara Vatta* (1937–42) would fill an important gap in Cambodian historiography. Except for issues allegedly produced in 1945, which have not been cited, nearly the entire run of the paper is held by the Bibliothèque Nationale in Paris.

The demonstration, which involved approximately five hundred Buddhist monks and a sprinkling of civilians, was to protest the arrest by French officials of two Buddhist monks accused of plotting a *coup détat*.[24] Chhoeun had apparently miscalculated the amount of support that the Japanese (whose forces had been in Cambodia for fourteen months) were willing to provide. He was arrested while presenting a petition, and was sentenced to life imprisonment. The edition of *Nagara Vatta* scheduled for the day of the demonstration failed to appear. Son Ngoc Thanh, who was implicated in the demonstration, used his connections with the Japanese to flee to Battambang and then to Bangkok. At the end of 1942, he obtained permission to take up residence in Tokyo, where he lived under an assumed name, under official protection, until the end of May 1945.[25]

In his petition to the Japanese, addressed from Bangkok in 1942, Thanh began to style himself the "representative of the Khmer Nationalist Party", a group which would have been illegal inside Cambodia itself.[26] According to Thanh, the party's constituency consisted of

> the entire peasant population of Cambodia, all Cambodians who were not functionaries, the entire population of the territories ceded (to Thailand in 1941), as well as of the Khmer portions of Thailand, the entire Cambodian population of Cochinchina, and all the Cambodians living in Bangkok. In Cambodia itself, only the King, his close associates, the royal family and those functionaries loyal to France are ineligible to participate in our movement.

[24] On the demonstration, see Reddi, *A History*, p. 85ff, and Bunchhan Mul, *Kuk Niyobay*, pp. 49–62. For a tendentious account, see Norodom Sihanouk, *Souvenirs doux et amers*, pp. 75–77. The demonstration is also discussed in Porée-Maspéro, "Journal", 20 July 1942. Laau Thouk (Interview, 20 September 1984) claims to have encountered part of the demonstration on his way to work.

[25] On the date of Thanh's return. see *RNS*, 546 and Ollivier, p. 209.

[26] Son Ngoc Thanh papers, "Le Parti Nationaliste Khmer pour l'indépendance du Cambodge", undated typescript, probably composed in August 1942, corrected in Thanh's hand.

Until 1943 at least the Japanese kept Thanh's presence in Tokyo a secret, providing him with lodging, an allowance, and a spurious Burmese identity, while he tried to learn Japanese and to remain in contact with Cambodian nationalists at home.

Five of his letters to colleagues in Cambodia, all composed in 1943, have survived.[27] They are in French. In the first of them, Thanh set forth a five-point programme for himself, involving studying Japanese, informing the Japanese about Cambodia ("It is pointless to tell you that our Cambodia is completely unknown here; the French have concealed it well"), making Japanese intentions known to Cambodians, undergoing "political education, to understand more deeply the New Order of things in Asia and in the world", and studying the practical details of Japanese life.

In the letters, Thanh struggles to clarify his political ideas, which contain elements of racism, anger at the French, optimism about Japan, and hopefulness that the Japanese ideal of "familialism" will catch on among Cambodians. In one letter, he gives vent to anti-Semitic ideas, probably picked up earlier in France, remarking that "Jewish occidentalism, with scientific progress, has spilled over onto Asia".[28] Other letters attempt to spell out Cambodian history in terms of foreign exploitation. The letters see Cambodia's future as tied to Japan's victory, and to the future of Indo-China as a whole.

It is not surprising, of course, that much of what Thanh wrote from Japan was poorly thought-out and contradictory. Out of touch with his compatriots, he was trying to blend his

---

[27] Son Ngoc Thanh papers; the letters are dated 22 February, 3 March, 10 April, 26 April and 25 July, 1943.

[28] Son Ngoc Thanh papers, letter of 10 April 1943.

[29] See, for example, Son Ngoc Thanh papers, "Raisons de l'antagonisme khmer-thailandais" dated 18 May 1943 and "L'Indochine dans la sphère de la Grande Asie Orientale", dated 25 June 1943.

own anti-colonial ideas (themselves fuzzily expressed) with unfamiliar Japanese proposals for the future of Southeast Asia. These proposals often ran counter to Thanh's own ideas about the intrinsic grandeur of the Cambodian "race".[29] His ideas about Cambodian history, in fact, are not nuanced, but this is not surprising because no historical texts had yet been published in Khmer, none was readily available in French, and Cambodian history was treated summarily in Cambodian schools.[30]

Because Thanh's correspondence from 1944 and 1945 has not survived, it is impossible to trace the evolution of his ideas in the latter stages of the war. It is clear, however, that the Japanese regarded him largely as an instrument of their policies rather than as a skilled political leader, along the lines of Ba Maw, Sukarno, or Chandra Bose.[31] This is not surprising either, given the lack of political experience that plagued Thanh and his associates.

On 13 April 1945, at the Buddhist New Year celebration, King Sihanouk pleaded for cooperation with the Japanese, promising that Cambodia would soon regain the greatness it had enjoyed as "the city of Angkor Wat" [sic]. Under the French, he said, Cambodians had not felt responsible for their actions, and had remained "asleep".[32] The ideas that Cambodian greatness in the past was entirely of its own making, while modern difficulties fell onto the country from outside, foreshadowed the ideology of several Cambodian governments later on.[33] Dazzled by "Angkor", and perhaps by the importance placed on their past by their colonial masters, many Cambodians were unwilling to examine the social relations that had informed that earlier civilization or to accept the changes that had occurred in Cambodia since its demise.

---

[30] On later interpretations of Cambodian history, see David Chandler, "Seeing Red: Perceptions of Cambodian History in Democratic Kampuchea", below p. 233.

[31] See Alfred W. McCoy (ed.), *Southeast Asia Under Japanese Occupation* (New Haven, 1980).

[32] *RNS*, p. 507.

[33] See David Chandler, "The Tragedy of Cambodian History", below p. 297.

Angered by "the French", they were unwilling to assume responsibility for the indigenous conditions that had led to French protection. In other words, the "nation" which Thanh and his followers hoped to establish had roots in the thirteenth century, and was nourished by recent animosities. Someone besides the Cambodians themselves, it seems, kept Cambodia from becoming a new "Angkor".

In May, the king delivered another address, dealing with Cambodian education.[34] He stressed that Cambodians should cast off the sense of inferiority foisted onto them by the French and the French-oriented educational system. The speech proposed phasing out French-language instruction in Cambodian schools until by 1949, classes at all levels would be taught entirely in Khmer, "and the problems of teaching in the French language will no longer exist".

In order to place the Cambodian royal family in the mainstream of the nationalist movement, the king also asserted that the protectorate of 1863 had been an "alliance" between the French and Cambodia's King Norodom, while the agreement of 1884 had involved the cession of Cambodian territory to the French:

> At the time when Cambodia fell under French control [in 1884] the French deceptively altered the Cambodian chronicles to say that the king [in 1863] had asked the French to come and protect Cambodia.[35]

In his memoirs, which fail to mention these addresses, Sihanouk claims to have begged the Japanese to allow Son Ngoc Thanh to return to Cambodia, although this is unlikely.[36] The two men were never close. The rationale for the Japanese decision to bring him back was probably that he was so demonstrably pro-Japanese.

---

[34] *RNS*, pp. 542–45.
[35] *RNS*, p. 545.
[36] *RNS*, p. 546; Ollivier, 208n; Sihanouk, *Souvenirs*, pp. 98–105.

Throughout the summer of 1945, the French government was accelerating its plans to return to Indo-China. This planning had been curtailed to an extent by President Roosevelt's almost obsessive opposition to French colonialism in Asia;[37] with Roosevelt's death in April, de Gaulle's provisional government (which had declared war on Japan in December 1941) moved swiftly with plans to restore French power in the Far East.

Some French writers pointed out the difficulties which such a return might entail. In June 1945, for example, a Colonel Stagnard seemed to agree with Thanh's analysis when he minuted that

> Our principal support in Indo-China can be found among intellectuals with jobs and of a certain age, attached to French culture; the mandarinal cadres whose destinies are linked with ours; Annamite Catholics; and retired military personnel who have remained loyal to us.[38]

Despite the thinness of this indigenous support, the French were confident that most of the population were indifferent to their colonial endeavor. One analyst even contended that

> I will not hesitate to affirm that the opinion of the rural masses . . . has remained where it always was, which is to say non-existent when it comes to issues of importance. Their preoccupations are primarily alimentary.[39]

For much of the colonial period, Cambodia had occupied a special place in French thinking about colonialism in general and Indo-China in particular. The temple of Angkor Wat, reproduced

---

[37] See Walter Lefeber, "Roosevelt, Churchill and Indo-China", *American Historical Review*, 80 (1975), pp. 1277–95, and Gary R. Hess, "Franklin D. Roosevelt and Indo-China", *Journal of American History*, 59 (1972), pp. 353–68.

[38] AOM/P 125/1117, "Bulletins et télégrammes": Lt. Col. Stagnard, "Note de reseignement".

[39] AOM/P 124/1091, "Notes sur la situation en Indochine: Septembre 1944".

in miniature at colonial expositions in France, had become a symbol of the genteel mysteries of French colonialism, and as time went on many French observers, beguiled by the politeness of most Cambodians, and the Francophilia of so many of the elite, thought that their *mission civilisatrice* was deeply rooted in the consciousness of the people. In sharp contrast with Vietnam, Cambodia had been politically quiet in the 1930s. No political parties or agitation ruffled the decorum of French rule. At the same time, young and comparatively forward-looking people began to filter into the French administration, and by 1935 one of them could write glowingly of the "awakening" of the Cambodian people under French protection. As material conditions improved, so did education, and Cambodian participation at higher levels of the administration.[40]

Against this background, *any* anti-French behavior by Cambodians was viewed by the French, particularly in 1945, as "opportunistic" rather than sincere.

As for the "independent" government in power in Phnom Penh, its freedom of action was almost entirely symbolic. There was very little it could do, for example, to improve communications, raise revenue, organize international trade, conduct elections, or arm Cambodians in their own defence. The government was dependent on Japanese support. The Japanese, for their part, saw Cambodia not as a nation but as part of a military zone and as a source of supply for its occupying forces.[41]

In July, quite late in the day compared with politics elsewhere in Southeast Asia, the Japanese encouraged the organization of

[40] See H. de Grauclade, *Le reveil du peuple khmer* (Hanoi, 1935). For a less optimistic view, see G. de Pourtalès, *Nous, à qui rien n'appartient* (Paris. 1931). 131ff. According to Mme Porée-Maspéro (personal communication) the number of French administrators fluent in Khmer increased significantly in the 1930s.

[41] See D. S. Detweiler and C. B. Burdick (eds.), *War in Asia and the Pacific 1937–1949* (New York, 1980), Vol. 6. map 6, which shows the Japanese military zones in Indo-China as of May 1945.

a militia, the so-called "Green Shirts", who numbered perhaps a thousand men by the end of the war.[42]

Although Ung Hy's government lacked freedom of manoever, it seems likely that younger members of the Cambodian *élite*, and much of the population at large, were slowly becoming accustomed to the absence of French supervision, and more tempted to listen to nationalist fulminations. Perhaps they had begun to think of the kingdom of Kampuchea as different from the protectorate under which they had always lived.

On 20 July, Cambodia celebrated the third anniversary of the monks' demonstration. Large crowds assembled outside the royal palace to cheer King Sihanouk, independence, and the Japanese. To mark the occasion, the Japanese turned over the French *résidence* supérieure (where Pach Chhoeun had been arrested three years before) to the Cambodians as a government guest house.[43] Ten days later, they arranged for Major General A.C. Chatterji, the so-called Foreign Minister of Chandra Bose's Free India Government, to come to Phnom Penh on an official visit.[44]

Events in the next three weeks were crucial to the *coup* of 9–10 August, and to Son Ngoc Thanh's activities from late August to October 1945, but available sources unfortunately provide no information about what must have been increasing Japanese support for Thanh and his nationalist entourage, increased

[42] The formation of the militia was announced in the official (French-language) newspaper, *Cambodge* on 17 July 1945 (Michael Vickery, personal communication). FOM (Aix-en-Provence; hereafter AOM/A), *Cambodge*, 2 F 29 (4), 5, estimates the strength of the Cambodian militia at 3,000 men, roughly equivalent to the number of Japanese posted to Cambodia. Hardly any of these were armed. Reddi, *A History*, p. 94 quotes the militia's leader as saying, "I am convinced that myself and my compatriots are the best Cambodian troops because we have been chosen among the intellectuals".

[43] *RNS*, 533 estimates the crowd on this occasion at 30,000.

[44] Chatterji had served with Chandra Bose's Indian National Army (INA) since 1943. He became Foreign Minister of the Free India Provisional Government in January 1945. See Joyce Lebra, *Jungle Alliance: Japan and the Indian National Army* (Singapore, 1971), pp. 145–46.

militancy among his younger supporters, and growing impatience in elite circles with the cabinet installed in March. By 6 August, of course, a nuclear device had been exploded at Hiroshima, but it is unlikely if news of this event, even if it reached Phnom Penh, would have made much difference to Son Ngoc Thanh.

In any case, early in the morning of 10 August 1945, eleven members of the Cambodian militia stormed into the palace, waking the king and demanding that he dissolve the Ung Hy cabinet.[45] In the ensuing *melée*, Sihanouk's secretary, Nong Kimny (in the 1950s and 1960s Cambodia's Ambassador to the United States) was shot at several times and lightly wounded. Earlier in the evening, it seems, most of the cabinet, excluding Thanh and Sihanouk's uncle, Prince Sisowath Monireth, had been detained although they were released soon after the king acquiesced to the demands of the people who had stormed the palace. Nothing of their demands is included in Sihanouk's chronicle, which treats the incident in terms of *lèse majesté*, remarking only that "in the night (of 10 August) a band of Cambodians transgressed the law and broke into the royal palace".[46]

The incident later became a rallying-point for Cambodian nationalists. According to Ollivier, two of the assailants had volunteered earlier to serve as *kamikaze* pilots;[47] while this is unconfirmed, it is certain that five of the group were active in subsequent Communist-led resistance to the French, and one of them, Mey Pho, became in the 1950s a member of the central committee of the Cambodian Communist Party.[48] Many

[45] On the *coup*, see Ollivier, 225, AOM/A 7 F 29 (4), 9, and Sihanouk, *Souvenirs*, pp. 106–109. See also Bpunchhan Mul, *Charet Khmaer* (Khmer Mores) (Phnom Penh, 1974), pp.19–20, which refers to the *coup* as a "revolution" (*padevat*).

[46] *RNS*, p. 549.

[47] Ollivier, p. 226.

[48] Kiernan, "Origins", pp. 179–80.

students at the *Lycée* Sisowath near the palace were excited by the event.[49]

On the following day, Mme Porée-Maspéro noted in her journal that

> There is talk of a 'people's movement' against the palace, with posters saying that the king continues to amuse himself while the people suffer.[50]

The *coup* certainly had Thanh's approval, and occurred with Japanese permission, but the anti-royalist component, and its violence, were new to the nationalist struggle, and alarmed the king. In the view of a French doctor who was free to circulate in the city, the *coup* had occurred because

> The popular party of Pach Chhoeun, under the pretext that the leaders of the government were 'Chinese' wished to knock them from their pedestal. The king, under the influence of his father, signed the papers at 2:00 a.m . . . [51]

A good deal about the *coup* resists analysis. For one thing, although Thanh was a direct beneficiary of the cabinet dissolution, he did not take office as Prime Minister for another five days – exactly the time it took authorities in Japan to decide to surrender to the Allies. The role played by Prince Monireth, suspected throughout the war of anti-French machinations (he had been passed over as king in 1941 in Sihanouk's favor) has never been clear nor have Thanh's motives in ordering the *coup* participants imprisoned as a condition of obtaining office.

---

[49] Keng Vannsak, interview with Ben Kiernan, Paris, 12 August 1979. Vannsak asserted that "around twenty" students stayed up all night to see what happened in the *coup*, about which they apparently had some foreknowledge.

[50] Porée-Maspéro, "Journal", 11 August 1945.

[51] Porée-Maspéro, "Journal", 13 August 1945.

It is likely that the 14 August date was selected by the Japanese to coincide with the installation, in Saigon, of a pro-Japanese "National Unity Front", replaced within ten days by officials sent south for the purpose by Viet Minh authorities in Hanoi.[52]

In any event, the cabinet proclaimed on 14 August and installed on the following day contained several hold-overs from the March cabinet, as well as three of Thanh's nationalist collaborators – Pach Chhoeun, Khim Tit, and Pitou de Monteiro. Khim Tit, as Minister of Defense, was to play a crucial role in Thanh's demise. Thanh, taking office as Cambodia's first Prime Minister (Ung Hy, it seems, had held only the finance portfolio). also retained his post as Minister of Foreign Affairs.

Sihanouk did not preside at the cabinet's installation on 15 August, although Thanh, in his speech at the time, proclaimed his loyalty to the throne, and announced a nine-point policy declaration, which has not been discussed elsewhere.[53]

Domestically Thanh promised to "nourish and defend" Buddhism, the king and the royal family, to consolidate the Cambodian people, to defend the state, to strengthen independence and to improve education. His foreign platform displayed little awareness of the realities of August 1945. He proclaimed the importance of a continuing alliance with Japan, as well as of new alliances with other Asian nations, and suggested a further alliance with the Vietnamese as well as all the "yellow-skinned people" of Indo-China.

Nothing in Thanh's speech explained how the government would pay for these programmes, or what the future might hold for the French interned throughout Indo-China, to say nothing of the Allied powers who were clearly in the process of winding up the war against Japan. It is hard to recapture, from the sources, whether Thanh believed what he was saying, or was

---

[52] See Philipe Devilliers, *Histoire du Vietnam de 1940 à 1952* (Paris, 1952), pp. 140–41; and D. Gareth Porter, "Imperialism and Social Structure in Twentieth Century Vietnam" (Ph.D. dissertation, Cornell University, 1976), p. 158.

[53] *RNS*, pp. 564–65.

going through the motions, aware that in the medium term his government was doomed. His behavior over the next two months as it can be reconstructed from the sources, indicates that in playing for time, Thanh presumed that something – an alliance with Thailand, a Vietnamese victory over the French – would turn up to keep Cambodia independent. Certainly he made no effort to retract or conceal his nationalist ideas.

On 22 August a "four-engined Allied plane" circled over Kompong Speu, to the west of Phnom Penh, dropping leaflets which proclaimed the imminent return of the French to Indo-China.[54] A week later, another plane parachuted eight French officers into Cambodia. They were brought into Phnom Penh by Cambodian officials. Two of them, Gajean and Huard, played roles in the ensuing weeks, although the former, according to Mme Porée-Maspero, "played up" to Thanh in the period immediately following his arrival.[55]

Perhaps to demonstrate his government's legitimacy to these newcomers (before anyone else arrived to question it), Thanh on 3 September proclaimed that a national referendum would take place, which would ask the Cambodian people if they wanted "to be as free as they were under Jayavarman, with the temples of Angkor Wat".[56]

In fact, Thanh had no time, and perhaps no inclination, to carry out a real referendum. Instead, the five questions to be asked and the answers to be given to them were circulated to government departments. When the "results" were announced it was said that over 541,000 citizens (men "between the ages of 18 and 60") had answered all the questions correctly, even though no Cambodians

[54] *RNS*, p. 566. The leafletting is noted in the chronicle immediately after Thanh's program, even though it occurred a week later.

[55] Porée-Maspéro, "Journal", 16 October 1945. *RNS*, p. 570 reports that on 11 October, the day after the anniversary of the Chinese revolution in 1911, a dinner was given for French, British and Cambodian officials by Chinese entrepreneurs in Phnom Penh.

[56] *RNS*, p. 568. See also Ollivier, p. 232, and Sihanouk, *Souvenirs*, pp. 110–11.

had ever voted for anything before. To add verisimilitude to the "results", two ballots were reported to be invalid.

By the middle of September British and Indian forces under Major General Douglas Gracey had arrived in Saigon and had begun to disarm the Japanese and to release French prisoners of war.[57] Gracey, and the French soldiers whom he had released, came into conflict immediately with the Viet Minh, who considered themselves to be the representatives of an independent state. As Gracey recalled eight years later, "They came to see me, and said 'welcome' and all that sort of thing. It was an unpleasant situation and I promptly kicked them out."[58] In fact, the British situation in Saigon in September and October became increasingly precarious and Gracey's decision to intervene in Cambodia was related directly to these events.

On 6 October Thanh dispatched a special delegate, Pann Yun, to Bangkok, to negotiate with the anti-colonial Thai government dominated by Pridi Phanomyong. According to later anti-Thanh reports, Yun was authorized to offer the Thai, in exchange for military support, continued control of the provinces of Battambang and Siem Reap which had been ceded to them by the French in 1941.[59] Although Pridi's group had sponsored anti-French guerrilla activities in Laos and along the Cambodian frontier, it was apparently unwilling to entangle itself with Thanh's endangered regime. Similarly, Thanh's attempts

[57] See Louis Allen, "Studies in the Japanese Occupation of Southeast Asia, 1944–1945", *Durham University Journal 64* (1972), pp. 120–32; George Rosie, *The British in Vietnam* (London, 1970); and Christopher Thorne, "Indo-China and Anglo-American Relations 1942–1945", *Pacific Historical Review 45* (February, 1946), pp. 73–96.

[58] Gracey's remarks, made in 1953, appear in the discussion following Melvin Hall, "Aspects of the Present Situation in Indo-China", *Journal of the Central Asiatic Society 40* (1953), pp. 213–14. Col. Hall, an American officer, commented on this occasion that "I have some questions as to whether the average Vietnamese soldier, like the average American Negro soldier, will obey and follow his Vietnamese officers to the death".

[59] Sihanouk, *Souvenirs*, p. 112; SNT papers, letter from Pann Yun to President Felix Gouin of France, 17 April 1946 mentions the mission.

in September to formalize an alliance with the Viet Minh failed primarily because of poor communications.[60]

Indeed, as conditions in Cochinchina continued to deteriorate, from General Gracey's point of view, it became urgent for the Allies to secure Cambodia. Street fighting had broken out in Saigon; more than 100 French civilians had been massacred in a residential district; the Viet Minh had imposed a blockade around the city. Food supplies from Cambodia, particularly rice, were vital to the survival of a Western presence in Saigon, and thus to the chances of a French return to power. Moreover, the political loyalties of Cambodia's large Vietnamese population were in doubt. On 11 October Lieutenant Colonel E.D. Murray, who had arrived in Phnom Penh as Supreme Allied commander only three days before, flew to Saigon to ask his commander, General Gracey, to authorize the French to arrest Son Ngoc Thanh.[61] Gracey and the newly arrived French military commander, General Leclerc, agreed to the proposal, which echoed others from French officials in Phnom Penh and from Thanh's own Secretary of Defense, Khim Tit. The royal family had been strangely silent on the issue; in Mme Porée-Maspero's view, Prince Monireth particularly was adopting tactics of *attentisme*.[62] By accident or design, on 14 October King Sihanouk departed Phnom Penh on a pilgrimage to a Buddhist *wat* half a days' journey from the capital.[63]

Thanh's arrest, in Murray's office at mid-day on 15 October, took him by surprise. General Leclerc and an armed French NCO hustled him out of the building, and from there to a plane that flew him off to Saigon. Having presided, as Prime Minister,

---

[60] *RNS*, 533; Reddi, *A History*, p. 108; Ben Kiernan, interview with Nguyen Thanh Son, Ho Chi Minh City, 28 October 1980.

[61] Anthony Barnett (personal communication) drawing on his interview with Col. Murray in 1982.

[62] Porée-Maspéro, "Journal", 7 November 1945.

[63] *RNS*, p. 561. The prince was accompanied by his parents, and twenty palace guards.

over ceremonies at the Lycée Sisowath in the morning, Thanh had lunch in the Saigon central prison.[64]

A six-man Cambodian ministry was sworn in three days later, after Sihanouk had been brought back from his pilgrimage with an allied escort.[65] Only one of the new cabinet members, the king's uncle, Sisowath Monipong, had not served in the cabinets of March or August. Two others, Sun Hieng and Var Kamel served in all three, while another two, appointed in August, remained in their positions, and Chan Nak, removed in August, now rejoined the cabinet.[66]

The delay between Thanh's arrest and the new cabinet being installed seems to have been due to Sihanouk's reluctance to declare Cambodia's independence null and void. By 18 October however, the fight was over. Sihanouk received Col. Murray in audience, and five days later, in a poignant example of what Paul Mus has called the "monologue of colonialism" he officially welcomed the reimposition of the French protectorate, reading aloud from a message composed for the purpose by the reinstated *résident supérieur*.[67]

Aside from some loose ends still to be tied up – such as the abolition of 9 March and 20 July as national holidays – the interval discussed in this paper closes with the torn fabric of French controls sewn back together. Nearly all the French and many members of the Cambodian elite, after months of turbulence and uncertainty, were reassured, and it is possible to read much of Cambodia's post-war history in terms of a reinvigorated *status quo*. At the same time, the interregnum of March-October 1945 had important long-term effects on Cambodian politics, and on Cambodian views of their own history.

---

[64] Ollivier, p. 242. See also *Renlités cambodgiennes*, 9 and 16 July 1967. Porée-Maspéro, "Journal", 17 October 1945, points out that Thanh's chauffeur escaped to warn Thanh's cabinet members, some of whom, including Pach Chhoeun, fled Cambodia to escape arrest.

[65] *RNS*, p. 562.

[66] *RNS*, p. 573.

[67] Porée-Maspéro, "Journal", 27 October 1945.

For many members of the Cambodian elite under twenty-five years of age, the seven months in question provided previously unthinkable opportunities for political action. Thousands of people, perhaps without knowing precisely what to make of them, attended "national" parades, or marched in them.

Thousands also listened to anti-French, pro-Japanese harangues or marched up and down as members of the Japanese-trained militia. In the countryside, thousands of young boys had heard from their Buddhist teachers about the monks' demonstration in 1942, and the death in 1943 of one of the arrested monks, Hem Chieu, on the French penal island of Poulo Condore.[68] Students in secondary schools at this time – including such future luminaries as Saloth Sar (Pol Pot), Khieu Samphan, Hou Yuon and Keng Vannsak, watched the French drop away from Cambodian history, and felt themselves, however briefly, forming a sort of vanguard. Older bureaucrats, like Nhek Tioulong, Lon Nol and Ieu Koeus, now perceived the attractions of factional politics, long forbidden them by the French. During Cambodia's independence, orators and journalists reshaped Cambodia's recent history into a ragged sequence of Cambodian gestures against the French. Anti-French heroes of the 1860s and 1880s, the anti-tax demonstrators of 1916, and the murderers of a French *résident*, Felix Bardez, in 1925 were given heroic status, which was smothered by the French when they returned to power, but was encouraged by the Viet Minh and by the anti-royalist Cambodian Democratic Party.[69]

The catalyst for much of this activity was Son Ngoc Thanh. The French found it easy to dismiss him as a *pirate arriviste*, and certainly his capacity to misread the politics of October 1945 suggests dreaminess at best, but in fairness to him it is unlikely that French residents of Cambodia would have thought

---

[68] The monk's name was used for a Viet Minh training camp inside Cambodia in the early 1950s. Interest in him revived under the Khmer Republic in 1970–75, and briefly under the PRK in 1979.

[69] See David Chandler, "The Assassination of Résident Bardez" above p. 139.

competent anyone who demanded their departure or rejected their protection. Ernest Gellner has argued persuasively that nationalist "thinkers" like Son Ngoc Thanh need not be either accurate or profound.[70] Thanh's writings and speeches are a *mélange* of garbled history, race pride, and half-digested Japanese ideas. At the same time, we should not discount the appeal of such ideas, or of such a leader, to Cambodians accustomed to being treated as *bons enfants*. It is by no means certain, indeed, that the interregnum, and Thanh's period as Prime Minister, convinced Cambodians who paid attention to politics – admittedly a small number – that French protection was, after all, preferable to freedom. To make such an assertion, in fact, was tantamount to admitting a permanent, crippling ineptitude.[71]

Another effect of the interregnum was to introduce many Cambodians to a world outside their borders. The influence of Japanese ideas *per se* does not appear to have been wide or deep. Few Japanese could speak Cambodian; fewer Cambodians could speak Japanese. However, it seems likely that the Asian emphasis of Japanese propaganda led many Cambodians, for the first time, to see that their experiences under the French were shared by millions of others in Southeast Asia, and particularly in Vietnam. In the late 1940s, several hundred Cambodians became attached

[70] Ernest Gellner, *Nations and Nationalism* (Oxford. 1983), p. 124. As late as 28 September 1945, before the situation in Saigon became so critical, General Gracey had favored forming an alliance with Son Ngoc Thanh along the lines of the one being worked out in Burma at this time with Aung San. See Daniel B. Valentine, "The British Facilitation of the French Re-Entry into Vietnam" (Ph.D. dissertation, University of California, 1974), p. 365n.

[71] Tramoni, op. cit., p. 226 reports that when he returned to Phnom Penh at the end of 1945, after his internment under the Japanese, he noticed that "everything had changed. The Cambodians held the reins themselves, and we found ourselves at the margin, without knowing what this would involve . . . we sensed the irreversability of the situation, all the more when our Cambodian friends didn't come to see us as they had done in the past. Oh, when we met, they were friendly enough, to be sure. But a certain reticence, something vague, a sort of mist was floating between them and ourselves . . . Did they cherish their independence, which had fallen out of the sky? . . . In effect, the past had evaporated forever".

to the Vietnamese-controlled Indo-China Communist Party, convinced that an Indo-Chinese struggle against the French was part of an international struggle against colonialism in general. Non-Communist resistance groups, on the other hand, adopted recognizably nationalist positions.

The divergence of views between those who saw Cambodia's future as woven inextricably into Vietnam's, and those who saw it as primarily Khmer is still perceptible today (1984), between the ideologues of Heng Samrin's People's Republic of Kampuchea (PRK) on the one hand, and the remnants of Democratic Kampuchea on the other – to say nothing of more or less anti-Vietnamese, apolitical Cambodians, now living in large numbers overseas. Whereas PRK spokesmen see Cambodia's history largely in terms of international relations, and the acceptance of Vietnamese protection, DK speakers before adopting "liberal capitalism" in 1984 perceived it in terms of Cambodian racial achievements, and its "traditional animosity" with Vietnam.

In the summer of 1945 and for some time thereafter, Son Ngoc Thanh and his followers (most of whom were active in the Democratic Party in 1946–55) kept these contending views in some kind of balance. Thanh himself, for example, managed to be both racist, in Cambodian terms, and relatively pro-Vietnamese. Like Sihanouk, he probably saw Cambodian nationalism to an extent as his own creation, and the country therefore in some sense as a personal fief. As the "father" of Cambodian nationalism, Son Ngoc Thanh, himself half-Vietnamese, played down the autarkic, anti-Vietnamese components of nationalism inadvertently encouraged by the French, and later more openly by Sihanouk, Lon Nol and Pol Pot, while never succumbing to the extreme PRK position which suggests Cambodians are peculiarly deserving of protection.

Son Ngoc Thanh remained outside Cambodia until 1951. In 1952, in a miscalculation which some would probably see as typical of him, he went into exile in northwestern Cambodia, hoping, but rapidly failing to attract non-Communist guerrilla support for his proposed politics of "national socialism".[72] Thanh had been overtaken by events, but remained a hero to many in the Democratic Party. He returned briefly to power, even as Prime Minister, in the Lon Nol regime of the early 1970s, but by then his long flirtation with foreign patrons, particularly Thailand, South Vietnam, and the United States, had rendered him largely irrelevant as an actor on the Cambodian scene.

It seems clear, in conclusion, that the forces set in motion in Cambodia in the summer of 1945 continued to affect Cambodian politics and international relations in the years that followed. The French were never able to regain the reformist momentum of the 1930s; King Sihanouk did not long remain such a complaisant accomplice; and in Phnom Penh at least party politics became widespread as early as 1946.

One striking aspect of recent Cambodian history, traceable to this period as well, seems to be that those who pursue an ideal of Cambodian grandeur and self-reliance run the risk of being taken apart by larger neighbors, while those who believe in Cambodia's membership in a larger family of nations run the risk of becoming once again, as they were under the French and the Japanese, the "younger brothers" of a protecting power.

[72] At that time, *La Liberté*, a French-language newspaper in Phnom Penh, reported that in September 1945, Cambodian customs police had intercepted a Vietnamese barge containing arms as it came into Cambodia from Vietnam. The crew of the barge, flashing a *laissez-passer* issued by Son Ngoc Thanh, had stated that the arms were destined for Vietnamese workers on Cambodia's rubber plantations: *La Liberté*, 27 March 1952. For a slightly different version, see Pierre Christian, "Son Ngoc Thanh", *Indochine-Sud-Est Asiatique* (July 1952), p. 48. The possibility that these reports were "planted" by French authorities should not be discounted but they make sense in the context of Thanh's behavior in September 1945.

CAMBODIAN ROYAL CHRONICLES (*RAJABANGSAVATAR*), 1927–1949: KINGSHIP AND HISTORIOGRAPHY AT THE END OF THE COLONIAL ERA

The chronicle histories (*bangsavatar*) of King Sisowath Monivong (r. 1927–1941) and of his grandson, King Norodom Sihanouk (r. 1941–1955, the chronicle stops at the end of 1949),[1] are the last examples of a venerable Cambodian genre derived from the tradition of royal chronicles (*phraratchaphongsawadan*) in Thailand.[2]
The manuscripts are of very different lengths. Monivong's takes 132 pages to cover fourteen years, while Sihanouk's uses over 800 pages to deal with nine. This difference reflects changes in what it was thought proper for a *bangsavatar* to include – Sihanouk's chronicle contains decrees and speeches, for example, while Monivong's does not[3] – as well as a change of style from

---

In revising this paper for publication, I benefited from discussions with Barbara and Leonard Andaya, David Marr and Craig Reynolds.

This paper was first published in *Perceptions of the Past in South East Asia*, 1981.

[1] The chronicles, entitled *Rajabangsavatar brah Sisowath Monivong* (hereafter RSM) and *Rajabangsavatar brah Norodom Sihanouk* (hereafter *RNS*) were photographed in Phnom Penh by the Centre for East Asian Studies in Tokyo and are available on microfilm.

[2] For a discussion of this tradition, see D. Wyatt, 'Chronicle Traditions in Thai Historiography' in C.D. Cowan and O.W. Wolters (eds.), *Southeast Asian History and Historiography: Essays presented to D.G.E. Hall*, (Ithaca: Cornell U.P., 1975); Charnvit Kasetsiri, The Rise of Ayudhya, (Oxford, O.U.P., 1975).

[3] On the parameters of the genre at this time, see my 'Duties of the Corps of Royal scribes: an undated Khmer Manuscript from the Colonial Era', above p. 159.

that of a sixty-five year old brigadier in the French Army *en retraite* (as Monivong was when he died) to an eighteen year old boy. More importantly, the expansion of the format reflects changes in the ideology of kingship, forced on the French by the pressures of World War II, and thus in the way that people in the palace, including Sihanouk, came to view this institution, and its role in Cambodia's past.[4]

Monivong's chronicle is the only Cambodian account we have of his reign. Writing history has never been as honored or as popular in Cambodia as in Thailand or Vietnam, but there is evidence that the number of *bangsavatar* in circulation fell sharply with the institutionalization of French control, after the death of King Norodom (r. 1860–1904). Before that time, as Professor Cœdès has shown,[5] copies and versions of *rajabangsavatar* were to be found not only in the palace, but also in monastic libraries throughout the kingdom.

With Norodom's death and, ironically, the advent of printing in Khmer, manuscripts of *rajabangsavatar* no longer circulated outside the environs of the palace, no *bangsavatar* with a provincial focus appear to have been written, and no edition of the chronicles was published in Khmer.[6] These developments contrast sharply with the flowering of historiography in the same period in Thailand and Vietnam.[7] To compound the irony, the years 1927–1949, which lacked local historians, accessible texts and indigenous students of history were ones in which French scholars were successfully reconstructing Cambodia's past, at

---

[4] The view of the past outside the palace was quite different, with less emphasis on kingship, and more on rebellious (or loyal) rural heroes. See, for example, Anonymous, *Roieṅ robalkhsat sruk khmaer* (Phnom Penh, 1958) drawn from a manuscript in verse dating from 1869–1870.

[5] G. Cœdès, 'Essai du classification des documents historiques cambodgiens conservés a la bibliothèque de l'EFEO', *BEFEO*, XVIII, ix (1918), pp. 15–28.

[6] Eng Sut (comp.) *Akkasar mahaboros khmaer* (Phnom Penh, 1969) was followed by Dik Keam (ed.), *Bangsavatar khmaer: sastra sluk rut vat Setbur* (Phnom Penh, 1975). Eng Sut's chronicle ends with Norodom's death, and Dik Keam's in 1860. In the colonial era, a severely truncated version was F. Poulichet (ed.), *Histoire du Cambodge* (Phnom Penh, 1935).

[7] See K. Breazeale, 'A Transition in Thai Historical Writing', *JSS*, 59, ii (1971), pp. 25–50.

Angkor and elsewhere, as a small part of what one of them has called the 'monologue' of colonialism.[8] In the colonial period, then, it seems that foreigners took more interest in Cambodia's history than the Cambodians did themselves. This inertia stemmed from the private nature of the genre, a lack of interest in history as a literary form, the limited audience for secular books, the French orientation of Cambodian schools, and perhaps from the colonial situation itself.

With this in mind, it is not surprising that Monivong's chronicle is uneventful and pro-French. This is less a result of censorship after the fact than censorship beforehand stemming from Monivong's own fondness for the French, from obvious constraints against his speaking out, and from the fact that palace affairs, including the compilation of *bangsavatar*, were throughout his reign in the hands of a powerful pro-French official named Tiounn.[9] But would the format be very different had it been compiled, in 1941, in an independent kingdom? Probably not, for the traditions of the genre favored a flat recital of events, the suppression of 'voices' and the accurate recording of the ceremonial actions of the king. Monivong's *bangsavatar* is repetitive and dry, but this reflects the character of the genre at that stage in its development rather than colonial restraints upon it. Pre-colonial *bangsavatar* are also repetitive and flat, partly because they record the performance each year of rituals sponsored by the king which were thought to assure the well-being of the kingdom and to enhance the king's own fund of merit. The monarch's merit in the eyes of his subjects was linked to his ceremonial life which was geared to calendars maintained within the palace.[10] In ceremonial terms, the king brought the year to life, and the *bangsavatar* records his doing so. The details

---

[8] Paul Mus, *Le destin de l'Union Française* (Paris 1954), p. 53.

[9] On Tiounn, see RSM, p. 64; M. Osborne, *The French Presence in Cochinchina and Cambodia: Rule and Response* (1859–1905) (Ithaca, 1969), p. 241.

[10] In form, the *bangsavatar* resembles the classical Chinese 'Diaries Activity and Repose' (*chi' chu chu*) compiled during an emperor's reign and later absorbed into the dynastic annals. See Lien-Sheng Yang, 'The Organization of Official Chinese Historiography', in W.G. Beasley and E.G. Pulleyblank (eds.),

of timing are important; there is little that can be heightened or foreshortened in a posthumous account, and certainly no dates can be omitted. 'Dullness' in a sense, is what the chroniclers were trying to convey; they saw the past as something that repeats itself; the alternative was chaos. The question then arises: convey to whom? And the answers would seem to be: to nobody, to posterity, to themselves. Historians outside the palace were not meant to read the chronicles, and neither was the general public. The *bangsavatar*, unlike the hikayat, were not written for recital or to entertain. In the case of Monivong's chronicle, the primary purpose of the original text was probably to form part of his regalia after he was dead; the break in Sihanouk's chronicle while he was still alive and the recopying of both texts in 1949 is impossible to explain.[11]

Monivong's chronicle is austere. The king's words are never quoted directly, and we learn nothing of his reaction to events until the last pages of the chronicle, which record his grief at the French defeat in the Franco-Thai War.[12] The substance of discussions with his ministers, or with the French is not reported, and there are only three quotations from royal decrees, all relating to reforms in the Buddhist monastic order. His non-official life, beyond his sponsorship of ceremonies and his movements from place to place, is not discussed and for someone looking for intimate information or revelations about his reign, the chronicle is almost useless. Its interest lies in its traditionalist flavor – especially when placed alongside Sihanouk's *bangsavatar*, discussed below – and in the way its view of the world is tailored to meet the exigencies of the genre. These are not the exigencies of narrative *per se*. The chroniclers' perceptions of the past are

---

Historians of China and Japan (London: O.U.P., 1961), p. 45. David Marr has also suggested (personal communication) that the genre resembles the remembrance books maintained by some Western parents for each of their young children.

[11] The office of royal scribes, however, was still in existence 1971 and chronicles were compiled there until 1966 (Kin Sok, personal communication). This is in sharp contrast to its counterpart in Thailand, which appears to have been phased out after the death of King Rama V (Chulalongkorn) in 1910 (M.R. Prudhisan Jumbala, personal communication).

[12] RSM, pp. 131–2.

contained in a dynastic model, although the *bangsavatar* by definition looks at Monivong's reign as a whole, it does so by recopying the raw data of his reign, in the order that events occurred, and never strays for insights outside the limits of the reign.

A large part of the chronicle, then, describes ceremonies performed or sponsored by the king. These included those connected with agriculture and reverence for ancestors, that punctuated the Cambodian year,[13] ceremonies associated specifically with Buddhism and others connected with Monivong's travels, or with the reception of visitors to his court. In each case, the *bangsavatar* gives the date, using at least two calendrical styles of notation, the time of day, the costumes prescribed for officials, the gifts exchanged with visitors, and, in the case of a coronation or a funeral, the order of march. The specific prayers or speeches recited at a ceremony are omitted and so are personal descriptions.

We hear Monivong's voice, in indirect quotation, only twice. The first time is in July 1933, when he travelled by car with French and Cambodian officials to several provinces giving talks to local farmers, urging them to work hard, save their money and pay their debts to the Chinese. The second occasion was in 1935, when he spoke at the consecration of a Buddhist *wat*, and urged the monks to avoid splitting into rival sects.

Inside the palace, the chronicle records such things as royal births and deaths, the promotion and retirement of concubines and high officials, changes in working hours, wages and official costumes, and the arrival of the king's French automobile (an Arjudat in transliteration) valued at 10,000 *riel*. It also reports the king's sponsorship of particular *wat*, his trips inside the kingdom and improvement to his two estates.

Outside this range, the world is dimly drawn. The chronicle mentions French public works, such as Monivong bridge, the railway to Battambang and the central market in Phnom

---

[13] See E. Porée-Maspéro (ed.), *Cérémonies des douze mois* (Phnom Penh, [1952]); and my 'Duties', note 6.

Penh; the inauguration of Cambodia's first *Lycée*, named after Monivong's father in 1935; an agricultural fair in the same year; and the invention by a French mechanic, near the central market, of a bicyclepowered rickshaw, or *cyclopousse*. In the provinces, which are usually mentioned only in connection with royal visits, there are two reports of malfeasance by Cambodian officials, later pardoned by the king. Eclipses and poor harvests are also noted.[14] At the national level, we learn of the appointment of each French *résident supérieur*, but no information about these men is supplied, and the only activities that are mentioned are their official encounters with the king. The chronicle is silent, too, about events in other parts of Indo-China, or indeed anywhere in Asia except Thailand, which is the subject of several entries, including a full-page report using royal language where appropriate on the anti-monarchic *coup* in Bangkok in 1932. As for events in the rest of the world, the *bangsavatar* mentions the assassination of the French president, Paul Doumer, referring to him as 'Mr. Republic, the King of France'; the accidental death of King Albert of Belgium; and the early stages of World War II, where Pétain's terms of surrender to the Germans occupy two pages. The Ethiopian War is mentioned, but not the war in Spain.

The chronicle closes with a terse account of the Franco-Thai War of 1940–1941 that blames the French defeat on a shortage of military aircraft. According to Sihanouk, the war broke his grandfather's will to live,[15] and while the chronicle records that he 'said nothing' about it, a French official later asserted that in the closing months of Monivong's reign the monarch refused to speak French.[16] He died in April 1941, and the French chose his daughter's son, over several other candidates, to take his place.[17]

[14] RSM, 67 and 87. These entries suggest a royal connection with the energies of the soil; none existed, apparently between the king and the kingdom's commercial well-being.

[15] Norodom Sihanouk, 'L'oeuvre de sa Majesté Monivong', *Realités cambodgiennes* (16 August 1958), p. 7.

[16] Decoux, p. 284.

[17] See M. Osborne, 'Kingmaking in Cambodia, Sisowath to Sihanouk', *JSEAS*, 3, iii (1973), pp. 169–85, which discusses rivalries between the Sisowath and Norodom branches of the royal family.

Like the dog in the Sherlock Holmes story that 'did nothing in the night-time', the omissions in Monivong's chronicle are as significant as what is included. The absence of the king's voice has already been mentioned; so has the absence of an audience. Controversy is also left out, although we know from other sources that the French community in Cambodia was faction-ridden,[18] as were segments of the Buddhist clergy;[19] the Cao Dai religion caused serious problems, too.[20] The chronicle says nothing about social friction in the kingdom, or about demography, and its treatment of economic issues is limited to recording changes in *sala*ry for Khmer officials and the circulation of new coins or paper money. Although the administrative aspects of Buddhism are often stressed, Cambodia's cultural life, in which Monivong took a great interest, is not mentioned. The most useful conclusion we can draw from the chronicle is that it was viewed upon completion as a religious object, useful in ceremonies honouring Monivong's reign and the dynasty as a whole. This would explain the fastidiousness about dating events and why the recurrent, role-enhancing and merit-making aspects of the king's life – such as his patronage of Buddhism, for example, or his gifts to French officials – are stressed at the expense of what was mundane, 'political' and idiosyncratic (such as his annual grant of opium, for example, from the French authorities).[21] In this way, Monivong's *bangsavatar* fits into a widespread Southeast

[18] Cf. the vitriolic campaign carried out against *résident supérieur* Silvestre, in the French language *Le Khmer* in the second half of 1936.

[19] Cf. G. Cœdès' review of Buddhist Institute's Cambodian dictionary, which discusses the infighting that delayed its publication, in *BEFEO*, XXXVIII (1938), pp. 314–31.

[20] On the Cao Dai, see Khy Phanra, 'Les origines du Caodaisme au Cambodge (1926–1940)' *Mondes Asiatiques* (Autumn 1975), pp. 315–48.

[21] The grant was abolished at the beginning of Sihanouk's reign (see below, note 24). Under Sisowath the opium was presented annually as a new year's gift to the king by the *résident supérieur*. See H. Franck, *East of Siam* (New York, 1926), p. 24.

Asian tradition and into perceptions of the past that this tradition implies.

Monivong's chronicle is incomplete, uninteresting and biased, but the flavor of the period which it imparts is not necessarily false. The unruffled surface of the text (and its lack of depth) matches French accounts of 'peaceable' Cambodia at this time, and reinforces a colonial official's statement in 1936 that Monivong had kept the political 'health' of his kingdom 'intact'.[22] Put another way, as it was by a nationalist writing in 1945, this meant that Cambodians were 'unconscious' or 'asleep' for most of the colonial era – for the portion of it, in fact, when writing history was out of fashion.[23] There were economic and social changes in Monivong's reign that helped to pave the way for Cambodian nationalists in the 1940s, and persistent inequalities that led some Cambodians to Marxism but the *histoire evénémentiel* of Monivong's era has not, so far, tempted Cambodian writers.

Sihanouk's chronicle, on the other hand, like Sihanouk himself, is a rich if erratic primary source that maintains a royal focus while widening its parameters to include the text of speeches by the King and others, newspaper clippings, legends and decrees. For our purposes, the chronicle can be broken into three parts: 1941–1945 (133–492); March-September 1945 (493–552) and 1945–1949 (553–929) which saw the return of the French, negotiations for independence and, inside Cambodia, the growth of political parties. In this last period, which has been studied by V.M. Reddi and Philippe Preschez,[24] the day-to-day format of the *bangsavatar* collapses and long sections of the text read as if they have been transferred *verbatim* from the press. For these reasons, I will

---

[22] *Le Khmer*, 4 January 1936. The full sentence is: 'Aussi bien la situation de votre royaume reste-t-elle tout à fait satisfaisante: santé politique intacte, libre acceptation des disciplines nécessaires, courageuse résistance à une crise economique grave . . .'.

[23] *RNS*, p. 494. See H. de Grauclade, Le Reveil du Peuple Khmer (Hanoi, 1935).

[24] P. Preschez, *Essai sur la démocratie au Cambodge* (Paris, 1961); and V.M. Reddi, *A History of the Cambodian Independence Movement* (Tirupati, 1970).

concentrate on the period 1941–1945, which saw at least two reassessments, one by the French and the second by the Khmer – of both kingship and historiography.

With Monivong's death, the French moved swiftly to reassert their hegemony in Cambodia. They did so to meet unprecedented threats stemming from events in Europe, their military defeat by the Thai, Japanese occupation, and increasing anti-French feeling among Cambodia's elite. The method they chose was to conclude a protocol with Sihanouk raising his allowance, broadening his powers and encouraging him to introduce reforms.[25] Over the next four years, the French 'unleashed' the young king under close supervision, allowing him far greater visibility among his people than previous monarchs had enjoyed, and encouraging him to give speeches and to take an active role in the mobilization of Cambodian youth. These developments and the retirement of Tiounn in August 1941 changed the format and style of the *bangsavatar* and also the relationship between the king and various segments of Khmer society.

In favoring and manipulating Sihanouk, the French helped to discredit him with the two groups who were opposed to their control – the Buddhist clergy and the bureaucratic elite – who made up the readership of the faintly nationalistic newspaper *Nagara Vatta* ('Angkor Wat', 1936–1942).[26] After isolating Sihanouk from these groups, the French encouraged him to reach out, behind the elite, to the 'non-politicized' segments of the society, especially peasants and students. The rift between the king and the *Nagara Vatta* group widened after 1942 when

[25] Decoux, pp. 287–8, fails to mention this agreement, a copy of which was in the Royal Palace in Phnom Penh in June 1971, and also in the Bibliothèque Nationale in Paris. The convention raised salaries of palace officials and of Sihanouk's immediate family, abolished the royal opium allowance, and promised to build Sihanouk a villa at Bokor. The agreement is not mentioned in the *bangsavatar* discussion of Decoux's visit (*RNS*, pp. 138–9) which states, however, that Decoux gave Sihanouk an automobile at this time worth 22,000 *riel*.

[26] For a discussion of this periodical, which deserves systematic attention, see Bunchhan Mul, *Kuk Niyobay* (Phnom Penh, 1971), pp. 10–26.

the paper's editor was arrested, narrowed briefly in 1945 when Cambodia was independent, and widened again through the 1950s and 1960s; in fact, several members of the group, like Son Ngoc Thanh and Pach Chhoeun, were active in deposing Sihanouk from power. In the early 1940s, Sihanouk's increasing visibility changed him, in the eyes of his people (hardly any of whom had ever seen a king before), into a political figure as well as a ceremonial one.

The change in style from one reign to the next is noticeable from the early pages of the *bangsavatar*, where Sihanouk is quoted as noticing that there were 'too many people in the palace, and many of them were over-age'.[27] His cosmetic reforms to palace procedure in 1942–1943 received ample coverage, and so did his frequent trips to the provinces and elsewhere in French Indo-China. On many of these trips he was called upon to speak and his words were recorded both in the *bangsavatar* and in the press. The royal focus of the chronicle tends to block out foreign news, but the greater detail shows Sihanouk to have been both more manipulated and more politicized than his grandfather had been. The chronicle records, for example, his honoring a jar of soil brought from the two provinces ceded to Thailand in 1941; ordering civil servants to desist from smoking opium; and eliminating Vietnamese and Thai toponyms from the Cambodian countryside, and substituting ones in Khmer. The chronicle also records Sihanouk's attendance at lectures on Cambodian history, given by French historians; the foundation of the *Commission des Moeurs et Coutumes Cambodgiens* (CMCC), a body set up to record and conserve Cambodia's folk heritage; and an extraordinary trip, by elephant, that took Sihanouk and some French and Khmer companions from Pursat to the Gulf of Siam. In 1943 a Cambodian literary contest was held, with the first prize named after the governor general, Admiral Decoux, and the others after Sihanouk and the Angkorean monarch, Jayavarman VII. The

[27] *RNS*, p. 150.

chronicle also discusses the legendary origin of several royal ceremonies, when noting that they took place.

Even with this widened focus, the chronicle is still royal and chronological, recording little about social change, war, or the economy. The expansion of Sihanouk's activities was part of an extension of French control – for Sihanouk always travelled with French officials, and always spoke in support of French policies – rather than a change in the way Cambodia, France or the past was looked at from the palace. The policy of mobilizing the non-politicized segments of the society (into youth groups, for example) may have worked against the French in the long run. In the early 1940s, however, with one important exception, the French policy of using Sihanouk to maintain and embody the *status quo* was a success.

The exception was the monks' demonstration of 20 July 1942.[28] On this occasion less than a thousand people, perhaps half of them members of the *sangha*, demonstrated against the arrest of two Buddhist monks who were accused of preaching anti-French sermons to the Cambodian militia. The demonstrators assembled at the headquarters of the *résident supérieur* after a peaceful march through the city led by the editor of *Nagara Vatta*, Pach Chhoeun. Despite its size, the French had little trouble in dispersing the demonstration and over the next few weeks they arrested the civilians who had been involved. The two monks, one of whom died in prison, were treated as martyrs by Cambodian nationalists in 1945 and again in 1971 when the anniversary of the demonstration was celebrated. The demonstration, in fact, was the only one of its size between the so-called peasant demonstrations of 1916 and Cambodian independence.[29] Its importance for our purposes is that it is not mentioned in the 1942 portion of the chronicle, but in retrospect from the summer

---

[28] On the demonstration, see Fillieux, p. 166; Bunchhan Mul, pp. 44–50, and Reddi, pp. 85–86.

[29] See M. Osborne, 'Peasant Politics in Cambodia: the 1916 Affair', *Modern Asian Studies*, XII, ii (1978), pp. 217–43.

of 1945. In the 'Sihanouk years' (1946–1969) the demonstration was pointedly ignored.[30]

Until early 1945, when Phnom Penh was bombed twice by Allied aircraft, there are very few references to World War II in the chronicle. Most of its pages are taken up with accounts of Sihanouk's travels and especially with his role as the patron of Cambodian sport. Tours by the *résident* and by some of Sihanouk's close advisers are also noted. The Romanization crisis of 1943–1944, in which the *résident supérieur*, Gautier, sought to change the Cambodian writing system, is mentioned in passing, but Sihanouk's unhappiness with the proposal (a view he shared with the *sangha*) is not.[31]

During this period the chronicle, like the Cambodian-language press, often stressed Cambodia's past greatness, and continuities between Angkor and the present. But history was not seen in terms of struggle, or of stages, and the colonial era, still in full swing, was not seen as a phase of Cambodian history worth examining by itself.

This aspect of Cambodian historiography, like much else in the kingdom, changed dramatically in March 1945 when the Japanese interned or imprisoned the French throughout Indo-China, and informed the chiefs of state of the region that they were independent.[32] The next few months were feverish ones from the standpoint of Cambodian nationalism, as they were in other parts of Southeast Asia. The *bangsavatar* for this period is a valuable primary source, especially since others, like the French-language *Cambodge*, are no longer accessible.[33]

---

[30] *RNS*, p. 493. For Sihanouk's disingenuous recollections, see his *L'Indochine vue de Pekin* (Paris: Seuil, [1972]), 42, where he refers to the demonstration as 'tragi-comic'.

[31] *RNS*, p. 293; Sihanouk, *L'Indochine vue de Pekin*, 38–9. The pro-French newspaper *Kambuja* carried some romanized columns in 1943–1944, but these never occupied a major part of the paper. Gautier's reforms were abrogated in the summer of 1945, and romanization was never reimposed.

[32] Reddi, 87–8; Decoux, pp. 325–7.

The most interesting entries are those that describe the ceremony celebrating the monks' demonstration, described above, and an anonymous essay entitled 'New Policies of the Cambodian State' that appears among the entries for July 1945.[34] In these entries and in the newspaper Cambodge (where the anonymous essay may have appeared originally in French) the colonial era, now thought to be over, was discussed for the first time as an era, and Cambodian historiography was revised to stress anti-French activities among the people rather than continuities in kingship and folk culture. If the Cambodians had been 'unconscious' under the French, the essayist complains, this was because the French stressed their own values, culture and language, rather than Cambodian ones, in the government and in the schools: someone who was fluent only in Khmer, he said, was 'not the equal of a French dog'.

But what were 'Cambodian' values, and what was 'Cambodian' history? The writers of 1945 had little training in approaching questions of this kind, since so much of their literature and schooling stressed obedience, hierarchies, conservatism and continuity. In attacking the colonial regime, however, the writers of 1945 turned to the tradition of popular rebellion against the French and earlier against the Vietnamese and the Thai, a tradition which, if not forgotten, was not officially allowed to be remembered.[35] In the 1945 entries, for the first time in a colonial *bangsavatar*, these confrontations are openly discussed, and the activities of young intellectuals in the 1940s are placed in the context of the anti-monarchic rebellions of 1860 and 1866, the anti-French revolt of 1884–1885, the demonstrations of 1916, the

---

[33] Reddi, pp. 91–101, has some excellent quotations from *Cambodge*, which he consulted during his research in Cambodia in the 1950s. Copies from this period are no longer (1996) available in Phnom Penh.

[34] *RNS*, pp. 494–5, 546–7.

[35] For discussions of this undercurrent in Cambodian life, see C. Meyer, *Derrière le sourire khmer* (Paris: Plon, 1971), 32–43; A.S. Rolland, 'Les pirates au Cambodge' *BSEI*, XXV (1950), pp. 427–37; and my 'An anti-Vietnamese rebellion in early nineteenth century Cambodia: precolonial imperialism and a pre-nationalist response, above, pp. 61–75.

so-called Bardez Incident of 1925 (placed, in this account, for symmetry, in Monivong's reign) and the monks' demonstration of 1942.[36] Seen in this way, Cambodian history was history with the kings left out, a sequence of assaults by recognizable heroes on those in power. Unsurprisingly, this version of the past was set aside after the French returned to Cambodia in October 1945, and it was not revived officially until the early 1970s, when, predictably perhaps, the historiography of the summer of 1945 was repeated rather than enlarged.[37]

The inclusion of such material in a royal chronicle shows how far the genre had come since Monivong's death in 1941. Over the next few years, the chronicle became once again primarily a record of the king's activities, culminating in France's *de jure* recognition of Cambodian independence.[38] These years also saw the French gradually loosen their control over Sihanouk and his generally pro-French entourage, until he was able to say (and perhaps believe) that independence was something he had won rather than something he had been given. The *bangsavatar* records Sihanouk's trips, celebrations and speeches along with the ups and downs of Cambodia's faltering parliamentary government. The focus, as always, is on the person of the king, although the rules about what can be included in the text have loosened a good

---

[36] See Osborne, *The French Presence*, pp. 206–30; and *idem*, 'Peasant Politics'. The Bardez Incident involved the murder of a French official of that name by villagers from whom he was collecting taxes. See "The Assassination of Résident Bardez" above p. 139.

[37] By 1970, of course, forbidden historiography became that with a Marxist viewpoint: this gives the anti-colonial literature published during the Lon Nol regime, which inherits the historiography of 1945, a curiously dated quality. The tradition flourished, however, in the Communist-oriented Issarak movement in the early 1950s. See, for example, *United States Foreign Broadcasting Service (FBIS) Daily Report*, 2 March 1951, which lists 'heroes' of the resistance, and *FBIS Daily Report* 28 November 1951, which carries a translation of a speech by the Issarak leader, 'Son Ngoc Minh' stressing the continuities between anti-royal and anti-French rebellions.

[38] *RNS*, p. 928ff. This independence was lightly won; see Anonymous, *Le Cambodge Moderne* (Phnom Penh, 1950) p. 46, which notes benignly that Cambodia's 'national sentiment is unaccompanied by any xenophobia'.

deal. The text closes as we have seen with Sihanouk still alive and on the throne.

We know too little about the sociology of rural Cambodia in the colonial era or about the elite to say how (or if) the transformation of royal politics, recorded in these two *bangsavatar*, affected people's lives or changed their own ideas. But I suspect that an unrelieved royal focus is not especially helpful if we want to write *A History* of Cambodia from 1927 to 1949, or if we are to generalize from the vantage point of 1976 about Cambodian perceptions of the past. Sihanouk's own periodization of Cambodian history in the years 1941–1970 as 'pre-Sihanouk' 'Sihanouk', and 'post-Sihanouk'[39] can be discounted. What characterized these years, and to an extent probably earlier ones as well, was not just the activities of the king but also a far-reaching and perhaps statistically inaccessible set of social, economic and ideological changes (not necessarily consonant with 'modernization') which broke to the surface in *Nagara Vatta*, anti-French and anti-Sihanouk rebellions, in the *coup* of 1970, and the savage destruction wreaked by both sides (and above all by the United States) in Cambodia's civil war. Some of the roots of the Cambodian revolution are to be found in this period. Sooner or later the incumbent regime will develop its own historiography, using sources like the *bangsavatar* and others, to write 'Cambodian' history – that is, history with the kings left out – which the writers of 1945 were hinting at: they will do this because, in Bernard Lewis' words, 'a new future [requires] a different past'.[40]

---

[39] Sihanouk, *L'Indochine vue de Pekin*, p. 37.

[40] B. Lewis, *History: Remembered, Recovered,* Invented (Princeton: Princeton U.P., 1975). Looking back at this sentence in 1996, I'm embarrassed by its glibness and shamed by its misconstruction of what was happening in Cambodia in 1976. I recall Hemuth Loofs quite correctly taking me to task for writing it, but I recall paying no real attention to what he said.

PART IV

CAMBODIA SINCE 1975

I began writing about the Khmer Rouge in 1976, over a year after the evacuation of Phnom Penh. The essay "Transformation in Cambodia", published in April, 1977, was written six months earlier. I see now that it was a naive, unduly optimistic assessment of the Cambodian revolution. I've included it here because it reflects views that were widely held in "anti-anti-Communist" academic circles in the backwash of the Vietnam War and because I think it gives a picture of the first year of the Pol Pot era, in view of the narrow range of sources available at the time.

In July 1981, the SSRC organized a workshop in Chiang Mai, Thailand, dealing with the revolution in Cambodia and its aftermath. Soon afterwards, I visited Phnom Penh for three days – my first time in the city since 1971. Papers from the workshop were later collected in a volume, along with some supple-mentary ones, including my essay "Seeing Red" which was written in 1982, at about the same time as "A Revolution in Full Spate" and "Revising the Past in Democratic Kampuchea". "A Revolution in Full Spate" was prepared for an international conference on Cambodia at the Woodrow Wilson School of International Affairs at Princeton University, organized by two intrepid undergraduates, Marlowe Hood and the late David Ablin.

The final essay in this section was written in Bangkok in November 1984, after I had spent three weeks in refugee camps along the Thai-Cambodia border as a consultant to the United Nations, interviewing over 200 survivors of the Khmer Rouge. The interviews convinced me that my next project should be a book length study of Cambodia's history between 1945 and 1979. A by-product of my work on that book, published in 1991 as *The Tragedy of Cambodian History*, followed by my biography of Pol Pot, *Brother Number One* (1992) was that for several years I wrote no scholarly papers.

TRANSFORMATION IN CAMBODIA

"Two thousand years of Cambodian history have virtually ended."

– Phnom Penh Radio, January 1976

Since the liberation or Phnom Penh and Battambang in April 1975, the former Buddhist kingdom of Cambodia, which had weathered two thousand years of recorded history, a century of French control, several years of American bombing and perhaps five centuries (c. 800–1400) of grandeur, has transformed itself into what seems to be the most radically altered country in the world.

The transformation affects every aspect of Cambodian life. The country is no longer a kingdom and Buddhism is no longer the state religion. The regime – which calls itself Democratic Kampuchea, but is known to most of its people as *angkar*, "the organization" – has moved millions of people out of towns and cities onto rural work-sites, in a process aimed at increasing agricultural production, fostering self-reliance and destroying what it calls the "old society." Money is no longer used. Shops, schools and monasteries are closed. Transportation and property have been collectivized. There is no postal service. Western medicines are not prescribed and the Cambodian language has

This paper was first published in *Commonweal*, April 1, 1977, reprinted with permission.

been overhauled to root out foreign words. The population, officially a blend of workers, peasants, and the revolutionary army," dresses in black cotton pyjamas traditionally worn at work by poor Cambodian peasants. Gambling, drinking, polygamy and extramarital sex are frowned upon or worse; people who had called each other in the past, "Sir", "Brother" and "Uncle" – to name only three Cambodian pronouns" – must now address each other as "friend."

Political leadership has been collectivized, too, in contrast to the personalized rule of Prince Sihanouk (1941–1970) and the befuddled dictatorship of Field Marshal Lon Nol, whose Khmer Republic (1970–1975) was called (by Nixon) a "model of Nixon Doctrine." The "old society" is seen as foreign, unequal, exploitative and corrupt. Its habits, hierarchies and economic relations have been swept aside.

What has taken their place? Is the revolution a "Cambodian" one? What are its roots, ideology, tactics and plans?

Nearly all the information we have comes from refugees or from officials of the regime. Cambodians who are happy with the revolution are inside Cambodia, but there is no way of hearing their opinions. Refugees, on the other hand, have by definition run away. Another problem with their testimony is that so many of them have escaped from northwestern Cambodia, where radical politics before liberation were weak, rural class differences especially pronounced, and agricultural production higher than elsewhere in the country. For these reasons, the liberating forces there seem to have been especially vengeful and undisciplined. Stories about harsh conditions and atrocities come largely from this part of the country. But information on this point is ambiguous. The lack of refugees from other regions could mean that conditions there are better than in the northwest, or merely that the Thai border is too far away to reach on foot. Other refugees have gone to Vietnam; Cambodian officials told a Swedish diplomat early in 1976 that these included the entire

Vietnamese population of Cambodia – perhaps 150,000 people – but unlike refugees in Thailand, they are inaccessible to outsiders.

Peasants have been "outside history" for many years. Cambodian records compiled before the arrival of the French in 1863 were written by and for the literate elite and reflect their values. This means that we know very little, in quantitative or political terms about the mass of Cambodian society, many of whom for most of their history appear to have been slaves of one sort or another. The frequency of locally-led rebellions in the nineteenth century – against the Thai, the Vietnamese, the French and local officials – suggests that Cambodian peasants were not as peaceable as their own mythology, reinforced by the French, would lead us to believe. To understand their picture of the world, we should remember that for the first thousand years or so of the Christian era, Cambodians were heavily influenced by India, which gave them an alphabet, a court language, art-styles, two religions (Hinduism and Buddhism) and a fairly rigid sense of social hierarchies. In isolated villages – especially after the abandonment of Cambodia's great capital, at Angkor, in the fifteenth century – Cambodian peasant-slaves, harassed at will by people in authority, developed little sense of community or strength. The word for "to govern" an area was the same as the word "to consume." As in India, language and behavior were oriented toward difference in status. The hope of reincarnation in Buddhism was to improve one's place; conversely, power, however ruthlessly applied, was taken as proof of meritorious behavior – in another life.

How did this legacy affect peasants in the colonial era? The French were not drawn to this kind of question, preferring to reconstruct Cambodia's ancient temples, nurture a small elite, and modernize the economy to provide surpluses of rice and rubber. Scholars know little of what actually went on. Did old elites break down, persist, or reappear? What happened to rural attitudes towards authority and success? Did families grow more or less cohesive? What were the effect of monetization, schooling and printed books? I put these questions to show how shaky our knowledge of Cambodian rural history often is. The same is true of the early independence period (1953–1970), the so-called "Sihanouk years." The Prince himself occupies the foreground, obscuring such important things as Cambodia's population boom, poorly planned mass education, the "revolution of rising expectations" and the effects on daily life of the Vietnamese civil war. To understand why so many Cambodians chose revolution in the 1970s, we need to know more about patterns of land ownership, malnutrition and indebtedness in the 1950s and 1960s, as well as the growth of personal fortunes and corruption among the Phnom Penh elite; U.S. bombing patterns, after 1969; and the ideology of Cambodia's students, including those who went abroad.

The ideology of Democratic Kampuchea draws its strength and wording from Marxism-Leninism especially as acted out in China without formally acknowledging the debt. Many leaders of the regime have Marxist pasts, some going back to the 1940s, when several thousand Cambodians – especially among those living in or near Vietnam – cast their lot in the war against the French with the Communist Viet-Minh. After the Geneva Conference of 1954, when France withdrew from Indochina, an estimated 2,000 of these men and women chose to go to North Vietnam rather than live under Sihanouk or Ngo Dinh Diem. Leftists who stayed in Cambodia and formed a People's Party were ruthlessly suppressed by Sihanouk and his police. Others went underground, especially in the mountainous southwest. Meanwhile, in the 1950s and 1960s, a younger generation of Marxists, including many Cambodians trained abroad or by French Marxists teaching in Cambodia, came of age and challenged Sihanouk's "Buddhist Socialist" regime. These "young intellectuals," or "Khmer Rouge," as Sihanouk called them, included many men who became leaders in Democratic Kampuchea – Pol Pot, Khieu Samphan, Hu Nim, Son Sen and Ieng Sary, to name only five.

In the late 1960s, the two strands of Cambodian radicalism – old Viet Minh and young intellectuals – merged. At the height of the Vietnam war, many intellectuals fled to remote parts of the kingdom to escape Sihanouk's police and to revolutionize their countrymen along Maoist lines. The northeastern part of the kingdom, already a base and corridor for Vietnamese liberation forces, was occupied by the Khmer Rouge fairly early probably with Vietnamese help. By 1971 after Sihanouk had been toppled by a rightist *coup* the Khmer Rouge occupied roughly two-thirds of Cambodia's territory and controlled perhaps half its population. The youngest and poorest segments of society, it seems, responded enthusiastically to the revolution. Those who disliked it fled, if they could, to government zones, swelling the population of Phnom Penh to some two million people. Others were "re-educated," or killed as American bombing – one of Dr. Kissinger's "bargaining chips" – and the violence of the civil war forced everyone in Cambodia to take sides.

In 1973, after the Paris Agreements, Vietnamese influence over the Khmer Rouge diminished. This development reduced Prince Sihanouk's freedom to maneuver, as head of an ostensibly pro-Chinese government-in-exile, and allowed the Khmer Rouge to replace pro-Sihanouk cadres with their own people as they accelerated their experiments, on Cambodian soil, with Maoist ideas of revolution. So-called "co-operative farms" (*sahakar*) were introduced in 1973. Other features of life in liberated zones included all-night political and cultural rallies, called *miting*, after the English word, in both Cambodian and Vietnamese; systematic puritanism affecting dress, hair-styles and sexual behavior; the abolition of money, badges of rank and private property; and a stress on collective leadership, ownership and self-reliance. Foreign models were played down to make the revolution seem a Cambodian one without roots in the "old society." In some areas, the process went on for several years; in others, especially those liberated late in the war, it was violent and brief.

The first months of peace in Battambang, for example, were harsh. After years of propaganda from their leaders and pummeling from U.S. and Lon Nol aircraft, Khmer Rouge soldiers, filled with what one of them called "uncontrolled hatred" took apart a pair or T-28 aircraft with their bare hands, and "would have eaten them, if possible," according to a witness. At the same time, people who held authority under Lon Nol began to disappear for "study." A morbid jingle declared that *"Khmaer krohom somlap, min del prap"* ("the Khmer Rouge kill, but never explain"). By mid-summer, however, the killings stopped, and the transformation of Cambodian rural society, in the northwest, began in earnest.

By this time, the people of Battambang and Phnom Penh – perhaps two and a half million of them – had been forcibly moved into the countryside by the revolutionary army, organized into work-teams and ordered to produce their own food. The work-teams were made up of groups of 10, 30, 100, 300 and 900 people, led at each level, except the lowest, by three workers placed in charge of "work" (the tasks at hand), "politics" (culture and morale) and "economics" (food and tools). This structure, modeled on a military ones, proved to be an effective instrument of Khmer Rouge control. Hours were long and food as scarce, although the "organization" made a point of feeding work-teams better than they fed "unproductive" people.

What was revolutionary about the process, in Cambodian terms, was the value placed on manual labor almost as an end in itself. In the "old society" peasants placed a premium on individual freedom and on leisure of an unsupervised kind. To make up for this, they are now told that they own the land and factories where they work, and even the revolution itself. Collective self-reliance or autarky, as preached by the regime, contrasts sharply with what might be called the slave mentality that suffused pre-revolutionary Cambodia and made it so "peaceful" and "charming" to the elite and to most outsiders – for perhaps two thousand years. A refugee from Battambang recalls a Khmer Rouge cadre making this point at *miting* in dramatic terms. The speech went something like this:

In the old days, the big people told us we had independence. What kind of independence was that? What had we built? Well, they built an independence monument. Where did they build it? In the capital. Who saw the thing? The big people's children. Did country people see it? No, they didn't; they saw only photos. The big people's children went in and out of Cambodia, going here and there, and then they came back, to control our kind of people. What do we do, now in contrast to all this? We don't build monuments like that. Instead, by raising embankments and digging irrigation canals, the children of Cambodia build their own independence monuments, ones that they can see and their children, too . . .

The theme of self-reliance is stressed in Cambodia's constitution, promulgated in January 1976, and derives in part from the dissertation that one of Cambodia's leaders, Khieu Samphan, wrote in France in 1959. The phrase is sometimes known as autarky, and Khieu Samphan used this word in his address to the Conference of Non-Aligned Nations held in Colombo last year. In cultural and economic terms, the word has been attacked by T.S. Eliot, used by Stalin, and defended by Mussolini. In the Cambodian case, in 1976, autarky makes sense, both in terms of recent experience – American intervention, and what is seen as the Western-induced corruption of previous regimes – and in terms of Cambodian's long history of conflict with Vietnam. Cambodians are urged daily by their radio, and four times in the constitution, "to build and defend" their country against unspecified enemies. What was wrong with the old society, these broadcasts suggest, was exploitation (literally, in Cambodian, "riding and stomping") and outsiders. Words that suggest foreign influence – such as "Communist," "socialist" or "Marxist," to name only three – do not appear in the constitution; French words are no longer used in Cambodian conversation; and the constitution condemns "so-called humanitarian" aid. Autarky is the keynote of Cambodian ideology today, and certainly explains changing "Cambodia," in English ("Cambodge" in French) to "Kampuchea," reflecting local pronunciation, as if Argentina, for foreign consumption, had changed the "g" in its name to "h."

Self-reliance also explains turning away from Cambodia's past to make a society where there are "no rich and no poor, no exploiters and no exploited," and where, in the words of the constitution, people are free to "have no religious beliefs." Instead, everyone is at work, "happily" building dams, canals and embankments to provide water from two or even three rice crops a year – an achievement unequaled since the days of Angkor. Can the regime recapture the grandeur of Angkor without duplicating the slavery (and by implication, the elite) that made Angkor what it was? Is the price for liberation, in human terms, too high? Surely, as a friend of mine has written, we Americans with our squalid record in Cambodia should be "cautiously optimistic" about the new regime, "or else shut up." At the same time, I might feel less cautious and more optimistic if I were able to hear the voices of people I knew in the Cambodian countryside fourteen years ago, telling me about the revolution in their own words.

REVISING THE PAST IN DEMOCRATIC KAMPUCHEA: WHEN WAS THE BIRTHDAY OF THE PARTY?

On September 20, 1976, Keo Meas, a veteran Cambodian Communist then working in the office of the party's central committee, was arrested by Democratic Kampuchea (DK) security personnel and taken to the regime's interrogation center at Tuol Sleng on the outskirts of Phnom Penh. For at least a month he was questioned and tortured before being put to death, along with several other communists with thirty-year histories of involvement with the Communist Party of Kampuchea (*CPK*) and its precursors. These other victims included Suan Nan (known as Chhuuk), and former Central Committee member Non Suon.[1]

While at Tuol Sleng Keo Meas was made to compose at least two confessions. One of them, twenty-two pages long, parried

---

This paper was first published in *Pacific Affairs* Vol. 56 No. 2 Summer 1983, reprinted with permission.

[1] Ben Kiernan, personal communication. Keo Meas (b. 1926) had joined the anti-French resistance soon after World War II; by 1954, he was secretary of the Phnom Penh Committee of the Khmer Peoples' Revolutionary Party (KPRP, discussed below). After Geneva, he contested national elections twice (in 1955 and 1958) and in 1960 was elected to the central committee of the Workers' Party of Kampuchea (*WPK*). He lost this position in 1963, but remained a Cambodian communist in good standing. From 1970 to 1973, he served as the Royal Government of National Union of Kampuchea ambassador in Beijing and, from 1973 to 1975, with the movement's radio station in Hanoi. Throughout his career, he was part of what Pol Pot came to see as the "pro-Vietnamese" element in Cambodian radicalism.

accusations that he had been "secretary" of a "rival party" to the *CPK*. The other, of twenty-seven pages, was entitled "1951 or 1960?" The issue at stake in this latter document, and in what follows, was the founding date of the *CPK*. The party's existence was not made public until 1977, so the controversy about its foundation was, for the time being, known only to party members.

Confidential histories of the party were circulated to members between 1971 and 1975. These traced the party's origins to the foundation of the Khmer People's Revolutionary Party (KPRP) on September 30, 1951, roughly twenty-five years before Keo Meas' arrest.[2] Indeed, the September 1976 issue of the party's youth magazine, *Yuvechon nung Yuvanearei padevat* (Revolutionary Youth) presumably printed before the arrest opened with a 16–page article celebrating this very anniversary, noting:

From the moment of its creation on September 30, 1951, the Communist Party of Kampuchea led everyone, including revolutionary Cambodian youths, in the struggle against French imperialism. In 1954, imperialism was driven from Cambodian soil.[3]

Soon afterwards, however, a "special issue" of the party's official journal, *Tung Padevat* (*Revolutionary Flags*), dated "September-October" went to press. The flyleaf depicted a Communist Party flag, as *Yuvechon* had done; but, whereas the caption under the

---

[2] For histories of Cambodian communism, see Stephen Heder, "The Historical Bases of the Kampuchea-Vietnam conflict." unpublished manuscript, May 1978; S. Heder, "Kampuchea's Armed Struggle: the Origins of an Independence Revolution." in *Bulletin of Concerned Asian Scholars*, (*BCAS*), Vol. 11, No. 1 January-March 1979), pp. 2–23; Ben Kiernan, "Origins of Khmer Communism," *Southeast Asian Affairs 1981* (Singapore: Heinemann, 1982), pp. 161–80; and Timothy Carney, *Communist Party Power in Kampuchea* (Cambodia): *Documents and Discussion*, Cornell University SEAP Data Paper 106 (Ithaca, New York: Cornell University Southeast Asia Program, 1977).

[3] *Yuvechun nung Yuvanearei padevat* (*Revolutionary Youth*), September 1976, p. 3.

flag in *Yuvechon* applauded the twenty-fifth anniversary of the
CPK, the caption in *Tung Padevat*, identical in other respects,
celebrated the party's sixteenth anniversary. The issue opened
with a 32–page article, which reads like a speech, purportedly by
a "party spokesman." Stylistically, it seems likely that the article is
by Pol Pot who was the secretary of the CPK Central Committee
at that time. The spokesman explained that the birth of the CPK
should no longer be traced to 1951, but to a meeting convened in
Phnom Penh in September 1960. The explanation ran in part as
follows:

> Last year we informed people attending the big meeting on
> September 30, 1975 that our Party was twenty-four years old.
> Previously, we had celebrated this day as the twentieth, twenty-
> first, twenty-second and twenty-third anniversaries, right up to
> the twenty-fourth. But now we celebrate the sixteenth anniversary
> of the party, because we are making a new numeration. What
> rationale is there for this? The revolutionary organization, *angkar
> padevat*, probably a euphemism for the CPK politbureau] has
> decided that from now on we must arrange the history of the
> party into something clean and perfect, in line with our policies of
> independence and self-mastery.[4]

This article will examine this decision in terms of the history of
Cambodian radicalism, as traced by Heder, Kiernan and Carney[5]
and in terms of events in September and October 1976, when
the CPK central committee made several decisions including
this one which hastened the radicalization of Cambodian life and
unwittingly brought about the collapse of the regime when the
Vietnamese invaded Cambodia in December 1978.

---

[4] *Tung Padevat* (*Revolutionary Flags*) Special Issue, September-October 1976,
p. 4.
[5] See note 2, above, and Ben Kiernan, "Conflicts in the Cambodian
Communist Movement," *Journal of Contemporary Asia*, Vol. 10. Nos. 1–2
(1980), pp. 7–74; and Carlyle Thayer, "The 'Two Lines' Conflict in the Khmer
Revolution," in Malcolm Salmon, ed., *The Vietnam-Kampuchea-China Conflicts*.
Working Paper, Department of Political and Social Change, Australian
National University, 1979, pp. 20–28.

By changing the party's birthday, Pol Pot and his colleagues were cutting themselves off from nine years of Cambodian history (1951–60) to which their own contributions had been ambiguous, subordinate or non-existent. In the anti-French struggle (1946–54), many Cambodian radicals had perceived a community of interest among themselves and their counterparts in Laos and Vietnam. By cutting the CPK loose from this perception, Pol Pot was soon able to embark, as he probably had planned to do for some time, on a full-scale war against Vietnam as well as a radical program of collectivization inside Cambodia which owed nothing to Vietnamese models or advice. A byproduct of this decision was to purge those members of the party, like Keo Meas, whom Pol Pot suspected of plotting against him, of siding with Vietnam, and of harboring nostalgia for Cambodian communism as practised in the 1950s. Systematic purges of the party's ranks began in the summer of 1976, about a month before Keo Meas' arrest. They intensified in 1977 and continued unabated up to the collapse of the regime.[6]

The foundation of the KPRP in 1951 was kept secret from the outside world. The anti-French guerrilla radio, monitored by the United States, said nothing of the event, and neither did the Vietnamese. The decision to found a separate Cambodian party appear to have followed from a decision to disband the Indochina Communist Party (ICP) founded by the Vietnamese with Comintern approval in 1930. In its place came a Workers' Party in Vietnam and Peoples' Revolutionary Parties in Cambodia and Laos.[7]

Founded with Vietnamese patronage, the KPRP, like its predecessor, contained a strong internationalist component.

[6] See Anthony Barnett, Ben Kiernan, and Chanthou Boua, "Bureaucracy of Death," *New Statesman*, 2 May 1980.

[7] See Heder, "Kampuchea's Armed Struggle," p. 1; also Ben Kiernan and Chanthou Boua, *Peasants and Politics in Kampuchea, 1942–1981* (London: Zed Books, 1982), pp. 20–1.

According to an insurgent broadcast of October 7, 1951: "The world is now developing into two camps-that of the imperialists led by the Americans, and that of democracy and peace, led by the USSR. The Cambodian people have chosen the second camp.[8] Six months later, Keo Meas himself, a delegate to the Vienna Peoples' Congress for Peace, declared in a similar vein that Cambodia was united with the "world's people" in its struggle against the French.[9]

Party histories that circulated before 1976, to be sure, stressed the provisional character of the KPRP charter, and played down the matter of Vietnamese guidance, although a 1973 history is explicit about Vietnamese co-operation with the fledgling party.[10] By 1953, the party had trained and recruited several thousand guerrillas, particularly in the eastern parts of the country bordering Vietnam. In that year, French intelligence estimated that these forces, nearly all under communist leadership, and many of them led and staffed by Vietnamese, operated freely over nearly two-thirds of Cambodia, although day-to-day control appears to have been limited to a handful of rural zones.[11] The KPRP lacked strength in the cities, where its leaders were liable to surveillance. As a political force, the party was undermined by Sihanouk's so-called "Royal Crusade," for by the end of 1953 the French had granted Cambodia the framework of independence.

Because of this, KPRP spokesmen brought along by the Vietnamese to the Geneva Conference of 1954 were not granted a hearing.[12] Cambodian communists, unlike their colleagues

---

[8] United States, *Foreign Broadcast Information Service* (*FBIS*), 12 October 1951. See also, *FBIS*, 26 October 1951: "The revolution in Cambodia has also been inspired directly by the world forces of peace and democracy, led by Russia, and by the influence of Indo-Chinese peoples."

[9] V.M. Reddi, *A History of the Cambodian Independence Movement* (Tirupati: Sri Venkateswara University, 1973), p. 196.

[10] See "Summary of annotated party history, written by the military-political service of the Eastern Zone," a U.S. government translation of a captured document now in the Echols Collection, Cornell University Library.

[11] Kiernan, "Origins of Khmer Communism," p. 177.

in Laos and Vietnam, were given no place inside their country to regroup. As a result about a thousand KPRP members and sympathizers chose to take up what they may have expected to be a short period of exile in Hanoi.[13] Nearly all of them were to remain outside Cambodia until the early 1970s.

Those who stayed behind, in the words of the party spokesman writing in *Tung Padevat*, "re-entered an era of exploiting classes and class warfare." Some of them, like Keo Meas and Saloth Sar (later to call himself Pol Pot), took the opportunity to oppose Sihanouk's newly formed *Sangkum* movement, alongside the anti-monarchic Democratic Party, in the national elections of 1955.

In retrospect it is hard to understand why these quixotic young men chose to stand up and be run over by the machinery of the state. In any event they were defeated by huge majorities in an election marked by government harassment of anti-government candidates. The 1973 history of the party shrugs off their defeat by saying: "In 1955 our party was only three years old [sic]. It lacked three things: ideologies, policies and organization."[14] The party spokesman of 1976 is somewhat less dismissive:

[In 1955] we knew that people's opinions throughout the country supported us 99 percent, but state power was in the hands of our enemies, the army and the police. The ballot boxes belonged to them. The events of 1955 taught us that we had no way of winning an election. We could only defeat the enemy by fighting a revolution.[15]

[12] Vietnamese communist support for what U.S. delegates called these "ghost regimes" of Laos and Cambodia was a lively issue at the early (Indochinese) phases of the conference. See *Foreign Relations of the United States 1952–1954*, Vol. XVI: *The Geneva Conference* (Washington, D.C.: U.S. Government Printing Office, 1981), pp. 729, 750, 782, 812, 1173.

[13] Kiernan and Boua, *Peasants and Politics*, p. 265.

[14] "Summary of annotated party history."

[15] *Tung Padevat*, September-October 1976, pp. 8–9. See also *FBIS*, 28 April 1977.

The party contested the 1958 elections too but by election day only one of its candidates, the redoubtable Keo Meas, had survived incarceration. He polled 398 votes in one district of Phnom Penh and then went underground.

In the late 1950s, then, the KPRP was without a viable strategy, without much support, and apparently without coherent guidance either from Vietnam or from hundreds of its veteran cadre, who continued to "study" in Hanoi and were all but impossible to reach.

In this context, the twenty-one KPRP delegates who met in secret on the grounds of the Phnom Penh railway station on 28–30 September 1960, were eager to find a strategy, an ideological line, and an organization which would attract support inside Cambodia and eventually from overseas. It is likely that the failure of electoral politics in 1955 and 1958 was discussed. Party histories assert that the meeting drew up statutes for a new clandestine party organization, known from other sources to have been named the Workers' Party of Kampuchea (WPK).[16] Semantically at least, the party was now on the same level as its counterpart, the Lao Dong party in Vietnam. It is unclear whether approval for the change had been sought or given in Vietnam. In any case, with its new name the party was now able (or permitted) to elect a permanent central committee, nine years to the day after the foundation of the KPRP. Saloth Sar was elected to this committee, alongside such veteran ICP-KPRP militants as Keo Meas, Nuon Chea, and the party's new secretary general, Tou Samouth.

---

[16] Ben Kiernan (personal communication). In 1977–78, the WPK surfaced in some DK documents as a rival party to the CPK, rather than a predecessor. See, for example. "Salut à la victoire de notre parti dans le liquidation des dirigeants du parti du travail cambodgien à la solde de la CIA," a document dated June 1978 presented to the "genocide" trials of Pol Pot and Ieng Sary in the People's Republic of Kampuchea (PRK) in August 1979 (Document Number 2.5.16). Keo Meas' first confession, made in early October 1976, denies that he had anything to do with such a "rival" party, and even claims that he had been "a revolutionary for over twenty-five years"; notes by an interrogator, in the margin, suggest that further "thinking" would be required before Keo Meas could earn the "forgiveness" of the Party.

The years 1961–62 culminated in the collapse of the party's open politics organization, the Pracheachon Group, which had contested the elections of 1955 and 1958. The group began to contest the 1962 elections as well, perhaps in defiance of the WPK politbureau, only to have its candidates – including central committee member Non Suon imprisoned. In July 1962, Tou Samouth himself disappeared mysteriously, dissolving an important link between the WPK and its Indochinese past. Whether this was engineered by fellow WPK members or by Sihanouk's police (or the two in combination), it worked to Saloth Sar's benefit: in February 1963, he was elected Secretary General in Samouth's place. He occupied the position for eighteen years, until the party was "disbanded" in December 1981.[17]

The 1963 election of party officials also elevated Saloth Sar's colleagues Ieng Sary and Sok Thuok (later known as Vorn Vet) at the expense of Non Suon and Keo Meas, who had sought to take part in the 1962 national elections. Soon afterwards, in July 1963, Saloth Sar and "ninety percent of the Central Committee" fled to eastern Cambodia cutting themselves off from urban elements of the party, from a good deal of its rural rank and file and from Sihanouk's police. Their flight apparently escaped Sihanouk's attention. As Ben Kiernan has suggested, he seems to have been unaware, throughout the 1960s, of changes in the leadership and ideology of the Cambodian communist movement. Instead, he retained the impression that the "Khmer Viet Minh," as he had styled the KPRP, retained a pro-Vietnamese, internationalist position, and thus offered no challenge to his rule, provided that he followed a similar line on the international scene.

In 1965–1966, Saloth Sar paid a long visit to Hanoi and Beijing. We know very little about this trip, except that his hosts kept Sihanouk in the dark about it, and that Saloth Sar

---

[17] Democratic Kampuchea, Central Committee of CPK, "Communique Concerning the Dissolution of the CPK." 6 December 1981.

was unable or unwilling to lure any Cambodian communists home from their sanctuary in Hanoi. It is possible that the Chinese encouraged him to think about a far-reaching social and economic mobilization in Cambodia along the lines of the Great Leap Forward and it is likely that the Beijing leadership also flattered him and gave him some assurances of support. But this is speculation. We know that in 1966, at a congress of the WPK held in the remote Cambodian province of Ratanakiri, the party's name was changed to the Communist Party of Kampuchea (CPK).[18] The change raised the party semantically to the level of the Chinese Communist Party. It seems highly unlikely that this change had been approved by Hanoi, and it was at about this time, according to DK sources, that the CPK broke off party-to-party relations with the Workers' Party of Vietnam.[19]

The process by which the CPK pulled away from Vietnamese guidance in the late 1960s has been analyzed by Kiernan and Heder.[20] For the purposes of this paper, it should be noted that the CPK's struggle against Sihanouk, which broke out in earnest in 1967, came to be seen by the party leadership as separate from the Vietnam War, although Sihanouk, like the Americans and the DRV/NLF, felt that the two were inextricably related.

In 1968–69, the CPK worked with some success to destabilize Sihanouk's regime, which was overturned in March 1970 by relatively pro-American and certainly anti-Vietnamese elements in the Cambodian elite. Subsequently, from overseas, Sihanouk

[18] Carney, *Communist Party Power*, p. 2, note 7.
[19] This action was announced in the DK's historiographically dubious "Black Book" in 1978. See Kiernan, "Origins of Khmer Communism," p. 178, and also Milton Osborne, *Aggression and Annexation: Kampuchea's Condemnation of Vietnam*, Working Paper no. 15, Australian National University, Research School of Pacific Studies (Canberra, 1979), p. 7. The wording of the DK text suggests that Vietnam was not informed of the break when it occurred. See also David Chandler, *Brother Number One: a Political Biography of Pol Pot* (Boulder, l992), pp. 75–77, drawing on the research of Thomas Engelbert and Christopher Goscha.
[20] See Kiernan, "Conflict in the Cambodian Communist Movement." and Heder, "Kampuchea's Armed Struggle."

adroitly took command with Chinese and North Vietnamese backing of the movement which had been trying so hard to overthrow him for the past three years. As Gareth Porter has shown, the North Vietnamese rapidly adjusted their Cambodian policy following the *coup*, and fell in alongside this rather unlikely "united" front.[21]

At this point nearly all of the KPRP-*CPK* exiles who had been in North Vietnam since 1954 chose to return to Cambodia or were sent back by the North Vietnamese to participate in the "anti-American" struggle which Cambodia now shared with Vietnam. Although some of these men were given responsible posts inside Cambodia by the *CPK* almost all of them were secretly executed at the party's behest in 1973 and 1974. Because Lon Nol and the Americans following Sihanouk's misguided thinking from the 1960s still believed the *CPK* to be largely a creature of Vietnam they were surprised when the Vietnamese following the peace agreements of 1972–73 were unable to deliver the *CPK* and bring about a cease-fire inside Cambodia as well. The leverage which the Vietnamese had hoped to possess in the Cambodian party, in fact, was in the process of being wiped out.

Because the *CPK* refused to negotiate with "the contemptible Lon Nol," preferring to continue its holy war against him and the United States and because the U.S. bombing of Vietnam had stopped at the end of 1972 the United States, between February and August 1973, dropped some 257,465 tons of bombs on Cambodia – nearly twice the tonnage dropped on Japan in World War II. Aside from killing and maiming tens of thousands of Cambodians who had never fired a shot at an American, the bombing had several political effects, all beneficial to the *CPK*.[22]

[21] Gareth Porter, "Vietnamese Policies toward Cambodia Since World War II." in David Chandler and Ben Kiernan, eds. Revolution and Its Aftermath in Kampuchea: Eight Essays (New Haven, 1983), pp. 57–98.

[22] William Shawcross, Sideshow: Nixon, Kissinger and the Destruction of Cambodia (New York, 1979), pp. 296–7.

One was to demonstrate the party's contention that Cambodia's principal enemy was the United States. Another was to turn thousands of young Cambodians into participants in an anti-American crusade, while driving hundreds of thousands of others into the relative safety (and squalor) of Phnom Penh, Battambang, and other Khmer Republic strongholds. The destruction of so many villages and the deaths and dislocation of so many people enabled the *CPK* to collectivize agriculture in the zones under its control, in May 1973, while the bombing was going on. When it stopped, the party was able to claim that the Cambodian revolution, unlike any other in the history of the world, had defeated the United States.

The bombing damaged the fabric of prewar Cambodian society and provided the *CPK* with the psychological ingredients of a violent, vengeful, and unrelenting social revolution. This was to be waged, in their words, by people with "empty hands." The party encouraged class warfare between the "base people," who had been bombed, and the "new people" who had taken refuge from the bombing, and thus had taken sides, in *CPK* thinking, with the United States.

The bombing was also an entirely Cambodian experience, connected only tangentially with the Vietnam War, just as the "revolutionary organization" was not connected, publicly at least, with the parties that were struggling against the United States elsewhere in Indochina. By keeping the *CPK*'s existence a secret, party leaders were able to take the line, at home and overseas, that Cambodia's revolution, like its victory, was incomparable, unprecedented and unconnected with the Vietnam War. In early 1977, the DK foreign minister, Ieng Sary, went so far as to say to some reporters that Cambodian leaders were not communists at all, but "revolutionaries."[23]

Secretiveness and subterfuge pervaded everything the party did. This was especially true between the liberation of Phnom Penh in

---

[23] Nayan Chanda, "Cambodia Looks for Friends," Far Eastern Economic Review, 28 April 1977, p. 11.

April 1975, and the party's assumption of state power ostensibly following a national election twelve months later. During these months, party members who objected to such Draconian policies as the abolition of markets were killed, and so were high-ranking officials of the Khmer Republic. But the systematic elimination of KPRP veterans, of "new people" in general, and of Cambodians returning from abroad, does not seem to have begun until the closing months of 1976. Ironically, the twelve months following the evacuation of the cities turn out to have been the most benign of the forty-four months in which the CPK controlled Cambodia.

A comprehensive development plan for the years 1977–80, which called for the complete collectivization of the country, was discussed by the CPK central committee at the end of August 1976.[24] Between these discussions and Keo Meas' arrest, a confusing series of events affecting the balance of power in Phnom Penh can be pieced together from broadcasts of Radio Phnom Penh.

At the beginning of September just before leaving for a two-week diplomatic mission to Mexico Ieng Sary made a point of attending a reception honoring Vietnam's national day.[25] At about the same time, negotiations were underway to establish regular air services between Phnom Penh, Vientiane, and Hanoi and a DK women's delegation was on an official tour of Laos and Vietnam.[26]

News of Mao Zedong's death on 9 September was received in Phnom Penh by an immediate and protracted period of official mourning.[27] In a eulogy of Mao, delivered on 18 September, the day that Ieng Sary returned from overseas, Pol Pot said that

[24] For a translation of this document, see David Chandler, Ben Kiernan and Chanthou Boua, ed. and tr. *Pol Pot Plans the Future: Confidential Leadership Documents from Democratic Kampuchea, 1976–1977*. New Haven, Yale University Southeast Asia Program Monograph Series, 1988, pp. 119–64.

[25] *FBIS*, 2 September 1976.

[26] *FBIS*, 8 September 1976.

[27] *FBIS*, 10 September 1976.

the "revolutionary organization" governing DK enjoyed "ties of militant solidarity and revolutionary friendship" with the Chinese Communist Party.[28] This statement came very close to publicly admitting the existence of the CPK and its Marxist-Leninist orientation.

Two days later, again according to the radio, Pol Pot resigned as prime minister of DK, a post he had held since April 1976, in order to "take care of his health."[29] Since most of his audience would not have been aware that he was concurrently secretary of the CPK central committee, nothing was said about his abandoning this position and it seems likely that he did not. According to the radio, Pol Pot's place as prime minister was taken by his deputy, Nuon Chea, a veteran of the communist movement since the 1940s.

The apparent detente with Vietnam, the political uncertainty in China connected with Mao's death and Pol Pot's absence from view may well have encouraged some Cambodian communists like Keo Meas to press the regime to celebrate the numerologically significant twenty-fifth anniversary of the founding of the KPRP when it occurred at the end of September. In so doing, it seems likely that partisans of this view wanted the party to come out into the open and thus locate its origins in a period of fraternal collaboration with Vietnam.

People who supported such a policy – or those whom the CPK leadership suspected of supporting it – were quickly arrested, tortured, made to confess to treason and put to death between September and November 1976. This suggests that Pol Pot's "retirement" may well have been a case of *reculer pour mieux sauter* – if, in fact, it had not been intended to lure his opposition unwarily into the light.

Confirmation of turmoil at the center comes from a member of the CPK who was captured inside Vietnam on a military

[28] *FBIS*, 20 September 1976.
[29] *FBIS*, 29 September 1976.

operation in November 1977.[30] He told his interrogators that arrangements had been made, in September 1976, to celebrate the Party's twenty-fifth anniversary, but:

> We received an urgent message from higher authorities ordering us to suspend preparations. Later on, a circular informed us that the party had been founded on September 30, 1960.

The prisoner went on to say that party memberships embarked on earlier than 1960 were to be made invalid, and that new members of the party were to be chosen from people between the ages of eighteen and twenty-eight.

Further evidence of a crisis comes from a typewritten party document entitled "The Activities of the Party's Central Committee – Political Tasks, 1976," composed at the end of the year.[31] Most of the text is concerned with the political aspects of collectivization, which was about to be introduced throughout the country; but one section discusses a decision, made in October, to keep the party's existence a secret from outsiders, at least for the time being. For our purposes, the passage is worth examining in detail.[32] Throughout 1976, it says, "[f]riendly parties begged us to bring our party into the open. In their view, conditions for doing so were propitious. Moreover, they needed our support." It seems likely that the phrase "friendly parties" refers to those of China and North Korea. We have seen that Pol Pot's eulogy of Mao on September 18 fell short of declaring the existence of the CPK. Chinese pressure to come into the open may have come earlier in the year, also, when the CPK took office. But the document continues:

---

[30] British Broadcasting Corporation, *Summary of World Broadcasts (Far East)*, 2 December 1977. Ben Kiernan's interview with CPK cadre Chim Chin, 28 July 1980, corroborates the sequence.

[31] For a discussion of this document, see below, pp. 252ff. A translation appears in Chandler, Kiernan and Boua, *Pol Pot Plans the Future*, pp. 182–212.

[32] Ibid., p. 204.

Enemies wanted us to bring the party into the open also, so that they could observe us closely and make things easy for the accomplishment of their objectives. Bringing the party into the open caused problems for the security of the central leadership, but in September and October [of 1976] we were on the point of deciding to come out. From then on, however, documents reveal that our enemies were trying to defeat us, using every method at their disposal.

Like many DK pronouncements, the text leaves plenty of room for maneuver. Were the party's "enemies" primarily inside the party (like Keo Meas), in the anti-communist United States, or in the "enemy" communist parties (in Vietnam, for example)? What were the enemies' "objectives"? Likewise, the "problems for the security of the central leadership" are not spelled out, unless they were simply a matter of telling the outside world who the leaders were. What are the "documents" which led the party to change its mind? Without knowing who the "enemies" are the documents cannot be identified. Perhaps they are the confessions that by the end of 1976 had begun to pile up in the archives of Tuol Sleng. Did the CPK leadership believe that these were true? The passage as a whole resists analysis.

Elliptically, the author concludes by noting that "a further difficulty in coming into the open is that doing so might give rise to disagreements with certain people." In September 1977, when Pol Pot triumphantly revealed the existence of the CPK, hundreds of these "certain people" had been snuffed out. The party's history, composed at last for public scrutiny, could begin, magisterially, with Pol Pot's own election to the central committee.[33]

Towards the end of 1976, therefore, the leadership of the CPK made a series of decisions to keep themselves in power and to

[33] *FBIS*, 2 October 1977, reporting Pol Pot's speech on 28 September 1977.

set Cambodia's course. One of these was to change the party's birthday from 1951 to 1960; another was to keep the party's existence a secret from outsiders; a third was to purge members of the party who were thought to believe that it had been founded in 1951. Still other decisions, embedded in the 1977–80 development plan, called for the collectivization of Cambodia, the intensification of class warfare, the transformation of the peasantry into an unpaid rural proletariat and the doubling of party membership within a year, so that newly recruited cadre could supervise the country's transformation. Cambodians were told to be ready to struggle (*tosu*) unremittingly against every kind of enemy. A party document from 1974 had already made this clear.

> When you are eating roots, you must struggle, and you must struggle [even] when you have noodle-soup and roast chicken to eat. You must struggle all the time.[34]

Internationally, the regime was now prepared to increase its dependence on China and North Korea so as to obtain economic assistance, arms, and political support for its own intensifying conflict with Vietnam. These agreements, which undermined Cambodia's policy of independence, were kept a secret from the people. The war against Vietnam served the interests of the Chinese, who probably encouraged it, and those of Cambodia's youthful army, nourished by what it had been told were victories over the United States and by "historical" claims to areas of southern Vietnam which had been, centuries before, under Cambodian control. If pressure to bring the CPK into the open had indeed come from China in 1976, Pol Pot appears to have been able to persuade these distant supporters that proclaiming the party's existence at that point would only have served the interests of the Vietnamese and their "lackeys" inside Cambodia.

---

[34] Anonymous, Kosang nung bongrung pak (*Building and Strengthening the Party*), n.p., n.d., but from internal evidence written in 1974.

The decision to purify the *CPK* was related to the decisions already discussed. "Old" communists were useless in a "new" kind of revolution. Anyone who suggested that Cambodians should take note of the balance of power in post-American Indochina was considered a traitor to a primarily national struggle which the Cambodians, by dint of their previous victories, were uniquely equipped to win.

The hubris of the DK regime encouraged its leaders to assume (or cynically to proclaim) that, by forcing the U.S. embassy to evacuate Phnom Penh in April 1975, or by bringing about the bombing halt in August 1973 (in fact an American decision wrung by the U.S. Congress from the Nixon Administration), Cambodia's revolutionaries had defeated the entire United States: "The Cambodian people have defeated the US imperialists and all other aggressors. Therefore all people, including the American people, will certainly achieve their victory."[35]

It is uncertain as to whether the Chinese encouraged the DK leaders to underestimate the Vietnamese, and to misconstrue their history; but, as I have shown elsewhere, flawed perceptions of their own history, transmitted largely by means of hortatory slogans and by word of mouth, had convinced many young Cambodians – and especially those in the revolutionary army – that, after April 1975, only victories were possible.[36] Cambodia's "true history," in other words, had only recently begun. To suggest that its communist movement had sprung up in 1951, under the tutelage of Vietnam, was to say that Cambodia shared some of its history with other countries. To the leaders of Democratic Kampuchea, the costs of making such an admission were prohibitive, in ideological and tactical terms, just as they

---

[35] *FBIS*, 1 May 1978. See, also, *Tung Padevat*, August 1975, p. 24: "The Cambodian revolution is a precious model for the world's people."

[36] See *FBIS*, 27 July 1978, which states that one result of defeating the Vietnamese would be that "our Cambodian race will be everlasting." For an analysis of *CPK* synchronic misperceptions, see W.E. Willmott, "Analytical Errors of the Kampuchean Communist Party," *Pacific Affairs*, Vol. 54, No. 2 (Summer 1981), pp. 209–27.

had been, psychologically at least, for previous, non-communist regimes.

And so to preserve Cambodia's "independence and self-mastery," to honor their perceptions of its history, and to maintain themselves in power, the leaders of Democratic Kampuchea at the end of 1976 embarked on a perilous and provocative course which was to lead, slightly more than two years later, to the disappearance of Cambodia as an independent state but also – although this does not seem to have occurred to them when they set out – to the survival of perhaps eighty per cent of the Cambodian people.

POST SCRIPT

In December 1981 some months after these lines were written the *CPK* dissolved itself. The action was announced by the Party's own Central Committee, most of whose members remained in place in the "non-Communist" coalition govern-ment of Democratic Kampuchea. In June 1982, officials of the People's Republic of Kampuchea (PRK) in Phnom Penh announced that its ruling party, the Kampuchean People's Revolutionary Party (KPRP) had been founded in June 1951, rather than in September, as previously stated. The party's new history parallels that of the KPRP as discussed in this essay up to 1960. Soon after the second party congress, however, held in Phnom Penh in October of that year the KPRP went off the rails, in the eyes of the PRK. From the early 1960s when Pol Pot took command of the party until the KPRP's "third" congress, on the Vietnamese frontier in December 1978, there was no authentic communist party in Phnom Penh, or anywhere else in Cambodia. The party's birthday is still a moveable feast, and its other anniversaries depend on the needs of the regime in power in Phnom Penh. *Plus ça change, plus c'est la même chose.*

February 1983

SEEING RED:
PERCEPTIONS OF CAMBODIAN HISTORY
IN DEMOCRATIC KAMPUCHEA

The Khmer revolution has no precedent. What we are trying to do
has never been done before in history.[1]

Ieng Sary, 1977

The regime of Democratic Kampuchea (DK) repeatedly
proclaimed that the revolution which began in Cambodia in
the 1960s under the leadership of the Communist Party of
Kampuchea (*CPK*) overturned Cambodian social relations and
gave birth to a new phase of Cambodian history. In power and
in exile, the regime has cast aside much of Cambodia's historical
experience while tailoring the rest to serve the revolution.

The DK view of history has at least five components. These
are closely related to one another.

The first of these is a tendency to separate Cambodian history
into two segments, broken at the liberation of Phnom Penh in
April 1975. What happened before that time is also broken down
into a sequence of phases (e.g. "primitive communist," "feudal,"
"colonial," and so on) which sometimes reflects orthodox Marxist
notions and occasionally does not. This concern with phases and

I am grateful to Ben Kiernan, Ian Mabbett and Michael Godley for their
comments on this paper.

[1] Ieng Sary's interview with Terzani, United States, *Foreign Broadcast
Information Service, Daily Report* (*FBIS*) 4 May 1977.

"evolution," familiar in other Communist parties, pays lipservice at least to an organic view of national development.[2]

A second ingredient is the tradition of Angkor, which is seen in terms of the collective capacities of ordinary people, and thus as a period in which Cambodians organized themselves for greatness. The kings themselves are never mentioned in DK by name and while their motives are derided and the "slavery" of ordinary people is bemoaned Angkor's place in DK historiography is as a model of exemplary behavior, a reminder of Cambodia's grandeur. Pol Pot recognized this by declaring, "If our people can make Angkor, they can make anything."[3]

Angkor is not seen, moreover, as a purely national event forming part of what a recent DK publication has referred to as the "essentially endogenous" character of Cambodian history.[4] To take this view (which DK shares with earlier and subsequent regimes) is to argue that outside influences such as those entering Cambodia from India or the West have been ignored or rendered indigenous to such an extent that comparisons of Cambodia with other nations and attributions of indebtedness to others are unhelpful. Not only are there no precedents for the Cambodian revolution in Cambodia's own past. There are also no connections between what has happened in Cambodia throughout its history and what has occurred in other countries. This grandiose and

---

[2] For a discussion of Marxist historiography in a Chinese context, see Arif Dirlik, *Revolution and History* (Berkeley: University of California Press, 1978), especially pp. 229–258. Interestingly, DK spokesmen never discussed the idea of an "Asiatic Mode of Production," even though Michael Vickery has argued that this Marxian notion can be fruitfully applied to Angkorean Cambodia and more arguably to the economy envisaged by DK. (Michael Vickery, "Angkor and the Asiatic Mode of Production," seminar at Monash University, November 27, 1981). I am grateful to Vickery for allowing me to refer to his unpublished paper. For an astute discussion of the problem in a Chinese context, see Arif Dirlik, pp. 95–136.

[3] *FBIS*, 2 October 1977 (speech of 27 September). My wording translates the Cambodian text.

[4] Democratic Kampuchea, Permanent Mission to the United Nations, Press Release 4 May 1982. "The Marvellous Monument of Angkor and its Tragedy," p. 1.

self-regarding view of history, the third component in my list, often interfered with the internationalist elements of the CPK's allegedly "socialist" (which is to say, generically recognizable) revolution. At the same time, it constituted a carry-over from preceding non-Communist regimes.

A fourth component is the element of struggle between enemies (*khmang*) within and outside the state on the one hand and the peasant masses inside Cambodia on the other. Enemies have exploited Cambodia's poor, DK spokesmen argue, ever since the country moved away from "primitive communism" some "2,000 years ago" into a world of class discrimination. Before 1977–1978 in public documents at least enemies inside Cambodia were seen primarily in terms of class. Peasants were told to "sharpen the boundaries between classes" to heighten their awareness of *khmang*. In confidential CPK materials as early as 1975, however, enemies inside the state also included those in the Party who disagreed with its leaders' political line. After the outbreak of extensive fighting with Vietnam in 1977, internal enemies were identified as those who sided with the enemy outside Cambodia's borders.

In 1978, as the war began to go badly for DK, enemies outside the state also came to be identified almost exclusively as Vietnamese. When the regime went into exile, the survival of the Cambodian race rather than the state or the revolution, became its acknowledged *raison d'être*.

The final component of these perceptions is made up of the tactical and strategic needs of the CPK. In published documents, these changed from time to time, and Cambodian history was realigned to correspond to them. For example, the "crucial role" of the CPK itself was withheld from the people until late 1977, when the party's existence was officially revealed. Similarly, a "radiant tradition" of peasant communalism began to be emphasized earlier in that year, when communal eating, part of the 1977–1980 CPK development plan, went into effect throughout the country.[5] Private property, once the bane of Cambodia's past, became a commendable "tradition" once again in the 1980s when the Party's leaders found themselves in Thailand.

These five ingredients of "history", of course, are not uniquely Cambodian, although it would be hard to find anything exactly parallel to the idea of Angkor in other countries with a similar heritage. What seems uniquely Khmer about the DK approach to history – at least for a partly literate society – is the absence of any historical texts, aside from histories of the CPK that circulated among Party members. When a speaker in 1978 enjoined his listeners to "read history and be fully confident" he was speaking metaphorically for at the time there were no written histories of Cambodia (or anywhere else) in circulation in DK and none accessible to ordinary people, since libraries, bookshops, publishing houses, universities and high schools had all been closed after "liberation" in April 1975. By "reading" history, the speaker probably meant that people should reflect on the oral versions of the past transmitted to them from time to time by Party spokesmen, consider the history of the CPK and recall their own experience of events. Instead of reading books they were to be guided by the ongoing *praxis* of revolution.

Documents and research of a conventional kind were spurned by DK. A 1973 text asserted that the history of the Party, for example, had been

> written with the flesh, blood, bones, sweat and physical, moral and intellectual strength of the people, combatants, party members. . . and cadres, living and dead.[6]

[5] The four-year plan, introduced in January 1977, had been discussed among CPK leaders on 21–23 August 1976. See David Chandler, Ben Kiernan and Chanthou Boua (eds. and tr.) *Pol Pot Plans the Future* (New Haven, 1988) pp. 119–163 for the text of a document discussed at this meeting.

[6] *FBIS*, 15 January 1976.

Similar phrases appear in a 1974 history of the *CPK*, in Khieu Samphan's remarks in 1976 about the DK Constitution, in Pol Pot's marathon speech of 27 September 1977, which unveiled to the Cambodian public the existence of the Party and in the DK's polemical "Black Book" attacking Vietnamese intervention which was published in 1978.[7] What "wrote" the revolution was the revolution itself.

With no texts for comparative study, no history curricula and the Party's monopoly of the subject it is not surprising that Cambodia's history in the DK period was often treated simplistically in terms of "2,000 years" of unrelieved class warfare, slavery and foreign intervention broken by the appearance of the *CPK* (with birthdays that began to vary after 1976) and its "inevitable victory" in April 1975.

In examining the periodization of Cambodian history then – the first of the five ingredients to be discussed – I should emphasize that what had happened in Cambodia before the 1960s rarely attracted the attention of the regime except insofar as the darkness of these eras could be illuminated by subsequent events. At the same time, as *CPK* requirements and leadership varied, certain phases diminished in importance, while others rose to command attention.

The *locus classicus* of DK periodization is Pol Pot's speech of September 27, 1977, in which he announced the existence of the *CPK* and gave his own idea of the periods that had marked his country's past. In his words:

> The history of Cambodia dates back more than 2000 years. It shows that like all societies in the world Cambodian society had experienced many social phases.[8]

---

[7] See Milton Osborne, *Aggression and Annexation: Kampuchea's Condemnation of Vietnam* (Canberra: Australian National University, Research School of Pacific Studies) Working Paper No. 15, 1979.

[8] *FBIS*, 2 October 1977. Until September 1976, the founding of the *CPK* was always traced to the foundation of the Vietnamese-sponsored Khmer Peoples' Revolutionary Party (KPRP: *Pak Pracheachon Padevat Khmae* in Cambodian) in September 1951. The foundation date was pushed forward to September 1960

The stages which Pol Pot reveals are familiar to students of Marxism but less so to most students of Cambodian history:

> In the era of primitive communism, there were not yet any divisions between classes. In the era of primitive communism, there were thus no struggles between classes. When Cambodian society entered the era of slave society, society had class divisions, which is to say that there were slave-owners and slaves. These were called masters of slaves, masters of workers, and those who were slaves, and workers for other people. In the feudal era, and in the capitalist era, but especially in the feudal one, there were landowners and rural workers. In capitalist society there were [also] capitalists and wage-laborers. These are the essential characteristics of the social phases through which our society has passed.[9]

Pol Pot went on to say that an additional dimension of recent Cambodian history had been exploitation at the hands of foreigners. He named these as the French, Japanese and American imperialists, adding that until recently Cambodia lived in a "semi-colonial" situation.

He said little about primitive communism, but other DK texts from 1977 and 1978, citing a "tradition" of communalism among Cambodian peasants, may be referring obliquely to this classless era as one toward which the regime was cautiously returning.

(and the KPRP consigned to limbo) in a speech by a "representative" of the CPK, probably Pol Pot himself, allegedly delivered on 27 September 1976, and reprinted in a special issue of *Tung Padevat* ("Revolutionary Flags," hereafter TP) September-October 1976, pp. 1–32, see "Revising the Past in Democratic Kampuchea: When was the Birthday of the Party?" above p. 213.

[9] *FBIS*, 2 October 1977.

Pol Pot then discussed the class conflicts which characterized later eras of Cambodian history. Introducing his remarks, he assured his listeners that

> several comrades have studied the texts of Cambodian history from earliest times. Our history clearly shows that for a long period of time, there have been classic struggles between the exploiting classes and the exploited ones.[10]

In the slave era, he asserts, slaves and masters constituted a revolutionary contradiction. Although slaves united to rebel on several unspecified occasions, he says, they failed because they lacked appropriate leadership, organization, and ideology. When rebellions succeeded momentarily, former slaves became masters and even kings, thus renewing social contradictions.

The speech is vague about the colonial era *per se*, and resistance to the French is dated only from the end of World War II. Pol Pot's mishandling of so much of the historical record raises doubts about how much he expected his audience to know about what he was discussing and questions about whether he believed what he was saying. In any case, he spoke of two strands to anti-colonial resistance. In the first of these

> the Japanese fascist clique and the American CIA give birth to a political movement demanding independence, calling it the 'peoples' Movement or the 'Free Khmer,' with the contemptible Son Ngoc Thanh as leader.[11]

By telescoping Japanese support for Son Ngoc Thanh in 1943–1945 into American support for Thanh's anti-Sihanouk movement after 1953, Pol Pot ignores any other non-Communist resistance to the French and, incidentally, the years in which the most

---

[10] Ibid.
[11] Ibid.

resistance of any kind took place (1945–1954).[12] At the same time, to demonstrate the legitimacy of the *CPK*, he apparently feels obliged to give the Party an ancestry from the period of resistance and liberation. The so-called "fascist" strand is unacceptable and so is the radical one he fails to mention, which was sponsored by the Vietnamese and in 1951 organized as a Cambodia-based, Vietnamese-supported Communist Party (KPRP). Rejecting these contending and occasionally cooperating forces, Pol Pot places the roots of the *CPK* among anonymous, leaderless peasant masses which, he asserts, fought long and courageously against the French. There is no evidence that such a movement ever existed, although it provides the *CPK* with forerunners who are uncorrupted by "fascism" and by cooperation with the Vietnamese.

The period 1955–1960 is of special interest to *CPK* historians because these years laid the basis, in a manner still unclear (and unclarified by official statements) for the foundation, or renewal, of the *CPK* under most of its subsequent leadership in September 1960. What we know about factionalism among Cambodian radicals in this period suggests that those who had remained in Cambodia (to differentiate them from perhaps a thousand cadre who emigrated to the DRV) were split about what line to follow, unsuccessful in attracting popular support and ambiguous in their relations with Hanoi. Earlier confidential party histories explore this period in some detail.[13] The main problem which these historians face is related to the failure of the radical Pracheachon Group and its ideology to attract continuous or extensive support among people who had in many cases, been happy to fight alongside Communists to gain Cambodia's independence from France. Unlike their counterparts in South Vietnam, Cambodian Communists in the late 1950s were unconvincing when they argued, as Pol Pot and his supporters did, that Cambodia's

[12] For a discussion of Pol Pot's misreading of Cambodian social conditions which parallels his misreading of history, see William Willmott, "Analytical Errors of the Kampuchean Communist Party," *Pacific Affairs* (Summer 1981), pp. 209–27, especially 220–23.

[13] See Chandler, "Revising the Past." Party histories are available from 1973, 1974 and 1976 (two).

independence was a sham, or irrelevant to resistance to the United States, whose dominance was still poorly understood by ordinary people. In fact, it seems likely that several thousand Communist-affiliated guerrillas laid down or concealed their arms in 1954–1955, agreeing with their leaders that the armed struggle was over. The strength of radicalism was tested in the 1951 elections when Sihanouk's political movement, the *Sangkum Reastr' Niyum*, won an overwhelming victory by co-opting rightist opposition, playing up to voters in the countryside and harassing such radical candidates as dared to run.[14] Because the notion of people willingly lending support to non-Communist political candidates is unthinkable to Pol Pot, he blames the radicals' defeat in 1955 on the strength of those in power:

> The people were unable to elect progressive figures because the power-holding class had guns, weapons, laws and courts, as well as other institutions with which to oppress the people.[15]

In 1976, an anonymous party spokesman, possibly Pol Pot, took a more fanciful approach in the pages of the *CPK*'s theoretical journal, *Tung Padevat*:

> We know that popular opinion throughout the country supported [radical candidates] by 99 percent but state power lay in enemy hands . . . The lesson of 1955 was that we lacked the means to win an election. Only by fighting a revolution could we defeat the enemy.[16]

---

[14] On the 1955 elections, see David Chandler, *The Tragedy of Cambodian History* (New Haven, 1991), pp. 81–84 and Ben Kiernan, How Pol Pot Came to Power (London, 1985), pp. 153–64.

[15] *FBIS*, 2 October 1977.

[16] TP, September-October 1976, p. 7.

The author gives no evidence to support his contention that "99 percent" of the people supported radical solutions to Cambodian problems in 1955. Had this been the case, surely something might be said (or might have survived in print) about radical programs tailored by anyone for these supporters. If radicalism had been as threatening to the "exploiting classes" in the late 1950s as Pol Pot suggests it is hard to explain the elite's indifference to the left or why the left was so ineffectual in this period. To highlight the importance of the foundation of the CPK, Pol Pot hypothesizes repression at the hands of Sihanouk's government after 1955. The repression is far in excess of anything which other evidence suggests. In fact, radicalism in Cambodia, as an October 1976 broadcast came close to admitting, was withering on the vine:

> In this period, we lost all sense of national soul and identity. We were completely enslaved by the reactionary, corrupt and hooligan way of thinking, by the laws, customs, traditions, political, economic, cultural and social ways and life-style, and by the clothing and other behavioral patterns of imperialism, colonialism and the oppressor classes.[17]

Stephen Heder makes the same point adroitly when he asserts that by 1960 "what was left of a communist movement in Kampuchea, and this was not much, was *without a party* and was largely bitter, or new, or both."[18]

Despite Pol Pot's claims to the contrary, the KPRP meeting convened in the workshops of the Phnom Penh railroad station on 28–30 September 1960 did not come up with dramatic new directions for Cambodia's Communist movement. The Party had little to show for its leadership activities before the so-called

---

[17] *FBIS*, 16 October 1976.
[18] Stephen R. Heder, "Kampuchea's Armed Struggle: The Origins of an Independent Revolution," *Bulletin of Concerned Asian Scholars*, (*BCAS*) 11, No. 1 (January-March 1979), p. 17.

Samlaut uprising of 1967 which the *CPK* leadership cashed in on after it had begun.[19]

Because documents prepared at the meeting were kept secret from outsiders, Pol Pot was able to link decisions reached at the meeting to subsequent victories and political emphases of the party. At no point in his 27 September 1977 speech, however, does Pol Pot suggest that developments inside the *CPK* were affected in any way by the intensifying warfare in the 1960s in Vietnam. In fact, a 1981 DK press release went so far as to assert that the *CPK* was founded in 1960 "*in order to fight the Vietnamese* [!]"[20]

The importance of the meeting for Pol Pot's purposes and those of Cambodian history as he perceived them was that he was elected to the Central Committee of the Party at this time.

Under DK the 1960 meeting became the earliest of several anniversaries to be celebrated publicly after the *CPK* had admitted its existence. Others honored the foundation of the revolutionary army in January 1968, the inauguration of rural communes in May 1973 and the liberation of Phnom Penh in April 1975. After September 1977, Cambodian "history" as celebrated by nationally-observed days off was dated from the foundation of the *CPK* seventeen years before. What had happened earlier than that was of little interest and was not seen as post-1960 developments were perceived, as a diachronic process. Instead, what had filled these "2,000 years" was the unrelieved, repetitive exploitation of man by man. While in some ways, perhaps, Cambodian society had lumbered along from one evolutionary phase of history to another on its road to socialism in the *CPK* view its history was

[19] For differing views of the 1960 meeting, see Heder, "Kampuchea's Armed Struggle," p. 3. At least one document emanating from the meeting surfaced in Vietnam in the late 1980s, when a Vietnamese translation came to the attention of the American and German scholars Christopher Goscha and Thomas Engelbert. See Engelbert and Goscha, *Falling Out of Touch* (Clayton, Australia, 1995).

[20] Democratic Kampuchea Permanent Mission to the United Nations, Press Release 11 December 1981, "Communiqué of the Central Committee of the Communist Party of Kampuchea Concerning the Dissolution of the Communist Party of Kampuchea," p. 2.

hardly progressive, for enemies from previous phases always remained in place. Each phase, in other words, only added a new form of exploitation. In words of a 1976 CPK text, "Capitalism and feudalism, having existed for 2,000 years, are [still] very much alive in Cambodian society."[21]

Before leaving this discussion of periodization, two periods of time that trouble DK writers need to be pointed out once more. These are 1945–1955 and 1955–1960. The first is troubling because so many older listeners would recall Vietnamese assistance in the fight against the French and in sponsoring the Cambodian Communist movement from its beginnings in the aftermath of World War II. The second period is embarrassing to the CPK because it was characterized by indecisiveness and by diminishing popular support. CPK historians also avoid discussion of the role played by Norodom Sihanouk from 1946 to 1960 by the simple expedient of hardly ever mentioning his name.[22]

It is possible also to see the experience of Angkor as troubling to the ideologues of Democratic Kampuchea. Its usefulness as an exemplar is limited by the reasonably accurate way in which DK speakers tend to describe its social structure. How can such an unjust society be useful to the revolution? The answer would seem to lie primarily in the realm of public relations. Privately circulated CPK documents hardly mention Angkor at all. As public relations, Angkor is used to demonstrate that ordinary people, when mobilized in vast numbers by the state can do

[21] See also *Yuvechun nung Yuvanearie Padevat* [Revolutionary youth] (hereafter YYP) No. 67 (December 1976), pp. 10–11

[22] In this context, Sihanouk (unnamed) was in charge of the "enemy" government against which the CPK began its armed struggle at the beginning of 1968; this government became legitimate by default when overthrown by the "treacherous" Lon Nol in 1970. The fact that Sihanouk joined forces with the CPK in 1970–1976 is seldom mentioned, and he is never mentioned at all after his retirement from office in April 1976.

extraordinary things. Angkor also fits into the boastful framework of DK foreign relations.

On the surface at least, some periods of Angkorean history, and especially the reign of Jayavarman VII (r. 1178–1220) offer striking parallels to the DK regime.[23] In both eras, a small, more or less invisible directorate – the king and his advisors, i.e. the "organization" – soaked up the time and dictated the activities of the entire population. Both had the policy of mobilizing labor and resources on an unprecedented scale to produce surpluses which could be used for their own ends. Unpaid laborers were put to work in the service of an arcane set of ideas, held by a few – Mahayana Buddhism or communism – which was used in turn to justify the alteration of social forms and to set in train the "liberation" of those who understood it. In both regimes history was thought to have ended and begun afresh after a ruinous war. These incidental connections, of course, can be pushed too far. They probably aroused little interest among the leaders of Democratic Kampuchea.

It is impossible to say, however, what Angkor meant to them. At least some probably saw it as a public relations tool. Others may have believed pre-revolutionary myths that it was the well-spring of Cambodian history and that Cambodia's grand identity stemmed from the experience. With Angkor behind it, Cambodia was a great power diminished in size, endowed with an ability to inspire, to lead and to give advice.

In his September 1977 speech, Pol Pot compared the monuments of Angkor favorably with the liberation of Phnom Penh:

Long ago, there was Angkor. Angkor was built in the era of slavery. Slaves like us built Angkor under the exploitation of the

[23] I developed this comparison initially in a seminar for the Department of History colloquium, University of Michigan, 21 February 1977. As I re-read these lines in l996 it seems forced. For more detail, see David Chandler, *A History of Cambodia*, paperback edition (Boulder, Colorado, l996) Chapters 4 and 9.

[24] Pol Pot speech, *FBIS*, 2 October 1977.

exploiting classes, so that these royal people could be happy. If our people can make Angkor, they can make anything.[24]

The laborers at Angkor and what they built served the revolution by providing an analogy of national grandeur which could be re-enacted in the 1970s. Because "Angkor" and "Cambodia" were synonymous the DK regime was perhaps compelled to use Angkor on its flag while discarding the rest of Cambodian history. Angkor was simply too *Cambodian* to be discarded. At the same time, DK spokesmen were unwilling or unable to look at Angkor in an historical way. They said nothing about Angkorean leadership, ideology or culture, and nothing about differences between successive periods of time. Why the civilization began, how it flourished, and why it shifted east and south in the fifteenth century are not discussed. Angkor had been built; it was marvelous; it was *there*. DK historians returned Angkor to the jungle but they were unable or unwilling to abandon it altogether. DK's flag, like those of all Cambodian regimes since the 1950s, featured an image of Angkor *wat*.[25]

The third ingredient of DK perceptions of history is harder to define than either "Angkor" or "periodization," because it constitutes a point of view. Primarily, it can be found in the refusal of DK spokesmen to accept or discuss either the precedents for the Cambodian revolution or conservative foreign influences on Cambodian history. This point of view, of course, is common to all revolutionary movements which lay claim to starting history afresh and emphasize the energy of participants at the expense of such contigency, foreign assistance or an inept

[25] Since independence, the Kingdom of Cambodia, the Khmer Republic and Democratic Kampuchea have all featured three-towered images of Angkor on their flags. The flag of the Vietnam-affiliated resistance of the 1940s featured a five-tower image, and so does that of the Peoples' Republic of Kampuchea (PRK). This flag was altered in 1990 to include a partly blue background. In 1993, the flag that had flown under Sihanouk until 1970 was reintroduced, along with Sihanouk himself.

ancien régime. When a Communist regime like DK allows itself no precedents, however, it plays down two important elements of Marxian ideology, namely its historical thrust and the propriety of similar revolutions throughout the world.

DK spokesmen often try to have the arguments both ways. They deny foreign influences over the Cambodian revolution but boast of its international impact; they assert that only in the hands of a Communist Party could the revolution succeed, but say nothing about where "Communism" comes from. They claim that the CPK is a Marxist Leninist Party, but say nothing about the writings (or even the nationalities) of Marx and Lenin.[26] In this context, it is interesting that Pol Pot's tribute to the crucial role played by Mao Zedong's thought in the Cambodian revolution, contained in a speech he delivered in Beijing on 29 September 1977 was not re-broadcast over Phnom Penh radio.[27]

There is some evidence from the last months of the DK regime that Pol Pot increasingly saw himself as a major figure on the world scene, comparable to Mao and Kim Il Sung, and it is likely that if the Vietnamese invasion had been postponed, a full-scale cult honoring his personality might have taken root in Democratic Kampuchea.[28] The usefulness of such a cult, moreover, would not only be to entrench and legitimize Pol Pot's hold on the Party; it could also be used to explain how the

[26] The first public admission that the "revolutionary organization" was Marxist-Leninist in its orientation came in the memorial services for Mao Zedong, held in Phnom Penh on 18 September 1976 (*FBIS*, 20 September 1976).

[27] See *Peking Review*, Vol. 20, No. 41 (7 October 1977). In his speech, Pol Pot said: "The most precious aid from Chairman Mao, the Chinese Communist Party and the Chinese people has been Mao Zedong's thought."

[28] By late 1978, Pol Pot's photograph was posted in many communal dining halls throughout the country (Ben Kiernan, personal communication). His frequent interviews with foreign journalists in 1978 also contained (often misleading) biographical data, and at least two busts of him were recovered by the Vietnamese when they occupied Phnom Penh in early 1979. See Anthony Barnett, Chanthou Boua and Ben Kiernan, "The Bureaucracy of Death," *New Statesman*, 2 May 1980.

Cambodian Communist movement achieved so many victories without any foreign inspiration and without a history previous to Pol Pot's election in 1960 to the party's Central Committee.

The notion that the Cambodian revolution was incomparable was already in place in August 1975, when Pol Pot asserted that this revolution without models was already providing inspiration to other countries, all impressed by the fact that such a marvelous revolution had, in his words, never occurred in the history of the world:

> When Cambodia won, the rest of the world was amazed. [Victory came because] the people were mighty, the revolutionary army was mighty and our Party leading us was mighty. Ordinarily, people might say, 'Surely unseen gods helped them win this rapid victory' ... [29]

The twin victories of April 1975 – the flight of the U.S Embassy staff on April 12, and the liberation of Phnom Penh five days later – were compared by Pol Pot and by other DK spokesmen to the grandeur of Angkor as we have seen but they were *incomparable* in extra-Cambodian terms. Indeed, the extreme chauvinism and xenophobia which has so often colored Cambodian political thought was a feature of DK pro-nouncements from the beginning and intensified along with the fighting with Vietnam. A 1978 broadcast asserted that:

> When you compare our revolution with other countries' revolutions, you will see that there is a great difference between us and other countries. For example, other countries have a currency, a wage system, market places and private property. In a word, we are not like other countries. In this case, should you stand on our side or the side of other people? If you opt for the latter, willingly or not, you have deserted our side. So, without a clear line

---

[29] *TP*, August 1975, p. 27.

between us and other people, little by little the enemy's view and ideology will creep into your minds and make you lose all sense of distinction between us and the enemy. This is very dangerous. is possible that several of our comrades have fallen into this trap.[30]

Interestingly, this self-regarding strain is more pronounced in internal CPK documents than in relatively public ones broadcast over the radio or delivered as speeches and monitored overseas. These are the places to look for genuflections to the revolutions of China and North Korea, or to the revolutionary thought of Mao Zedong and Kim Il Sung. The pages of *Tung Padevat* and the CPK youth magazine, on the other hand, say very little about foreign countries except in derogatory terms – although China and North Korea are not insulted.

DK spokesmen frequently claimed that the revolution, by liberating ordinary people, enabled them at last to *write their own history*. Up to the colonial era, Cambodian history had been written by foreigners and by the wrong Cambodians. Under the French, this false history was made worse by the intervention of the imperialist culture, carried on by "Japanese fascists" and eventually the United States. All these powers took turns at writing Cambodi*A History*; pure Cambodian history was impossible to compose until the emergence of the CPK.

This leads us to the next ingredient of DK history, namely that it is best described in terms of a never-ending struggle. We have encountered the participants in the struggle already. On one side are the slave-owners, feudal landlords, capitalists, imperialists, unfriendly foreign powers, lackeys of the United States and so on. On the other are Cambodia's poorest peasants who came to the revolution with "empty hands". These men and women became its principal beneficiaries and the backbone of the revolutionary army.

---

[30] *FBIS*, 14 April 1978.

Throughout the DK period, enemies and the tendencies they represented were subsumed by Cambodian history itself. The frequently repeated statement that "2,000 years" of Cambodian history had come to an end in April 1975 meant that poor Cambodians were no longer responsible for their past. By their victory they had broken the social relationships, which is to say the chains that had bound them for two millenia. Those who had been acted on by history were now enacting it. In the words of a broadcast in November 1977 they were now free to do anything at all that served the *interests of their class*.[31]

But what did "writing their own history" and the "interests of their class" really mean? To be sure, perennial patterns of exploitation and defeat had been broken and a new pattern of autarkic victory had been set. If history was a struggle, however, victory could not be taken for granted and had nothing to do with magnanimity or compromise. Unlike their counterparts in Vietnam, the leaders of Democratic Kampuchea had no interest in forgiving, reforming or abandoning their enemies, even though these had been so thoroughly defeated. Perhaps because they believed what they said about their almost supernatural success the leaders seem to have connected more success with struggles of a similar kind. They saw themselves as swifter, purer and more correct than the Vietnamese. They remained alert and maintained their revolutionary violence which they saw as the key to their success. As early as August 1975, Pol Pot had urged members of the *CPK* to root out enemies implanted in its ranks,[32] a process which would culminate in 1978 with accusations that some high ranking members of the Party had been working simultaneously for the CIA, the Vietnamese and the USSR.

The multiplication of enemies and the intensification of vigilance led DK historians toward the end of the DK era to depict Cambodian history as a struggle against the forerunners

---

[31] *FBIS*, 11 November 1977.
[32] *TP*, August 1975, p. 41.

of these enemies warning ordinary people that the marvellous, unprecedented victories of 1975,were precarious and under threat. The darkening of history and the corresponding shrillness of DK documents in 1978 reflected the progress of the war with Vietnam, instability and dogmatism at the top levels of the CPK and factional-regional disputes that undermined Pol Pot's authority at this time.

The CPK preferred a conflict model of society and history to one that emphasized consensus. They believed that revolutionary violence was akin to national liberation. Consensus, in their view, was a sham imposed by rulers on the ruled. When the rulers were removed from power conflict had to continue, not only *inside* people striving for improvement, but also between the traditionally warring classes: as in Mao's China, which provided many models for DK, feudalists without land and capitalists without money remained legitimate targets of the regime and were to be "weeded out." So were capitalist "tendencies" in Party members whose "life histories" were otherwise unblemished. The ambiguity of such antagonims, combined with the literalism of untrained, enthusiastic cadre, led to tens of thousands of executions of "class enemies" in 1977–1978, long after the revolution had supposedly been won. These successive purifications of Cambodian society were intended to produce a country in which everyone was eligible for membership in the CPK as Anthony Barnett has suggested.[33] In this regard, DK efforts since going into exile to take up a more pluralistic and liberal model for Cambodian society, emphasizing the unity of all social groupings *vis-à-vis* the Vietnamese – is an unconvincing tactical necessity.

It would make a tidy conclusion if I could assert that the fifth ingredient of DK perceptions of Cambodian history, namely the needs of the CPK at a given moment, always or generally governed the other four.

[33] Discussion at SSRC-sponsored Chiang Mai Seminar, 15 August 1981.

[34] Khieu Samphan told an Australian visitor in 1980 that he wished his Ph.D. thesis, completed in the 1950s, had addressed "the real issue" (Vietnamese ambitions) rather than French colonialism or economic inequities. (Kelvin Rowley, personal communication.)

There is some evidence that this was true from time to time. In 1977–1978, for example, and culminating in the "Black Book," Cambodian history was vigorously rewritten so as to focus on the iniquity of Vietnam.[34] Similarly, histories of the CPK written between 1974 and 1978 gradually de-emphasized the role played by Cambodian radicals before the CPK was authentically "founded" in 1960. In both cases, it is easy to connect these shifts to the tactical requirements of the Pol Pot faction. More obscurely, these requirements are probably served by the emphasis which party leaders have placed on the survival of the Cambodian race at the apparent expense of the CPK itself, which "disbanded" at the end of 1981.[35]

To suggest that the CPK was not entirely in charge of DK perceptions of history, moreover, is not to assert that anti-CPK history or dissident historians ever flourished under the regime, or that Cambodian history is now a subject for discussion. At the same time, there are three components of recent DK historiography – that is, since the overthrow of the regime – that owe as much to pre-revolutionary thought patterns as to Marxist-Leninist ones. These are the experience of Angkor, the transformation of the Vietnamese into national *khmang*, and the self-regarding view that Cambodia is a major state, impervious to improvement or advice and incomparable to other nations. These ideas flourished under the regimes of Sihanouk and Lon Nol. Their roots can be found in part among the ideologies of the anti-French movement in the 1940s although only the experience of Angkor was used understandably by the pro-Vietnamese radical faction which evolved into the KPRP, the Pracheachon Group and, most recently, the ruling party in the People's Republic of Kampuchea (PRK).

The PRK has also chosen to play down the chauvinistic aspects of Cambodian Communism and historiography. Unlike Pol Pot

---

[35] Democratic Kampuchea, Permanent Mission the United Nations, "Communiqué."

and his colleagues (and unlike Sihanouk and Lon Nol, in earlier times) the leaders of the PRK have pressed no territorial claims, they picture the country as belonging to one family of a socialist nations and they emphasize the role of the Vietnamese in the history of the CPK by returning the Party's birthday to 1951. Interestingly, the PRK also picks up a thread of historiography from the Lon Nol regime which was abandoned under DK – of listing anti-colonial martyrs, usually anti-monarchic as well, who surfaced briefly in the 1940s but vanished when Sihanouk was in power.

Ideologues under Sihanouk and Lon Nol, when speaking about the "dangers" of Vietnam, sounded very much like the authors of the "Black Book" and occasionally made similar territorial claims. To them as to DK historians, Cambodian history was a series of territorial losses, inflicted largely by the Vietnamese. To them, Cambodia was a diminished nation. It could be argued, in fact, that emphases in Angkorean grandeur, Vietnamese depredations, and the autonomy of Cambodian history served the tactical interest of the regimes in the same way as they served the Pol Pot faction after 1976. What is more difficult to assess is the effect of these ideas on ordinary people. How many of them were widely *believed*? It seems likely that anti-Vietnamese feeling was more prevalent among the Cambodian elite than among peasants, although violence against Vietnamese could easily be orchestrated by Cambodian regimes. Angkor probably remained a mystery to most Cambodians who were happy that their ancestors had built the temples but failed to gain much intellectual nourishment from the idea. The self-regarding character of Cambodian ideology is not surprising in such an overwhelmingly rural country although the persistent incapacity or unwillingness of its leaders to accept the news that Cambodia was a small nation unable to escape from its surroundings may suggest an ideological choice similar to the one made in the late 1970s by the leaders of the CPK.

I am suggesting, then, that in launching attacks against "enemies of the state" in order to recapture Cambodia's national greatness, Pol Pot and his colleagues appear to have been swept along by considerations which pre-dated the arrival of socialism in Cambodia and which, they assumed, ran more deeply among ordinary people than many of their more recently acquired socialist ideas. In the eyes of the Pol Pot faction, the Cambodian "race," locked in combat with Vietnam as they had been against the Chams under Jayavarman VII was acting out the essential drama of its history.

Exactly why the Pol Pot faction embraced this course is impossible to determine. Some of their rationale probably dated back to ideas absorbed in the 1940s and 1950s, and some of it, as Stephen Heder has suggested[36] from their perceptions of Vietnamese ambitions *vis-à-vis* the Cambodian revolution. It is ironic, to say the least, that these ideas and perceptions should lead them into perceptions of history which were identical to those of the Khmer Republic. To say that they chose their course of action merely to meet their tactical requirements is inaccurate if these requirements sprang from their perceptions of history as they seem to have done rather than the reverse. For the same reason, using the evidence available it does not seem useful to question that they believed what they were saying, or to suggest that they were willing to say anything in order to remain in power. The course they chose involved enormous risks for them and for the rest of the country. This would suggest an element of sincerity, as well as a misguided reading of the past which they shared with every other doomed Cambodian regime.

---

[36] See Stephen R. Heder, "Kampuchea's Armed Struggle," *passim*.

A REVOLUTION IN FULL SPATE:
COMMUNIST PARTY POLICY
IN DEMOCRATIC KAMPUCHEA
DECEMBER 1976

The Peoples' Republic of Kampuchea (PRK) in many respects is a post revolutionary society. Democratic Kampuchea (DK), nearly two years after the abolition of the Communist Party of Kampuchea, has repeatedly disavowed any revolutionary intentions. For its part, the PRK regime has so far been unwilling and probably unable to bring the people of Cambodia to heel to serve its avowedly socialist goals. For millions of people in the coiuntry, such loyalty as they feel toward the regime is connected directly to the contrast between PRK behavior toward them since 1979 and DK behavior over the preceding years.

It seems likely that *internal* politics in the PRK will be acted out against this background for the next few years at least. For these reasons, as well as the intrinsic interest of Kampuchea's recent past, it seems worthwhile to examine the DK revolution in full spate, using a fifty-eight-page document prepared by the CPK for private circulation at the end of 1976.[1]

This paper was first published in *International Journal of Politics*, 1987.

[1] *Mapheap reboh mochumpak raam pear'kech niyobay ruom chnam 1976*. ("Report on the activities of the Party Center according to the general political tasks of l976" 58–page tyewritten text dated 20 December 1976. I'm grateful to Ben Kiernan for providing me with access to the document and for his comments on this paper. For a full translation, see David Chandler, Ben Kiernan and Chanthou Boua (eds. and tr.) *Pol Pot Plans the Future* (New Haven, l988), pp. 177–212.

We must be especially grateful for a document of this kind (and there are not very many of them) because so little was printed in Democratic Kampuchea between April 1975 and the end of 1978. The scarcity of documentation, which reflects official policy, is compounded by the regime's contempt for paperwork and research, and its much publicized preference for practice at the expense of theory. To a PLO visitor in 1976, Ieng Sary remarked, "We did not act with the guidance of definite theories, but followed our feelings and carried out the struggle in a practical way . . . What is important is the determination and faith of the principal revolutionaries. We did not study in ideological schools, but practiced a struggle in the light of the concrete situation."[2]

In a speech commemorating the eighteenth anniversary of the founding of the CPK in 1978, Pol Pot was even more schematic, remarking that "theory helps practice, and practice helps theory, but practice remains the basis. In this way the masses can accomplish their goal. Theory alone is too much for the masses. Practice alone will not go far. For these reasons we must combine theory and practice."[3]

These passages raise questions about the "feelings" mentioned by Ieng Sary, and the "determination and faith of the principal revolutionaries," as well as about whose practice and whose theory were to be combined and, more importantly, what sorts of practice "[remained] the basis" of the Kampuchean revolution.

Another characteristic of Democratic Kampuchea that deflects inquiries is its preference for being clandestine, for verbal ambiguity, and for subterfuge. This cast of mind meant, for example, that the existence of the CPK itself was kept a secret from the Kampuchean people until September 1977, and that the secretary general of the party, "Pol Pot," preferred to reveal to

[2] Quoted in Hamad Abdul Aziz al Aiya, "Modern Kampuchea," News from Kampuchea 1, 4 (October 1977), p. 35.

[3] See United States, *Foreign Broadcast Information Service* (*FBIS*), Daily Broadcasts, October 2, 1978.

nobody that for the first fifty years of his life he had been known as Saloth Sar. Examples such as these could easily be multiplied. In 1976, a party spokesman, writing in a *CPK* journal, went so far as to suggest that secrecy itself was to be taken as the "basis" of the revolution.[4] Certainly the number of facts kept from the Cambodian people between April 1975 and the end of 1978, and the methods Democratic Kampuchea employed to keep anyone from sharing or receiving information, suggest a conscious choice, by DK leaders, to run the country secretly, and to explain themselves, if at all, on the basis of a person's "need to know."

Moreover, Ieng Sary's phrase "determination and faith," like a great many DK declarations, suggests that the attitude of the regime toward information was ambiguous, to say the least. The preference for being clandestine encouraged the DK leaders to listen, for the most part, to themselves. The decision to carry their conspiratorial style of government over into the late 1970s, after the liberation of Phnom Penh, is difficult to assess. Did it reflect enormous self-confidence on the part of the leaders, or none at all? Had the revolution succeeded so spectacularly because of clandestinity, or was it on the verge of collapse unless clandestinity was maintained? Who trusted the party? Whom could the party trust? These are fascinating questions, and they have been tackled by several scholars. What interests me is the attitude toward information that prolonged isolation and clandestinity had fostered among these men and women at the center of the party. As William Willmott has shown, it is clear that not much serious research lay behind the *CPK*'s ham-fisted "analysis" of Cambodian rural sociology, or its decision to single out "feudal landlords" for special blame, rather than local Chinese and Sino-Khmer who dominated the economic life of the country.[5] It seems likely that information *per se* was of little interest to them until it could be harnessed to their ideas of strategy and tactics. Despite lip-service in texts and speeches

---

[4] *Tung Padevat* [*Revolutionary Flags*], (September-October 1976), p. 27.
[5] William E. Willmott, "Analytical Errors of the Kampuchean Communist Party," *Pacific Affairs* 54, 2 (Summer 1981), pp. 209–227.

studying Cambodia's "objective conditions" it is unlikely that much studying took place and while this is unsurprising in the grueling civil war of 1967–1975, the self-assurance of the CPK after 1975 reflects their frequently stated view that victory was identical to "practice."

Pol Pot and his colleagues were entranced by the exercise of power and by the *praxis* of prolonged and unrelenting warfare. To bring about a millenial transformation of the nation and its people through internal and external war DK leaders depended on the hard work and loyalty of everyone in the country. They sought to insure these by controlling everyone's access to food, leisure, movement and information. The balance of evidence and the document discussed below suggest that the leaders knew very little about the "people" and distrusted them en masse. Information reaching them that class warfare and national transformation were proceeding slowly, painfully, or expensively seems to have made little difference to their 1976 decision to accelerate these two procedures. Even though regional differences of fertility, personnel and leadership (to name only three) were often extreme, as Michael Vickery has shown, CPK policies aimed at a full-scale, consistently paced revolution. In 1976–77 at least, what was actually happening to the "new" people, in terms of their own health and sanity, made little difference, as the widely circulated slogan about "new people" – "sparing them's no profit; losing them's no loss" – suggests. On the other hand, information that conveyed the impression to the leadership that everyone's loyalty was open to question – i.e., that everyone was potentially disloyal – appears to have been accepted at the party center in a comparatively uncritical way.

Spokesmen for the regime spoke often of "contradictions" (*tumno'h*) and suggested that the clash of opposites itself rather than any synthesis between them that might develop was what gave life to the revolution. The regime's own relations with the majority of the people, of course, represent a contradiction of another kind. On the one hand, the masses (*mahachon*) were the ones on whose behalf the revolution was ostensibly taking place. On the other, revolutionaries must always be on their guard against them, at least on an individual basis. In the war with Vietnam that began in 1977, the people were ordered to "fight to the death" but the regime gave them no weapons to fight with. And although the regime claimed in late 1975 that there was only one stratum in Cambodian society – the worker-peasants – everyone was enjoined to wage warfare against "class enemies." These enemies were never defined by the regime with much precision. Although "99 percent" of the masses ostensibly supported the revolution, those who opposed it were thought to permeate every level of the society, including the ranks of the CPK itself. Pulverizing this embedded segment gave the revolution a *raison d'être* (and the party center, incidentally, carte blanche). In other words, forming all of Cambodia's people into collective life, swiftly and thoroughly, was not intended merely as a means of transforming society in a rewarding way. Rather, as some documents assert, the main purpose of collectivization was to expose its enemies and prevent the old society from reemerging: "Why do we make revolution?" a Party spokesman asked in 1976. "We have not come to make revolution blindly. Nobody has forced us to do it. We have consented to all sacrifices for this cause because we want to shake off the domination, oppression, and repression of the enemy and help liberate our worker-peasant class."[6]

The CPK held power in Phnom Penh for less than forty-one months. In the first year or so, operating as a front with Prince Sihanouk as chief of state, the party concentrated on transferring "nearly four million people" (its own estimate) from the cities to the countryside, and on tackling the "problem of water" so as to achieve national self-sufficiency in rice. Less openly, the party center used this time to consolidate its hold on the army, and on the military regions that had operated with a good deal of autonomy during the civil war. Although it was clear to foreign

---

[6] *FBIS*, September 4, 1978.

observers such as Timothy Carney that the CPK was identical to the "organization" (*angkar*) supposedly running the country, the party kept its existence secret from the masses throughout 1975 and 1976.

When Democratic Kampuchea assumed state power in April 1976, the party center took several steps to inaugurate what it referred to secretly at first as a "socialist revolution" (padevat *sangkum* niyum). At the end of August 1976, an economic development plan for the years 1977–1980 was discussed at a three-day meeting sponsored by the party center. The plan, which was instituted at the beginning of 1977, called for the collectivization of industry and agriculture and set targets for agricultural production. Shortly afterward, the CPK set in motion the first of many purges against "traitors" (kbot) allegedly embedded in its ranks. Veteran members of the party, like Keo Meas and Non Suon, were arrested, interrogated, tortured, and killed. I have argued elsewhere that the purges were probably connected with a controversy connected with the birthdate of the CPK and its implications for relations with Vietnam, and with arguments within the party about making its existence known.[7] The party center decided to set 1960, rather than 1951, as the birthdate of the party, and to keep the party's existence a secret from nonmembers.

On December 20, 1976, the party center completed a fifty-eight page document for internal distribution entitled "Report on the Activities of the Party Center: Political Tasks, 1976." Its style suggests that it represents the transcription of a speech, probably delivered by the secretary of the CPK, Pol Pot. The typescript offers a rare glimpse of Democratic Kampuchea examining itself, evaluating its performance and setting its priorities at a turning point in its short career.

The report is divided into three parts following a one-page introduction. The first of these, entitled "Revolutionary Tasks,

---

[7] See David Chandler, "Revising the Past in Democratic Kampuchea: When was the Birthday of the Party?" above p. 215.

1976," opens with a discussion of the party's plan to introduce and intensify the socialist revolution. Three aspects of society still impede such a revolution: exploiting classes, individualism, and privilege. In 1976, however, exploiting classes fell "even farther down" than in 1975 but remnants remained to be "beaten, pulverized and uprooted," and class enemies existed even in the ranks of the party. As for individualism, the key to obliterating it was to abolish private, personal property. Privilege, which still existed "especially inside the party" needed to be eradicated as well.

The report goes on to make a case for an all-embracing socialist revolution, claiming that "if our revolution is not all-embracing the party will be confused, the army will be confused, the people will be confused, officers and ministries will be confused and the 1976 development plan will be defeated."

But the diffusion of clarity is not sufficient reason to wage a revolution, as the next three pages of the text make clear. A major reason for doing so is to extirpate its enemies, compared to "microbes" (*merok*) embedded inside it. The "people's" and "democratic" revolutions of the 1960s and early 1970s had allowed some of the microbes to take shelter inside the *CPK* itself:

> The heat of the peoples' revolution and the democratic revolution were not enough . . . The level of people's struggle and class struggle meant that [when] we searched for evil microbes inside the party, we couldn't find them. They were able to hide. Now that we are advancing on an all-embracing socialist revolution . . . in the party, in the army, among the people, we can find the evil microbes. They emerge, pushed out by the true nature of the socialist revolution.

Throughout the text, "enemies" and "traitors" inside the party and abroad are never identified by name or in terms of ideology.

The tendency to leave readers and listeners guessing about such things was widespread in DK texts before 1978 when all enemies became generically Vietnamese. This 1976 text, however, fails to clarify who the "traitors" were who have lingered on from the earlier stages of revolution and must now be pushed aside.

Perhaps they were Sihanouk and his entourage; perhaps they were those like Keo Meas who had argued against the party's continued clandestinity (or some of its policies); perhaps they were the DK ambassadors recalled from their posts at this time for "consultation" and arrested for treason soon after they arrived. The text, in other words, gives us no criteria for judging "friends" or "enemies." Categories of people to guard against and the kinds of offenses they are likely to commit are not made clear. As in so many DK documents, one gets the impression that a major purpose is to provide the party center with freedom to maneuver.

There is no need for more precision, the text contends, because a socialist revolution provides party members with correct behavior on its own: "We must resolve the errors that we encounter in our ranks, but no ministry of state security will reveal them. The socialist revolution [itself] will do so, and will seep into the party, the army and the people, sorting good from evil."

The revolution proceeds by the collectivization of food, supplies, the means of production, workers, and peasants. In 1976, we are told, the process had already made enormous progress, against enormous odds: "We had empty hands. We lacked food. We lacked tools. Cattle and buffaloes were sick, and many died. Enemies from outside and enemies within continued their activities. We had no assistance from anywhere in the world."

There are no answers here for the important questions: Who were the enemies? What were they trying to do? Moreover, nothing is said of any *human* deaths connected with the acceleration of social change.

The report goes on to suggest that the only way to counter the hostility the revolution has met inside Cambodia and elsewhere is to prepare for a people's war; guerilla warfare inside the country, and a full-scale war along the frontiers, particularly since there are secret agents (*phtai knong*) working for unnamed powers everywhere.

The second section of the report deals with what it calls "Two Key Tasks for 1976": organizing collectives into larger units than villages, and solving the problem of water. The expansion of collectivization was delayed because there were insufficient party members to supervise the process – an issue taken up in more detail at a later stage of the report. Solving the water problem means, in essence, providing all collectives with enough water to deliver the three-ton *per annum* per hectare quota or to exceed it. According to the report, the population of Cambodia, estimated at 7.7 million people, consumed thirteen thang (i.e., approximately 780 pounds) of *padi* per capita per year. At 1976 production rates, calculated in some detail, the party center estimated that this would already allow for an exportable surplus of milled rice of between 100,000 and 150,000 metric tons.

The report goes on to review the production of *padi* throughout the country in 1976. Four zones (Northwest, East, Southwest and West) are deemed to have produced sufficient rice for food and seeds, and to maintain enough reserves for some of the surplus to be exported. Exportable surplusses in the East and Northwest, traditionally the "rice-baskets" of Cambodia, are set at 50,000 tons apiece. The less favored West and Southwest are asked to export 20,000 and 30,000 tons respectively. The North (an area including Kompong Thom) was short of *padi* for food to the extent of 12,117 tons in 1976, according to the report; the Northeast was similarly a deficit area. Region 106, which included Siem Reap, enjoyed a 10,000–ton surplus of *padi* and was asked to set nearly all of it aside for export.

One point that emerges from this passage is that the Northwest (largely liberated in 1975, and then repopulated with hundreds of thousands of "new people") is asked by the party to export less than half of its alleged surplus of *padi*, while the East, with its healthy workforce, its competent cadres (and, perhaps, its proximity to Vietnam) is levied more than two-thirds of its surplus.

With exports out of the way, the report goes on to discuss five problems that may impede the acceleration of agriculture. The first of these is the problem of water. More work is needed, the report asserts, on water shortage tanks, feeder canals, ditches, and reservoirs. The second problem, treated in less detail, involves the labor force: "In 1976 the labor force was feeble. It was only in the East that it was not feeble. Thus in the coming year we must arrange things properly and persuade people to follow the party's plan, and to rest according to the party's plan. Resting three days a month is sufficient for health, but when people work nonstop, it has ill-effects on them."

There are two things of interest in this passage. The first is that it confirms the conclusions of several scholars, derived from interviews, that conditions in the DK Eastern Zone were somewhat more benign, and that the labor force was handled somewhat more humanely than elsewhere in the country.[8] One reason for this is that the region had a long tradition of radicalism and an unusually high proportion of indigenous peasants. Many *CPK* cadres operating in the East had become affiliated with the Vietnamese communists during the war against the French (1945–1954). This long association gave them not only some sympathy for the revolution but also some experience of working both as cadres and as farmers among the local population. The passage itself implies that inexperienced cadres elsewhere in DK feeling pressure from the party center and indifferent to the fate

---

[8] See the essays by Ben Kiernan, Michael Vickery, and Anthony Barnett in David Chandler and Ben Kiernan, eds. *Revolution and Its Aftermath in Kampuchea: Eight Essays* (New Haven: Yale University Southeast Asia Studies, 1983).

of inexperienced newcomers, were prepared or even delighted to work some of the newcomers to death.

The remaining problems obstructing the achievement of CPK goals have to do with seed-rice, fertilizers, tools and medicine for the peasants. Throughout this section, the party center deals rather mechanically with what it perceives to be a mechanical problem.

There is nothing here about increasing one's awareness of contradictions. Instead, the "labor force" is seen as an ingredient of the problem, rather than its solution; it is akin to tools and water. Like livestock, the labor force needs food, rest, and medicine. In the context of the passages being discussed, the aspirations and "liberation" of people inside the work force are neither here nor there.

The report then sets forth the Party Center's plans for the future in other areas than self-sufficiency in rice. These involve increasing production of secondary and plantation crops, raising more animals for food, producing more medicine, repairing transportation facilities and so on. Interestingly, "culture" is mentioned briefly and last of all:

> Progress in the work of abolishing illiteracy has been good. Some places manage to set some time aside, specifically for studying. But other places have failed to do this. Arrangements should be made carefully. Books should be prepared that are identical throughout the country. It is important that these books be easy, so that people can learn [from them] to follow the revolutionary path.

Here again, the people are treated as objects rather than subjects and education (a word that is not mentioned in the report) is defined as the absorption of simple, standardized texts that enable otherwise uneducated people to follow the revolutionary path.

The report's final section carries the title "Tasks of All Sorts Which Are Subservient to the Political Central Tasks of 1976." The first of these is seen as the problem of developing the party and its central organization. The report claims that all party members have been informed by now of the decisions of the party center that led to the policy of accelerating a socialist revolution in Kampuchea. Once again, as in the first section of the report, the main obstacle to this object is a lack of understanding, and therefore, "We must grasp the essential character of Kampuchean society more clearly, so as to know who friends are, and who enemies are, and in what ways the class struggle in Kampuchea must be carried out. This is a real necessity, especially in forming cadres at every level."

The report goes on to give an "example" of what is required:

> In order to defend the country well, one must grasp the situation inside the country firmly, the situation all around us firmly, and also the situation of the world. If these are not grasped firmly, the enemies' weaknesses and the enemies' strengths cannot be seen; nor can our strengths and weaknesses. Wrong measures will be taken, leading to disorder.

To avoid "disorder," cadres must be trained carefully to be in tune with party strategy for the next "ten, twenty, thirty . . . hundred years." The report admits the difficulties of inculcating so much subtlety at the pace required by the revolution, but it also stresses – in a brief paragraph – the need for unspecified, intensive study.

A major problem the Party Center faced at the end of 1976, which the report discusses next, was the need to expand party membership to provide cadres capable of understanding the principle of collectivization on the one hand and of administering collectives on the other. Although the number of party members already in place in each collective is not given, the speaker suggests that the figure be increased in each collective by 40 percent in the first half of 1977 and by 60 percent in the second half so as to double by December 1977.

How were new members to be selected? Each *sruk* was to provide "several" candidates per quarter, chosen in terms of their "life histories" (pravatt'rup) and from recommendations. Candidates would be told that "higher authority has called them away to study." When the (unspecified) studying was done, candidates would be made to prepare their own life histories. If these failed to conform with information received from the candidates' base areas, they would be asked to reexamine the profiles, and then the candidates would rewrite them until the two reports converged.

People's life histories, the report contends, are the strongest recommendation for new members of the party-far better than someone's deceptive record of activities, which might allow enemies to appear eligible for inclusion. What one did was important during the war against Lon Nol, says the report – the closest it comes to saying that the war was fought by a united front – but people's class background – i.e., whether they were born poor or not – is now more crucial. Collectives in the hands of these properly screened people, under the leadership of the party, will provide a bulwark (kampeng) of defense.

The next section takes up the question of whether the party should "come into the open or remain clandestine." The section is worth quoting in full.

> The situation inside the country and outside the country is sufficiently developed for the party to come into the open.
>
> Friendly parties express the wish that our party come into the open. For one thing, they see that the situation would allow the party to come into the open. For another thing, they need our support.
>
> Enemies also want to see us come out, so as to see clearly; this would enable them to pursue their own ends.

But if the party came into the open, this would pose problems of protecting the leadership of the party. During September and October 1976, we were on the point of coming into the open. But since that time, documents have revealed that the enemy has sought to beat us, more than ever.

Still another problem is that if the party came into the open, difficulties would be created with certain people. We have therefore decided to defer a decision on the issue of the party's coming into the open.

It seems likely that while pressure to bring the CPK into the open probably came from China, and perhaps from North Korea, further pressure came from within the party, particularly as the numerologically significant twenty-fifth anniversary of the founding of its predecessor party, the Khmer People's Revolutionary Party (KPRP), approached on September 30, 1976. Pressure to celebrate this anniversary probably came from elements in the party opposed to its anti-Vietnamese stance. The KPRP had been founded, after all, under the patronage of the Indochina Communist Party (ICP) soon after that party's "dissolution." The "documents" referred to here may be confessions extracted from some of these long-serving party members, like Keo Meas, who had been arrested in late September; one of his confessions in the archives at the Party's interrogation center at Tuol Sleng, where he was incarcerated before being killed, is entitled "1951 or 1960?" – a reference to the founding anniversary (1960) preferred by Pol Pot and his colleagues.[9]

While it is likely that the text refers to this sequence of events the speaker gives no clear assurances as to who the "enemies" were, or what their "activities" involved. And how would bringing the party into the open have endangered the Party Center? It

---

[9] I'm grateful to Ben Kiernan for information about Keo Meas's confession, which I discuss in more detail in "Revising the Past," above.

is possible that what is meant is that the pressure to bring the party into the open was accompanied by pressure for a *coup d'etat*; certainly DK spokesmen often said as much, in 1977–78, when referring to September 1976. But there is no way of knowing this from the passage as it stands.

The report turns next to the problem of inducing the people to strengthen their syndicates and collectives "so as to develop the worker-peasant alliance under the leadership of the party."

Previously, the speaker admits, political training had been ignored or insufficient. In many places distrust had built up between the people and CPK cadres. By improving cadres' political consciousness, the report declares, the people's confidence in the cadres will increase. Those who live apart from the people and don't suffer from the same shortages are not respected. Cadres must live among the people and serve them unafraid: "Don't be afraid of enemies buried among the people. Whenever we serve all of the people, even though there are one or two enemies among them, they cannot stay buried for long."

These pages reveal lyrical confidence in the capabilities of ordinary people, unique in the report; in fact, they encourage an open dialogue about a limited number of subjects which the Party Center appears to shy away from. In a revealing passage, the report goes on to say that "some comrades seem to believe that all 'new people' are enemies and so they do not pay attention to expanding their awareness of politics, and do not pay attention to solving problems of their livelihood. This is a very great error, for it would mean not gathering everyone up on the side of the revolution."

One way of "stirring up the people," and of increasing their understanding of the revolution, is to hold short, frequent meetings to explain the party's plans. There are problems even here, however, for

If we stir up the masses in this way, one crazy fraction will take advantage of us, and will raise this difficulty, that difficulty, beg for this, beg for that. But we shouldn't be afraid. Our path is correct, our rationale is correct, we serve the people, the people support the party. In the beginning, one or two people [presumably cadres] are able to mistreat the people, but as time goes on, the people gain awareness, they understand.

The next section deals with the expansion of the party's control of state power. The "very poor class" nourishes the party and protects its dominant position by uprooting "secret networks of the enemy." These can be found in collectives and in factories. The frightened and menacing tone of this passage contrasts sharply with the benevolent one before it. Why is this so? Perhaps because the "enemies," unlike the "people" are unspecified, "buried," hard to find. If "the people" are those who believe in the revolution (as defined by the party center), enemies are those who actively oppose it, and those who only seem to give it their support. How are these hypocrites to be ferreted out? Primarily by verifying everyone's class status and by taking advantage of the heightened clarity of vision that accompanies one's understanding of the revolution.

The "enemies" of the Party Center at the end of 1976 appear to have been a transitional group. On the one hand, in the past, lay the Americans, the Lon Nol "lackeys," capitalists and landlords of the "old society," making up "new people" who had been "rounded up" into collectives particularly in the Northwest. On the other hand, perhaps, in the future, but clearly hinted at in the report, are the Vietnamese. The enemies of the moment, in other words, are those who might tend to support those of the past, those of the future, or both. By keeping their identities imprecise, the Party Center had the options of attacking the enemies it liked.

At the end of 1976, the report suggests, however, that there were parts of the country where the CPK was not sufficiently in control:

In some places, particularly in the Northwest, the proportion of new people is far too high. For this reason, former soldiers and former government employees have insinuated themselves into positions of responsibility in many collectives. For this reason the party has been unable to develop sufficient influence, so far, and so a number of combatants and a number of revolutionary youths must be chosen to take charge of these collectives to prevent enemies from taking over.

No one can transform himself into a revolutionary, in other words, unless his class origins allow the transformation to take place. The report makes this point, by warning against accepting people from the "upper stratum" for positions of responsibility in the collectives, because they may belong to "enemy networks," while "as for people from lower strata who have just come out of the cities, don't choose them yet [for positions of responsibility]. They are too diverse."

Turning to DK foreign relations, the report makes the point that the *CPK* has established friendly relations with a number of "Marx-Lenin" parties, including parties in and out of power. In the future, the speaker continues, DK plans to increase the number of noncommunist countries with which it has diplomatic relations, partly to overcome the insults it has received from "American and French imperialists," who have taken unfair advantage of Democratic Kampuchea's inability to defend itself abroad. Characteristically, no other friendly or unfriendly countries – and particularly China and Vietnam – are mentioned at this point. The section closes by stating,

Our only failing overseas has been a shortage of cadres in the revolutionary movement who are able to work in the field of foreign affairs. Some [foreign affairs] personnel have come back from outside the country, and thus are separated from the movement. Others have acceptable life histories, but lack the skills to serve the movement. At the moment we need several new ambassadors. We beg those attending this meeting to put their minds to solving this problem.

The last line indicates that the report was delivered orally for discussion. Some of those at the meeting would have been aware that on the very day this report was tabled – December 20, 1976 – DK ambassadors and diplomatic personnel, summoned home for "consultations," had been arrested at Phnom Penh airport and taken off for interrogation and torture at Tuol Sleng, thereby creating personnel vacancies in DK missions overseas. These vacancies were difficult to fill, because diplomacy was the only area in which Democratic Kampuchea was required to behave by foreigners' conventions.

The following section of the report takes up the issue of implanting the ideas of revolution through Democratic Kampuchea: "We are not thinking merely of forests and mountains, we are paying attention to the entire country: the countryside, the cities, the collectives, the factories, offices, and ministries, all of them can see how the revolution has progressed . . ."

An issue of concern to the party center, however, was that "certain places, some in the interior, others along the frontiers, are not yet firm, or reliable enough . . . there are problems here. People are running off to Vietnam, to Siam [sic], to Laos. The places are not reliable, for one thing, because of new people. And yet there are also base areas of long standing, from which people are fleeing to other countries."

To combat this problem, the report suggests "toughening" the army and expanding the role of the CPK. In practical terms, people who lack "good characteristics" should be moved from frontier areas and their places taken by "old, reliable people" (i.e., hardened revolutionaries).

The closing pages of the report exhorts listeners to protect the party by remaining vigilant "without making their alertness known," and by working in secret to ferret out enemies wherever they may be found.

The report concludes by pledging its listeners' obedience to the tasks imposed on them by the party center, "no matter how much initiative or creativity you may show."

Inadvertently, the report tells us a good deal about the mentality of the DK regime and the ways in which it governed Cambodia from 1975 to 1979. The stress the document places on clandestinity and "enemies," for example, and the ways in which it seeks rather than avoids ambiguities of language, probably derive in large part from the experience and preferences of the men and women who made up the Party Center.

Throughout the history of the CPK and its predecessor parties, the membership of the Central Committee, party policies and everything else about the party had been kept a secret. Such clandestinity was normal for a party intent on seizing power and was forced on the CPK by Sihanouk's anticommunist policies. Moreover, it worked: before 1970, Sihanouk himself seems to have had no idea of the membership of the party center. After 1963, when this group of people, led by Saloth Sar (Pol Pot), sought refuge in the countryside the disjunction between them and the Cambodian political process became even more pronounced. From then on, the center seldom explained itself, even to party members, or argued the feasibility of the policies it was developing in secret, on its own. No party congresses were held between 1963 and 1971.[10] Instead, at the core of the party was an anonymous "organization" (*angkar*) impervious to attack (or consultation) and indifferent to information. Anonymity served the leaders well during the civil war that broke out in 1967–68, but why did Saloth Sar's secretiveness about himself, and the CPK's reluctance to come into the open, persist after April 1975? Three explanations suggest themselves. One is that Pol Pot, who assumed this pseudonym at about this time, felt

---

[10] Ben Kiernan, personal communication.

no obligation to reveal himself to his enemies who had lost the civil war. From 1975 to 1979, indeed, the "organization" treated survivors of the Khmer Republic as if they were citizens of another nation, rather than fellow Khmer. A second explanation is that the leaders of the CPK, by keeping under cover, were not required in public to honor the internationalist components of communist ideology, or to express fraternal solidarity with other parties, particularly with Vietnam. The Vietnamese knew who was in charge of the CPK without being told, and they were aware of the anti-Vietnamese policies the CPK had pursued since 1971. Moreover, the mere expression of solidarity between two communist parties does not preclude contrary behavior. Thus it seems likely that the CPK kept its identity a secret primarily to convince people inside the country that the "organization" owed nothing to communist history or models. It served purely Cambodian ends. Because it was incomparable, the Cambodian revolution was idiosyncratically national rather than recognizably communist. Enemies were identified as foreigners, or those who served them.

The question then arises: why did Pol Pot and his colleagues persist in calling themselves communists at all? They did so, perhaps, to retain the support of China and North Korea, to retain the services of CPK cadres tempered by the civil war, and because they saw themselves not as schismatics but as communist revolutionaries of a particularly pure sort whose victory offered a model for revolutionaries elsewhere in the Third World.

By remaining clandestine and anonymous, the party center maintained its freedom of maneuver. By using ambiguous language, it was able to keep its "enemies" – who changed from day to day – off-balance. The idea that the Cambodian revolution was exemplary and incomparable, coupled with the notion that the party center was always right, may have led the CPK to force the pace of the revolution in 1976–77, with little regard, if any, for the human costs involved. In December 1976 the leaders of the CPK may well have been uncertain of Chinese support, following Mao's death; uncertain about relations with Thailand, following the right-wing *coup* in Bangkok in October 1976; and uncertain, as they had been for several years, about Vietnam's long-term geopolitical plans. These uncertainties intensified the Party Center's search for "enemies" inside Kampuchea's borders and inside the CPK. A sense that time was running out may have encouraged the CPK's leaders in their belief that the revolution in Kampuchea had to be accelerated and completed as rapidly as possible. Once again, the absence of historical precedents for such a transformation does not seem to have worried Pol pot and his colleagues. In fact the absence of models appears to have encouraged them to push ahead.

As things turned out, the Party Center had little cause to be alarmed about China or Thailand in 1977 and 1978. On the other hand, encouraged by Beijing, the CPK soon chose to embark on a provocative policy toward Vietnam, to preserve Cambodia's independence and to focus the virulent energies of the revolutionary process in general, and the army in particular, on a new target. It is impossible to say whether those in the party center believed that Vietnam could be defeated militarily, or that Vietnam would never dare to invade Cambodia in strength. In the process of "purification" that swept through the country in 1977–78, as the war was waged, hundreds of thousands of citizens were executed as "enemies" or died of malnutrition or disease as they were mobilized for all-out war. There is no way of telling how far this process would have continued had the Vietnamese postponed or cancelled their attack, but it seems likely that the policies of 1977–78, many of them foreshadowed in the 1976 report, laid the basis for millions of survivors turning against an indigenous nationalist regime and welcoming a foreign invasion. In this sense, the CPK's estimate that its enemies were everywhere may turn out to be one of its very few accurate assessments.

CAMBODIA IN 1984:
HISTORICAL PATTERNS RE-ASSERTED?

In the third century B.C., Ch'in troops attacking Yueh strongholds along what is now the frontier between China and Vietnam discovered that

> the Yueh people fled into the depths of the mountains and forests, and it was not possible to fight them. The soldiers were kept in garrisons to watch over abandoned territories. This went on for a long time, and the soldiers grew weary. Then the Yueh came out and attacked; the Ch'in soldiers suffered a great defeat. Subsequently, convicts were sent to hold the garrisons against the Yueh.[1]

Skillful resistance to Chinese encroachments was to form a leitmotiv of Vietnamese history over two millenia. Without altering the sense of the passage very much, we could even read "French" or "Americans" for "Ch'in", retaining a picture of foreigners bogged down in a hostile country.

But what if we were to alter the passage to read "Vietnamese" for "Ch'in" and "Cambodian guerrillas" for "Yueh"? Many

This paper was first published in *SEASI Southeast Asian Affairs*, 1985, reprinted with permission.

[1] Keith Taylor, *The Birth of Vietnam* (Berkeley: University of California Press, 1983), p. 24.

reports in 1984, emanating from the "Coalition Government of Democratic Kampuchea (CGDK)" read alarmingly like the passage I have quoted. As Mark Twain remarked, history may not repeat itself, but it can often be said to rhyme.

In this essay, I propose to examine some of the "rhymes" between events in Cambodia in the 1980s and events at earlier stages in its history. Vietnamese interference in Cambodian life goes back to the early seventeenth century, and intensified gradually over the next two hundred years. The period 1811–1845, when the Cambodian court fell under systematic Vietnamese control, offers some interesting parallels with the situation in Cambodia today when a Vietnamese-sponsored regime, the People's Republic of Kampuchea (PRK) holds office in Phnom Penh, threatened particularly in the north and northwest of the country by Cambodian guerrillas of several political persuasions supported from Bangkok and from further afield as well.[2] The parallels between the two eras, however, are misleading ones. For one thing, Vietnamese influence in Phnom Penh, extensive in both eras (and perhaps exaggerated by hostile witnesses) was merely Vietnamese in the nineteenth century, and could not be interpreted as action at a distance on the part of a larger power. Nowadays, on the other hand, Pol Pot's Democratic Kampuchea (DK: the most effective segment of the Coalition Government of Democratic Kampuchea, in military terms) and Heng Samrin's PRK are seen by many observers as surrogates for China and the United States on the one hand and the Soviet Union on the other.[3] Another sharp difference between Cambodia in the early nineteenth century and 1984 has to do with Thai military ambitions and capabilities. In the nineteenth century the Thai mounted several important military expeditions to remove the Vietnamese from Phnom Penh and to assert Thai influence

[2] David Chandler, *A History* of Cambodia, paperback edition (Boulder, Colorado: Westview Press, 1996, Chapters 6 and 7.
[3] See Anthony Lake, "Dealing with Hanoi", Indochina Issues, 49 (August 1984.)

over the Cambodian court. In the twentieth century aside from campaigning against France in 1940–1941, the Thai have never mounted systematic expeditions against Cambodia. It is ironic, in this regard, that while the Thai have invaded Cambodia so often, the Vietnamese have never invaded Thailand, particularly when spokesmen in both countries are busily searching for historical analogies and pointing to "historical" threats. Finally, while in 1984 there is a good deal of evidence to show that the Heng Samrin regime's popularity with ordinary Cambodians springs in large part from the Vietnamese army's capacity to keep the DK forces at bay, Vietnamese protection of Cambodia in the 1830s appears to have confused and intimidated all but a few Cambodians without attracting any compensating support.

It is clear that the "rhymes" of Cambodian history should not be forced into anything stronger, particularly in the service of national interests which have no parallels in the 1840s. Moreover, it is fatuous to suggest that Vietnamese policies in the 1840s are identical to policies in the 1980s or that Cambodia itself has remained passive and susceptible to these pressures for 140 years.[4]

Despite these cautions, it is possible to say that what is happening in Cambodia in 1984 has often occurred before. Since the seventeenth century, in fact, Cambodian history can be seen as an alternation of brief periods of autonomy with longer periods of dependence. This alternation is partly due to Cambodia's proximity and accessibility to powerful, heavily populated neighbors, and partly to the xenophobia which so often characterizes independent Cambodian regimes. Foreign powers convinced that they have been, in some sense, "born to rule" Cambodia – I refer, for the period since 1848, to the Thai, the French, and now the Vietnamese – have never had much respect

---

[4] The remarks of U.S. Assistant Secretary of Defense, Richard Armitage, delivered on the occasion of "Cambodia Day", 11 September 1984, suggest that some policy-makers for rhetorical purposes at least consider the twentieth century a replica of the nineteenth insofar as Cambodia is concerned.

for the concept of Cambodian autonomy, and Cambodian ideas about politics or international relations, nor for what is different about Cambodian values from their own.

Particularly since the 1790s the settled central area of Cambodia has been a battleground between Thai and Vietnamese interests, or more precisely between what appears to be the forward defense policies pursued by Bangkok, Hué, Saigon and Hanoi. In the 1830s, the Vietnamese emperor, Minh Mang, referred to Cambodia repeatedly as his country's "fence". During the French colonial period, Cambodia and Laos served as convenient buffer zones, and the concept of "Indochina", primarily one of administrative convenience, became, for Vietnamese communists at least, an article of faith.[5] For the Thai, Cambodia lay within a Bangkok-centered Theravada Buddhist cultural zone.

In this sense at least, the mid-1980s "rhyme" with the first half of the nineteenth century. Along the border between Thailand and Cambodia, Thai and Vietnamese forces (aided, and in the Thai case, egged on by larger states) are maneuvering against each other in an effort to insure that any government in Phnom Penh will act predominantly in Thai or Vietnamese political interests. The Thai carry out this struggle within ASEAN as well. Both states are assiduously seeking international support for the "legitimate" Cambodian regimes which they sustain in office.

The cultural differences between Thailand and Cambodia on the one hand and Vietnam on the other, no longer as perceptible as they were in the 1840s, have now been perhaps transferred into the realm of ideology. The components of the CGDK and the Thai Government proclaim a free enterprise orientation while the SRV and the PRK are socialist regimes. There are many ironies here. In Vietnam's attempt to personalize and

---

[5] See Gareth Porter, "Vietnamese Communist Policy toward Kampuchea, 1930–70", in David Chandler and Ben Kiernan, eds, *Revolution and its Aftermath in Kampuchea* (New Haven: Yale University, Southeast Asia Studies. 1983), pp. 58–60.

condemn the "Pol Pot" regime its spokesmen scrupulously avoid mentioning that Democratic Kampuchea was for over two years recognized in Hanoi as a "fraternal" fellow-socialist state. For the Vietnamese to admit Cambodia's brief socialist past would be to undermine their own claims to be setting in motion rather than continuing a Marxist-Leninist revolution inside Cambodia.

Because previous Vietnamese interference in Cambodian life took place so long ago in a largely illiterate country the "historical" aspects of the Vietnamese threat have passed into folk memory. Peasant refugees from Cambodia today, when asked why they fear the Vietnamese, often refer to nineteenth century events.[6] How justified are they in doing so? Again, some rhymes or half-rhymes appear to be involved.

In the early nineteenth century courtiers in Udong or Phnom Penh, the alternate Cambodian capitals, as well as most ordinary Khmer saw their cultural forms and values largely indistinguishable by this time from those of their counterparts in Bangkok and the Thai countryside as threatened by the Vietnamese, whose hair-styles, clothing, eating habits, architecture, religious practices and village organization – to say nothing of differences in language, self-perceptions, concepts of history and literary genres – were radically different from their own. In a time of poor communications, isolation, widespread illiteracy and random violence the strangeness of foreigners aroused fear and animosity. In the Vietnamese case, these were exacerbated by the fact that unlike other minority populations in Cambodia – the Chams, Chinese and hill tribes – the Vietnamese in this period attempted to overturn Cambodian values on a national scale. Like the French who followed them, the Vietnamese appear to have believed that they had a *mission civilisatrice*; to them, the Cambodians were benighted.

[6] Author's interviews with refugees in Khao-i-Dang Holding Center, October 1984. Several elderly refugees referred to stories told them by their grandparents, passed down from the 1840s, about persistent Vietnamese behavior.

Under the French administration of Indochina (the dates for Cambodia are 1863 to 1954) many of the barriers between Khmer and Vietnamese eroded. For one, half a million Vietnamese, often encouraged to do so by the French, eventually settled in Cambodia, and came to dominate some sectors of the economy such as fishing in the Tonlé Sap, labour on the French rubber plantations, and petty artisanry in the towns. Hundreds of Vietnamese, at any given time, occupied positions in the colonial civil service. Cambodia's most prominent nationalist in the 1940s, Son Ngoc Thanh, was half-Vietnamese. The Prime Minister of the CGDK, Son Sann, also has Vietnamese blood, and so does the high-ranking DK official, Ieng Sary. At the time, Cambodia was linked closely in financial terms with southern Vietnam, then known as Cochin China. In the colonial era, Cambodia had no deep water port; its international trade, controlled by the French, passed through Saigon. Moreover, in the first Indochina war (1945–1954), Vietnamese strategy in Cochin China dictated the behaviour of Vietnamese-supported guerrillas inside Cambodia. From the beginning of the 1950s, Vietnamese communists guided their counterparts in Cambodia. The Cambodian Communist Party, founded at Vietnamese insistence in 1951, was known then as now as the KPRP, although the word "Khmer" in the title Khmer People's Revolutionary Party in 1951 was changed to "Kampuchean" when according to the Vietnamese the party came back to life at its "third congress" in 1979.[7]

Between 1954 and 1979 the Cambodian Communist Party, under various names struggled and then succeeded in breaking loose from Vietnamese control, particularly when, in the late 1950s, the Vietnamese Workers' Party continued to co-ordinate its strategies in South Vietnam with its tactics inside Cambodia. One faction of the KPRP, led after 1960s by Saloth Sar (who changed his name in 1975 or 1976 to "Pol Pot"), followed the

---

[7] David Chandler. "Revising the Past in Democratic Kumpuchea: when was the Birthday of the Party?" above p. 215.

same policies as Sihanouk's government – that is, an alliance with China and independence from Vietnam – while retaining what it saw as its mandate to overthrow Sihanouk himself, a policy discouraged by the Vietnamese, who saw an unaligned Cambodia as essential in their plans to liberate the South.[8]

Rifts between communists in Cambodia and Vietnam were papered over in the late 1960s and early 1970s because of exigencies of the Vietnam war and also because of Vietnamese assistance to the Cambodian communists in their opposition to the anti Vietnamese government headed by Lon Nol. Ironically, while one element of Cambodian history was "rhyming" with the past in this period – that is, in the case of an anti-Vietnamese faction inside Cambodia – this faction failed to seek an alliance with the Thai whose ideology was incompatible.

In examining Vietnamese patronage nowadays in the PRK, it is important to stress that Cambodia has had a socialist government since 1975. During the DK era, and especially in 1977–1978, hundreds of Cambodian communists were tortured and killed because they were suspected of colluding with Vietnam, and of perceiving continuities in Cambodian radicalism which were being effaced by the leadership of the Communist Party of Kampuchea (*CPK*). One of these was the notion of a fraternity of socialist states. Whereas DK preferred to act alone, concealing its financial and political links with China, the PRK has wrapped the "resurgent" KPRK with fraternal rhetoric, beginning with an "historical" alliance among the components of Indochina which is imperceptible, I suspect, to most scholars of the region. In referring to these links, Heng Samrin has remarked that

An historic lesson people have learned over the past ten years at the cost of blood and tears is that separation from Laos and

[8] For an analysis of this period of Cambodian history, see Porter, "Vietnamese Communist Policy", *passim*.

Vietnam means death, while unity with Vietnam and Laos means victory.[9]

In a similar vein, the PRK Foreign Minister Hun Sen has insisted that

Our party has come to the conclusion that the solidarity of the three Indo-Chinese countries is the law of evolution of the Kampuchean revolution.[10]

Examples of similar statements could be multiplied. References to Cambodian independence, correspondingly, are rare.

It seems likely that continuities between the aberrant socialism of DK and the allegedly correct socialism of the PRK are sufficient, as William Shawcross[11] has suggested, "to have encouraged the PRK and the Vietnamese to personalize their attacks on DK, to overlook its Marxist-Leninist components," and to suggest that its policies were limited to the un-Marxian ones of declaring war on Vietnam and deliberately killing off the Cambodian people. To buttress these assertions, the PRK in August 1983 stated that over 2.7 million Cambodians had "died horrible deaths" in the DK period.[12] One reason for the regime's lack of legitimacy, in PRK eyes today, is that the KPRP had run off the rails between its "second" congress in 1960 (when the Saloth Sar faction gained control) and its "third" congress in 1979. Ironically, it was during these very years that many PRK leaders such as Heng Samrin himself and Hun Sen joined the party, perhaps drawn to its fervent policies and aware in any

---

[9] See United States, *Foreign Broadcast Information Service*, Asia and Pacific (hereafter *FBIS*), 10 January 1984.

[10] *FBIS*, 5 January 1984.

[11] See William Shawcross, "The Burial of Cambodia", New York Review of Books, 10 May 1984, and William Shawcross, *The Quality of Mercy* (London: Andre Deutsch, 1984), pp. 200–21, and Paul Quinn-Judge, "Too Few Communists", *Far Eastern Economic Review* (Hereafter *FEER*), 16 February 1984.

[12] *FBIS*, 22 August 1983.

[13] *FBIS*, 1 July 1983.

case that "fraternal" links continued to exist between the *CPK* and its counterpart groupings in Vietnam and Laos. Now, of course, PRK spokesmen must assert that with the liberation of Phnom Penh in April 1975, "Pol Pot and Khieu Samphan began the barbaric acts which destroyed the revolution and killed the Kampuchean people".[13]

Many of these people remained loyal to the party, if not perhaps to the Pol Pot faction until the purges of 1977 and 1978 when many of those who could went over to the Vietnamese, not only because they feared for their lives, but perhaps because they thought that the future of socialism in Cambodia lay with Vietnam rather than with Pol Pot's policy of protracted war. The fact that many of these people took so much time to realize what was wrong causes them some embarrassment today. Speaking to a Swedish journalist Heng Samrin admitted that

> There was no possibility of collecting people for a revolt [before 1978]. Pol Pot took full power over the whole country and the Kampuchean people believed in Pol Pot. It was impossible to build up a resistance front; it was too early. [14]

Towards former DK supporters, the PRK has adopted a generous amnesty policy.[15] While it accuses "Pol Pot" of following "Nazi" policies, it has not embarked on any efforts to "de-Nazify" Cambodia. In Hun Sen's words, "We will not close our eyes to those who awaken in time".[16] Instead, the PRK allows repentant DK supporters including cadres to return to productive work within the framework of the Cambodian revolution. It is precisely because adherents of Sihanouk and Son Sann refuse to accept such a framework (as well as Vietnamese control) that they are treated as "traitors" to Cambodia in a way that repentant

[14] *FBIS*, 15 February 1984.
[15] *FBIS*, 10 April 1984 and 16 May 1984.
[16] *FBIS*, 3 April 1984.

cadres now "pledged to be loyal to the correct line of our party" are not. People who see the DK era as an aberration in socialism, rather than as one in Cambodian history can be re-absorbed into a successor communist regime.

At this point, it is convenient to question the so-called conversion of the DK faction to what a spokesman in August 1984 referred to as a "liberal capitalist regime". There is little understanding of capitalism offered in the DK rationale:

> In the current geographical situation of the world . . . and in the situation where the existence of Kampuchea remains constantly in suspense, Kampuchea can in no way espouse socialism, it will be unable to mobilize the national union force of all social strata . . . [17]

Those of "all social strata" who had been mobilized under Sihanouk's banner to overthrow Lon Nol between 1970 and 1975 might be forgiven for some scepticism at this point, provided they have lived long enough to listen. In the so-called "Khmer Rouge" camps along the Thai-Cambodian border, visitors are not allowed, and rare reports indicate that DK policies of unthinking obedience, regimentation, and chauvinism remain intact, behind a veneer that permits personal possessions such as watches. There are reports that soldiers loyal to Sihanouk and Son Sann are occasionally the targets of DK patrols.[18] No one in the DK regime has disowned Pol Pot, who remains in charge of its military forces, now estimated at approximately 40,000 men and women. Khieu Samphan has admitted that he consults Pol Pot "frequently" on political and military matters.[19] Moreover,

---

[17] *FBIS*, 21 August 1984, in an article punchily entitled, "In Order to Safeguard and Prepetuate the Kampuchean Nation and Race, Kampuchea Should Adhere to a Liberal Capitalist Regime".

[18] See R. Tasker, "Stabbed in the Back", *FEER*, 30 September 1984 and John Macbeth, "Fear of Khmerization", *FEER*, 9 August 1984.

[19] *FBIS*, 17 April 1984.

the "errors" which some DK officials now admit, particularly when travelling abroad, are never traced to policies laid out by the central committee of the Communist Party of Kampuchea. If indeed, as a Bangkok newspaper asserted in 1983, the DK faction is trying to conduct reforms "to erase the 'Red' image that has been criticized in the world",[20] there is no evidence that the leaders of the CPK are genuinely repentant, and it seems likely that the party's infrastructure remains intact.

The extent of Vietnamese control over the PRK is difficult to determine. Defectors assert that it is particularly systematic in the fields of foreign affairs, defence, and in matters affecting the expansion of the party, and rather less so in such areas as the collection of taxes, and the collectivization of agriculture.[21] Indeed, according to a PRK agronomist, only 20 per cent of the peasantry in Cambodia today have been collectivized at all.[22] Although Vietnamese guidance is seldom openly admitted, the broadcasts of Radio Phnom Penh and scattered reports from visitors to Cambodia do not suggest any differences of opinion between Cambodians and Vietnamese, although it is impossible to say if the slavish tone adopted in so many PRK pronouncements is imposed by Vietnamese advisers or merely represents a desire to please them on the part of officials of the PRK. The effect is the same. It seems accurate to describe Cambodia today as a satellite of Vietnam. Nonetheless, the imposition of foreign control, however humiliating it is, perhaps particularly to people serving in the government itself, does not seem to arouse emotions as intense as the possibility that "Pol Pot" might at some stage return to power. The Vietnamese are assiduous in connecting their presence to the "wishes of the Cambodian people" not to be governed by "Pol Pot". At the same time, their efforts to create an indigenous army have been slow

---

[20] *FBIS*, 26 July 1983. As part of this effort, DK soldiers no longer wear black uniforms.

[21] *FBIS*, 13 April 1984. See also "The Vietnamization or Kampuchea", Indochina Report (October 1984).

[22] See *Le Figaro*, 27 April 1984, interview with Chea King.

enough to suggest that they perceive such a force as possibly contrary to Vietnamese national interests. In other words, if Cambodian troops could prevent "Pol Pot" from returning to power, without the assistance of 140,000 Vietnamese, it might also be possible for the Cambodian people, so rarely consulted about their wishes throughout their history, to declare that they wanted a government that was neither socialist nor dominated by Vietnam. These possibilities might be ventilated if Cambodians were allowed to talk freely with foreigners in Cambodia, as they are not, or if the Vietnamese were to admit that an independent, non-socialist Cambodia might not pose a serious threat to Vietnam's national interests. In the meantime, it seems clear that these interests are entangled with notions of a civilizing mission inside Cambodia, inseparable at this stage of Vietnamese history from the imposition of the Vietnamese version of socialism.

To justify their continuing presence in Cambodia the Vietnamese have dramatized the excesses of DK. Every 20 May, a "day of hate" is officially celebrated,[23] when the horrors of the DK era are recalled. How much longer this will continue to strike a responsive chord among Cambodians with access to official pronouncements is difficult to say. For the moment, however, it seems clear that Pol Pot and his colleagues created a nation of enemies in their pursuit of independence.

Like the French in the 1860s, the Vietnamese chose a convenient time to impose their control over Cambodia. Like the French, they have been able to justify themselves by saying that without them Cambodia would have disappeared. Going further, they suggest that the rationale for their continuing presence in Cambodia springs from the Cambodian people's inability to manage their own affairs. PRK pronouncements repeatedly assert that Vietnam intervened in Cambodia to "save it from genocide" – a policy which they blame not on policies or

---

[23] For an analysis, see Elizabeth Becker, "Kampuchea in 1983". Asian Survey, 24/1 (January 1984), pp. 37–48. See also *FBIS*, 22 August 1983.

a regime but on on a handful of murderous people. No previous Cambodian regime is treated as legitimate. In other words, the Vietnamese have delivered the Cambodians from themselves and have allowed Cambodian history of an acceptable sort to begin. Similar assertions of starting afresh were also, ironically, frequent under DK.[24]

Perhaps the strongest statement of the rationale for the Vietnamese presence in Cambodia appeared in a PRK radio broadcast in April 1984, after first having been published in a Cambodian-language journal entitled *Great Solidarity under the Banner of the Front*. The passage reads:

> By nature Kampucheans are loyal, gentle, kind and polite. They have already done well in preserving the Kampuchea-Vietnam bonds of solidarity and in impartially abiding by the fundamental principles of this solidarity from the bottom or their hearts . . . while defending and building their own country towards progress. As for the Vietnamese people, who are champions of independence and freedom and for this sacred cause have fought most persistently . . . for decades against French imperialism, Japanese fascism, and aggressive U.S. imperialism . . . have proved their traditional heroic abilities in helping free the Kampuchean people from the danger of genocide . . .[25]

The ineffectual Cambodians, in the passage, are seen as having been liberated from foreign domination by the heroic (and independent) Vietnamese. Vietnamese control of Cambodia is not comparable to foreign control of Vietnam, by implication, because Vietnam and Cambodia are not comparable to each other. What passes for national interest in Vietnam is reducible in Cambodia to *folie de grandeur*. Even if, as I have suggested

[24] See David Chandler, "Seeing Red: Perceptions of Cambodian History in Democratic Kampuchea", above p. 233.
[25] *FBIS*, 18 April 1984.

earlier in this essay, the roots of anti-Vietnamese sentiments among Cambodians in the 1980s are not as deep as opponents of the Vietnamese might prefer, it is easy to see how such roots might well be nourished by unrelenting colonialist statements of this kind, as well as by the requirement that Cambodians celebrate Vietnamese national holidays – such as the anniversary of Dienbienphu – as well as what are left of their own.[26]

In 1984, activities on the diplomatic front affecting Cambodia revealed a reluctance to compromise on major issues on the part of most of the principal actors. Just as the United States, ASEAN states, and China, despite expressing abhorrence for DK, were reluctant or unable to neutralize this important "bargaining chip", so too, the Vietnamese and their Soviet patrons saw no reason to retreat from the territory which they had gained for themselves at such a comparatively low cost. Similarly, the government of PRK, while hoping to detach Sihanouk from the CGDK and while continuing to welcome DK defectors into its ranks remained reluctant to open up the political process inside Cambodia or to suggest in any public forum at least that the erosion or deferral of Cambodian independence was causing them great concern.

Militarily, 1984 saw an intensification of fighting along the Thai border, as well as increasing insecurity inside Cambodia, suggesting (although this is impossible to confirm) that guerrilla forces belonging both to the DK faction and to the anti-communist forces presided over by Son Sann have been able to operate more freely inside the country than in previous years, perhaps because they are able to capitalize on increasing weariness with Vietnamese control. Of course, from the PRK point of view, beginning to govern the country instead of presiding over it has meant introducing measures such as taxation, conscription, and state-controlled enterprises which, in the heady days following the demise of DK, many ordinary Cambodians may well have

---

[26] *FBIS*, 24 June 1983.

hoped would never re-appear. Similarly, even if considerable cynicism is attributed to the Vietnamese, their desire to shift some of the military burden in Cambodia onto indigenous forces is easy to understand. At the same time, with an audacious disregard for what has been happening in Cambodia since 1970, DK spokesmen have asserted that "Khmer do not fight fellow Khmer", referring to this misreading of history as a "sacred slogan."[27] It may well be true that many Khmer no longer wish to fight their countrymen, particularly to maintain a Vietnamese-sponsored regime in power in Phnom Penh.

In November and December 1984, Vietnamese forces stepped up their attacks on KPNLF and DK population centers along the frontier. Most experts now predict a more prolonged and more intense dry season offensive in 1985 than occurred in 1984, citing the recent disembarkation at Kompong Som of tanks supplied to the Vietnamese forces by the USSR. Thai military authorities are understandably nervous about Vietnamese intentions; in November, skirmishes inside Thai territory resulted in several casualties on both sides.

To accompany this intensification of military activity, and perhaps in response to the rebuff to the PRK that occurred at the U.N. General Assembly in October, discussed below, the Vietnamese continued their diplomatic pressures on the CGDK, hoping perhaps to woo Prince Sihanouk back to Phnom Penh in some sort of figure-head position – a shrewd move on the part of the Vietnamese, since Sihanouk, to many foreigners, remains in some sense the "real" government of Cambodia (whatever most Cambodians may think), and since in recent months his long-standing feud with Son Sann has frequently boiled over into bitter polemics on both sides.

In economic terms, the PRK has been seriously hampered in 1984 by disastrous weather: severe flooding in the east and late, insufficient rain in the northwest led to a 200,000 ton

---

[27] *FBIS*, 6 March 1984.

shortfall in the 1984 rice harvest. This crisis, exacerbated by poor communications inside the country as well as the demands of the Vietnamese army, and insecurity produced by the guerrilla war, has raised widespread fears of famine. Whether these are justified or not, they have impelled thousands of ordinary Cambodians to the Thai border where they hope to be fed without falling into the hands of any political faction at a time when the Vietnamese and the PRK, to remain in power, have had to make greater demands on their time, energy and labour. Aid from the Soviet bloc, while generous in terms of bloc aid elsewhere, is insufficient to get Cambodia back onto its feet.

Ironically, as the PRK has come to rely less and less, in much of its daily work, on Vietnamese advisers, Vietnamese efforts to re-arm the Cambodians to defend themselves against their countrymen have not apparently accelerated at the same pace, probably because, for many Cambodians, there is some truth in the DK spokesman's adage, quoted above, and perhaps because armed Cambodians might, at some point turn more effectively against the Vietnamese than unarmed ones. At the same time, evidence about Vietnamese behavior in the countryside is contradictory, and it seems likely that the continuing Vietnamese presence (Vietnamese Foreign Minister Nguyen Co Thach now speaks of anything from five to ten more years) will induce increased resentment, if not outright resistance.

On the international scene, the PRK has failed to gather any additional support. On 30 October 1984, the U.N. General Assembly voted 110–22 (with 18 abstentions) in support of an ASEAN-sponsored motion demanding the removal of all "foreign troops" from Cambodia. Earlier, the Assembly had agreed to honour the CGDK's credentials, making the regime the only government-in-exile to fly its flag at United Nations Plaza.[28]

Looking towards the future, it seems safe to assert that the next 12 months will see no slackening of Vietnamese control over

---

[28] Le Figaro, 13 April 1984.

the important levers of Cambodian political life, while KPRP control over the countryside may become more systematic, as cadres are recruited and trained. Vietnamese troop withdrawals can be expected as PRK forces come into their own, but changes in the military order of battle in Cambodia are likely to be slight. Diplomatic support for the PRK, risking disapproval by China, the United States, and ASEAN, is unlikely to increase, and efforts to arm the Son Sann and Sihanouk factions of the CGDK will probably intensify. Corresponding efforts to neutralize the DK faction, as long as it enjoys Chinese support, will probably be unavailing, and the DK faction, under a leader who cared little for his "image" overseas, will remain the best-trained, best equipped, and most aggressive of the forces opposing the Vietnamese. For ordinary Cambodians living inside their country, increasing PRK interference with their lives may become irksome, without provoking armed resistance, or conversion to the CGDK, although fatigue with warfare may prevent them from telling the PRK about guerrilla incursions. The PRK, for its part, is eager to increase its role in governing the country; so are the Vietnamese, who need their own experienced cadres at home.

In saying that more of the same is in store for Cambodia in 1985, it is important to note that weariness with war and politics may well impede the PRK in its policies towards ordinary people, and also slow down Thai efforts to have their national interests pursued by surrogate Cambodian troops. While most ordinary Cambodians, if consulted – perhaps an unthinkable scenario – would probably say that some sort of non-socialist "good old days" would be preferable to the dour alternatives proposed by a socialist regime, many have probably learned at enormous cost that the "good old days" were not very good at all. The Cambodians who remain in Cambodia know for the first time in their history about class warfare and class solidarity. It is unimaginable that many of them would welcome the return of the Cambodian élite, which has been blown out of history, and its survivors scattered overseas. More importantly, young

Cambodians now undergoing training in the Soviet Union and Eastern Europe – many of them orphan "pioneers" favored by the PRK – when they return to positions of responsibility and relative comfort will probably perceive the advantages of working in a socialist environment.[29] It is to be hoped, of course, that some of them will also perceive that being relatively open to the world, as parts of Eastern Europe have become, might be advantageous to Cambodia; others will decide that socialism as practised in the Soviet bloc has little to offer. In any case, it seems likely that these people will run Cambodia in the 1990s.

As for the CGDK, it seems unlikely that its leaders, separated by chasms of animosity for more than 20 years, will make their marriage of convenience into anything more durable in 1985. As long as the DK faction retains Chinese military support, and logistical support from Thailand, it will continue to dominate and frighten its coalition partners, and encourage the Vietnamese to keep large numbers of troops inside Cambodia. Despite wishful thinking on the part of many in the west, bemused by Cambodia's "charm", it seems clear that Prince Sihanouk has lost credibility among Cambodians, bewildered, to say the least, by his persistent alliance with DK. As for Son Sann, it is unlikely that enough educated Cambodians have survived inside Cambodia to staff a free enterprise regime, or that others, having begun new lives elsewhere, could be persuaded in sufficient numbers to return.

In thinking about the future of Cambodia, the historical rhymes I discussed at the beginning of this paper are not particularly useful. This is because neither the Thai nor the French, to say nothing of larger powers, is inclined to mount an expedition into Cambodia which would sweep the Vietnamese back into Vietnam. In the 1840s, the Vietnamese were removed by a Thai army; in the 1860s, Thai protectors of the Cambodian court

---

[29] In 1983, Heng Samrin claimed that 1,479 Khmer were studying abroad in "fraternal socialist countries" (*FBIS*, 28 August 1983). He later announced that roughly three million Cambodians were enrolled in the state education system (*FBIS*, 27 September 1983). My long term prediction here was wrong.

were brushed aside by the French. While Thai and Vietnamese national interests apparently require some kind of interference in Cambodian affairs (at least until Vietnam and Thailand come to terms with each other), thus perpetuating nineteenth century confrontations, no other power is willing to risk war with Vietnam as the price of liberating Cambodia. The survival and, ironically, the eventual liberation of Cambodia depends entirely on its opening up to the rest of the world, rather than remaining, with Vietnam, in a kind of isolation ward – a "Z-nation", in American terms. At the same time, students of Cambodian history, or of realpolitik, or both, would be prudent to remain pessimistic about the welfare of ordinary Cambodians or about their happiness, to use a more appropriate word. After nearly a decade and a half marked by intensive foreign intervention, indigenous brutality, and continuing civil war, the longing of these people for peace and the unimpeded renewal of family life has seldom been in the forefront of other peoples' minds, when the "Cambodian problem" is discussed. The continuing economic, political and military crisis in Cambodia is fueled by foreign ambitions and foreign money. This honor has been bestowed, as usual, by larger states on the Khmer.

PART V

TRAGEDY AND HISTORY

In 1978, soon after the conference at Cornell where I presented "Songs at the Edge of the Forest" my friend Alexander Woodside invited me to talk at the University of British Columbia, and suggested the title "The Tragedy of Cambodian History". I gave the talk in November 1978, revising it for publication after the collapse of the Pol Pot regime. I used the title again in my book on Cambodian history since World War II, and finally in a talk I prepared in 1994 in two successive versions while a resident fellow at the Woodrow Wilson Center in Washington, DC. This last essay, "The Tragedy of Cambodian History Revisited" places my writings in an autobiographical context and seems a pleasing way to close off a collection that represents a quarter century of my work.

THE TRAGEDY OF CAMBODIAN HISTORY

Pity and fear can arise from the spectacle and also from the very structure of the plot, which is the superior way and shows the better poet. The poet should construct the plot so that even if the action is not performed before spectators, one who merely hears the incidents that have occurred both shudders and feels pity for the way they turn out.

Aristotle, *Poetics*, Chapter XIV

"Il n y a de detruit que ce qui est remplace," c'est un mot profond de Dantou, et it ajoutait: "Nous ne remplacerons rien."

ST Beuve, *Car net Vert*, U67

The word "tragedy" springs to mind in writing about Cambodia, I think, because of the price its people have been made to pay for their Republic and their liberations, for their alliance and their war with the United States, for independence in the 1840s and French protection after that, for Jayavarman VII's visionary Buddhism, which swept up so many people in the twelfth and

This paper was first given as a lecture at the University of British Columbia in November 1978. In revising it, I benefited from comments by R. E. Elson, Tony Day, and J.D. Legge.

This paper was first published in *Pacific Affairs*, Vol. 52, No. 3, Fall, 1979, reprinted with permission.

thirteenth centuries, and for the deeply ingrained notion that there are "big" and "little" people in society, which is in turn woven, rightly or wrongly, in a hierarchical design.

Why were these sufferings so intense? Five reasons come to mind. These include Cambodia's location between two populous, antagonistic countries, Thailand and Vietnam, its ethnic singularity and the righteousness that flows from it; the weight of an imperial past, looming behind a time of powerlessness; the kinds of leaders (and the ideas of leadership) which preceded the revolution; and the popular ideology which, until recently, blended the notions of high social standing, power and merit, as well as their opposites – poverty, powerlessness, and spiritual shortcomings.

Of these reasons the first is probably the most important. Modern Cambodian history has been shaped to a large extent by the fact that its capital, Phnom Penh, lies on a cultural fault-line between the Indianized, Theravada Buddhist culture of Thailand and the Sinicized, Confucian culture of Vietnam. Cambodia itself, of course, was until recently a Theravada kingdom – but its capital region, where most of its people live, has always been more accessible to Saigon than to Bangkok. These facts led to the country being invaded by the Thai (ostensibly to free Cambodia from Vietnamese protection) in 1811, 1833 and 1840.[1] Between 1834 and 1847, much of the country was occupied by the Vietnamese; Cambodia returned to Thai protection between 1847 and the imposition of French hegemony in 1863. Until gaining independence in 1953, Cambodia, unlike her large neighbors, had been exploited (the Khmer phrase, *jih joan*, means literally, "ridden on and kicked") and colonized for a hundred and fifty years .

In the colonial era Cambodia's foreign trade and internal economy were geared to the needs of the French in Indo-China

---

[1] For a detailed treatment of this period, see David Chandler, *Cambodia before the French, Politics in a Tributary Kingdom, 1794–1847* (Ann Arbor: University Microfilms, 1974).

as a whole, and to the export economy of southern Vietnam (Cochin-China) in particular. One price the Cambodians paid for what the French often called their "docility" was the highest per capita taxes in Indo-China. Moreover, while the French allowed governing elites, including the monarchy, to function ceremonially, the bureaucracy was largely staffed with French-speaking Vietnamese.[2] It is not surprising, therefore, that Cambodians associate periods of powerlessness with periods of Vietnamese control and periods of nationalist unrest (such as the 1840s, 1970–72 or 1976–78) with killing Vietnamese. Little of this animosity would have arisen perhaps, if Cambodia's demographic center of gravity had remained in the north western part of the country near the site of Angkor beyond the reach of the Vietnamese but accessible to the post-Angkorean Thai kingdoms of Ayudhya and Bangkok.

Turning to the weight of Cambodia's past, one of the intriguing features of nineteenth-century Cambodian history is the collective amnesia of the population regarding its relationship to Angkor. Between the ninth and fourteenth centuries, after all, Cambodia had been at several times the mightiest state in Southeast Asia. Its monarchs had com missioned temples, hospitals, roads and enormous irrigation works. After the rise of Ayudhya in the fourteenth century, Angkor faded in importance; it was abandoned, finally, in 1431. Although Cambodians remembered the kingdom's greatness in the nineteenth century by including the name of the city in the king's royal titles, by half-remembering the names of certain ruins, and by using some of them – notably the twelfth century tomb/observatory of Angkor Wat – as Buddhist pilgrimage sites, they ignored the fact that the ruins were evidence of a *Cambodian* kingdom.[3] Had Cambodia's greatness – or her fall from greatness – been so heavy, in a sense, as to encourage this amnesia? In the 1960s, Cambodians would

---

[2] See, for example, France. Archives d'outremer (Aix en Provence) *Cambodge*, 3 E 11 (2), Report from Kompong Chhnang, November, 1907.

[3] See David Chandler, "Maps for the Ancestors: Sacralized Topography and Echoes of Angkor in Two Cambodian Texts," p. 25 and "Folk Memories of Angkor in Nineteenth Century Cambodia: The Legend of the Leper King,"

often say that the temples were the work of gods or giants even after French *savants* had proved they had been built by people who spoke and wrote recognizable Cambodian, or Khmer.

Another reason for this forgetfulness is that Cambodia's archives appear to have been destroyed several times between 1431 and 1800. Surviving royal chronicles say nothing about Angkor except in garbled form; instead, they commence their allegedly historical as opposed to mythological sections with the founding of Ayudhya, in 1350!4 It would appear that because of what happened to Cambodia *vis-a-vis* the Thai, it became impossible in the eighteenth and nineteenth centuries at least for people who had been powerless for so long to believe that they had powerful ancestors. Alex Haley poses a similar dilemma in his autobiographical study, *Roots*.

During the colonial era the French gave Cambodia back its past by deciphering inscriptions, refining chronological frameworks and roughing out notions of Angkorean law, religion and society. Whether the gift was usable or not is another matter and regimes since independence have used Angkor in several different ways. Prince Sihanouk for example, saw it as foreshadowing his policies of "Buddhist socialism" and allowed his entourage to compare him favorably with the Angkorean monarch Jayavarman VII. Lon Nol as President of the Khmer Republic thought of Angkor as evidence of what he called "Khmer-Mon" hegemony over much of Southeast Asia. The Pol Pot regime, whose ideology focussed unblinkingly on the importance of national pride and self-sufficiency, perceived the Angkorean era as a time when an enslaved people, naturally endowed with creative skill, built

p. 3. More recent work by Ashley Thompson and Ang Choulean, based on inquiries in the vicinity of Angkor in the 1990s promises to deepen and enrich scholarship on this topic.

[4] See Michael Vickery, "The Composition and Transmission of the Ayutthayan and Cambodian Chronicles," in David Marr and Anthony Reid (eds.), *Southeast Asian Perceptions of the Past* (Singapore: Heinemann, 1979).

hundreds of temples and kilometres of irrigation canals – not for themselves as a group, as they were in theory to do after 1975, but for their masters, whose ideology or style the Communists made no effort to explain.[5]

The weight of the past, the embarrassment of prolonged dependence, and Cambodia's precarious location have meant, among other things, that nationalist statements in Cambodia often take the form of diatribes against the Vietnamese – one of the few historical traditions which the Pol Pot regime allowed to flourish. Cambodia's ethnic singularity, in a sense, amounted to a tendency for Cambodians to visualize themselves as being not Vietnamese, rather than as members of what Benedict Anderson has called an "imagined community" – made up of Theravada Buddhists, Communists, or "Southeast Asians."[6]

An irony that flows from this kind of self-perception is that prerevolutionary depictions of Cambodians stressed their innate docility and at the same time described the same people killing large numbers of Vietnamese. In nineteenth-century texts, Cambodians explained this by saying that the Vietnamese, not being "Buddhist," were subject to different rules – exactly the charge the Vietnamese levelled against them, as being non-Chinese. What emerges from the Cambodian view, enshrined in the official "Black Book" of 1978 is a kind of smouldering self-righteousness, identifying what is "Cambodian" with what is not Vietnamese, and the Vietnamese with what is evil in the world.

Cambodian history is the history of a few survivors but this has not made Cambodian writers cautious, or encouraged them to place their history in a comparative perspective. Perhaps they have failed to do so in part because Cambodia's helplessness *vis-a-vis* its neighbours reads poorly in connection with Angkor. Until the revolution, Cambodians blamed hardships on foreigners or failures of merit, and successes on the enduring power of the

---

[5] All five flags of independent Cambodia have included images of Angkor Wat.

[6] Benedict Anderson, *The Imagined Community*, London, 1994.

builders of Angkor. With so much past grandeur, and so little, sociologically, to show for it, Cambodians like Sihanouk, Lon Nol, and Pol Pot have been unable to join the so-called first or second worlds and unwilling to sink back into the third. Like a superpower, Cambodia since independence has chosen to say that its history is unique, and that large powers have much to learn from it.

Another component of Cambodia's tragedy lies in the leadership which the country has perennially enjoyed. The essence of leadership in traditional Cambodia was exploitation rather than service, patronage rather than cooperation. The word to "govern," as in many Southeast Asian languages, was the same as the word to "eat." Traditional leaders, though perhaps not always kings – were judged by their followers or slaves on a spectrum of relative injustice rather than in absolute terms. The relationship between master and slave was the one on which the society was based; the notion that one could be without a master was not widespread; and while slaves often shifted in times of crisis from one master to another, mastery as an institution that governed Cambodian social behavior remained in force. Interestingly the Cambodian word for servant (*nak bomrao*) means "one who is told," rather than "one who renders help."

A tragic light always plays around the edges of such leaders who do not have to account to others for their behavior. Ideologues like Pol Pot, Ieng Sary and Khieu Samphan possess *hubris* in an Aristotelean sense, as anyone does who seeks to dismantle, melt and recast a nation's history and to alter at once, the bases of everybody's lives. There is hubris, I think, in the Communist leaders' declarations that their policies in Cambodia had so few roots in the millenia before 1975.

Earlier leaders, also, may be seen in terms of tragic flaws. Sihanouk, for example, seems to have believed – from time to time at least – the mythology about himself to the point of confusing himself with Cambodia, and of thinking that he could *outwit* a power like Nixon's United States. Likewise, Jayavarman

VII (r. 1178–1220), whose massive building program seems to have accelerated the kingdom's decline, probably believed what his inscriptions say – i.e., that he was an incarnation of the Buddha, placed on earth to deliver his people from suffering and from time. Other Cambodian leaders like King Chan (r. 1806–1835) and Lon Nol, were powerless for major tragic roles; but their misconceptions, based on a faith in alliances with Vietnam and the United States, accelerated the punishment of their country (and, in due course, the defeat of their patrons, too).

Throughout its history with the possible exception of the colonial era and the early years of independence, Cambodia has been governed (or at least, "headed") by figures whose power has, theoretically, been absolute. In practice, these kings and officials have been pestered by the demands of subordinate (and also absolutist-minded) leaders. When kingship weakened as a political institution, after the fall of Angkor, very little power or riches filtered past provincial leaders either to the people they "consumed" or to the king they theoretically revered. Because power, leisure, surpluses and elegance – in literature and clothing, for example – were in the hands of a few (having been extracted from the many), ordinary people came to believe and were told, by people in charge – that the orderliness of the society came from the existence of "haves" (*nak mean*) and "have nots" (*nak kro*), and also from there being a graded spectrum of hierarchy, whereby those at the top enjoyed more merit (the Buddhist term *bon*) than those at the bottom.[7] This does not mean that their behavior was more meritorious – in fact, the opposite was usually the case. Rather, it meant that people thought they owed their position, viewed in vertical terms, to

the meritoriousness of their former lives. In a sense, people thought they were poor because their ancestors (or predecessors, *nak tā*) had wanted them to be poor. Because of the merit of their

---

[7] See Jasper Ingersoll, "Merit and Identity in Village Thailand," in G. William Skinner and A. Thomas Kirsch (eds.), *Change and Persistence in Thai Society: Essays in Honor of Lauriston Sharp* (Ithaca, NY: Cornell University Press, 1975), pp. 219–51.

former lives, officials did not live like ordinary people: they did not have to grow their own food. To free oneself from subsistence farming, a man had to lead a meritorious life (and a woman, first of all, had to be reincarnated as a man!) This ideology, if it can be called that, helps to explain the gaps that are so often perceptible, in terms of politeness, between the behavior of a poor peasant and a rich policeman. It also explains the apparent acceptance of servility, which French administrators half admired, on the part of the population as a whole.[8]

Sihanouk tried to weaken this fatalistic view of the world by attacking it piecemeal, allowing people a few more avenues out of the bottom levels of the society, particularly by means of expanded primary education. But he never questioned his right to govern, or his people's obligations to obey. Peasants were not allowed to call the tune; they were expected to perform it: as at Angkor, peasant volunteer labor was an essential ingredient of Sihanouk's (Buddhist-Socialist) regime.

Thus the history of Cambodia before 1970 was tragic, I suggest, because its people were exploited by their leaders and, in a sense, by their own way of looking at the world. Powerlessness encouraged further exploitation which was seen as "correct" or "inevitable" perhaps because it so frequently succeeded. It is hardly surprising that powerlessness, fatalism and individualism were high priority targets of the Pol Pot regime. A problem facing people wanting to move systematically against a hierarchical view of society (and the word for "I" in Khmer is still the word for "slave") is that it appears that ranking itself may have produced a sort of self-assurance, even while "classes" (if we can talk about these in traditional Cambodia; the Cambodian word derives from

---

[8] For a classic statement of this notion, see Adhemard Leclere, "Veducation chez les cambodgiens," *Bulletin de la Societe d'Etknographie* (1895), p. 185: "Celui qui est bon mandarin, me dit un lettre, sera mandarin dans une existence terrestre future; celui qui est mauvais mandarin, renaitra homme du peuple et sera toujours en butte aux mauvais traitements et aux injustices des mandarins."

the Sanskrit varna) were, in a Marxist view, exploiting others.[9] Hierarchy in the Cambodian case was related to good manners, especially between two people, face to face; it was reinforced by the kinds of pronouns one employed. The encounter was subject to what Clifford Geertz, writing about Java, has called "linguistic etiquette."[10] While the solidarities and intensity of family life might seem removed from such a scheme, actually families at the linguistic level again were like theaters where relative status was repeatedly acted out. The loyalties which however mistakenly were reassuring to many ordinary people (reverence for teachers and grandparents, for example) stood in the way of liberation. Only liberated people, after all, could be brought to enjoy the uneasy solidarity of unranked groups. And it was in these "solidarity groups," as they were called, that liberated citizens were asked to submerge themselves, no longer for the pleasure of a larger person, but for the greater good. It might be argued in fact that almost every aspect of traditional Cambodian behavior stood in the way of such a liberation. Like the city of Ben Tre in the Tet Offensive in the Vietnam war, Cambodian society had to be destroyed in order to save it.

And here we come up against the problem of perspective. As this is written (1979) it is easy for some to diminish Cambodian history and American (or French) involvement in it by calling that history "tragic," while meaning merely "sad." We must be wary of confusing our judgment of what has happened to Cambodia with our regret as "friends" for having been removed so unceremoniously from it. Can we really say, looking back at pre-revolutionary Cambodia, that for Cambodians it was a happy, equitable place? Is it the failure of *that* society (its "tragedy," perhaps) and our perceptions of it, that should attract our attention – or is it the failure of the revolution? Put another

---

[9] See Ian Mabbett, "Varnas in Angkor and the Indian Caste System," *Journal of Asian Studies* (*JAS*), Vol. 36, No. 3 (1977), pp. 429–42.

[10] Clifford Geertz, *The Religion of Java* (Glencoe, IL: Free Press, 1960), p. 248: The rest of the paragraph benefits from discussions with Ward Keeler.

way, is it the persistence of old ideas that made the revolution fail or merely, as Pol Pot would argue, treasonous notions, and the Vietnamese?

Perspectives vary. Those who set themselves the task of imprinting Cambodia's future on its people saw the past in terms of "2,000 years of exploitation." At one point, Pol Pot even proclaimed that in five years Cambodia had passed through the fourth and fifth stages of evolution (capitalism and socialism), having taken two thousand to overcome the other three (primitive communism, slavery, and feudalism).[11] His genuflections to theory, are in sharp contrast to the acuity of more anonymous Communist thinkers, reported by Radio Phnom Penh, who emphasized the second phase – slavery – as far more deleterious, and resistent than the other four. What kept the country from self-sufficiency, and therefore from power *vis-a-vis* its neighbors, the argument ran (skirting the edges of tautology), was the psychological and social powerlessness of its people, enmeshed in a world of masters and servants, patronage and respect. The acceptance of hierarchy, ironically, made the people easier to exploit, even after they were commanded to be free. They remained easy to exploit because they were not allowed, after 1977, to eat together as families, to look for their relations, to escape or to write letters. With Andre Gide, the leaders of Democratic Kampuchea might have said, "*La famille, je vous hais,*" and this suggests, I think, that they were trying to root out more than "feudal" deference to authority; they were trying to extirpate parents, in order to free their children from obligations and from love.

In traditional Cambodia, being free usually meant that one was – momentarily – self-sufficient in food and unmolested by superiors. After 1975 being free entitled one to take revenge against anything that had held the poorer strata down: i.e., every social relationship which has preceded the revolution (except of

---

[11] Pol Pot, *Discours prononcie . . . au Meeting commemorant le IT anniversaire de la fondation du parti communiste du Kampuchea* (Phnom Penh, September 1977).

course, the fraternity of the international Communist movement, which took a little longer to deconstruct). Since all of society was to blame who was exempt from vengeance? Only the "poor and blank;" and these, increasingly, had the power being heavily armed – to name themselves and intuitively to come to grips with "law."

And so the Cambodians from 1975 to 1979 were revisited by leaders – many of them very young – who "consumed" them, in the course of promising them something else, or explaining nothing at all, as leaders often do.

There was also the matter of work. Under the Pol Pot regime, people in the countryside worked all year, in ten-day bursts, without salaries or leisure time. In the eyes of the leadership, there was no other effective way to "build and defend" the country; but for the people, informed that they were now the "masters" of their country, the labor surpassed anything any of them had ever known. The people were overwhelmed and revolutionized supposedly on their own behalf but also in the service of an ideal – which is to say, an idea from somewhere else. Thousands came to share this ideal to the point of dying for it; tens of thousands of others died without any understanding of the ideal.

And this is often the outcome, after all, of *missions civilisatrices*. Cambodia has been on the receiving end of these more often than any other country in Southeast Asia. Leaving aside the intricate process of Hinduization which preceded the foundation of Angkor, and the period of Thai hegemony which followed Angkor's decline, Cambodia has been victimized since 1800 or so by five countries – Thailand, Vietnam (twice) France, the United States and China. Before 1850 it was the battleground for Thai and Vietnamese notions of hegemony. From 1863 to the 1950s, it was preserved in catalepsy by the French who, after injecting novocaine at various points in the society, often remarked that Cambodians were "docile" as compared to the "vigorous" Vietnamese. Since 1970 the Cambodians have been the playthings of the Nixon Doctrine,[12] the discarded Chinese notion of permanent revolution, and Vietnamese ideas of presentable Indo-Chinese behavior. Remnants of the Pol Pot regime fighting in the Cardamom mountains may not realize that like the Lon Nol forces before them they are fighting someone else's war – in this case, China's against the U.S.S.R.

Glimmers of humanitarianism have emerged from the early public statements by the Heng Samrin regime and from scattered eye-witness reports, but if we see Cambodian history, in a sense, as ending (or taking stock) in 1979 then the future does not seem especially bright. There is the possibility of widespread famine. Cambodia, also, is still too close to its neighbors, and there are too few Cambodians to impose their will on them.

At the same time, their "merely personal" values (I owe this marvellous phrase to an Australian social scientist), perhaps more buffeted than any others in the twentieth century, have apparently persisted in parts of the society, where many are now trying to walk away from the past and from the war. These values, in turn, which to outsiders have endowed the people with "charm" have traditionally given them no protection from each other, when enraged, or little cohesion or confidence in themselves, when unarmed.

The leaders of Democratic Kampuchea argued that between 1975 and 1979 the people changed all this, and set forth on an uncharted, supposedly socialist, fully autonomous history. These leaders talked about the immediate past and the immediate future and the "thousands of years" in which Democratic Kampuchea would inevitably flourish. In view of what has happened since 1975 these predictions which still emanate from the defunct regime are difficult to read. They are fragments of a script whose

---

[12] See ex-President Nixon's interview with David Frost on March 12, 1977 (*New York Times*, March 13, 1977), where Nixon reports that Kissinger occasionally suggested that the American incursion into Cambodia in 1970 had been a mistake. "And I said, 'Henry,' I said, 'We've done it.' I said, 'Remember Lot's wife. Never look back.' I don't know whether Henry had read the Old Testament or not, but I had, and he got the point."

authors, now in hiding, no longer understand. We can refer to them and those who are suffering on their behalf as "tragic" from the safety we enjoy. Closer up, for most of the Cambodians themselves, I suspect it is impossible, in Yeats' phrase, to tell the dancer from the dance; and as Andre Malraux foresaw as long ago as 1935, "la danse de mort. . . n'a guere change que son pas."[13]

[13] Andre Malraux, preface to Andree Viollis, *Indochine SOS* (Paris: Gallimard, 1935), p. xi.

THE TRAGEDY OF CAMBODIAN HISTORY REVISITED

"Tragedies should properly be classed as the same or different mainly in virtue of the plot, that is to say those that have the same entanglement and denouement. Many who entangle well are bad at the denouement."

Aristotle, *Poetics* XVIII.3

I have used this title, without the "revisited," three times before: the first time was for a talk I gave at the University of British Columbia in 1978, published as an article a year later. I used it again in 1991 for a book that dealt with Cambodian political history since 1945. Earlier this year I used the title for a talk I gave at SAIS. Since that talk events in Cambodia have led me to alter the ending of the paper, swinging from cautious optimism to cautious pessimism about Cambodia's future.

In these works I meant different things by the word "tragedy." The talk, the article, and the book were written at different times in my life and at different points in Cambodia's recent past. Because I have spent thirty-four years as an observer of Cambodian history, my views have altered as history has altered

This essay is based on a talk given at Johns Hopkins University in February 1994 and, in expanded form, at the Wilson Center five months later. I would like to thank Dr. Mary Brown Bullock of the Wilson Center's Asia Program for her support and Professor Frederick Z. Brown of SAIS for his helpful comments on both occasions.

course; my own ideas have changed in response to events in Cambodia or to other stimuli.

On the earlier occasions the word "tragedy" seemed to describe the wastefulness and losses that so many Cambodians had suffered, partly at the hands of their political leaders and partly from outside forces. And, although I wanted to evoke the sadness that "tragedy" implies, I realized that "tragedy" also describes a narrative pattern of Cambodian political history, in terms of such ingredients as leadership, social structure, and power relations. Inside this tragic format it was easy to see the history of Cambodia's leaders in terms of changes of fortune, tragic flaws, pride, and huge, unmanageable forces, as well as what the Greeks called *moira*, or "fate."

In 1978, when I first used the phrase, Cambodia's tragedy was not so much historical as it was a case of ongoing suffering. As I spoke in Vancouver, Cambodians were saddled with the Khmer Rouge, home-grown fanatics who were still in power at that time. It was the "home-grown" aspect that attracted my attention and bewildered me. So did the apparently limitless ferocity of the regime, which was at odds with my sentimental, Orientalist recollections of the country, where I had lived and worked in the early 1960s.

By the time I revised the paper for publication the Khmer Rouge had been overthrown. An untried, Vietnamese-sponsored regime had taken their place. The tragedy had progressed into another act-perhaps the last, if "nation-state" were to be part of the title. The Vietnamese occupation of Cambodia, after all, seemed to fit into long-standing Vietnamese notions whereby Cambodia and Laos would become federated with Vietnam, reconstituting the hybrid "Indo-China" that the French had invented a century before and reimposing Vietnamese imperial boundaries that had existed circa 1825.

As the 1980s progressed and the Vietnamese occupation evolved into an open-ended, relatively peaceable protectorate I asked myself: did Cambodia's disappearance as a nation-state really matter? Were protectorates and the loss of independence the worst that could befall a people? Was nationalism as virtuous as it had seemed when clothed in anti-colonial or anti-American garb? What was more important in this case, it seemed to me, was that Pol Pot and his apparatchiks had left the country. The massacres were over. Those who had survived were busy rebuilding their society and their lives. I probably wouldn't have given a talk or a paper with this title in those days.

Nonetheless, watching Cambodia in the 1980s was a depressing avocation. I visited Phnom Penh very briefly in 1981 and was saddened by the waste and suffering I saw. I could not blame this condition on the regime as much as on its isolation from the world, imposed by the United States, China, and their allies. All the same, it was sad to think that the county where I had lived and worked twenty years before was becoming a dreary socialist state, echoing the satellite status of Eastern European countries. Not a "tragedy," perhaps, but nothing to cheer about either.

When I began writing *The Tragedy of Cambodian History* in 1988 the situation in Cambodia had altered somewhat. The Cold War was fading and Cambodia, like Vietnam, was edging into a wider world. In that same year Cambodia's Communist party adopted some economic and social reforms that pleased the people, enriched important figures and were impossible to repeal.

These reforms widened opportunities for Buddhism, awarded people titles to real estate, and opened up the country to investment. In September 1989 Vietnamese troops and advisors, bereft of Soviet assistance and perhaps despairing of building a permanent satellite in Cambodia, ceremoniously went home.

Privately, I applauded these developments but left them out of my book, which I decided to close with the arrival of the Vietnamese. I believed that the long-term tragedy I was writing about – Cambodia's tyranization throughout recorded history at the hands of its political leaders, its victimization by its neighbors, its role as a football in the Cold War – had altered in the 1980s, although I could not be too sure. After all, I had spent only three days in Cambodia during this period, and I have no knowledge of Vietnamese.

What did I mean by "tragedy" as a title to describe Cambodia's history from 1945 to 1979? I argued that the tragedy had several aspects. The first was geopolitical. I wrote that Cambodia's vulnerability to outside pressure had been exacerbated by its leaders who were influenced in turn by other aspects of the tragedy such as Cambodia's location, their perceptions of the past, and the crushing weight of Cambodian power relations. They were influenced, in other words, by the way they expected and were expected to behave.

The story that emerged was adorned with tragic heroes and contained their falls from grace, including examples of confrontations, occasionally fatal, between their pride, their visions, and reality.

In Norodom Sihanouk, the man who has dominated a half-century of Cambodian politics, we have a tragic hero *par excellence* as well as an indefatigable impresario: gifted, prideful, loquacious, self-absorbed. Here was a man with a quick intelligence, genuine fondness for his people, a lively sense of *realpolitik*, and an overwhelming, even suffocating style. Here was a man who was overtaken in 1970 by his shortcomings, by teacherous colleagues, and by forces larger than himself: what could have been more tragic? Soon afterwards, as he went into exile (cause and effect were not, despite his claims, this simple) Cambodia was torn apart.

After 1970 two less talented figures – Lon Nol and Pol Pot – wrestled for the leading role. Both came equipped with hubris and cloudy perceptions of the world. They had less common sense than Sihanouk and a more distorted sense of the power relations that governed the 1970s. Both men believed, for example, that Cambodia could defeat Vietmam.

What bound the three men together, from a tragico-historical perspective, was their authoritarian style, their distrust of Vietnam, and their recurrent bouts of *folie de grandeur*. All three commanded loyalties that are sometimes difficult to understand, even if charm travels badly and is in the eye of the beholder. Sihanouk, to be sure, benefited from the deference he received as a former king and busily courted popularity throughout his years in power. Pol Pot and Lon Nol, on the other hand, fitted other, more pedestrian expectations that many Cambodians have of leaders. They were (and Pol Pot remains) smooth featured, taciturn, and genteel in face to face relations, driven by an unseen, grandiose agenda – racialist/utopian in Lon Nol's case, Utopian/racialist in Pol Pot's. All three men shared visions of Cambodia's destiny and of themselves that were out of touch with reality and have been missing from other Cambodian politicians since 1979. People like Chea Sim, Hun Sen, and Prince Rannaridh have cut Cambodia down to size or been reduced by its catastrophes. They have been unwilling, unable, or too timid to take up tragic parts.

But the tragedy of Cambodian history, I went on to say in my book, was not confined to its heroes. Cambodian culture had a role to play as well. From this perspective it seems tragic to me that Cambodia's people have been entangled with so many clownish, incompetent leaders, and yet seemed defenseless against them. Throughout the country's history, power in Cambodia has been pervasive and unrestrained. What was it in Cambodian social structure and relationships that produced so many avid leaders and so many cowed, bewildered subjects? What was it about the society and its arrangements that angered Pol Pot and his colleagues and led them to try to take the society apart? Having asked those questions, it's fair to say that I have no clear answers, even after wrestling with the questions for many years.

Another part of Cambodia's tragedy, I wrote in 1990, arose from its location, caught between the jaws of Thailand and Vietnam: nine million people inhabiting a flat, accessible country are a tasty dish to set before twelve times as many neighbors. This situation became crucial in the nineteenth century when Vietnam established a protectorate over Cambodia. Then, following years of warfare, the Vietnamese were replaced as Cambodia's patrons by the Thai. The wars bled Cambodia white. If France had not established its own protectorate over Cambodia in 1863, the kingdom would have been divided up between Thailand and Vietnam, as it almost was again, informally, before the Paris peace accords in 1991. The specter of Cambodia's disappearance haunted the visions and dictated the behavior of Sihanouk, Lon Nol, and Pol Pot.

A legacy of these nineteenth century events is that to this day Thailand and Vietnam have difficulty perceiving Cambodia as a free and sovereign state. Their unwillingness to take Cambodia seriously has made it easy for these countries to subvert Cambodian regimes at various times since 1954. In this evolving context, Cambodia was used by its neighbors and by their patrons as a participant in the Cold War regardless of its interests. The fact that Sihanouk's neutralist foreign policy "immoral" in the eyes of John Foster Dulles – met these interests fairly well was of no importance to outside powers whose views of Cambodia, when they had any, were almost always instrumentalist, patronizing and dismissive.

Another legacy from the colonial era was that under the French, the Americans, the Vietnamese, and most recently the United Nations Transitional Authority in Cambodia (UNTAC), many Cambodians became fonder of protection than of risking their hand at independence, given their weakness *vis-a-vis* Thailand and Vietnam. Anticolonialism never struck very deep roots in Cambodia, where people were probably better off under France than they would have been as a backwoods minority in Thailand, Vietnam, or both. The French enjoyed Cambodia, in an unashamedly Orientalist way, and many Cambodians enjoyed the French, whose rule was neither strenuous nor intrusive. Moreover, the notion of patronage was deeply entrenched, and habit-forming.

Of course, Cambodians could never choose to be truly independent, because the country's far more powerful patrons were reluctant to leave Cambodia alone. Its weakness in relation to its neighbors was a fact of life. In this regard it is poignant that Pol Pot laid such stress on "self-mastery" and "independence." Utopia, as conceived by Thomas More, was an island, separated (as Pol Pot tried to separate Cambodia, permanently) from its neighbors.

Another tragic aspect of Cambodian history, I wrote, was the weight of its past and the effect of that weight on politicians and ordinary people. Between the ninth and fourteenth centuries the Khmer-speaking kingdom of Angkor dominated much of Southeast Asia. In the fifteenth century, as the region's center of political gravity shifted toward Thailand in the west, Cambodia diminished in size. Its rulers abandoned Angkor, although the principal monument, Angkor Wat, was still an important pilgrimage site when the French claimed to have discovered the temples in the 1850s. Over the next century or so French savants deciphered over a thousand Cambodian inscriptions, dated a similar number of ruins, and established the chronology of Cambodian history. At the same time, they felt obliged to tell the Khmer about their present-day helplessness and their long-term "decline," noting en passant that without the French the country would have disappeared. I have argued that giving Cambodian intellectuals (and semi-intellectuals, like Sihanouk, Lon Nol, and Pol Pot) a grandiose, unusable past produced among them a *folie de grandeur*. Sihanouk flagrantly allowed himself to be compared with Angkorean rulers, a practice continued by Lon Nol, who saw himself as presiding over a triumphant Cambodian "race." And as for Uncle Secretary Pol Pot, "If our people can build Angkor," he said on one occasion, "they can do anything."

The final dimension of Cambodia's tragic history, in structural terms, stems from the Cambodian peoples' attitudes toward power and the attitudes of powerful Cambodians toward those they perceive as below them. Cambodia's language and institutions are suffused with the notions of hierarchy and ranking, deference and command, hegemony and servitude. Society is seen in familial, authoritarian terms rather than in terms of voluntary, supposedly "horizontal" associations. "Lop-sided friendships," as one anthropologist has called patron – client relationships, describe the relations between masters and servants, monks and lay people, elders and youth. In Cambodia the teacher-student relationship was another crucial place where power and subservience were deployed; it is not accidental that so many Khmer Rouge leaders were schoolteachers by profession, adept at controlling rooms full – to say nothing of a country-full – of potentially unruly people. For all its Maoist rhetoric, Cambodia's revolution, like most revolutions perhaps, was a revolution from above. There were no schools, but former teachers played a prominent role in dispensing revolutionary wisdom, strategy, and tactics. Pol Pot, Ieng Sary, Son Sen, and Khieu Samphan had all been teachers and were in most cases beloved by those they taught.

Until recently Cambodians had no words for "society" or "consensus" but many words for relationships among people. There were words for "exploit," "command," and "persecute," and words for "obey," "honor," and "respect." In many ways Cambodia was held together by the relations enforced between those with power and those without, between those who commanded (*nak prao*) and those who were commanded (*nak bomrao*). In Buddhist thinking, there was also thought to be a correlation between power and merit, which reinforced the legitimacy (but seldom improved the behavior) of those in power. Victory made a warrior meritorious; power reflected a leader's merit. This was a closed system that favored the status quo. In this respect, Cambodia resembles many other countries in Asia and elsewhere that have no tradition of pluralism or peaceful succession, and none of questioning those in power. Acquiescence and fear were the better parts of valor. Terror was an indispensable ingredient of rule. Cambodia's precarious location and the mutability of support made most post-Angkorean leaders frequently scared and relatively prudent – a tradition kept alive since independence. Thus, in his foreign policy pronouncements, Sihanouk defied the world; privately, he made secret alliances. Lon Nol boasted that his "friendship" with Richard Nixon was a "secret weapon" that would defeat Vietnam. In private, he often burst uncontrollably into tears. Pol Pot and his colleagues exercised total control of Cambodia, but remained concealed behind barbed wire and revolutionary names – totally powerful, perpetually afraid.

When I finished writing my book in 1990, I assumed that neither Pol Pot nor Sihanouk, both discredited by their behavior, would rise from the ashes to take the stage again, as tragic heroes or anything else. I was mistaken, but I wrote at the time, taking a chance, that they might return less as heroes than as clowns.

Here I think I may have been partially correct. Neither man enjoys genuine power today.

Pol Pot retains the ability to frighten people and to charm his entourage. Sihanouk, depending on your point of view (the matter of "charm" again) maintains the power to beguile, bamboozle, or annoy. In 1990 I felt that these two people, plus the late Lon Nol, plus many impersonal forces – call them "society" or "fate"—had wrought the terrible damage to Cambodia and its people that led me to use the word "tragedy" in the first place. I was happy to see them off the stage. I was not sure, however, what other Cambodians had learned from their experiences as they walked away from them, in a state of shock.

On the last page of *The Tragedy of Cambodian History* I wrote:

> The fifth act of Cambodia's tragedy has been reserved for those Cambodians whose health and personalities have been broken by events the 1970s and 1980s. Many of these men and women are living thousands of miles from Cambodia, in Long Beach, Tacoma, Creteil, Toulouse and Cabramatta. The older ones are besieged by memories, losses, and longings, aware that something has happened to them – probably history – which they are not in

a position to explain. Their children, cut off from Cambodia, have become citizens of other countries. Over nine million Cambodians continue to live inside Cambodia and continue to lose their arms and legs to land mines and their children to malnutrition and disease. What is a game for outside powers entranced by their perceptions of the Cambodian problem is a continuous disaster for these Cambodians, who are trying to mesh their personal priorities and their life histories into a society in which politics as they have always considered the term-that is, as visitations from above-has lost its value, probably for good.

Four years have passed since I wrote those words. Some of them still ring true, but in the interval my own relationship to Cambodia and its history has altered drastically.

Between 1990 and 1993 I visited Cambodia six times. What I saw, read, and heard was depressing. I came to Cambodia prepared to find elements of tragedy closely linked to the country's recent past. I found some, as I expected, when I revisited the Khmer Rouge interrogation facility and prison in Phnom Penh, a former high school known in the Pol Pot era by the code name S-21. The Vietnamese transformed S-21 into a genocide museum in 1979, taking East German advice and employing a Vietnamese museologist. The bulk of the documents they preserved are 4,000 forced confessions of people accused of betraying Pol Pot's Communist party. In 1990 the haunting photographs of Pol Pot's victims there, and their horrendous testimony, hit me once again. Here, I kept telling myself, was runaway power, unchecked violence, meaningless malignity.

If S-21 held few surprises, I found unexpected elements of tragedy when I revisited Angkor for the first time in thirty years. On my earlier visits, as on this one, I found the ruins hauntingly beautiful and their woodland setting romantic and evocative in the extreme. In the 1960s, when I had visited Angkor many times, Cambodia was in a seemingly charming, post-heroic phase of its history; the ruins were beautiful reminders of past "greatness," contrasted to the country's powerless, but mesmerizing "charm". When I returned to Siem Reap in 1992,1 was struck not only with how much beauty the monuments conveyed , but also how so many of them, and Angkor Wat in particular, could also be read as expressions of unchecked power and control. Angkor Wat, in this reading, was a statement made in the twelfth century AD by and for a single man, King Suryavarman II, whose tomb the temple was to be. This was not only the largest religious monument in the world: it was the world's largest individual tomb. Wandering inside the temple and marvelling at its grandeur increased my sense of powerlessness. This effect had been intended when it was built, and the ratio of builder to visitor remained in force. On the bas reliefs I found the themes of power and control repeatedly and graphically expressed: men, monkeys, and elephants were locked in ferocious combat. Prisoners of war were being led off in chains to slavery or to be killed. Before my eyes, people were being led into Buddhist hell to be tortured, as they were so often under Pol Pot. There was nothing festive or benign about this display of power, nothing that reached out and "down," if you like, "among the people." There was nothing for a visitor to patronize, either. The temple retained its awesomeness, and it was totally Khmer.

With my S-21 and Angkor Wat experiences as background, I can say that my most important visit occurred in November 1992, when I took part in a three week research mission with Amnesty International to investigate widespread reports of human rights abuses in the period prior to the UN-sponsored national elections. During this visit I travelled widely for the first time since 1962. On my travels I came to think that the word "tragedy" as a description of Cambodian history was still valid, but with wider applications than Sihanouk, the Khmer Rouge, the country's political decline, its disappearance as a nation-state, or the sufferings of Cambodia's many victims. A cruel, exploitative flavor pervaded Cambodian politics, as conducted by the incumbent party. Although this may have always existed, I was able to observe for the first time, however, its effects in situ and at close range, rather than on paper or in conversations with people overseas.

I had the same impression of power and control when in the course of our investigations we examined human rights abuses perpetrated, in most cases, by the ruling political party, which remains in de facto control of Cambodia today. Prior to the elections the party went out of its way to terrify the recently formed, inexperienced, and unarmed opposition parties, whose members often displayed the stubborn, foolhardy courage that is another characteristic of the Cambodian people. Agents threw grenades at peoples' houses at night or, posing as robbers, wounded or assassinated people who had defected from the ruling party. The government denied complicity – Hun Sen even blamed the opposition for killing some of its own supporters but the UNTAC human rights component built up formidable dossiers implicating those in power. Other dossiers implicated the Khmer Rouge, who had embarked on their own reign of terror, targetting Vietnamese civilians in the country. We confirmed the information in the dossiers in interviews we conducted with survivors. As I spoke to the widows of victims and people wounded by grenades, and as I went through the daunting files of offenses assembled by UNTAC, I was overwhelmed by a sense of *déjà vu*. Here, in living color and on a smaller scale were the bas reliefs at Angkor, the cruelties of the nineteenth century upheavals, Sihanouk's sordid political killings, the massacres of Vietnamese civilians by Lon Nol, the murderous purges of Pol Pot. I was tempted to see these ruthless demonstrations of power as a permanent feature of the landscape, and the victimization of Cambodia's people (especially the more helpless among them) stretching on forever. Exhausted by two decades of warfare, trauma, and destruction, isolated from developments in other countries, the ruling party of Cambodia, as it emerged from its Marxist-Leninist cocoon, seemed to have learned and forgotten nothing.

Alongside this depressing landscape were several touching features that seemed to me peculiarly Khmer, such as the widespread belief that UNTAC would linger in Cambodia indefinitely, to protect the people against themselves, or that Prince Sihanouk, by physically coming home, could stop history and politics in their tracks and reinstate the vaguely remembered, or misremembered, paradise that had existed when he was overthrown twenty-two years before. No one spoke of what might happen to Cambodia as it reentered a wider, voracious world. The stubborn conservatism of the Cambodian people now prevented its leaders from realizing that Cambodia faced a greater, more dangerous challenge from a rapacious Southeast Asia, led by Thailand and more recently by Singapore and Malaysia as well. Politicians who had sidestepped the revolution looked askance at social change. For them, the re-established status quo meant staying in office, making money, and controlling people: *déjà vu* again. The possibility of pluralism unnerved them. Pluralism, after all, opened the possibility of a social contract, and of a peaceful transfer of power.

At the same time, there was something very moving about the way that unarmed people responded en masse to this intimidation and to the possibility of political choice, before and during the election. I saw this process at close range in 1992, when registration gathered steam, and again in April 1993 when I returned briefly to Phnom Penh. I heard much more about it in July, when I visited once again with Amnesty, and discussed the elections that had taken place two months before. Most observers were surprised that the government party failed to win the election. Instead, a royalist party led by Sihanouk's eldest son won a majority of the seats. What had happened was very strange, and very moving: for the first time in Cambodian history millions of Khmer had voted freely and fairly, and a majority had opposed an armed, incumbent regime. In a sense, the vote was a massive statement rejecting politics as usual – the tragedy of Cambodian history – and proposing something different: peace and quiet, for example. Whether or not the leaders of the incumbent party paid any genuine attention is perhaps less important than the fact that over two million voters now remember making the statement and could, in similar circumstances, make the statement again. The parallel with the Burmese elections of 1990 – where the National Democratic party won handily but whose victory was dismissed by the military rulers – is a suggestive one.

Because of this new awareness of the possibility, however remote, that politics in Cambodia can be changed and that such concepts as the rule of law, civil society, and respect for human rights can take root in Cambodian culture, I might be mistaken to apply the word tragedy open-endedly to Cambodian history. This is particularly true now that we know the world can be changed and that Cambodians, like many other people, may be forced to alter their old habits. The elections provided grounds for optimism, but such optimism may not long endure. We can also be confident about the new openness of Cambodian society, although this may produce disorder and repression.

Hope lies among younger Cambodians, especially those living outside the country and willing to help, as well as in those outside the power structure-the survivors of the past who reject, when given the chance, the politics of the past that locked people into so much fatalistic subservience to others. Pol Pot's murderous revolution, if nothing else, weakened many hierarchical relationships and broke others for good. If changes occur in the way Cambodians perceive, exercise, and resist political power, if Cambodia's neighbors change their ways, and if leaders in the future fail to be attracted by spurious possibilities of greatness – and these are enormous "ifs"-we can perhaps stop referring to Cambodia as a tragedy, even though periods of its history, such as the period between 1945 and 1979, and above all the Pol Pot years themselves, can still be thought of in that way.

This is how I closed a talk with this title when I gave it in February 1994. Five months later, I'm afraid that the upbeat final paragraph needs to be toned down. Cambodia has a large capacity to ambush prophets and take historians by surprise, but I would be happier if the paragraph as written contained less wishful thinking, and if events since then had not heightened the sense of *déjà vu*, bordering on desperation, that stretches back into Cambodia's past.

Recent visitors to the country have spoken to me about runaway corruption, widespread violence and intransigent behavior by the dominant political party. They've mentioned factionalism and bickering at every level of the government, squabbling among donor nations and very little economic onward movement. To this chorus I can add questions such as: Why is King Sihanouk in Pyongyang? Why has no one arrested (or shot) Pol Pot? Is history intent on repeating itself as farce?

At ground level, millions of mines lie inches below the surface, and kill and maim dozens of Cambodians every month. The infant mortality rate remains one of the highest in the world. The Khmer Rouge have not been removed from Cambodian life, and politicians, unsurprisingly, have rejected the rejection of politics as usual. So the tragedy has reopened, perhaps as a black comedy or as a farce, after a noble attempt to shut it down. Elements in the Thai military establishment seem glad to give succor to Pol Pot and continue, as their ancestors did, to bleed Cambodia of its resources. Vietnamese policy toward Cambodia seems to be dormant, but Cambodia is still a

golden opportunity for Vietnamese guest workers, whom many Cambodians find unwelcome and are reluctant to invite. Indeed, Cambodian fears of Vietnam, however unwarranted, could erupt at any time into further massacres. It is disturbing that the anti-Vietnamese stance of the Khmer Rouge is widely supported by many Cambodians who are otherwise appalled by their former rulers.

Whether what happens in the near future will be described as a stalemate, a downward spiral, or more remarkably as "progess" of a sort, remains to be seen and impossible to predict. This unwillingness to predict the future, of course, is the historian's classic disclaimer. In my own defense, I can only refer again to Cambodia's skill at overturning prophecies; the election is the most recent example of this contrariness. In any case, the weight of the past is such that "tragedy" seems to be one of the more descriptive words, and most enduring explanations, for the ongoing process of Cambodian history.

INDEX

Ablin, David, 205
Albert, King of Belgium, 194
Amnesty International, 320, 322
Anderson, Benedict, 301
Ang Chan (Cambodian king). See Chan
Ang Duong (Cambodian king). See Duang
Ang Im (Cambdoian king). See Im.
Ang Mei (Cambodian queen). See Mei
angkar (organization), 59, 260, 273
Angkor Thorn, 34–5
Angkor Wat, 14,15–23, 36, 245, 246,
    299,316,320–21
Aninditapura, 37
Archaimbault, Charles, 126
ASEAN. See Association of Southeast
    Asian Nations.
Association of Southeast Asian Nations
    (ASEAN), 279, 289, 292
Athvea, 33
Australian National University, 137
Aymonier, Etienne, 7, 32, 122, 125
Ayudhya, 17

Ba Maw, 173
Ba Phnom, 30, 38, 40, 66–67, 119–135
babad, 101
Bakong, 31, 123

baku (court Brahmin), 31, 42
bangsavatar (chronicle), 62, 160–164
BanteaiSrei, 123
Barai, 88
Baray (dam), 33
Bardez, Felix, 137, 139–158, 185
Basak, 36
Bastian, E., 129
Baudouin, G., 143, 146
Bayon, 27
Ben Tre, 305
"Black Book" of 1978, 237, 251, 301
Bokor, 146
Bose, Chandra, 173, 177
Brah Ban, 15–23
Brahma, 34
Briggs, L.P., 38
Buddhist Institute (Institut Bouddhique),
    1, 125, 159, 161,170
"Buddhist Socialism", 300
Burmese election, 323

Camau, 123
Cao Dai, 195
Carney, Timothy, 217
Central Intelligence Agency (CIA), 239,
    250

CGDK. See Coalition Government of Democratic Kampuchea.

Chan (Cambodian king), 61–75, 86–98,102,105,303

Chantabori, 17

Chatterji, A.C., 177

Chaudoc, 64

chbap (normative poems), 45–60

Chea Sim, 314

"Chenla" (Zhenla), 37

Chikreng, 8

Chou ta Kuan (Zhou daguan), 4, 9

CIA. See Central Intelligence Agency

Coalition Government of Demo cratic Kampuchea (CGDK), 274, 276

Coedes, George, 8, 11, 13, 15, 32, 124, 190

Communist Party of Kampuchea (CPK), 215–232

Conference of Non-Aligned Na tions, 213

CPK. See Communist Party of Kampuchea

Dalet, R., 123

"day of hate", 287

de Gaulle, Charles, 175

Decoux, Jean, 197, 198

Democratic Kampuchea (DK), 233–54

Democratic Party, 220

devaraja, 35, 37, 40

dliarma (the law), 52

Dienbienphu, 289

Dik Keam, 154

direction (bestial), 140 DK. See Democratic Kampuchea.

DokThan, 121–122

Doumer, Paul, 194

Dulles, John Foster, 315

Duong, (Cambodian king), 14, 25, 58, 77, 100–118, 124

Durga. See Uma.

Eastern Zone of DK, 264

Echo du Cnmbodge, 142,156

Eng (Cambodian king), 102, 105

Errington, Shelly, 112

Ethiopian War, 194

Franco-Thai War, 192,194

Free Khmer, 239

"Funan", 124, 131

Gallet, Charles, 153, 156

Gautier, Georges, 169, 200

Geertz, Clifford, 107, 305

Gellner, Ernest, 186

Geneva Conference of 1954, 210, 219

Gia Long (Vietnamese emperor), 63

Gide, Andre, 306

Glaize, Maurice, 34

Godelier, Maurice, 116

Goloubew, Victor, 8–9, 35, 38 328

Gracey, Douglas, 182–184

Great Leap Forward, 223

Green Shirts, 177

Groslier, B.P., 9, 32

Guesdon, G., 125

Gulf of Siam, 64

Harihara, 32

Hariharalaya, 32, 34

Hatien, 64

Heder, Stephen, 217, 242

Heng Samrin, 187, 277, 282–83

hikayat (Malay chronicle), 101, 112, 192

holy man's rebellion, 61–75

Hood, Marlowe, 205
HouYuon, 185
HuNim, 210
Hun Sen, 283–4, 314

ICP. See Indo-China Communist Party
Ieng Sary, 210, 225–6, 256–7, 281, 302, 317
IeuKoeus, 185
Indo-China Communist Party (ICP), 186–7, 218, 268
Indravarman I, 31–2, 34
Indravarman II, 3–14
Indravarman III, 13
Institut Bouddhique. See Buddhist Institute.

Java, 122
Jayavarman II (Cambodian king at Angkor), 37
Jayavarman VII (Cambodian king at Angkor), 3–14, 35, 39, 245, 259, 297, 300, 302
Jung Khnes, 32

Kai, 64–73
Kali, 129
Kampot, 113
Kampuchea, Kingdom of (1945), 165–188
Kampuchean Peoples' Revolutio nary Party (KPRP), 232
Kandal, 89
Keng Vannsak, 185
Keo Meas, 215–232, 260–62, 268
Khieu Samphan, 185, 210, 213, 237, 284,302,317
KhimTit, 180
Khmer Nationalist Party, 171

Khmer Peoples' Revolutionary Party (KPRP), 216, 268, 281
Khmer Republic, 225, 300
Kiernan, Ben, 137, 142, 166, 215, 220–1
Kim II Sung, 247, 249
Kissinger, Henry, 211
Koh Sautin, 70–71
Kompong Chhnang, 147, 148
Kompong Svay, 30, 88, 128
Kompong Thorn, 30, 34
koun lok (child of man: a bird) 79–82
KPRP. See Khmer Peoples' Revol utionary Party and Khmer Revolutionary Party.
Kraang Laev, 139–58
kru (teacher) 48
Kuy, 69

Laau Thouk, 166–7
Lao Dong Party (Workers' Party of Vietnam), 221,281
Le van Duyet, 65
Leclerc, General, 183
Leclere, Adhemard, 30
Leper king (*Sdach komlong*), 3–14
Levi Straus, Claude, 82
Lewis, Bernard, 203
Lingaparvata. See Wat Ph'u
Loeng nak tā ("raising the ancest ors"), 31, 129
Lokesvara, 9–10
Lolei, 34
Lon Nol, 42, 58, 185, 188, 208, 224, 285, 302–3, 313–316, 318
Lovek, 18 329

Mahaballipuram, 122
Mahayana Buddhism, 11

Mahisa, 40

Malraux, Andre, 140, 152–3, 309

mandala, 28

Mao Zedong, 57, 226–8, 247, 249

Me Sa, 25–42

Meas, 86–98

Medaeng, 36

Mei (Cambodian queen), 102–103, 110

Mey Pho, 178

Minh Mang (Vietnamese emperor), 67, 73, 75, 86, 279

Monash University Library, 142

More, Thomas, 316

Mormoiron, 137

Moura, Jean, 7, 129

Murray, E.D., 183

Mus, Paul, 41

Mussolini, Benito, 213

Nagara Vatta ("Angkor Wat"), 170, 197, 200

nak chea (healthy person), 48

nak sel (holy man)

nak tā (ancestor people), 106

nak tā Me Sa, 119–135

Nakorn Ratchasima, 210

Ngo Dinh Diem, 210, 291

Nguyen Co Thach, 291

Nguyen dynasty, 63

Nguyen van Sieu, 66–7

Nguyen van Thuy, 63, 67, 75

Nhek Tioulong, 153,185

Nixon Doctrine, 307

Nixon, Richard, 208, 303, 318

Non Suon, 222, 260

Nong Kimny, 178

Norodom (Cambodian king), 114, 120, 124,130,174, 190

Norodom Rannaridh, 314

Norodom Sihanouk (Cambodian king), 42, 59, 165–188, 189–203, 208, 219, 241–2, 302, 313–15

Nuon Chea, 221

oknha luang (king's officials), 144

Ollivier, R., 178

Pach Chhoeun, 170–1,177,198–9

Pallava, 126

Parmentier, Henri, 122

Pech, 84

Pelliot, Paul, 9

Peoples' Republic of Kampuchea, 187, 232, 252

Peoples' Socialist Community. See Sangkum Reastr Niyum Petain, Philippe, 194

Phan Boi Chau, 152

Phan Chu Trinh, 152

Phnom Bakheng, 31–2, 34

Phnom Bok, 34

Phnom Chisor, 126

Phnom Di, 32

Phnom Kandal ("central mount ain"), 35

Phnom Krom, 31–4

Phnom Kulen, 7, 13

Phnom Prah, 31

Pimai, 40

Pitou de Monteiro, 180

Pol Pot (Saloth Sar), 43, 185, 217–8, 229, 234–43, 247, 252–4, 260, 273, 280, 284–7, 301–2, 305, 312–2, 315, – 324

Poree, Guy, 137

Poree-Maspero, Eveline, 5, 26, 40, 122, 137, 161

Pou, Saveros, 43, 47

Pracheachon Group, 222, 240, 252
Prak, Lady, 86–98
Pranidhan, 125
preah khan (sacred sword), 92
prei (forest, wild), 49, 77
Preschez, Philippe, 196
Prey Veng, 70,145
Pridi Phanomyong, 182
Pursat, 30–31
Pyongyang, 324

"raising the ancestors", 31
rajakar (royal business), 157
Rama I (Thai king), 93, 102
Rama III (Thai king), 90, 93, 102
Rama IV (Thai king) 102
Ramayana, 51
Reamker (Honor of Rama), 51, 58
Reddi, V.M., 196
regional kings (*sdach tran*) 30–1
Revolutionary Flags. See Tung Padevat.
Roluos, 34
Roosevelt, F.D., 175
Royal Crusade for Independence, 219
Royal Terrace, 6

S-21. SeeTuolSleng Saigon, 64, 183
sakdi na (dignity marks), 109
Saloth Sar. See Pol Pot Sambhupura, 37
Sambour, 81, 82
Samudvijana, General Channa, 137
Sangkum Reastr Niyum (Peoples' Socialist
    Community), 241
sangkum (society) 48
Santhuk, 30
Satta (Cambodian king), 16
sdach komlong, See Leper king.
sdach tran (regional king), 30–1,124

Sdok Kak Thorn, 35
Shawcross, William, 283
Siem Reap, 31–32, 34
Sijata. (Cambodian princess), 16
Sisowath (Cambodian king), 120
Sisowath Monipong, 184
Sisowath Monireth, 178–9,183
Sisowath Monivong (Cambodian king),
    151, 159–64, 189–203
Siva, 33, 34, 105–6, 124
Siwotha, 119,130
Social Science Research Council, 44
Sok Bith, 142,150–51
Son Ngoc Thanh, 137, 170–188, 198,
    239, 281
Son Sann, 281, 284, 289–90
Son Sen, 317
srei (free), 52
Stalin, Joseph, 213
Stern, Phillippe, 108
Sukarno, 173
Suryavarman II (Cambodian king), 320
Svay Rieng, 143

Tay Ninh, 64–66
Tayson Rebellion, 57
Tboung Khmum, 29, 70, 128
Tet Offensive, 305
Thammaraja IV (Cambodian king), 18–9
Theravada Buddhism, 11
Thon (a crocodile), 81
Tinh, 147–148
Tiounn, 191,197
Tmenh Chey, 97
Tonle Sap, 19–20,147
Tou Samouth, 221
Trang, 30

Tung Padevat (*Revolutionary Flags*), 216,
    217, 241, 249
Tuol Sleng (S-21), 215, 229, 268, 272,
    319, 320

Udong, 18, 25, 28, 31, 33, 81, 103–4, 280
Uma Mahisasuramardini, 40, 66, 119–135
Ung Hy, 169,177
United Nation General Assembly, 291
United Nations Transistional Au thority
    in Cambodia (UNTAC), 315, 321
United States bombing of Cambodia,
    224–5
University of British Columbia, 295
UNTAC. See United Nations Tran
    sitional Authority in Cambodia.
Utopia, 316

VarKamel, 169
Varenne, Alexandre, 152
Varuna, 80
Vickery, Michael, 258 331
Vinh te Canal, 64, 73
Vishnu, 34,105–6
Vorn Vet, 222

Vyadharapura, 37

Wat Ph'u, 38,126
Wat Sambaur, 64
Wat Srolauv, 84–99
wayang (Javanese puppet theatre), 56
Woodside, Alexander, 295
Workers' Party of Kampuchea (WPK),
    221–223
Workers' Party of Vietnam. See Lao
    Dong.
WPK. See Workers' Party of Kam
    puchea.
Wyatt, David, 1

Yasodharapura, 36, 38–39
Yasodharatataka, 33
Yasovarman I (Cambodian king), 6,
    14,26,31,33–8
Yeats, W.B., 309

"Z-Nation", 294
Zhenla. See Chenla Zhou daguan. See
    Chou ta Kuan.

Lightning Source UK Ltd.
Milton Keynes UK
UKHW011839170921
390604UK00010B/279